ISBN 978-1-332-61715-9
PIBN 10265187

ORDINARIUM MISSÆ.

In Dominicis ad Aspersionem Aquæ benedictæ.

EXTRA TEMPUS PASCHALE.

Repet. Ant. Aspérges me.

℣ *In Dominica de Passione et in Dominica Palmarum non dicitur* Glória Patri, *sed post Psalmum* Miserére *repetitur immediate Antiphona* Aspérges me.

BY

THE REV. DOM DOMINIC JOHNER, O. S. B.

OF BEURON ABBEY

(FROM THE GERMAN)

CUM PERMISSU SUPERIORUM

RATISBON, ROME, NEW YORK & CINCINNATI

FR. PUSTET

TYPOGRAPHER TO THE HOLY SEE AND TO THE CONGR. OF S. RITES

1906

Imprimi permittitur.

Beuronæ, die 2. Februarii 1906.

† **Placidus** Archiabbas.

Imprimatur.

Ratisbonæ, die 24. Martii 1906.

Dr. **Fr. X. Leitner,**
Vic. gen.

Translated by H. S. Butterfield and revised by the author.

Introductory.

This *New School of Gregorian Chant* is intended for practical purposes in the wide domain of ecclesiastical music, and by no means as an Academy solely for savants and professional musicians. Indeed, it is one of its most important and congenial tasks to elevate to a higher level those whose capacities are inconsiderable or but moderate, and to enable them to render Gregorian chants in a worthy manner and, so far as possible, in a really artistic style; more especially, however, to train them for their highly important duties in connection with the liturgy, and to enkindle their enthusiasm for it. Although in practice we have usually to deal with persons who possess little or no ability, yet it was necessary to consider those who are more advanced and capable of being developed, and at least to point out to such the path leading to excellence, so that, if God has bestowed upon them the talent and the will, they may do their best to follow it. For though Gregorian sung in a simple and devotional manner, let us say, by little children, may greatly please us, still its full beauty and the perfection of its varied forms can only be displayed when it is treated as artistic music. Consequently, the divisions of this work into *Preparatory School*, *Normal School*, and *High School* are not to be viewed as intended for three distinct Classes. On the contrary, at the commencement of the instruction and during the course of it the teacher should select from later Chapters, according to his forces and the time available, whatever may help to enliven the instruction or to elucidate points touched upon in a previous lesson. In an instructional work it is necessary to summarise to a considerable extent, and an intelligent teacher will make as good progress, or better perhaps, if he deals separately with some of the topics, anticipating or holding over this or that. For example, the preliminary Vocal Exercises in Appendix III. may suitably be interrupted by remarks concerning the contents and divisions of the Gregorian books, the Latin language, the Church Modes, the neums; or something can be gleaned from the Chapter on Liturgy, from the History of Plain Chant, and the like. In this way the teacher prevents the lesson from becoming dry and wearisome, the intelligence of the singers is quickened and their interest maintained. Moreover, the somewhat complicated subject being sub-divided is more easily mastered. Literature calculated to assist those who desire to investigate certain points more closely has been indicated in footnotes.

Choir-singers are seldom good singers, that is to say, they do not often possess the knowledge and practical experience indispensable for the methodical use of the human voice. That is probably the main reason why the results of strenuous efforts are at times so unsatisfactory, and why we have to complain of the manifold difficulties connected with the cultivation of plain chant and church music generally. Chapter III. in the *Preparatory School,* and the Vocal Exercises in Appendix III., are therefore specially recommended for instructional purposes. Thoroughness in training the voices is the only way to secure accuracy, firmness and uniformity in rendering the choral chants, just as it is always the foundation for a well-executed, vigorous, fluent solo. An hour judiciously employed in this manner will be well repaid. Later on it saves much time, and, in addition, prevents many disappointments, misunderstandings and mistakes.

In order that the beginner may thoroughly master all the details connected with the rhythm, and may be enabled to phrase the melodies properly, the notes which are to be accentuated are clearly indicated in the *Normal School* over the various groups of notes. It stands to reason that the importance and strength of the accentuation must be very different in different places, and that it must always be effected quietly and very smoothly, especially at closing cadences. Hence, the final notes, even when an accent is placed over them in the book, must always be delivered softly and gently, dying away softly and gently. Beginners can use these signs as means to help them to read and practise the music, just as a pianist at first gladly avails himself of fingering-exercises. More advanced pupils can test their method of execution by means of these signs, dispensing with them when in a position to do so.

The chief portion of the task naturally fell to the Chapters included in the *Preparatory* and *Normal School,* the object being to inculcate therein the correct method of rendering the chant; consequently, the matter for the *High School* could be arranged more in the form of hints and suggestions. In the Chapter on the Artistic Value of Plain Chant the purpose was to demonstrate in as lucid a manner as possible the principles that are carried out in the ancient melodies. Whoever has dipped into the rich treasury of the melodies in the *Kyriale* and *Graduale,* will, with the help of the characteristic phrases here brought to notice, be in a position to discover for himself most instructive illustrations, and to appreciate more and more the advantages of the traditional melodies both as regards their forms and contents. With regard to the Chapter on Organ Accompaniment, it is taken for granted that the organist has sufficient skill as an executant and harmonist. The examples given do not in any way pretend to exhibit the only correct method of accompanying plain chant, and they will not suit everyone; they are, in fact, merely offered as an attempt to surround the melody with harmonies in keeping with its character, and all in the same style, forming an accompaniment which, it is hoped, will be found of some interest from a musical point of view. The attention of Organists who require to have the music before them is called to the Accompaniment to the *Kyriale* by Dr. F. X. Mathias, lately published by Mr. Fr. Pustet.

The author of the *New School* is of opinion that the theory of equal measure for the plain chant notes, using this term in its accepted sense as equivalent to time-value, is not only the one that can be best defended from an historical point of view, but he also recognises in this interpretation the only possible method of rendering these expressive chants in a natural and logical manner, satisfying all the requirements of art, and in accordance with the convictions of those who have formed correct opinions on the subject. Nevertheless it would not be right to look upon this equal measure of the notes as the vital and essential point in the Gregorian rhythmic system, for it is not of itself the form-giving principle for the rhythm. The rules laid down in the book are the results either of generally accepted conclusions or of experiences gained by practical work and close attention to minute details, day by day. Where opinions differ on this or that point, as, for example, in regard to the importance of the *quilisma*, the retention of the *mediatio correpta* in psalmody, the *New School* allows perfect freedom. But no one should give up the whole system and decline to have anything to do with the restoration of the chant owing to the fact that certain questions of minor importance are still awaiting settlement. If in future one is only to take something in hand provided that both learned and unlearned are in perfect agreement, well, one would simply have to give up everything. Or, in other domains where something great has been achieved, has complete unity been attained in theory and practice? Even as regards the performance of the contrapuntal works of the Old Masters, the mode of conducting Beethoven's symphonies, or of rendering his sonatas — compositions which have long been the common property of the educated world — and also as regards the artistic conception of Wagner's musical dramas, there are to this day various personal views, indeed, distinct opinions of various schools of thought; and it will ever be so, and the world will not cease to enjoy these masterpieces and to derive from them food for the mind. Moreover, just because we choose to worry about the settlement of theoretical, historical or purely personal questions, it would be unreasonable to deprive ourselves of the pleasure of labouring on behalf of the restoration of the chant, to say nothing of losing the many beauties revealed in the ancient melodies. Those who have to instruct many must first learn from many, and that which is for the benefit of all has a claim to the help of all, and needs the help of all. Hence the author of the *New School* begs those who are interested in Gregorian chant not to be merely sympathetic friends, but also advisers and promoters when circumstances permit. Author and publisher will be grateful for any suggestions, and will do all in their power to improve the *School*, in order, with the blessing of God, to cooperate more effectually in the great work of the restoration of Gregorian chant, in accordance with the intentions of our holy Father Pius X., for the honour and benefit of holy Church.

A word of sincere thanks is due in this place to the Reverend Fathers of Solesmes for their kind permission to use the "white note" employed by them in psalmody; likewise to the Rev. Dom Gregory Böckeler, O. S. B., of Maria-Laach, who undertook the preparation of Chapter III. for the *Preparatory School*, and the Vocal Exercises in Appendix III.; also to the Very Rev. Dom Raphael Molitor, O. S. B., Prior of St. Joseph's Abbey, Coesfeld, who contributed the greater, and more valuable, part of the Chapters for the *High School*, besides evincing in various other ways his keen interest in the efforts to bring the task to a happy conclusion.

Beuron, near Sigmaringen, Feast of the Purification, 1906.

D. J.

Contents.

Part II. Different Species of Plain Chant.

High School.

Preparatory School.

Chapter I.

What is Gregorian Chant?

1. In order to reply briefly to this question we ask first of all: What is our ordinary national song or our popular hymn tune?

This can be seen from the following melody:

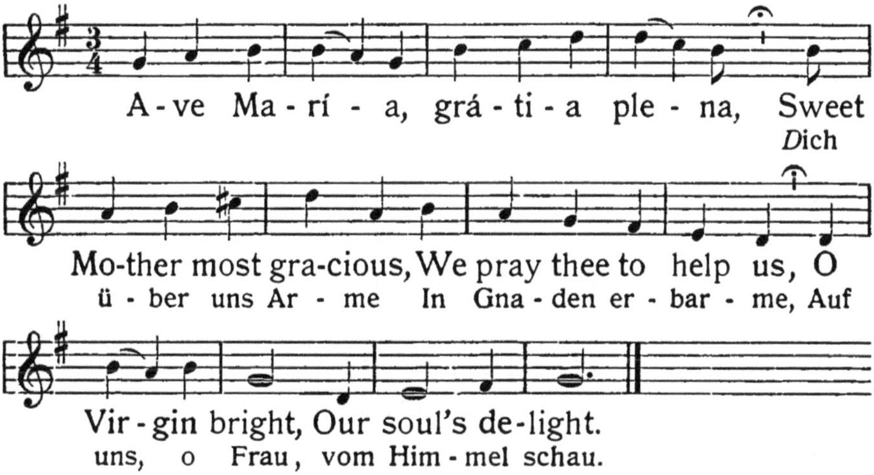

Looking at the musical construction of this devout hymn we perceive that it is written in a certain key — G major; that there is a definite order in the movement of the melody — $^3/_4$ time; that it has three members (periods) of equal length, each consisting of four bars, that the first period is under the influence of G major harmony, the second under that of D major harmony, the third, like the first, under that of G major harmony.

2. We find the same plan in most of the national songs and hymn tunes in use at the present time. The greater number of them are in the modern modes (24 keys), and in time; their members (periods) are symmetrically constructed so that the various parts exactly correspond to one another, and their melodies are formed on, and greatly influenced by, a harmonic foundation which is either actually added or more or less in the mind of the composer.

"Time" is brought about when the accented or "good" note recurs at intervals of the same duration; hence in $^3/_4$ time after the expiration of three beats, in $^4/_4$ time after the expiration of two or four beats.

The keys are recognised by the signatures (G major, one ♯, F major, one ♭, and so on).

3. Now try the following Gregorian melody:

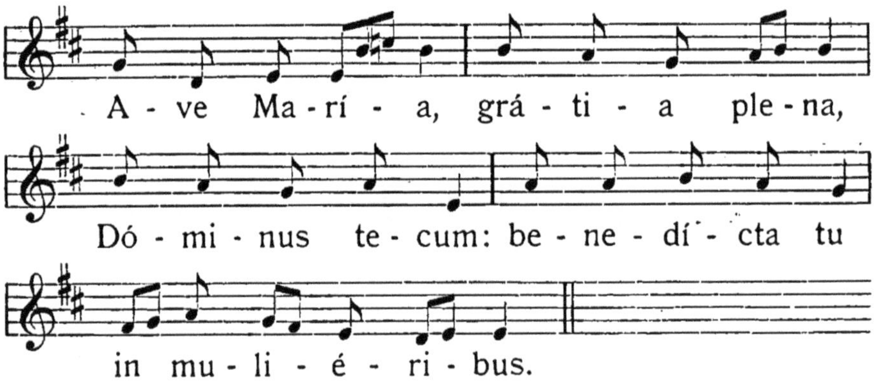

Observing this more closely one perceives that

a) The accented note occurs at different distances, therefore with more freedom than in time, and in fact time is absent.

b) The melody belongs to none of the 24 keys familiar to us.

c) Periods (sub-divisions) of the melody are there certainly, but they do not correspond to one another as regards length or construction.

d) Harmony or the succession of chords seems to have affected the melodic progression only to a trifling extent.

Nevertheless this melody likewise has a definite mode, a movement properly arranged with certain time-values and distinct members. It belongs in point of fact to the 1st Gregorian mode, the movement is in free rhythm (in contradistinction to time), and it is divided into two unequal halves with three against two subordinate members.

4. The melodies of the Gregorian chant therefore differ in many respects from our ordinary national songs and hymn tunes, as also from modern art songs. But it is precisely in this difference that an advantage worth noticing consists. We gain an art of a special kind, an independent art, richly endowed with its own means of expression. Still, the general laws relating to music of course hold good in Gregorian as in other music, though their application results in different forms and effects. A thorough knowledge consequently of Gregorian chant helps one to a thorough knowledge of music, and the old masters rightly viewed the study of Gregorian as simply a part of the study of music.

5. To the question, what is Gregorian? one must therefore give a reply something like this:

By Gregorian we understand the solo and unison choral chants of the Catholic Church whose melodies move in one of the eight Church modes, without time, but with definite time-values, and distinct divisions.

It is a peculiarity of Gregorian that

a) The various time-values are never formed, like modern music and its forerunner, *musica mensurata,* by division into $^1/_2$, $^2/_4$, $^4/_8$, $^8/_{16}$ and so on, but by combination of the time-unit, and thus we have two, three and more units (■ ■, ■ ■ ■, and so on);

b) As sung at the present day, beyond the simple ♮ it has no sign of alteration of the note, and therefore it is strictly diatonic.

6. What has hitherto been said about the Gregorian chant holds good also in regard to the Ambrosian (Milanese) chant,[1]) which is sometimes more elaborate and sometimes simpler than Gregorian; likewise for the Mozarabic chant (formerly in vogue in Spain). All these go back to one source and are very closely related. Further concerning this, together with information in regard to the later reforms, see Appendix I.

7. Gregorian chant has other appellations, viz., *cantus choralis,* choral chant (German, Choràl), *cantus planus* or *simplex,* or *firmus,* simple or unchanged chant (in contradistinction to measured harmonised music), plain chant, plain song; in French, *plain-chant;* in Italian, *canto fermo.*

Chapter II.

A) Remarks concerning Latin; *B)* Concerning High Mass and Vespers.

A.

8. The text to which the Gregorian melodies are set is in the language of the Church, i. e., the Latin language. It is called the language of the Church because it is employed in the Catholic Church officially in all her liturgical functions.

Hence, in order to sing Gregorian well we must in the first place know how Latin should be pronounced and enunciated.

Pronunciation: this differs from English in the following respects:

a. Vowels: *a* has always the open sound as *a* in the English word *father; e* as *a* in say when before *a, e, i,* and *u*; before consonants in general as *e* in met, *i* and

1) In regard to the relationship of the Gregorian chant to the Ambrosian, see *Mitteilungen aus dem Benediktiner- und Cisterzienserorden,* 1884 Heft 2, 3, 4. *Paléographie musicale* (Tournai, Desclée) V. and VI.

y as *ee* in seen; *o* as *o* in *no,* and *u* always as *oo* in *goose*; the diphthongs *ae* and *oe* (*sæculum, cœlum)* as the vowel *e,* i. e., as *a* in say; *eu* is only met with in the words *heu, eheu, seu, neu, neuter* and *neutiquam,* and the Greek words *euge* and *Euphrates,* and the first vowel is made the more prominent; in all other words *(Deus, reus,* etc.) the two vowels are sounded apart; *ei* is a diphthong in *hei,* in all other words it is sounded separately *(elé-ison, dé-inde,* etc.); *ui* is a dissylable in *huic* and *cui* and stress is laid on the first vowel and the second slurred: they should never be pronounced as the words *pike* or *sky*; those vowels are separate in *Spi-rí-tu-i, gé-nu-i,* etc. *Au* is always a diphthong pronounced as *ou* in *house.* Sometimes when the vowels are sounded separately two dots are placed over the last vowel (diaeresis) to distinguish them from other words of identical spelling.

β. Consonants: pronounce them as in English with the following exceptions: *c* before *e, i, y, ae, oe* and *eu* as *ch* in *cheese, ce-drus, ci-bá-vit* = tsche-*drus, tschiba-vit),* before other vowels and all consonants as *k.* When however *c* comes before *h,* it is pronounced as *k,* e. g. *chiroteca* should be *kirotheca*, *sc* before the same vowels is sounded as *sh* in should; *sch* is to be separated, *pas-cha, scho-la; xc* before *e, i, y,* etc., is as *gsh* in egg-shell (*ex-cel-sis* thus, eggshélsis); double *cc,* before the vowels mentioned, as *tc (ec-ce = etsche).* The letter *j* when used as a consonant *(Juda, Jerusalem,* etc.) is pronounced as *y* in *you; g* is always soft before *e* and *i (genui); x* and *z* are to be treated as *cs* and *ds.* When a vowel follows the syllable *ti,* this syllable is to be pronounced as if *zi (otium, gratias = o-zi-um, gra-zi-as),* exceptions are foreign names *(Ægypti-i)* and when another *t, s* or *x* comes immediately before this syllable (*ostium, mixtio). Qu, gu* and *su = kw, gw* and *sw,* when they form one syllable with the following vowel (*quan-do, san-guis);* when they form a distinct syllable as in *su-um* they are pronounced according to the rules given above.[1])

9. Correct Division of Syllables and Words. Lacking this the recitation would be unintelligible or misunderstood.

α. Syllables. A consonant between two vowels belongs to the vowel following it. Therefore do not pronounce thus, *bon-œ, tib-i,* but *bo-nœ, ti-bi, gló-ri-a.*

Consonants which commence a Latin (or Greek) word together belong to the following syllable *(pa-tris, a-gnus).*

Make the division particularly clear when two similar vowels occur together *(fílii, mánu-um)*; also when an *m* or *n* occur between two vowels; in this way the unpleasant nasal colouring of the first vowel is avoided, *(no-men, A-men, ho-nó-re, se-nes).* Guard against pronouncing a broad *e,* e. g., *say-nes* instead of *se-nes.* Pronounce the *e* as you would in the first syllable of "elder".

β. Words. Beware of uniting two words together, therefore read and sing, *sub Pontio,* not *súpontio, quia apud,* not *quiapud, Patri et,* not *Patret, dona eis,* not *doneis, De omnis,* not *Deomnis.*

10. Correct Accentuation. This is generally indicated in the Gregorian books as regards words of more than two syllables by a sign over the vowel (accent): *Magni-ficat.* Words of two syllables are always accentuated on the first syllable. Accentuation means strengthening the tone[2]) (originally elevating the tone), but not necessarily prolonging or sustaining it (cf. Dŏmĭnŭs dēstĭtŭŏ).

The accent is not usually given on capital letters; observe, if there be no accent on a word of more than

---

1) The above rules are taken for this English edition from Dr. Haberl's *Magister Choralis,* English ed. (F. Pustet).

2) Cf. Dr. Mühlenbein: *Über Choralgesang* (Paulinusdruckerei, Trier, 1900).

two syllables the last syllable but two (antepenultimate) is to be accentuated: *Omnia, ómnia.*

11. Rhythm. This means order in the movement. This order is brought about by the accents; they should be sufficiently prominent, but the accented syllable should not be prolonged (sustained): *Dixit Dóminus Dómino méo.*

So long as dissyllabic and trisyllabic words follow one another the rhythm presents no difficulty, but when words of more syllables or monosyllables occur the reader is in danger of hurrying or slurring over some of the syllables, or he unduly emphasises the accent, or his recitation becomes unsteady or jerking, and thus the proper order of the movement is interfered with. Therefore do not omit to employ secondary accents. A sequence of syllables like this: *Archiepiscopus Constantinopolitanus* must have several secondary accents in addition to the principal accents, otherwise the supporting points will be wanting. Read therefore: *àrchiepíscopus Cònstantinòpolitánus.*

"As rhythm is necessarily either binary or ternary, a word which consists of more than three syllables must have a secondary accent on one or two syllables in addition to the tonic accent (principal accent)" (Tinel[1]).

"One of three syllables following one another must have a principal or a secondary accent, in other words between two *ictus* (accents) there cannot be less than one and not more than two middle syllables (unaccentuated syllables)" (Gevaert[2]).

If an unaccentuated syllable follows a word accentuated on the antepenultimate, the last syllable of the word receives a secondary accent (\`): *Dóminùs ex Sion, Dóminùs magnificus.*

If two or three unaccented syllables follow a word of more than one syllable, the first of them usually receives a secondary accent: *glóriam dè te, Dómine àd-*

1) *Le chant grégorien* (Malines, Dessain, 1890) p. 12.

2) Gevaert: *Histoire et théorie de la musique de l'antiquité* (Gand, Anoot-Brœckmann) Tome II. p. 94, mentioned by Tinel l. c.

oránde, pálma mùltiplicábitur; the same when the unaccented syllables are at the beginning of the sentence: *bènedícimus, glòrificámus.*

Longer words must have several secondary accents: *ópportùnitátibus, cónsubstàntiálem, trìbulàtióne, dèprecàtiónem, cònglorificátur.*

Take particular care not to slur middle syllables, otherwise the rhythm suffers, and if several persons are reciting together uniformity is prevented: *réquiem,* not *requem; su-á-vis,* not *svavis; tentati-ó-nem,* not *tentatyonem; sǽ-cu-lum,* not *sǽclum; fí-li-us,* not *fílyus; ó-cu-li,* not *ocli, rèconcili-á-tio,* not *reconcilyatyo.*

Do not pronounce what are properly vowels as consonants: not *meyus, Kyriye,* but *me-us, Kyri-e.*

Here are two examples of rhythm to show how the text should be declaimed when the usual reading takes place:

Státuit[1]) éi Dóminus téstaméntum pácis | et[2]) príncipem fécit éum
3 2 3 2 2 2 1 3 2 2

rit.
út sit ílli sàcerdótii dígnitas ìn ætérnum.
2 2 2 3 3 2 2

Jústus[3]) ut pálma florébit | sícut cédrus Líbani mùltiplicábitur |
3 3 2 2 2 3 4 3

rit.
plantátus in dómo Dómini | in átriis dómus Déi nóstri.
1 3 2 3 1 3 2 2 2 2

12. Delivery in accordance with the Sense. Pay particular attention to the punctuation; make suitable pauses when necessary; give the accent rather more emphasis before a pause; lead up to the longer pauses at the last accent with a slight *ritardando,* but avoid separating the words in such a way as to spoil the sense.

Hence, do not read thus: *sémini | ejus in sæcula, dispérsit | supérbos | mente cordis sui; in die iræ | suæ reges; Deus in adjutórium | meum inténde.*

---

1) Introit from the Common of a Confessor and Bishop.
2) The syllable with 1 below it after a pause means an up-beat.
3) Introit from the Common of a Confessor not a Bishop.

13. Tone of Voice. Whatever is to be read is not simply to be "said off"; on the contrary, the words must be delivered with a soft attack, at a suitable pitch (not too low, *f* ♯, *g*, *a* ♭ or *a*, according to the reader's voice), expressively and solemnly. Beware, however, of closing every single sentence with a *ritardando,* for this makes the reading monotonous and heavy, weakening the effect of the needful *ritardando* at the close. The latter should never begin too soon; usually 2—4 words suffice to mark the close sufficiently. Without this *ritardando* of just the last words the listener never gets the impression of a satisfying and properly prepared close. Therefore do not begin the *ritard.* too soon, but on the other hand do not cut off the voice abruptly. This also holds good for the epistle and gospel at High Mass.

For practice read the *Credo* and particularly the Vesper psalms; by this means the chanting of the psalms is very greatly improved (steady, even flow of the words, neither hesitating nor hurrying). If the words to be read are under the notes, attention is to be paid only to the punctuation of the text, not to the signs for pauses in the melody.

This solemn reading on a sustained tone at the same pitch is usually called reciting, recitation *(recitare, recto tono canere,* i. e., straight away, the voice not rising or falling.

B) Concerning High Mass and Vespers.[1])

a) Gregorian Books for High Mass and Vespers.

14. The chants for Mass are contained in the *Graduale* (partly also in the Missal); the chants for Vespers are contained in the *Vesperale, Antiphonale.* The *Graduale*

1) Literature relating to Mass and Vespers: Duchesne: *Origine du culte chrétien* Paris, 3rd ed., 1903 — Dupoux: *Les chants de la Messe,* in *Tribune de Saint Gervais* 1903, pp. 129 *seq.* — Guéranger: *The Liturgical Year,* Duffy, Dublin.

takes its name from the most elaborate of the Mass chants; the *Graduale* (see p. 105); the *Antiphonale,* from its principal contents, i. e., the antiphons (see p. 75).

15. *Graduale* and *Vesperale* are each divided into four sections:

a) *Proprium de Tempore:* this includes the Sundays and week-days of the ecclesiastical year, most of the feasts of our Lord and the feasts of saints which occur between Christmas and the Epiphany.

b) *Proprium de Sanctis:* this includes some of the more modern feasts of our Lord and feasts of the B. V. M. and saints.

c) *Commune Sanctorum:* this contains Masses and Vespers for the following classes of saints: Apostles (*Graduale* for the Vigils of these feasts), Martyrs out of Paschal time *(Grad.* for a Martyr and Bishop, *Martyr Pontifex;* for a martyr not a Bishop, *Martyr non Pontifex;* for many Martyrs); one and many Martyrs during Paschal time (T. P.), a Bishop *(Pontifex),* Confessor *(Confessor non Pontifex) [Grad.: Abbot],* Virgins and Martyrs *(Virg. et Martyr),* Virgins only *(nec Virg. nec Martyr),* also Mass and Vespers for the feast of the Dedication of a Church, and Vespers for feasts of the B. V. M.

d) In an Appendix: (1) in the *Vesperale,* the psalm tones, *Benedicamus Domino,* feasts of our Lord and of saints which are not celebrated everywhere, votive Vespers; (2) in the *Graduale,* the same feasts, various votive Masses, Masses for the Dead and in particular the invariable Mass chants (Ordinarium Missæ).

β) Order of the Chants at High Mass and Vespers.

16. As regards the chants at Mass see pp. 93 *seq.* The order for Vespers is as follows:

After *Pater noster* and *Ave Maria* in silence the priest intones *Deus in adjutorium* (on *a* or *b* ♮ perhaps); the choir then sings *Domine ad adjuvandum* (see pp. 84, 85). The priest intones the first antiphon, which is continued by the choir; Hereupon the cantor intones in the mode of the antiphon the first verse of the first psalm, which is then sung through by two choirs alternately. This being concluded the whole of the antiphon is repeated without being again intoned. The cantor now intones the second antiphon and so on till the five antiphons and psalms have been sung. If the feast is a *semi-duplex, simplex* or *feria* (in the ecclesiastical Calendar shown thus: *sd., simpl.* or *feria* after the indication of the feast), each antiphon is only intoned the first time (sung as far as the sign * or ‖), and then the psalm immediately follows, after which the whole antiphon is sung through. After the repetition of the fifth antiphon the priest sings the *Capitulum* (Little Chapter) (see p. 125), if possible on the dominant of the psalms, the choir answering *Deo gratias* with the same close as that used by the priest.

The priest now intones the hymn, which is continued by one side of the choir; the second verse is sung by the other side, and this alternate singing is continued till the last verse which is sung by both sides of the choir.

Then the versicle is sung by the priest or cantors (2—4), the response = ℟. by the choir (see pp. 91, 92), either on the dominant note of the psalms, or if the *Magnificat* is sung at a higher pitch on the dominant thereof. Then follows the antiphon before the *Magnificat,* intoned by the priest; hereupon the cantor intones, or 2—4 cantors intone, the *Magnificat* which is sung in the solemn form (sustained notes), the *initium* (see pp. 61 *seq.*) being used with each verse. The antiphon having been repeated, the priest sings *Dominus vobiscum* (choir, *Et cum spiritu tuo*) and the collect for the day. One or more commemorations often follow (see below); after the last *Dominus vobiscum,* etc., *Benedicamus Domino* is sung by the cantors (or assistants), the choir answering *Deo gratias* (see pp. 139 *seq).* The priest sings on a rather lower note, *Fidelium animæ per misericordiam Dei requiescant in pace* ("May the souls of the faithful departed through the mercy of God rest in peace"), the choir answering *Amen* on the same note. After *Pater noster* in silence the priest sings *Dominus det nobis suam pacem* ("May the Lord grant us his peace"), again on one note, as likewise the choir when they sing the ℟.: *Et vitam æternam, Amen* ("And life eternal, Amen").

Then follows one of the four antiphons of the B. V. M. (intoned by the priest or cantor) with versicle and prayer (see pp. 92, 140, 141): from the first Vespers of the first Sunday of Advent to the second Vespers of the Purification inclusively, *Alma Redemptoris Mater,* but from the first Vespers of the Nativity till the Purification the versicle and prayer differ from those in Advent; from Compline on the feast of the Purification till Wednesday in Holy Week, *Ave Regina cœlorum;* from Holy Saturday to the first Vespers of Trinity Sunday, *Regina cœli;* from that time till Advent, *Salve Regina.* After the prayer the priest sings on one note, *Divinum auxilium,* etc., the choir answering *Amen.*

17. Many Vespers have one or more commemorations, i. e., after the prayer following the *Magnificat,* the *Magnificat*-antiphon, taken from the feast to be commemorated, is sung with ℣., ℟. and prayer. Thus when we read in the Calendar, *Com. seq.* (= *Commemoratio sequentis)* we take the *Magnificat*-antiphon, ℣., and ℟. from the first Vespers of the following day; if we read *Com. præc.* (= *præcedentis*) we take the *Magnificat*-antiphon, ℣., and ℟. from the second Vespers of the feast that was celebrated or commemorated in the Mass on that day (Calendar, *Com. simpl.*); if it be *Com. Dom.* (= *Commemoratio Dominicæ* — of the Sunday) we take the *Magnificat*-antiphon, etc., as in the office for the Saturday before the Sunday concerned; if we see *Com. de Cruce* (= Com. of the Cross); *Com. comm.* (= *Com. communes*) or *suffr.* (= *suffragia Sanctorum*) a commemoration is to be made of the Cross and of various saints which are indicated before Compline and occur in Vespers which are not of the *ritus duplex.*

If several commemorations follow one another only the last one has the long formula for the close of the prayer, the choir responding *Amen.* As regards the others the choir does not sing *Amen* after the prayer, but commences immediately the following antiphon.

The expression *Vesp. a cap. de seq. Comm. præc.* (= *Vesperæ a capitulo de sequénti, Commemorátio præcedéntis*), means that the five antiphons and psalms are from the second Vespers of the feast begun on that day; from the Little Chapter onwards all is taken from the first Vespers of the next day's feast, and after the prayer proper for that feast a commemoration (*Magnificat*-antiphon, ℣. and ℟. from the second Vespers) is made of the feast just ending.

γ) Liturgical Regulations in regard to High Mass and Vespers.[1])

18. Must everything be sung at High Mass and Vespers? According to the ecclesiastical precepts the following must be sung: the first verse of the canticle *(Magnificat, [Benedictus, Nunc dimittis]),* the first and last verse of the hymns, likewise those verses at which a

1) See *Cæremoniale Episcoporum,* Lib. I., cap. XXVIII and Lib. II., cap. VIII. and XX. — *Decreta authentica Cong. S. R. 1900.* — *Die Entscheidungen der h. Riten-Kongregation.* J. Auer (Ratisbon, F. Pustet). The Latin text of the more important decrees is given in addition to the German version — *Ecclesiastical Precepts in reference to Catholic Church Music,* by J. Mitterer, Catholic Truth Society, London.

genuflection is enjoined *(Veni Creator; O Crux ave* (feast of the Holy Cross) and *O salutaris* and *Tantum ergo* in presence of the B. Sacrament, and during the octave of Corpus Christi, if the B. Sacrament is on the High Altar, *Ave maris stella, Te ergo quæsumus,* etc., in the *Te Deum*; further those portions of the text at which all have to bow the head, e. g., *Gloria Patri* at the end of the psalms. (As regards *Gloria in excelsis* see p. 99.) The whole of the *Credo* must always be sung. In regard to the other parts of Mass and Vespers there is no precept ordering them to be sung.

19. Those portions of the liturgy which are not sung must, in accordance with the ecclesiastical precepts, be recited, and this is certainly of obligation for all Cathedral and Collegiate churches.

If circumstances are such that this cannot be complied with or only by greatly overstraining the choir, or in an unsatisfactory manner, the best way is to consult the *Rector ecclesiæ,* i. e., the parish priest, and abide by his decision, unless a relaxation of the rule has already been obtained through the Bishop.

Concerning *Dies iræ* see p. 116.

Those who only render such chants as they understand and have thoroughly practised, and who recite the remainder, serve the good cause better than those who go beyond their capacity; of course recitation must also be practised, and should be neither too drawled nor too hurried, but always dignified. The preparation for this need not occupy so very much time. If when a melody should be sung twice, recitation has to be resorted to once (e. g., Introit) a more solemn effect is produced by singing the text the first time.

20. Who is to sing? The Vesper chants could not easily be rendered by the whole choir, leaving out of consideration some of the longer *Magnificat*-antiphons, therefore the verses of the psalms and hymns should be sung by two choirs. The same as regards the *Gloria* and *Credo* at High Mass; how and by whom the other Mass chants are to be rendered will be explained later on (see pp. 93 *seq.*) At Vespers the priest intones *Deus in adjutorium* (see p. 84), the first verse of the hymn, the *Magnificat*-antiphon and the concluding antiphon of the B. V. M. The priest's intonations at High Mass are well known.

21. It is only in churches which are under an obligation to sing the Canonical Hours of the Divine Office that the performance of Vespers in strict accordance with the Diocesan Calendar (or general *Ordo*) is positively necessary; all other churches, therefore nearly all parish churches, can likewise do this, but they can also sing Vespers from another office, e. g., that of the B. Sacrament, the B. V. M., St. Joseph, etc., as votive Vespers; but such Vespers must accord in every respect with the Vespers of the office selected.[1])

Chapter III.

Voice Production — Points of most Importance.[2])

A. In General.

22. Position of the Body. Hold yourself in such a manner that the organs necessary for singing may have perfect freedom of action.

α) Always stand when singing, with both feet resting equably on the ground, not too far apart.

β) The chest must not be contracted or overloaded with clothes; arms not crossed; book held at a little distance and raised to about the level of the mouth.

1) *Decreta authentica*, 29. Dec., 1884.

2) This Chapter and most of the Vocal Exercises in Appendix III. have been contributed by the Rev. Father Gregory Böckeler, of Maria-Laach, whom I heartily thank for his kindness.

γ) Take care that there is no pressure on the larynx; the neck not to be craned even when the highest notes are sung; the chin not to be depressed too low even when the lowest notes are sung.

In short, "head erect, chest out, abdomen in". Stand firmly, but always in an easy posture and without constraint.

23. Position of the Mouth. *α)* Mouth open; teeth apart. Normal opening (for the vowel *a)* is when the middle of the thumb can easily be placed between the teeth; open the mouth gently and not too wide; unnatural straining of the muscles of the throat and pressure on the larynx would result in an unpleasant palatal *timbre*.

β) Half of the upper teeth, and the lower teeth almost entirely, should disappear behind the lips.

The lips, however, should not be pressed upon the teeth; that makes the tone muffled; nor should they be too far away, for that makes the tone too sharp. The form of the mouth should be more round than oval.

γ) The tongue must remain motionless so long as one and the same vowel is sounded.

Particular care must be taken to keep the back part of the tongue extended in a middle position otherwise the tone becomes palatal. The tip of the tongue should rest lightly on the back part of the wall of the lower incisor teeth.

24. Breathing. We can breathe

α) By depressing the diaphragm ("diaphragmatic breathing") [if the lower ribs have part in it, "flank-breathing"];

β) By raising the whole of the chest ("rib-breathing");

γ) By raising the shoulders ("shoulder-breathing" or "high-breathing"). Only the methods *α)* and *β)* are of use for singing.

Still, rib-breathing is rather a strain. For a long succession of tones diaphragmatic breathing united with flank-breathing is the easiest and quickest method, as it least interferes with the muscles of the larynx and throat.

Breathe

1. Quietly, not hastily;
2. Inaudibly; draw in the air; do not sip it in;
3. At the right time, i. e., not just when the last residue of air is utilised;
4. Only when needed, i. e., not after every small group of notes.

The exhalation of the air must be effected calmly, equably and slowly; the air must not be forced out; carefully economise the breath when singing the first notes.

B. Tone Production.

25. Attack of the Tone. The attack is either

1. Hard (marked), (shock of the glottis = $\overset{>}{a}$), or
2. Breathed = $h\overset{<}{a}$, or
3. Soft = a.

The soft attack is the usual one.

Still the two first are important for voice production: the hard attack for those who deliver the tone in an indefinite and stifled manner; the breathed attack for hard, piercing voices.

a) The tone must be attacked at once with the first breath, entirely, softly and very sharply indeed (purity of *timbre)*.

Therefore no growling or humming sound without a definite tone-colour; no audible breathing, still less an *m* or *n* or similar sound interposed.

β) The tone must be attacked with the utmost purity (purity of tone).

Therefore avoid the unpleasant method of attacking with a long or short note from above or below. Many, particularly basses, bring the tone quite out of the depths, and run through several tones before they lay hold of the proper one.

γ) The tone must maintain its proper pitch, hence it must not sink, rise, or tremble.

The sinking of the tone when it is sustained (mostly united with a diminution of its force) arises from a want of breath (almost always with shoulder-breathing); frequently also from a too vehement attack.

The raising of the tone (less frequent) comes from a too hurried forcing out of the air, or too great a strain when singing.

δ) Each tone must be attacked gently, with little breath, and then swell out; should the tone be strong (accented), the swelling out must of course proceed rapidly, almost instantaneously.

ε) The vowels and consonants to be sung must be attacked with correctness and precision (purity of letters).

This holds good chiefly of the vowels. Therefore do not prefix *m, n, ng, nd, h* or *r.* Do not sing *o-a, i-e.* Do not change the tone-colour of the vowel.

All the muscles taking part in the formation of a vowel must with lightning speed be put in proper position, remaining therein immoveable so long as the vowel lasts.

26. Attack of the Tone (continued). The tone formed in the larynx must be so directed as to strike a little behind the roots of the upper teeth. The simultaneous sounding of the air enclosed in the hollows of the facial bones and in the nasal cavities then gives it more retundity and power. If the tone is directed straight to the mouth it sounds colourless (flat); if it strikes further behind on the soft palate it becomes muffled and toneless.

Persons who have not acquired from youth upwards a good sonorous tone will only be able to obtain it under the guidance of a competent singing master.

The attack is good when without any strain it produces a full, strong, but at the same time soft-sounding tone.

27. Faults in the Tone: *a)* Throaty Tone; the lower part of the tongue with the lid of the larynx (epiglottis) is depressed too much and the voice sounds stifled.

This occurs with tenors in the higher notes; the fault is owing to craning the neck, the muscles of which are thereby strained and pressed.

As regards basses it occurs very frequently in the lower notes; here it is the reverse, namely the depression of the chin, that causes the fault.

Remedy: do not force either the high or the low tones. A tenor must develop his falsetto tone by tone upwards, and *piano*, gradually learning to use it *forte* without straining. A bass must at first be content with somewhat weaker lower tones, endeavouring to strengthen them little by little, but without any straining. A rather nasal, dark colouring of the vowels will be helpful to him in doing this.

β) Nasal Tone: it occurs when the *velum palati,* the soft part of the palate to which the uvula is attached, is depressed and too much of the stream of air passes up to the *choanæ,* the internal nasal cavities. The tongue is often raised, so that the entrance to the mouth is completely blocked.

Remedy: study the production of the vowel *a* before a looking-glass, closely observing both organs.

γ) Palatal Tone: the tongue goes too far back so that the tone is only directed by circuitous routes towards the soft palate.

This fault often comes from opening the mouth too wide, therefore most frequently with *a.* Nevertheless *o* and *u* are often given in rather a palatal tone, because in forming these vowels the tip of the tongue, hollowed in the form of a spoon, lies in rather a lower position than usual.

Remedy: the root of the tongue should be raised high when singing *o* and *u*; on the other hand, with *a* the whole of the tongue should be kept evenly balanced on the edges of the lower teeth.

A universal remedy for all these defects, and in fact the best way to produce a good tone, to acquire distinct pronunciation and facility in connecting the notes, is solfaing, i. e., reading and singing the notes to the Guidonian syllables, *do, re, mi, fa, sol, la, si, do.*

28. The exercises should not consist of more than 5—7 notes, with intervals not wider than a fourth. Practise them at first on a middle tone that can be taken comfortably, at a moderate speed, only once at first, then twice, thrice and so on, as your breath may allow. Little by little they can be taken at a quicker rate, the pitch can in turn be lowered or raised in order to extend the compass of the voice. — The exercises must always be sung *softly*.

After some weeks (supposing that daily practice has taken place, lasting for about a quarter of an hour), more extended exercises can be taken in hand and worked through in the same way. The short preliminary exercises should however still be kept at hand, but they must be sung slower and slower, with at last several notes to one vowel. In slackening the *tempo* however, great care should be taken not to change the vowel sound.

Not until a fair range of voice, united with flexibility and correct attack, has been acquired, singing *piano*, should the pupil attempt *mezzo forte; forte* exceptionally for a few minutes.

Two main conditions for the attainment of the desired object should be carefully observed:

1. The consonants must be pronounced very sharply indeed, the vowel sound being light and soft.

Those who do not form *r* with the tip of the tongue but at the back of the throat pronounce *re* as *way* or *nay*, instead of *ray*.

2. The tones belonging to each other must be carefully connected one with another.

By diligently solfaing the Gregorian melodies the singer will derive benefit from these exercises, and acquire facility in striking the note.

29. Release of the Tone: *a*) If a *new syllable of the same* word follows, the vowel of the syllable must continue to sound until the time comes for the new syllable; the transition must be effected briskly and with precision.

If *two vowels* follow one another the new vowel must be started faultlessly, without the interpolation of other vowels. Therefore not *Mari-æ-a.* In the same way consonants must not be inserted; e. g., not *Mari-ya; De-y-us; Jo-u-v-annes.* To avoid this fault many put the two vowels near each other but disunited; that is not beautiful in speech or song.

Diphthongs *(au, eu, ei)* are to be sung as double vowels, and in such a way that the first vowel may sound almost as long as the tone lasts, the second being inserted at the end quickly (thus *la - - udet, e - - uge, ele - - ison).* Consonants are always drawn to the next syllable; therefore one must sing *e-xspe-cta-ntes.* Interpolations between the consonants such as *ome-nes, ve-a-rbum, ver-e-bum,* must be particularly guarded against.

β) If a *new word* follows beginning with a consonant, it is to be taken at once like a syllable of the same word, provided that the words belong to one another according to the sense; e. g., *Deo Patri sit gloria* is to be sung as *Deopatrisitgloria.* The letter *h* must evidently be an exception, for of course it cannot be pronounced without breaking off *(pax hominibus).* — If two consonants alike in sound follow one another, it is easier and better to enunciate the same letter once only, making it however rather longer, e. g., *sedes sapientiæ* = *sede-ssapientiæ;* otherwise with *sedet* | *Deus*, in which case the consonants are not precisely alike.

If a word closes with a consonant whilst the second begins with a vowel, attack the second word afresh, excepting perhaps words which are very closely connected with each other, only the consonant must not be too indistinct; in fact it will be better if enunciated rather sharply, e. g., *ab‿illis, in‿eo;* not so good, *Deus‿est.*

A vowel must not be broken off before a pause, but must gently die away. On the other hand a consonant must be ended off distinctly. It is just the end consonants that are lost, and this to the disadvantage of the listener.[1])

1) Cf. Piel: *Über den Gesang* (Schwann, Düsseldorf, no date).

Normal School.

Part I. Principles.

Chapter IV.
Plain Chant Notation.

30. The notes now generally used for Gregorian or plain chant are as follows:

a) The square note or *punctum* ■, the usual sign, *b)* the tailed note or *virga, caudata,* or ; *c)* the lozenge, diamond, or *rhombus* ♦, *d*) the *quilisma*, *e*) the liquescent notes, as .

31. These notes are placed on four lines or in the spaces between them (stave or staff).

When the melody exceeds the limit of this stave a small ledger line is used.

32. The *time-value* of all these notes is of itself the same.

In converting them into our modern notation, therefore, it is best to change all the notes without distinction into quavers (♪).

The *difference in their shape* is explained chiefly by their relation to the pitch of the note (whether the note in the melody is a higher or a lower one).

The *punctum* indicates, in contradistinction to the *virga,* a lower note; the *virga,* a higher note.

The other signs are never used alone. The *rhombus* or lozenge is employed in descending passages, the upper note of which is generally a *virga*; the *quilisma,* in an ascending melody. Concerning the liquescents see pp. 36, 37.

33. Notice particularly that the *virga*

a) Can be used for accentuated syllables of words (syllables with an accent) just as well as for unaccentuated syllables;

b) Has not a longer duration of sound than the *punctum* or the lozenge.

34. The degrees of the scale in plain chant have the following names:

do, re, mi, fa, sol, la, si, si♭ (sa)
c, d, e, f, g, a, b, b♭.

35. A ♭ before *si (b* natural) lowers the note a semitone and in the Vatican edition only affects the note before which it is placed, but in other editions it holds good until the next mark for a pause, unless it has previously been restored to its normal position by a ♮.

The ♭ is only used for the note *si.*

A sharp ♯ (diësis) is unknown in plain chant.

36. To mark any particular sound as being higher or lower than another (the pitch), *clefs* are used, which are placed on one of the four lines of the stave.

There are two clefs, 𝄡 and 𝄢. Wherever 𝄡 is placed the note thereon throughout the whole of the melody, until the clef is changed, is always *do (c)*; hence this is called the *Do clef.* On whatever line 𝄢 is placed, the note thereon is always *fa (f)* until the clef is changed, and hence this is called the *Fa clef.*

The *Do clef* can be placed on the fourth, third or second line.

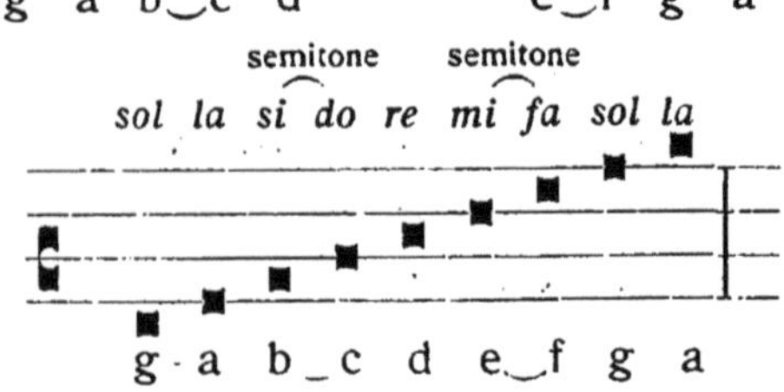

For practice read the notes of the *Kyrie* in the Mass for Easter, and those of the *Asperges*.

The *Fa clef* can be placed on the third line, seldom on the fourth.

For practice read the notes of the *Sanctus* in Mass XII., and those of the *Offertorium* for Holy Thursday.

Sometimes a ledger line above or below is needed:

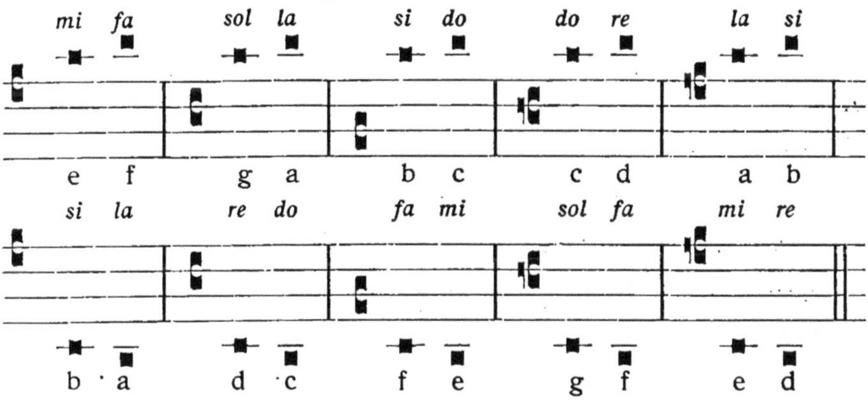

37. At the end of each line, seldom in the middle of the sentence, a small note is placed indicating the succeeding note, and therefore called *custos* (watchman, guide).

38. The following signs indicate *pauses:*

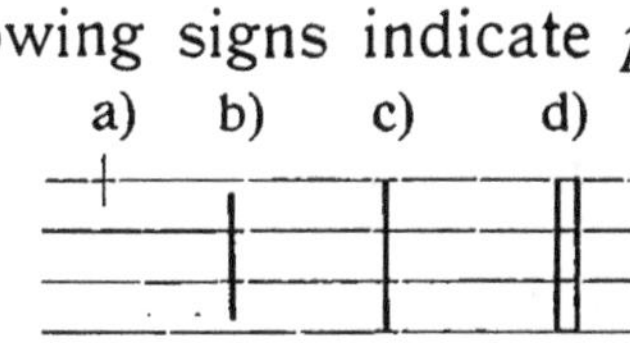

a) indicates that breath can be taken at this place; in many cases, especially if the melody is a very short one, it is better to employ a *mora vocis* (see pp. 52 *seq.*)

b) indicates half as long a pause as c), the latter occurring at the end of a melodic section.

d) occurs at the end of a principal sentence or verse in the Gradual or Tract; also after every sentence written for alternate choirs *(Gloria, Credo).*

A sign after the first or second word of a piece (* in the *Kyriale* of the Vatican edition) indicates how far the cantor has to intone.

If the chant is intoned by one or more singers and is then continued by the choir, this sign indicates at the same time a short pause; this however is not made when the whole choir repeats the chant from the beginning, or when the singers who intone the chant sing it through alone without the choir. Here a pause would in most cases have a bad effect.

As regards the *length of the pauses,* the purport of the words that are between them, the character and *tempo* of the piece, the acoustics of the church, etc., should be taken into consideration.

Further concerning this see Chapter on "Mode of Rendering".

39. Is the *virga* ▜ to be sustained longer than the *punctum* ■? Does it not occur on *accentuated* syllables?

Answer: In genuine plain chant according to the mediæval tradition, no.

Proof: *a)* When several words which only have one note for each syllable follow one another in MSS. wherein there are no lines for the notes, sometimes ■ only is used (generally when the melody moves on a lower note), sometimes ▜, without regard to the verbal accent or the length of the syllables. In codex 339 in the library of St. Gall[1] (10th century), fol. 45 according to the old, 13 according to the new numbering, we have in the Gradual for the feast of St. Stephen, *sālvūm mē fāc prōptēr mīsērīcōr(diam);* the same in codex 121 in the library of Einsiedeln[2] (10th to 11th century), fol. 34; similarly the Montpellier codex H, 159,[3]) always has the *virga* with the vertical stroke for this text (fol. 168).

This codex indicates by letters under the neums the exact tonal value of each note of the neums.

---

1) *Pal. mus.* II. 2) *Pal. mus.* IV. 3) *Pal. mus.* VII.

The psalm-verse of the Communio *Mense septimo,* fol. 427 in codex 121 at Einsiedeln, must, in accordance with the principles of modern plain chant notation, be transcribed in this way:

Attendite popule me-us legem me-am, inclinate aurem vestram

in verba oris me-i.

The notes for *(at)tendi-(te)*, *(in)clin-(ate)*, *o-(ris)*, *me-(i)*, are higher than the note immediately preceding them, hence the use of the *virga.*

b) In the *neumatic notation* of Aquitaine,[1]) which spread from Metz throughout the rest of Europe, in which even before the introduction of the stave the tonal position of the notes can be ascertained with a tolerable degree of certainty, the *virga* scarcely ever appears.

c) In MSS. with *lines for the notes* the *virga* is very freely employed, i. e., they very often use it when a *punctum* is given for the same passage repeated elsewhere in the same MS., or in other MSS., or melodies are entirely written, note after note, with the *virga* or with the *punctum.*

That the old theorists assigned no particular duration of sound to the *virga* is evident from the circumstance that many neums exactly alike are written in different ways, i. e., with and without the *virga.* One meets with , but still more frequently with ; or in the *climacus* (see p. 34) or ; or in the *clivis* (see p. 33) or .

As a matter of fact, the ancient notation has sufficient means of its own to enable it to express time-values of two or more time-units. It does this by the *pressus* and by simply doubling, and so on (concerning this see p. 46 *seq.*). Why then should in one case a double note, etc., be used if the *virga* already indicated this prolongation?

Moreover, one frequently finds the following combination . Why is it not , as in many other places? Answer: because the *virga* does not indicate a prolongation, but only the higher tone in the *climacus.*

d) (Pseudo-)Hucbald († 930) writes in his *Commemoratio brevis:*[2]) "The chant should be rendered with exact equality (æqualitate).

1) *Pal. mus.* II., Pl. 83 *seq.* and Vivell: *Greg. Ges.*, Graz, Styria, 1904 p. 80.
2) Migne: *Patrologia Latina*, 132, 1039 (Paris).

No neum and no tone should be lengthened or shortened at this or that passage without reason." And in *Musica enchiriadis* he explains his remark by an example in which on every syllable all the notes have the same duration, and only the notes on the last syllable of a sentence are doubled, and he expressly observes: "*Solæ in tribus membris ultimæ longæ, reliquæ breves sunt* (in the three members of the sentence only the last notes are long, all the others are short)."

Franco of Cologne (13th century) says: "*Musica mensurabilis* means music measured by long and short notes. It is called *mensurabilis* because in *musica plana* (i. e., plain chant) this measuring is not taken into account."[1])

Other authors expressly declare that the *virga* is not to be made longer than any other note, and that it is only prolonged through the abuse and ignorance of singers.

e) In *printed notation*[2]) at the end of the 15th and beginning of the 16th century the *virga* appears sometimes on accentuated, sometimes on unaccentuated syllables, on long and on short syllables.

f) The axiom "the notes in plain chant have the same duration" was still almost universally recognised in the 17th century, as Dom Molitor has proved in his work "Reformchoral" (Herder, 1901). The numerous authors therein quoted (pp. 3—7), sometimes appealing to St. Bernard, agree in part with Scheyrer (1663) who says: "In plain chant one note is worth as much as another."[3])

g) Finally, the *unsightly lines of notes* which became necessary owing to the *lengthening of the virga* and the *shortening of the lozenge* prove that this leads to a very defective rendering from an aesthetical point of view, and is therefore practically inadmissible. The comparatively very modern notion that the *virga* is a sign of prolongation and accentuation has helped very considerably to bring plain chant into disrepute.

40. But by keeping to the rule we have laid down does not plain chant become "tedious"? is it not condemned as a "pattering rhythm, like falling drops of water, or the tick-tick of a clock"? Answer:

a) The notes are to be of equal *length* but not of equal *strength*. Plain chant is no more opposed to dyna-

1) Coussemaker: Scriptorum de musica nova series (Paris 1864—76), II., 118.

2) Molitor, *Choral-Wiegendrucke* pp. 12 *seq.* and particularly Table 1 (Missal by Ulrich Han, Rome, 1476).

3) For further proofs see Vivell: l. c. pp. 79 *seq.*, and Wagner: *Neumenkunde*, pp. 230 *seq.*

mics, gradation in the strength of the tone, than any other music claiming to be art.

b) The *notes* are of the same length; the *tones* are not always of the same length; plain chant possesses various means such as the *pressus* (see p. 46), the *quilisma* (see p. 48), the *bistropha, tristropha* (see pp. 33, 34), *mora vocis* (see p. 52), by which it can effect a *different duration of sound.*

c) In regard to the rhythm of the syllabic chants (in which there is only one note for each syllable) what has been said on pp. 7 *seq.* holds good.

d) Apart from psalmody, purely syllabic chants do not frequently occur. In other chants as regards the number of notes to a syllable there is great variety, and this is also of advantage to the rhythm.

e) The theory alone of "notes of equal length" prevents the singers from adopting an unpleasant and often violent forcing of the tone, and renders it possible to produce a beautiful, calmly flowing, yet free and varied, movement.

Chapter V.
The Church Modes.

41. If we compare the melody of the *Asperges* with that of the *Gloria* in the first Mass *in Duplicibus,* we find that the two melodies differ from each other as regards position of notes, progressions, and general turn of the melody. Whilst the *Asperges* closes on *sol,* the *Gloria* ends on *mi.* We find the same thing with regard to the half-closes in the various parts of the melody. In the *Asperges* the half-close falls on *sol;* in the *Gloria,* 16 times on *mi.* This difference is not by chance; we find it in other melodies; the reason is that the character of the melody, the mode, is different in both chants.

By "mode"[1]) *(modus,* less frequently, *tonus,* tone[2]) is understood the peculiarity of a melody which is perceived from the position of the tones and semitones and their relation to the varying fundamental tone.

42. Plain chant has 8 modes. If above one of the 4 notes *re, mi, fa, sol,* on which the plain chant melodies usually close, and which are consequently called closing tones, fundamental tones, final tones, a diatonic scale of 7 tones is constructed, the material for the 4 authentic (genuine, original) modes is obtained, and for these the following scales form the foundation:

For Mode I.	(dorian)	re mi fa sol +la si do re
" " III.	(phrygian)	mi fa sol la +si do re mi
" " V.	(lydian)	fa sol la si +do re mi fa
" " VII.	(mixolydian)	sol la si do +re mi fa sol

43. Each of these modes has its relative mode. If the upper 4 tones of the scales (the first of these is marked in each case with a +) be placed under the 5 first tones of the scales, the material for the 4 plagal (derived) modes is obtained, and for these the following scales form the foundation:

For Mode II.	(hypodorian)	la si do re mi fa sol la
" " IV.	(hypophrygian)	si do re mi fa sol la si
" " VI.	(hypolydian)	do re mi fa sol la si do
" " VIII.	(hypomixolydian)	re mi fa sol la si do re

In the plagal modes the final is the same as in the authentic modes from which they are derived.

1) Cf. Brambach: *Das Tonsystem und die Tonarten des christl. Abendlandes im M. A.* (Leipzig, Teubner, 1881.)

2) *Tonus* indicates more especially forms of the *modus,* and is properly used for the *formulæ* for chanting the psalms, canticles, *Gloria Patri,* etc. We say "psalm-tones" just as we say "hymn-tunes". Trsl.

The arrangement of the authentic modes was formerly incorrectly ascribed to St. Ambrose, that of the plagal to St. Gregory. It is true that in the Ambrosian chant the modes are dealt with in a manner somewhat different from that adopted in the Gregorian chant.

If a chant closes on *re* it will be seen from the above scales that it belongs to

		Mode	I.	or	II.;
If it closes in	*mi*	to	III.	„	IV.;
„ „ „ „	*fa*	„	V.	„	VI.;
„ „ „ „	*sol*	„	VII.	„	VIII.

44. The *authentic* modes differ from the *plagal*

a) Owing to the *dominants being different.* By dominant (the dominating note, also tenor) is meant that note round which the melody preferably moves, upon which it rests in a certain way for support. Whilst the final seldom appears in the melody, sometimes only *quite at its close,* the dominant comes much more frequently; it is particularly prominent in psalmody wherein very few closing cadences fall on the final of the mode. The dominant in the *authentic* modes is a fifth above the final, except for Mode III. which takes the sixth, *do,* its dominant having for centuries been transferred to that note from *si.* In the *plagal* modes the dominant is a third above the final with the exceptions of Mode IV. *(la,* not *sol)* and Mode VIII. *(do,* not *si).*

b) Owing to the difference in the *melodic* movement:

α) in the authentic modes the tendency of their progressions is to ascend, in the plagal, to descend, i. e., below the final (Mode IV., almost always excepted);

β) certain progressions that are frequently found in the authentic modes are never or seldom met with in the plagal, and *vice versâ;*

γ) in the authentic modes the melodies move stepwise to the final, in the plagal by skips.

Of course none of these rules are without exceptions. What the old writers said about the differences between the two kinds has but little practical interest for us.

45. *Table of Modes.*

N. B. Final and dominant are indicated by double notes (bistropha), the final always first.

Authentic. Plagal.

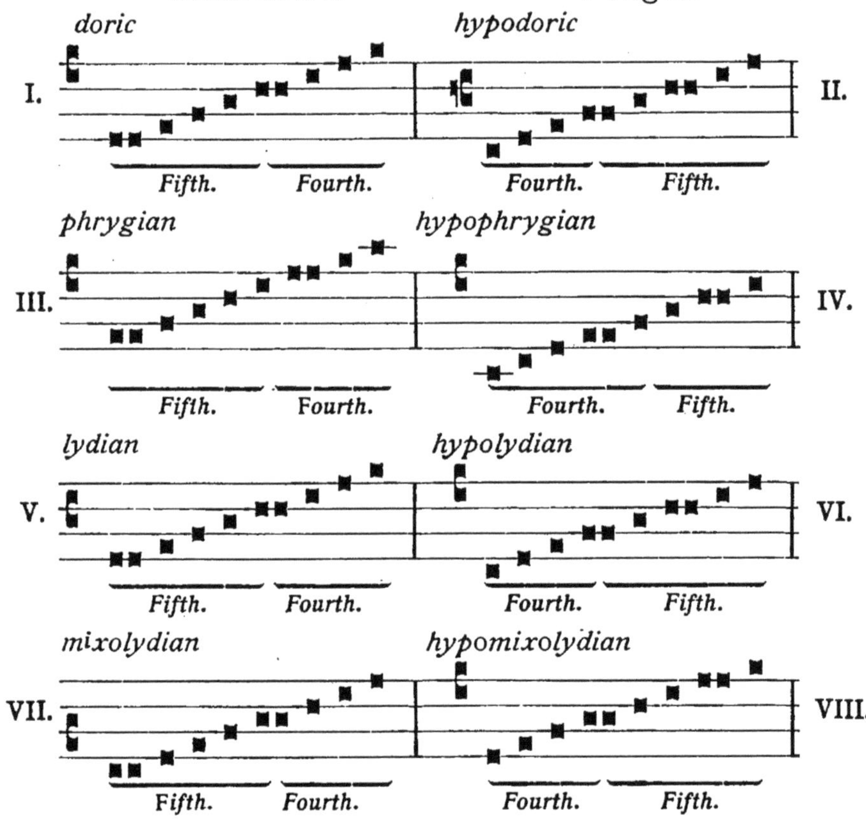

46. In the Vatican edition a Roman numeral at the beginning of the chant indicates the mode.

Occasionally we see I. et II., VIII. et VII.; in these cases there are passages which belong both to the authentic and plagal modes.

47. Sometimes progressions proper to one mode occur in another one, and then we perceive that a modulation (transition to another mode) has taken place.

Many of the more modern authors maintain that certain melodies belong to none of the modes. But this is incorrect. Though melodies with a very limited range can be assigned to *different* modes (e. g., to Modes I. and II.), it does not follow from this that they belong to *none* of the modes. The doctrine of an *absolute melody,* which permits of no harmonic basis, is also in plain chant inadmissible.

48. The mode is called "perfect" (*perfectus*) when it makes use of the whole range or compass (*ambitus*) of its scale, otherwise it is called "imperfect" (*imperfectus*); "more than perfect" (*plus-quam perfectus*, *superabundans*), when it extends the *ambitus* of the scale above or below; "mixed" (*mixtus*), when it has progressions proper to both an authentic and a plagal mode. — The doctrine concerning the *ambitus* is no longer of such importance as it formerly was for theory and practice.

49. When a chant does not close on *re, mi, fa, sol,* it generally means that a *transposition* has taken place, i. e., the melody, which remains unchanged, has been transposed to a higher or lower position (*modi affines* or *affinales*).

The *Liber Gradualis* of Solesmes has scarcely any transpositions excepting to the fifth, and these are based on the following scales:

For Modes I. and II.:

la si do re mi fa sol la

cf. *Communio* for the 3rd Sunday in Lent.

For Modes III. and IV.:

si do re mi fa sol la si

cf. *Kyrie* in Mass XV., *Sanctus* and *Agnus* in the Mass for Easter.

For Modes V. and VI.:

do re mi fa sol la si♭ (si) do

cf. *Resp. Cum audisset* for Palm Sunday and the *Communio* for the 6th Sunday after Pentecost; Modes VII. and VIII. are not transposed.

The melody of the Communio *Beatus servus* in the Mass *Os justi* is transposed a fourth, likewise an antiphon in Mode IV. that frequently occurs (see p. 78). According as one allows further transpositions, the number of the church modes is increased. Charlemagne, it is said, added 4 new modes to the 8 to show the Greeks that the Westerns having this invention were superior to them. Henry Loris of Glarean insisted upon 12 modes.

Transposition is chiefly employed in order to avoid *mi* ♭ (e ♭) or *fa* ♯ (f ♯).

The Communio *Passer* (3rd Sunday in Lent) and the antiphon *Gratia Dei* (see *Antiphonarium,* 25. Jan.) would have appeared in normal notation like this:

pul - los su - os. sed grá - ti - a.

50. As regards the *characteristics of the church modes* (the sentiments that each of them expresses) Kienle remarks in his *Choralschule,* p. 140: "We ought not to assign to one church mode a joyful character and to another a sorrowful one; for in each there are bright and jubilant strains, and each can be grave and mournful, but they all do this in their own way." With some justice, however, one may be allowed to say that the melodies of Modes V. and VI. are mostly spirited and joyful, those of Mode IV. sweet and attractive, almost dreamy, whilst the other modes may be described as solemn, majestic, and often sublime.

The peculiarities of the various modes can most readily be ascertained by continually singing and comparing melodies in the various modes, especially antiphons.[1])

Chapter VI.

Neums.

51. By the term "neum" is meant a combination of two or more notes, forming a distinct group of notes.

The simplest form is the combination of the *accentus acutus* with the *accentus gravis,* i. e., a higher tone with a lower one, and *vice versâ.*

---

1) Cf. Adam of Fulda in Gerbert's Script. III. pp. 329 *seq.* — Card. Bona: *Divina psalm.,* cap. 17, para. 4 — Ambros: *Musikgeschichte* (Leipzig, Leuckart, 2nd ed. 1880) pp. 13 *seq.* and 211 *seq.*

The word is derived from the Greek *neuma,* a sign (the leader or cantor indicated with his hand how the group should be rendered), or from another Greek word *pneuma,* breath (the notes of the group are sung in *one* breath). The former derivation is no doubt the more correct.

52. Neums a) with *two* notes are: the *clivis* ; union of a higher tone with a lower one.[1])

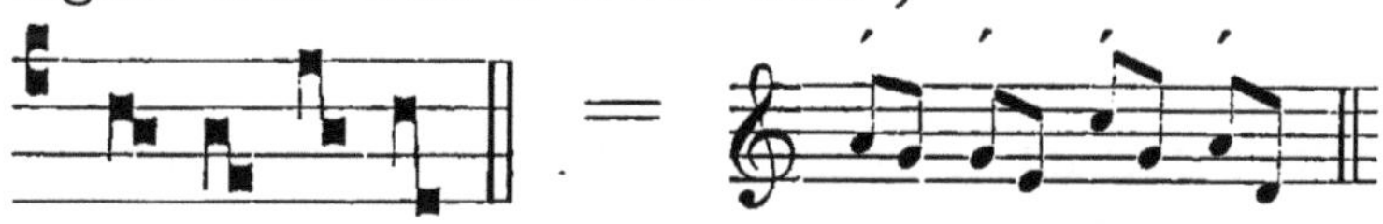

The *pes (podátus)* ; union of a lower tone with a higher one.

The *bistropha* (or ; this form is more conformable to the MSS.); the two notes are the same height of pitch.

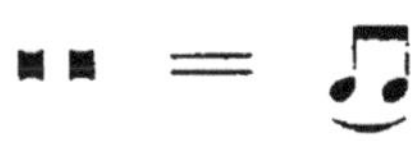

b) With *three* notes: the *tórculus* ; the middle tone is higher than the other two.

A note between 2 *torculus* (in some editions) is called *oriscus.*

The *porrectus* ; the middle tone is lower than the two others.

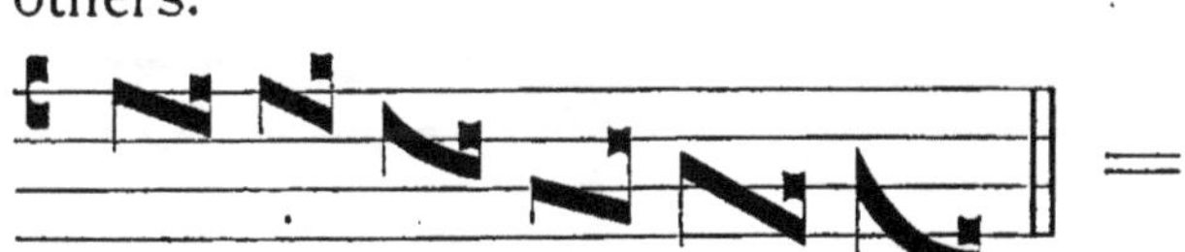

1) Vocal exercises for the various neums see Appendix III.

The *tristropha* (): the three notes are the same height of pitch (almost always on *fa* and *do).*

The *climacus* (*climax*, ladder) ; union of a *clivis* with a lower tone or tones.

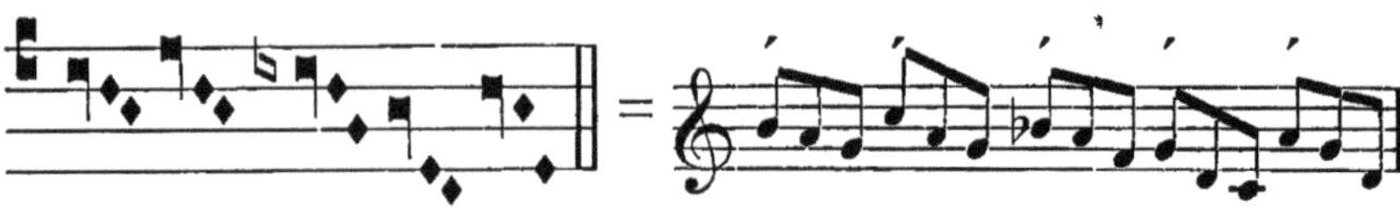

The *scándicus* ; union of a podatus with a higher tone.

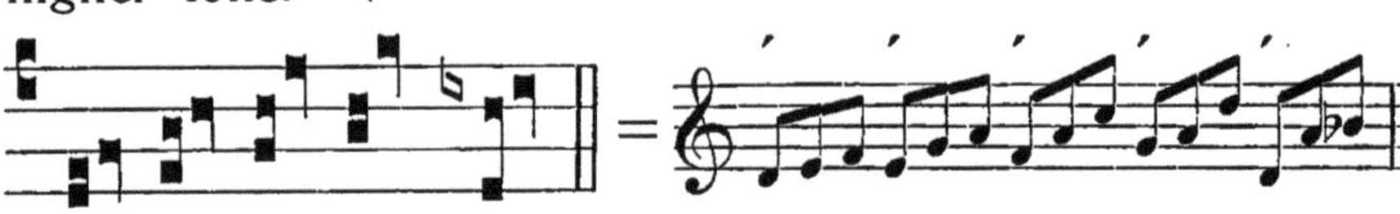

Concerning the *sálicus* see No 54.

c) With *four* notes: *α)* the fourth note is higher *(resupinus)* than the third:

The *climacus resupinus*

The *tórculus resupinus*

β) the fourth note is lower *(flexa)* than the third:

The *porrectus flexus*

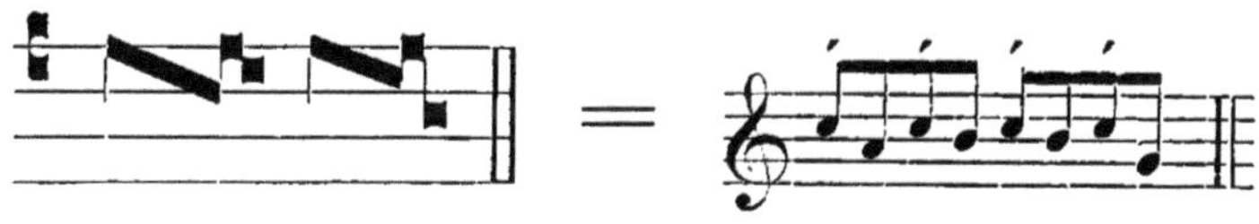

The *scándicus flexus*

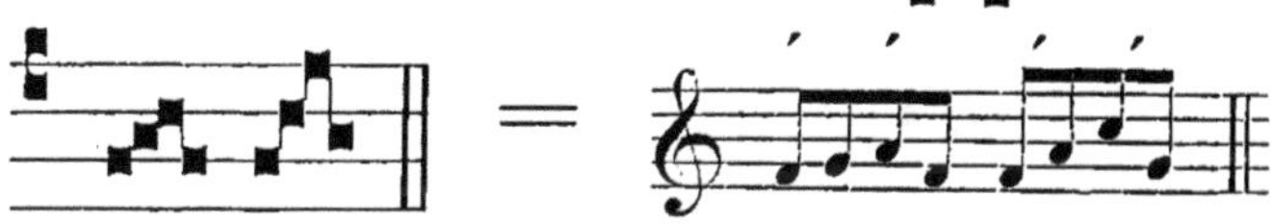

γ) the third and fourth notes are lower than the second: the *pes subbipunctis (pes* with two lower notes)

the *virga subtripúnctis (virga* with three lower notes)

d) With *five* notes: *α)* the fifth note higher than the fourth:

Virga subtripunctis resupina

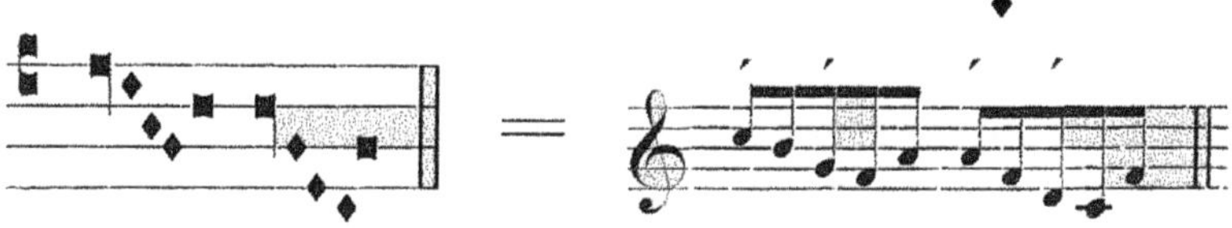

Pes subbipunctis resupinus

β) the fifth note is lower than the fourth:

Pes subtripunctis

Scandicus subbipunctis

Torculus resupinus flexus

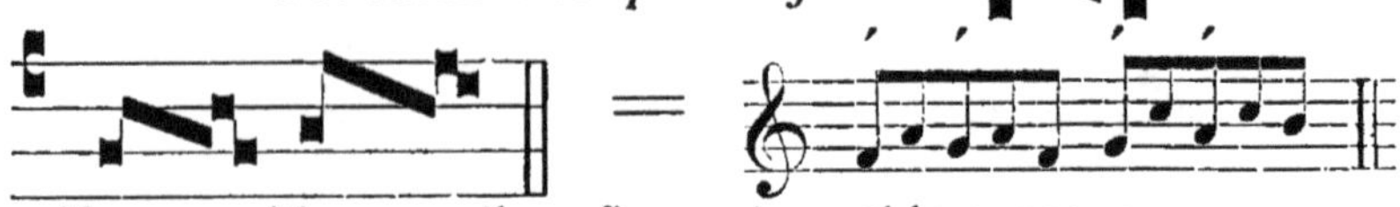

Neums with more than five notes seldom occur.

53. According to the way in which they are written, and partly according to the manner in which they are rendered, we distinguish:

a) Full neums; such are all those above mentioned.

β) Abbreviated in the notation: *liquescent* neums (*liquescens* = melting into one another). These are placed usually at the end of a group at the transition of one syllable (or word) to another, when the following letters occur together:

1) Two or three consonants, particularly when the first of them is l, m, n, r, s, t, d *sanctus*, a *dextris meis)*, also gn (*magnus*), or *j* after a consonant *(subjecit)*;

2) *j* between two vowels *(ejus)*,

3) at *au (gaudete)*.

To the liquescent neums belong:

the *cephálicus*, modified form of the *clivis*,
the *epíphonus*, „ *pes*,
the *ancus*, „ „ *climacus*,
the *torculus líquescens*.

The liquescent neums are easily rendered, like the full neums, as we Germans [and English-speaking persons] can pronounce the above mentioned combination of consonants without any trouble. Guido of Arezzo remarks in his *Micrologus*.[1]) "If you wish to make the tone fuller, not allowing it to melt away, it does no harm."

1) Migne, l. c. 141, 396.

When however a moderately accelerated rate of movement is preferred with these neums, a better effect can generally be produced.

54. In singing the notes belonging to a neum care must be taken to keep them closely connected and distinct from the preceding and following neum. This is done by the *accent* which is generally on the first note of each neum. The accentuated note has the same import as a note in measured music on the accented part of the bar.

The *salicus*, consisting of three ascending notes, which differs from the *scandicus* as to the space between the first and second note, has the accent on the second note.

The Vatican *Kyriale* does not use a different notation for the *scandicus* and *salicus*.

The accent of itself, as already remarked above, is not *a lengthening of the tone*. The *degree of strength* of the tone is determined either according to the importance of the syllable over which the neum is placed, or according to the position of the neum in the melodic phrase, but, above all, according to the *crescendo* or *decrescendo* of the movement. The strengthening of the tone on the accent must certainly be observable, but it must never produce a vehement tone. Likewise avoid all *forcing* or striking at the tone and do not attack it too impetuously. The accent must do its momentary task in a suitable manner, but the tone should always be full, and yet at the same time soft and rounded.

If a neum consists of more than three notes, it is necessary, as with a word of more than three syllables, to have a secondary accent (seldom two).

Generally the first note of each neum has the principal accent; the third or fourth note, the secondary accent.

Yet no general rule binding in all cases can be laid down; on the contrary, in each case one must consider the relation of the notes to the succeeding ones and to the whole melodic phrase.

In this example 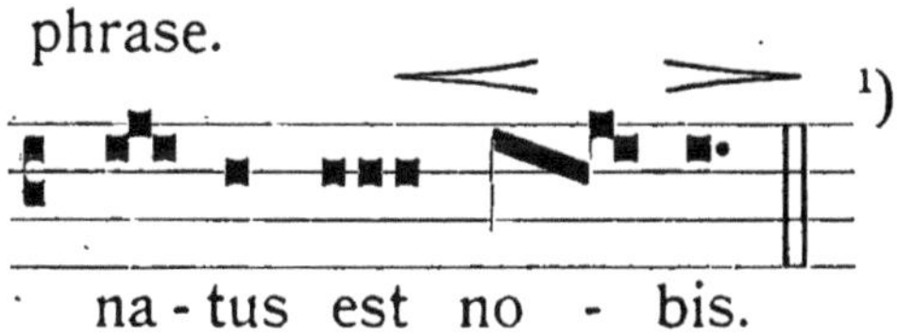

[1]

1) A dot after a note means that the duration of sound is doubled.

the accent on the note *re* would be best treated as a secondary one, that on *mi* as the principal one.

Neums with three accents are rare.

If a single note on an unaccented syllable follows a neum with three notes, the third note of the neum receives an accent (usually secondary), see p. 42 and pp. 7 and 8.

The unifying effect of the accent on the final note of each of the neums can be enhanced still further by a beautifully executed *legato* or *mora vocis*. Concerning this see pp. 52 *seq*.

55. If the notes belonging to a neum are to have their *full* and *complete* effect, beware of *a)* hurrying over one neum to get to another:

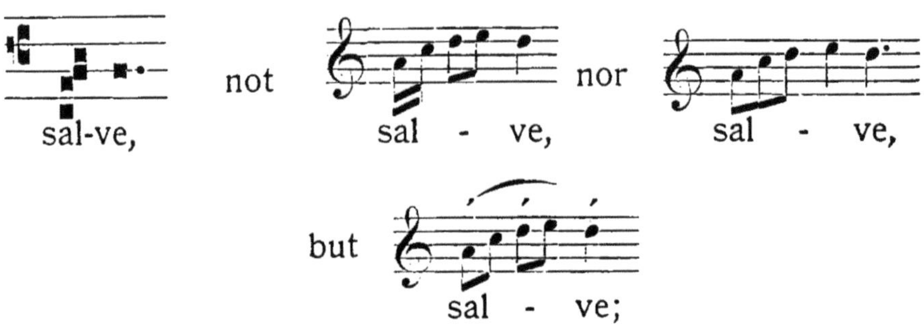

b) and of sustaining the last note before a new syllable:

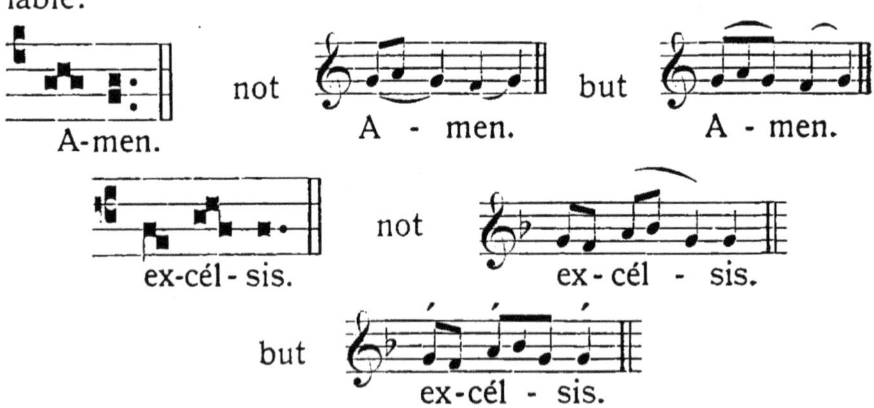

Chapter VII.
Plain Chant Rhythm.

Preliminary Remarks. 1) So soon as the pupil has mastered the most necessary rules (Nos. 56, 59, 60, 61, 74) he should pass on to the study of simple melodies, and only when cases arise for which these rules no longer suffice should he be made acquainted with a new rule to suit the particular case. In this way a beginner can learn easily and thoroughly an apparently complicated system.

2) The special rules, then, are not to be explained until in the course of practical work it has become necessary to do so, and even then the particular passage should be sung before the pupil as a pattern, and attention should not be drawn to the rule as such until a considerable number of similar cases have been practically treated and become familiar.

3) In reality the same idea is at the bottom of all the rules and apparent exceptions, namely, that the accent must be perpetually renewed and that the renewal has always to take place within three units.

4) Singers who seldom sing plain chant or only the Mass chants do not generally require to know these rules. *For them it suffices to know where there should be a stress in the melody, a pause or a sustained note,* and the choirmaster can make this clear by singing a pattern and adding a few words of explanation.

5) The work will be much facilitated for such singers if they make use of editions in which the necessary rhythmical signs are indicated (e. g., the Solesmes *Liber usualis*, 1903).

6) Hence *the least possible forcing of theories,* especially at the beginning and with untrained singers. *It is practical work that will best serve their interests and save their time.*

Of importance for the rhythm of Gregorian chant are, *a)* the rhythmical fundamental forms, *b) pressus* and *quilisma, c)* pauses and *mora vocis.*

a) Rhythmical Fundamental Forms.

56. The various neums with which we have been made acquainted in Chapter VI. are employed in a plain chant melody in great variety. One need only examine a few examples to perceive at once that

a) Sometimes neums with two tones, or

b) Those with three tones follow each other, or

c) Neums with three tones and those with two succeed one another in turn, or

d) They are connected together in groups like this: 2+3, 3+2, 2+3+2, 3+2+3, 2+2+3, and so on.

57. We *never* find in the *more extended* melodies *neums with only two or only three tones.* On the contrary, these figures appear in turn with perfect freedom, often interspersed with single notes (on single syllables of the text). This free alternation, defined or definable by no law, is like the free use of words in unfettered speech, words of two, three or more syllables following one another, as for example *Dixit (2) Dóminus (3) Dómino (3) méo (2).*

From this it follows that

a) The accent (the accentuated note) does not in plain chant recur at regular intervals of time;

b) The plain chant rhythm, i. e, the order in the movement of the melody, is in consequence *free;*

c) It is precisely this rhythm that can be called *oratorical rhythm,* or the *rhythm of speech,* owing to its relation to unfettered speech.

As the accent in plain chant melodies is renewed at unequal intervals of time, they differ from melodies in measured time.

58. Though the *rhythm of plain chant* is free it is not at pleasure, that is,

a) It conforms itself to the musical and rhythmical laws in general;

b) It is never left to the singer to place the accent where he likes;

c) With perfect freedom in the movement (apart from psalmody) there are definite time-values and time-units;

d) The axiom "Sing as you speak" is quite true as regards declaiming and expressing the melody, but for the rhythm of notes and neums can only be upheld to a certain extent in syllabic chants.

59. On an *accented unit* one or two, but *never three unaccented* syllables can occur. Cf. pp. 7, 8.

Where is the accent (accented unit) placed?

60. Answer: In *syllabic chants,* i. e., in melodies wherein only one tone falls on each syllable, the note which is placed over an *accented syllable* receives the accent:

The rules given for principal and secondary accents on p. 37 and 38 hold good.

In syllabic chants, then, different words can be set to the same succession of notes, with a different accentuation.

61. For *melismatic chants,* i. e., for melodies wherein neums with two or more tones often occur over single syllables, the rules are as follows: the accent is placed on the first note in the case of simple neums with two or three notes; see above, pp. 37 and 38.

Neums with four tones receive two accents, neums with five tones, also two accents (2+3 or 3+2); neums with six tones receive two accents to three tones, or three to two, according to the notation.

62. Very often *single notes* placed over an *unaccented* syllable are viewed as belonging to the preceding syllable (auxiliary notes or tones). Three cases have to be distinguished:

a) A neum with two notes: the single note is then simply treated as a *third* note, and the accentuation remains unaltered:

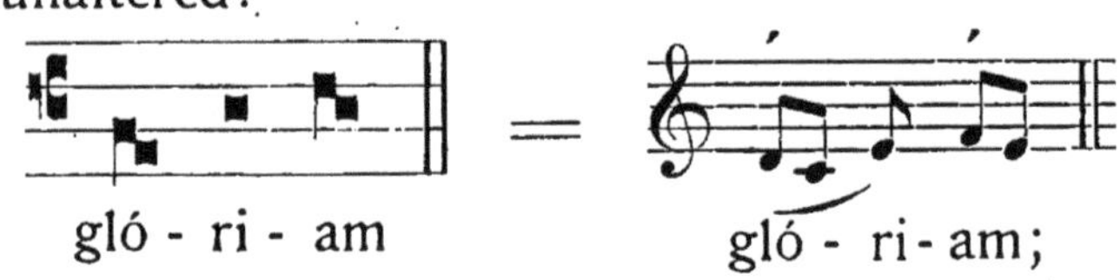

b) A neum with three notes; then there is a *superabundant* tone (four tones do not go to one accent, the fourth is therefore superabundant); in this case the final note of the preceding neum takes the accent:

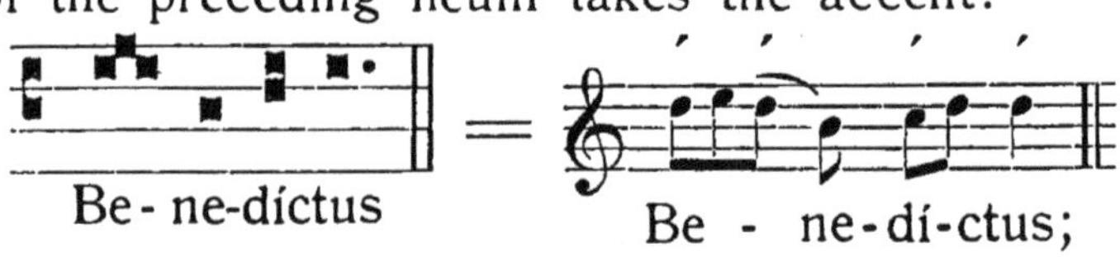

c) A neum with four or more notes; then the single note is considered to belong to the last accent (secondary) of this neum:

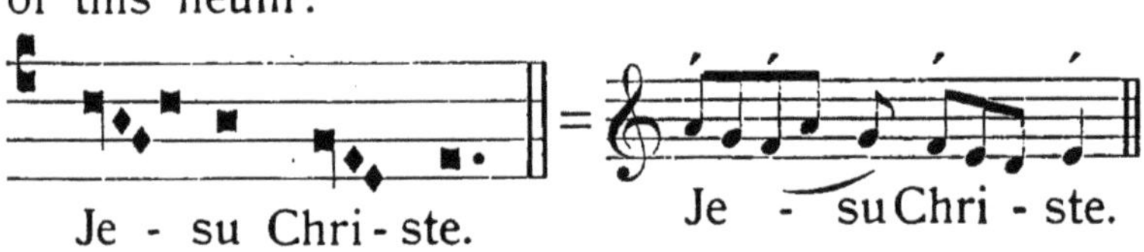

cf. a).

If two unaccented syllables with only one note between two neums (a) or between two accents (b), the first receives a secondary accent:

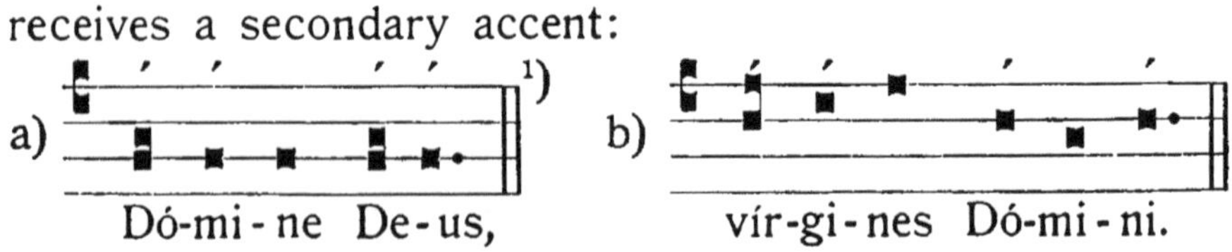

1) If 2 notes occur one above the other *(podatus, scandicus)*, the accent is always on the lower note.

63. If a single note appears over an *accented* syllable, between two neums, it belongs, according to the rules in No 62, to the last *accent of the preceding neum, yet the word is to retain its ordinary accent.* The neum that follows keeps its accent on the first note, whether it has two or three tones:

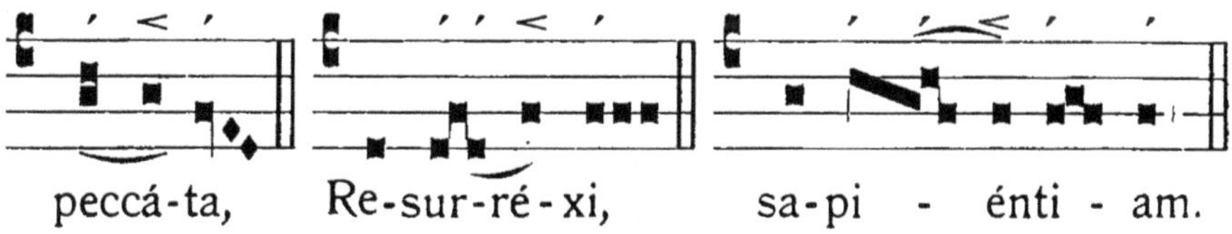

Here the verbal accent must *not* be prolonged.

Such passages are to be rendered as if three accents, of course of unequal strength, followed one another. But the single tones must be accentuated softly and gently. In the vocal compositions of the old masters similar passages occur very frequently. Compare, for example, a few bars from the motett *media vita* by Jakob Handl:[1]

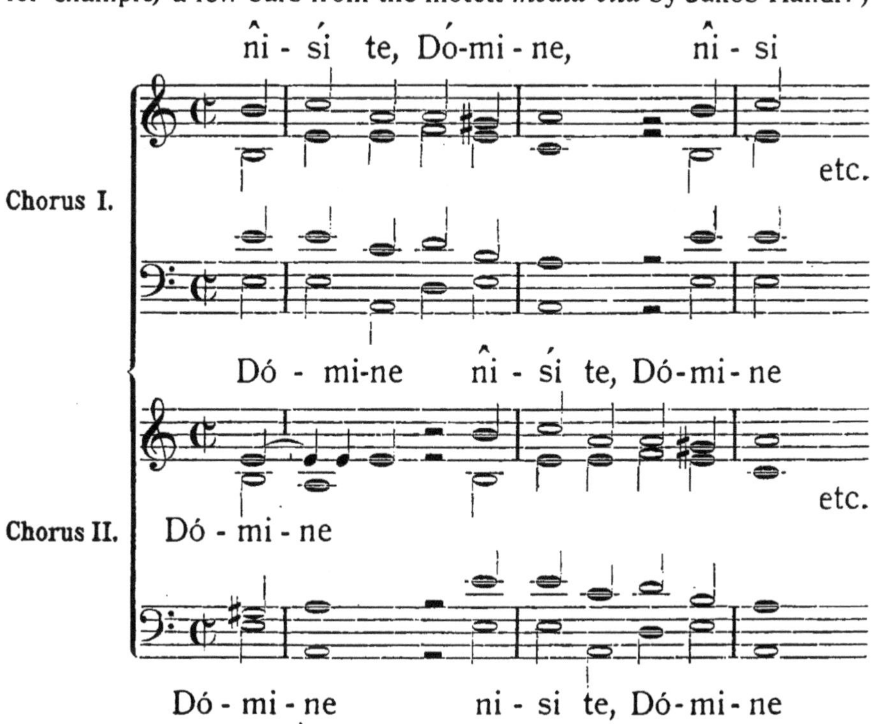

1) *Denkmäler der Tonkunst in Österreich* (Vienna, Artaria), Part I., p. I.

A well trained choir will accentuate *nisi té Dómine,* and yet find on the final syllable of *nisi* a rhythmic resting place. Notice especially in our example the entry of both choirs. — In practice the question as to whether we here have to deal with accents proper or not is immaterial. Phrases like *tu quoque, tu solus, Tu Domine,* can, especially if spoken with great emphasis, only be uttered, without an interval of rest, with two accents close to each other.[1])

Moreover, it is immaterial for practical purposes whether we *write* such passages like Dom Mocquereau (Pal. mus. VII., 252) in this way:

or whether we prefer to write them thus:

or instead of 

in this way 

only do not linger too long on the syllable *cá* and give the *climacus* over *ta* with a good, but gentle, soft, rounded accentuation. *And always strictly "legato".*

The same thing applies for passages like: 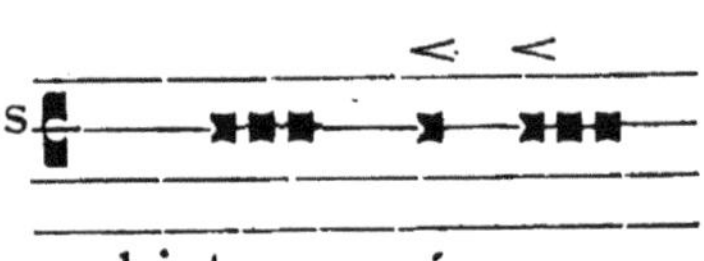

in which the syllable *no* is not to be sustained, but yet not hurried or jerked. Try the passage at first gently, the note-groups lightly soaring, and then lay a moderate stress on *no* and *men.*

In passages like those previously given *(Resurrexi)* and similar ones the accents should be given in a gentle and elastic manner, avoiding all heaviness and vehemence.

64. Single Notes at the Beginning of a Melody or after a Pause.

1) The author also gives the words *Óbstbäume, Frúchtwagen, Úrwälder,* but there are no exact equivalents for these in English as regards accentuation. Trsl.

a) If the syllable over which the single note is placed is *unaccented,* and a neum with two or more notes follows on the next syllable, it counts as an up-beat:

b) If the syllable in the same circumstances is accented, the rule in No 63 applies, therefore:

c) If there are *two* unaccented syllables with only one note at the beginning of the melody or after a pause, the first of them receives a secondary accent:

65. The first *note* (a) of the *salicus* and (b) of the *pressus* (see below), as well as (c) the note (placed lower) before the *bistropha* and *tristropha* or other neums, is to be treated as a single note:

a)

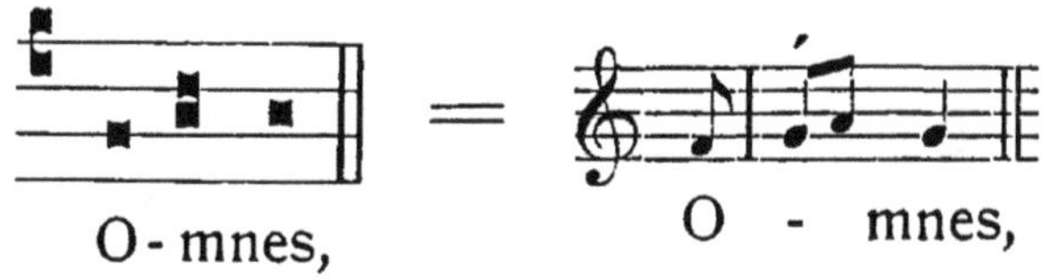

b)

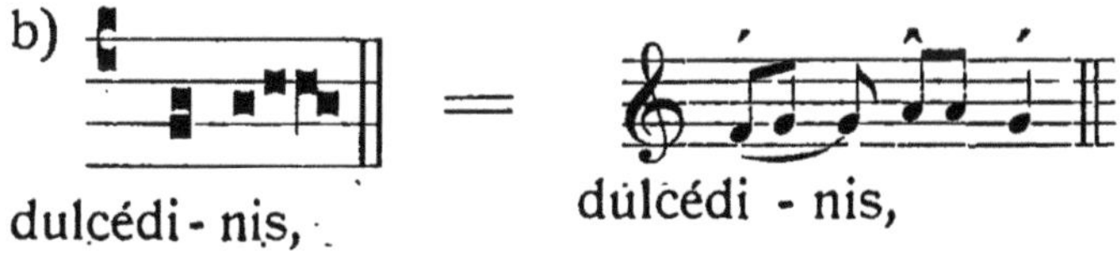

c) 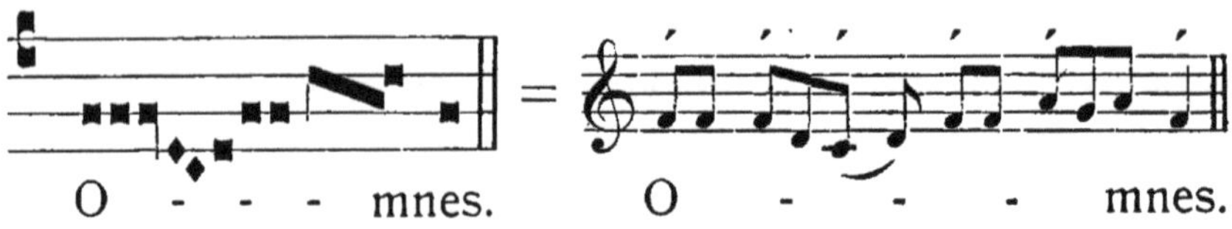

b) Pressus and Quilisma.

I. Pressus.

66. If two neums occur together over one syllable the second of which begins with the same note with which the first ends , a new form arises, the *pressus,* i. e., the new notes of the same height of pitch are drawn together, *accentuated on the first note* and sung with a moderate *sforzato.*

The most important forms of the *pressus* are:

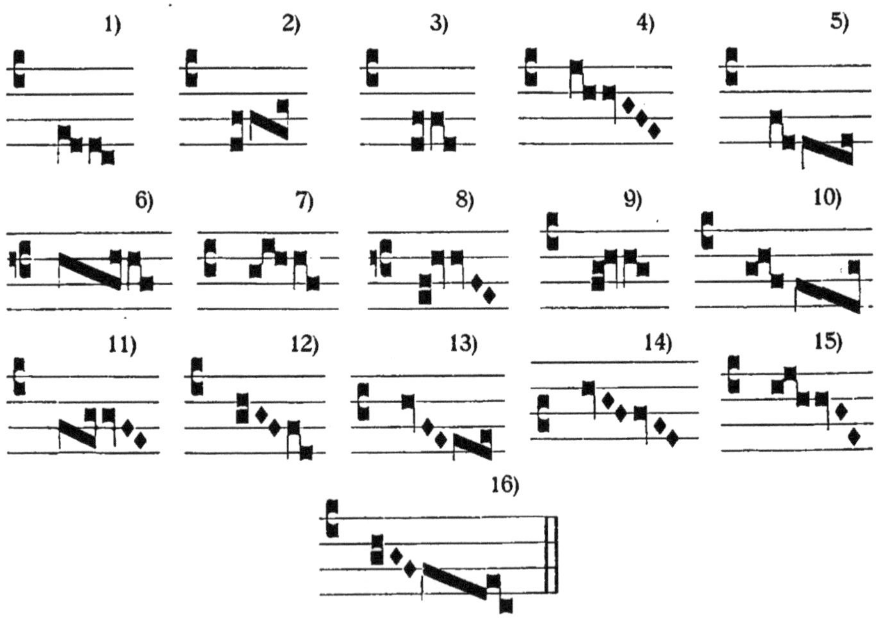

In modern Notes:

If before a *clivis* there is one *punctum* of the same pitch, a new form of the *pressus* arises:

But not if two *puncta* are placed before the *clivis:*

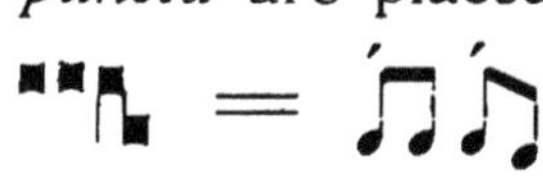

67. If the first neum in the *pressus* has *a) two* tones, the *initial note* is treated like that of the *salicus* (see p. 37); e. g:

The same in cases like

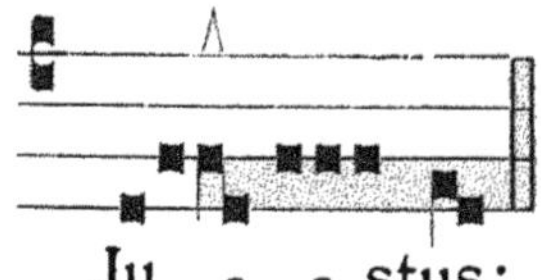

β) if it has more than two tones the rhythm should be as indicated on p. 51, e. g.:

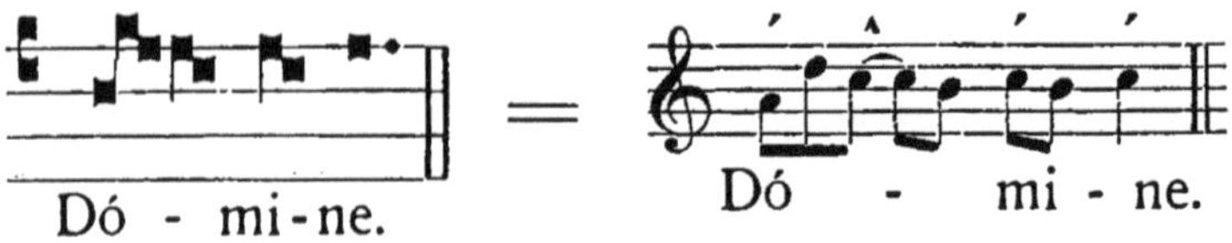

The note *after* the *"pressus"* *can* itself receive an accent:

Sometimes *several* *"pressus"* follow one another:

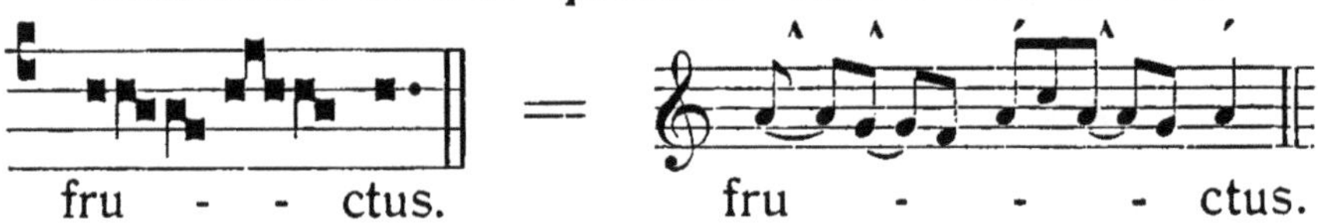

As regards the notes which have no *sforzato* the strength of the tone must not be diminished too considerably.

The apóstropha, which is appended to a neum, must be clearly distinguished from the *pressus*. Here then there should be no *sforzato:*

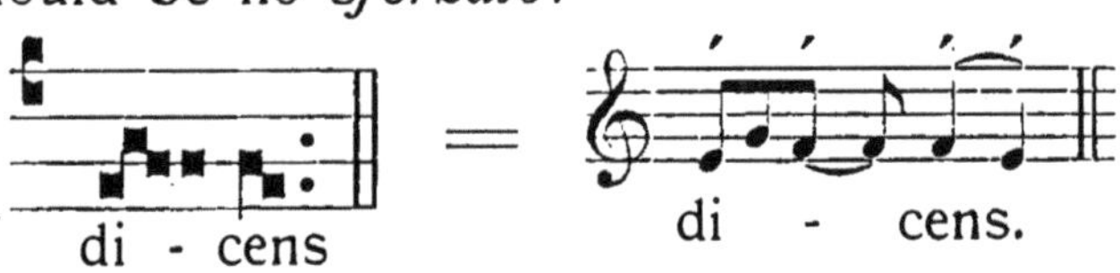

The *pressus* gives the melodies *a)* strong impulses and resting places, *b)* effective variety owing to the longer time-values (double time-units).

II. Quilisma.

68. If a *single tone* over the same syllable of the text precedes the *quilisma* (see p. 21) the single tone is *accentuated* and rather *sustained*; but if a *podatus* or a *clivis* precedes it, the first note of these neums is doubled, a slight *ritard.* being made on the second note.[1])

---

1) For another explanation of the quilisma see *Gregorianische Rundschau* (Graz, Styria, 1905).

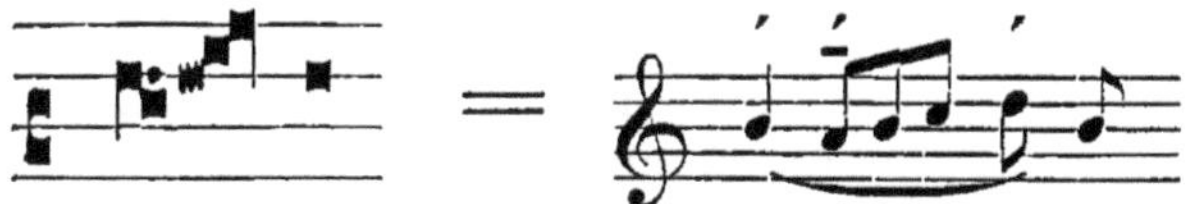

How effective the quilisma is when thus rendered is evident from passages like this:

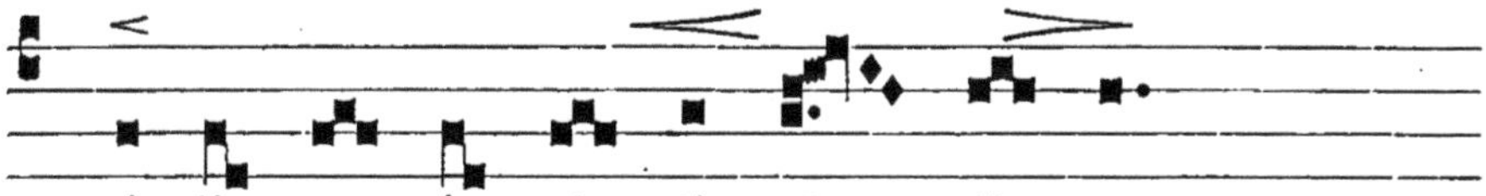

The quilisma most frequently occurs as the middle note in the progressions *re mi fa* and *la si do.*

The *quilisma* enhances the effect of the melody as it interrupts the even flow of the movement for a moment, thus causing a feeling of suspense and then of relief, and in this way the melody is enlivened.

Pauses and Mora Vocis.

I. Pauses.

69. The note before a pause must not be cut off; on the contrary, it should be rather sustained so that it may be about equal in time-value to the *bistropha.*

When the pauses are short, when there is a rest for a moment only, in order to take breath quickly, it is not always necessary to sustain the note; or the time of the pause can be reckoned in, so that the last sustained note and the pause may be equal to about two units.

Plain chant has only masculine cæsuras, i. e., *each phrase ends with an accentuated note;* consequently very often a note which of itself bears no accent, i. e., the final note of a neum, receives at the close of a musical phrase an independent accent.

The old masters of ecclesiastical polyphony close their periods, with very few exceptions, with the masculine cæsura; Bach and Beethoven had a special predilection for it, whilst Mozart preferred the feminine cæsura.

70. As regards this prolongation, attention should be paid to the following rules:

a) If the last syllable or the last monosyllable has *only one note* before the pause, only this last note is doubled:

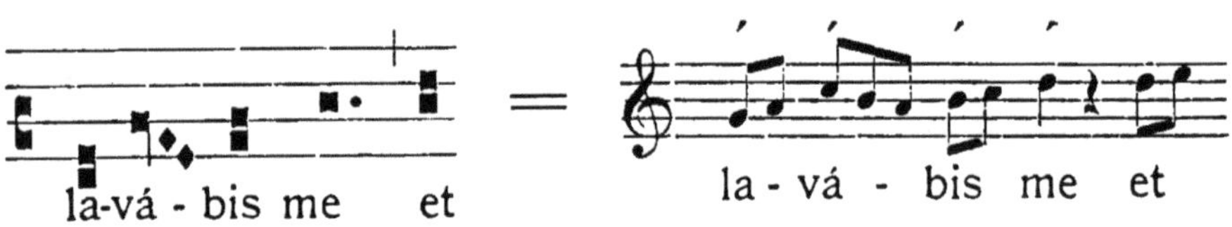

The same when a *dactylic* word has only one note to each syllable:

If, however, the *penultimate syllable* bears the accent and there is only one note to a syllable, the two last notes are doubled:

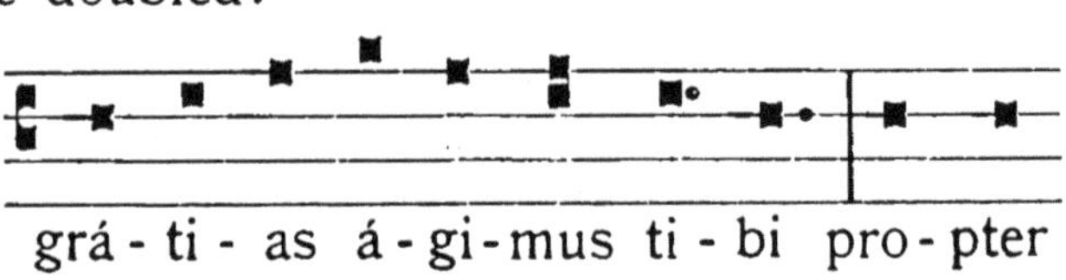

If several little phrases follow each other with similar words at the end, it is desirable sometimes to treat these phrases as a whole, sustaining only the final notes of the last phrase.

b) If the last syllable or the last monosyllable before the pause has *two notes* or several neums, of which the last neum has two notes, then the last two notes are doubled:

Take care that when singing the two doubled notes they are kept closely connected with each other, for this is easily overlooked; the MSS. with "Romanian signs" have in these cases a line over the *clivis,* or a *t (tenéte = hold).*

c) If the last syllable or the last monosyllable before the pause has *more than two notes,* then as a rule only the last note is doubled:

Neums of three tones owing to this prolongation receive at least four beats, and at least two accents (the same applies before the *mora vocis)*:

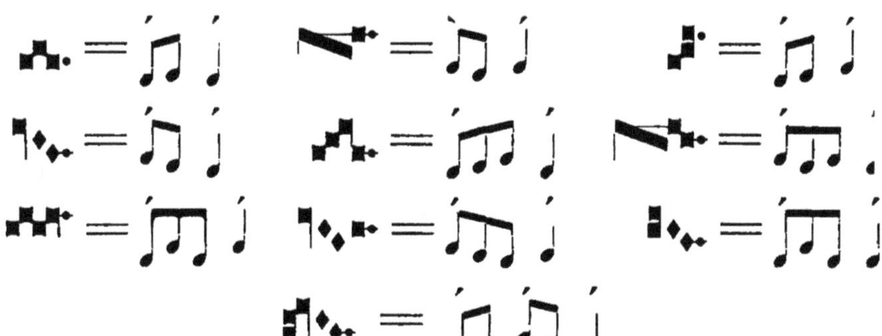

If for choirs that are not very well trained more pauses are needed than are given in the official books, they must be made at suitable places.

71. Immediately before a new syllable of the *same word* the melody should never be interrupted by a pause, as this would create the impression that another word had begun (regula aurea): it would seem as if the breath had not sufficed for the whole passage, and that a pause elsewhere would be *absolutely* impossible or undesirable.

It would also be incongruous to double the last tone immediately before the new syllable, see p. 38.

II.

Mora vocis.

72. If *several groups of notes* (neums) are placed over *one syllable of the text*, the duration of the final notes of a group is often doubled (sustained) before the movement passes on to the group immediately following. This "delay" is called *mora vocis*. Its object is not only to mark off the groups from one another, but also to connect them with each other.

This prolongation interrupts for a moment the even flow of the melody and attracts the attention of the listener. It has the effect of rest, the accent on the following neum the effect of energy. In this way the *tout ensemble* gains light and shade.

In view of its object the *mora* must be in relation to the following neum, which it has to introduce and make prominent, i. e., the momentum of rest (in the *mora)* must be proportionate to the momentum of force in the accent following.

If the new member begins with a note which is to be sung louder, it is well to close the prolongation on the *mora* with a slight *crescendo*, but if a softer note follows, the prolongation should die away in a slight, soft *decrescendo*.

73. The *mora vocis* is to be viewed as an independent beat and therefore a *new accent* will always be necessary. For this the same rules apply as for the pause above, see p. 51.

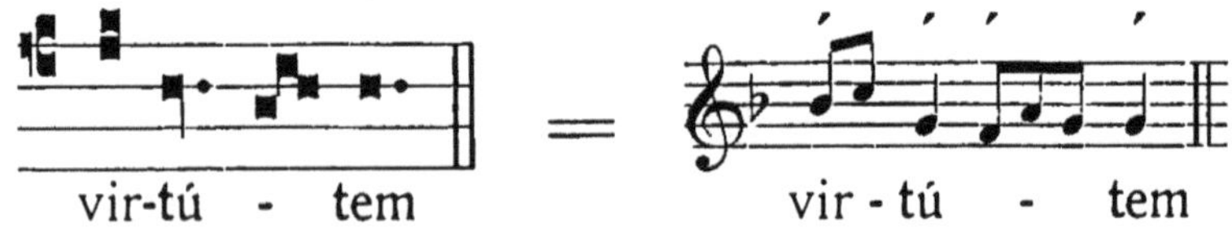

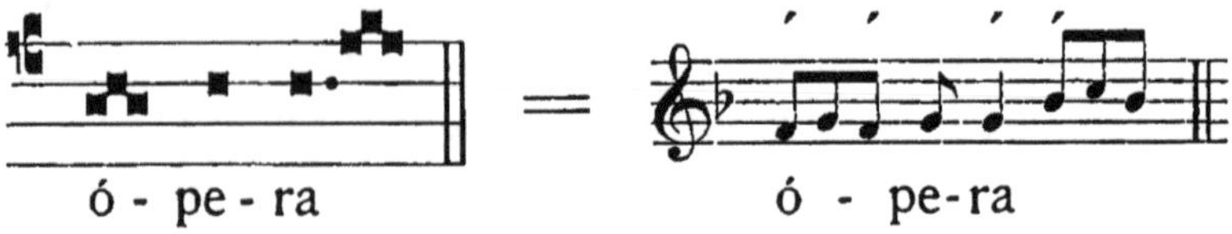

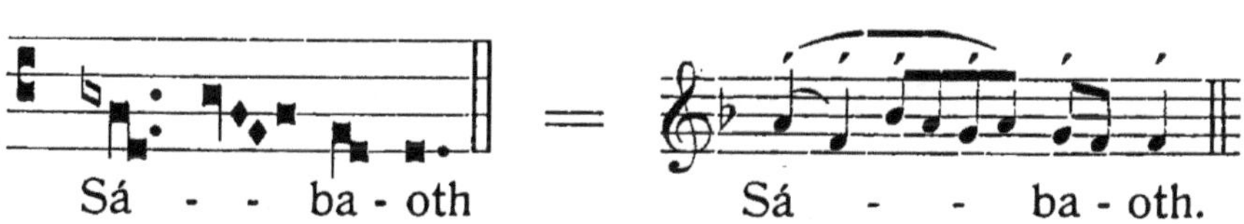

If on the other hand another neum precedes the *podatus* or the *clivis* before a *mora* on the same syllable, the initial note is treated like that of the *salicus* and only the second note is sustained, e. g.:

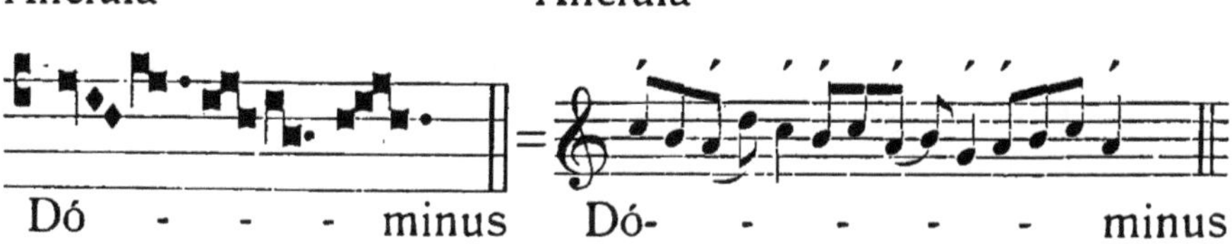

A *mora* never occurs immediately before a new syllable of the same word, e. g., in the word *Do-mi-nus*

the last note on *do* and the last one on *mi* cannot have a *mora*.

In many places plain chant is sung without a *mora*. Yet it cannot be denied that the melody gains in expression if the *mora* is rightly used.

In the Vatican edition, as in the MSS., the *mora vocis* is indicated by a wider space between the neums, in which another note could comfortably be placed.

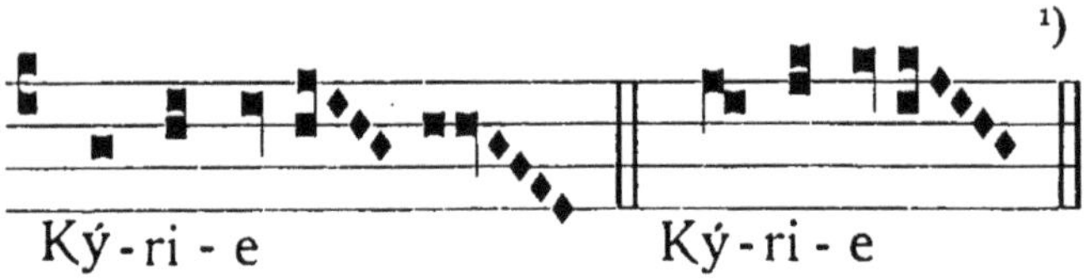

In the middle ages great importance was attached to the correct mode of connecting groups of neums belonging to one another, and to the separation of those to be kept apart, as appears from St. Bernard's introduction to his *Antiphonale*. This "School" indicates the *mora* by a dot behind the note.

Supplementary Remarks.

74. Briefly stated, the following are the principal rules for the rhythm of the Gregorian melodies:

In the syllabic chants the rhythm is indicated by the verbal accent.

In other chants pay attention to the following points:

1) The pauses: the note before a pause receives an accent.
2) The *mora vocis:* the note before a *mora* receives an accent.
3) The *pressus:* the first note receives an accent.
4) The *quilisma:* the note before it receives an accent.
5) The *apostropha:* the note before it receives an accent.
6) Neums with two or three notes have the accent on the first note.

1) Mass II of the Vatican edition.

7) Neums with more notes are to be treated as explained in N° 61 (2+2, 2+3, 3+2, etc.).

8) Finally, remember what has been said about single notes in N°s 62, 63, 64.

For practice let the pupil sing various pieces, the teacher showing him which notes bear the accent, and why, e. g., in *Asperges: sol, do, si, re, mi, sol, etc.*

Advanced pupils will find it useful to try and write down a melody whilst it is sung by one of their number.

75. Treatment of the Text in Plain Chant.

a) The German and English languages differ considerably from the Latin language, and in the latter there are many things that in German or English would be viewed as faults. If one attempted to set *German or English* words to music in the same way as *Latin* words are sometimes set to plain chant, the results would be highly unsatisfactory. *But it does not follow from this that plain chant gets the better of the Latin language.*

b) The Latin poet can, e. g., without committing any fault sing in the hymn at Sext:

Rectōr potēns verāx Deūs

whilst in ordinary speech everyone would pronounce thus:

Réctor pótens vérax Déus.

In German (or English) this kind of thing is impossible. But that does not give us a right to forbid the composer of Gregorian melodies to make use of this and similar licences.

c) We Germans [and English-speaking people] frequently pronounce Latin with such an exaggerated accent that the words fall too heavily on the ear. Other nations, the French, for example, pronounce the words more smoothly, with a lighter accent. Pains must be taken to modify this exaggerated accentuation. Can it be supposed that throughout the middle ages, when the traditional chant was daily nourishment, they did not know what was most in accordance with the spirit and peculiarities of the Latin language?

d) Indeed the *Instituta Patrum* said that in plain chant the verbal accent must certainly be taken into consideration, adding however, "so far as this is possible."[1])

---

1) Gerbert: *Script.* I pp. 6 and 7.

e) Then the masters of polyphony, Palestrina and others, also allowed themselves many liberties with the text. Compare Molitor's *Théorie et pratique du chant grégorien* (Desclée) and Pal. mus. VII.

Palestrina writes:

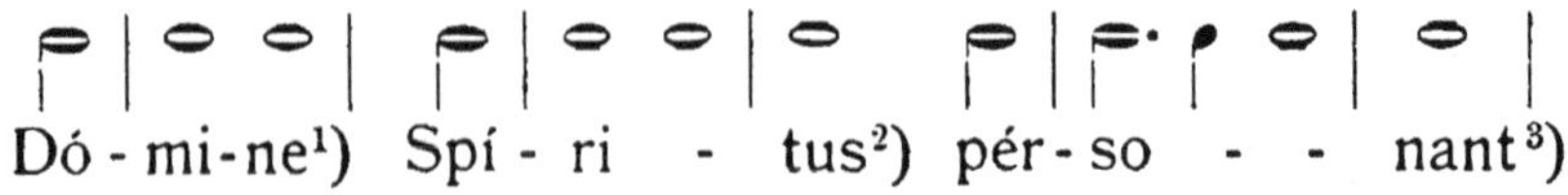

f) With regard to the old grammarians[4]) we may mention the following: *D*ionysius of Halicarnassus († c. 40 B. C.): "In vocal and instrumental music the words are subordinate to the music and not the music to the words"; Quintilian († 118 A. D.): "It is for the music to make the syllables longer or shorter according to her need".

g) Singers under instruction will do well to express their opinions on this and many other points with considerable reserve, remembering that they are dealing with an art that has its own principles, which for centuries have been carried out practically on well tried systems.

Normal School.

Part II.: Different Species of Plain Chant.

Chapter VIII.

Psalmody.

76. The psalms[5]) are divided into verses which are sung alternately by two choirs. Each verse consists of two parts indicated by an asterisk *.

---

1) Palestrina, Complete Ed. (Breitkopf and Härtel) Vol. XI., p. 4.
2) L. c. Vol. XII. p. 141. 3) L. c. Vol. VIII. p. 125.
4) Compare *Pal. mus.* IV. pp. 66 *seq.*
5) The excellent little book by the Benedictines of Solesmes: *Psaumes notés précédés d'un petit traité de psalmodie* (Desclée, 1903) serves as the groundwork for this chapter. [*Rules for Psalmody*, the English version of the treatise, may be had from the same publishers.]

The *Cantica* (Canticles) *Magnificat, Benedictus* and *Nunc dimittis* are treated like the psalms and are therefore subject to the same rules.

77. The *mode* of the preceding antiphon determines the *tone* of the psalm. Corresponding with the eight modes the present Roman psalmody employs eight psalm-tones, added to which is the *tonus peregrinus*[1]) (foreign tone) which may be assigned to Tone 1 or 8.

At the beginning of the antiphon the mode of the same and of the following psalm is indicated by arabic numerals: 1 = Tone 1, 2 = Tone 2, etc.; for the *Tonus peregrinus*[1]), P.

A) Constituent Parts of the Psalm Tone.

A psalm-tone consists of three parts: I. Intonation (initium); II. Recitation on the dominant; III. Middle cadence *(mediatio,* mediation), and Final cadence *(terminatio* or *finalis,* termination, ending or final).

78. I. The *Intonation* consists

a) Of *one* note and an inseparable group of notes (*podatus*) (in Tones 1, 3, 4 and 6), or of two groups (in Tone 7); in both cases the words are set to the same *regardless of the verbal accent:* the first two syllables of the psalms:

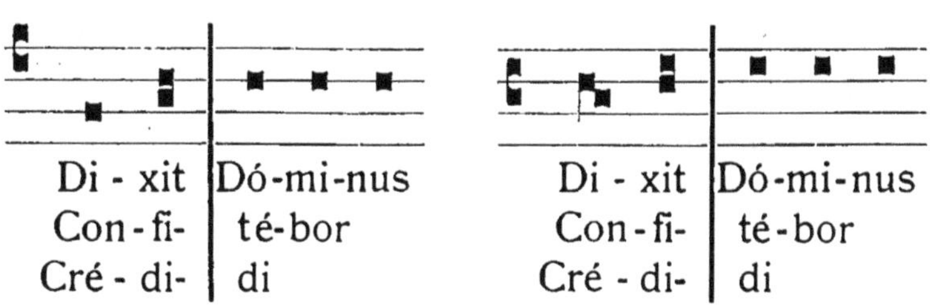

The group of notes retains its full time even if set to an unaccented syllable *(credidi),* but in such cases must be sung smoothly and flowingly, not in a heavy, clumsy manner.

1) This will be dealt with on pp. 69, 70.

β) Of *three* separated notes; then the first three syllables are set to them (in Tones 2, 5, 8):

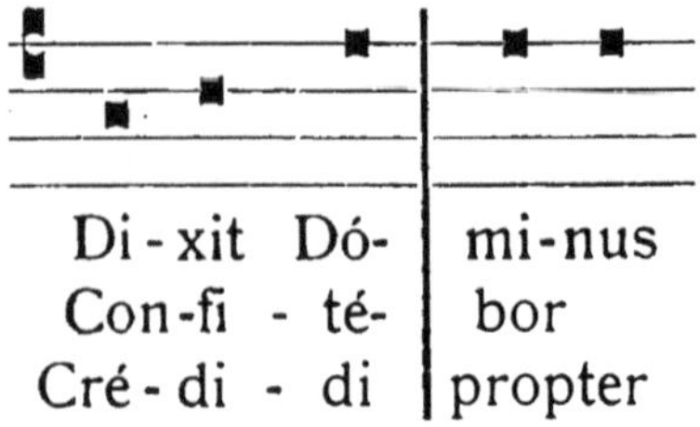

All the verses of the Canticles begin with the full intonation, but in the psalms only the first verse, the remaining verses commencing at once on the dominant.

79. II. All the syllables which do not fall to the intonation, mediation, or final, are sung on the dominant (the reciting note).

80. III. The *mediation*[1]) and *final* have sometimes *a)* only *one* musical accent (indicated in our examples with 1 over the note concerned), in which case the *last verbal accent* in the half-verse concerned falls to this accentuated note or group of notes.

The musical (cadence-) accent is as a rule also a rhythmical accent, but cannot occur more than twice in a half-verse against the rhythmical accent after every second or third note.

The *verbal accent* is either a principal accent (on the penultimate, *méo,* or antepenultimate syllable, *Dómino*), or a secondary one[2]) *(dè té, èxultávit)*, see pp. 7, 8 and pp. 73 *seq.:*

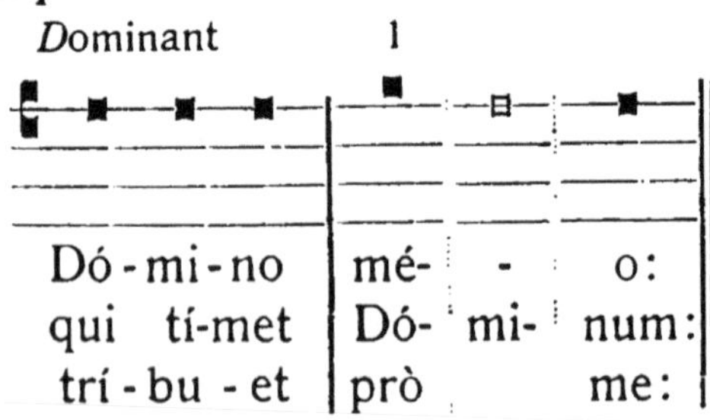

1) Concerning the *mediatio correpta* used in many places see p. 70.
2) Compare *Pal. mus.* III. pp. 36 *seq.*

β) Or sometimes the cadences have *two* musical accents (here marked 2 and 1 over the particular note) and in this case the two last verbal accents (principal or secondary) fall to the two accentuated notes or group of notes:

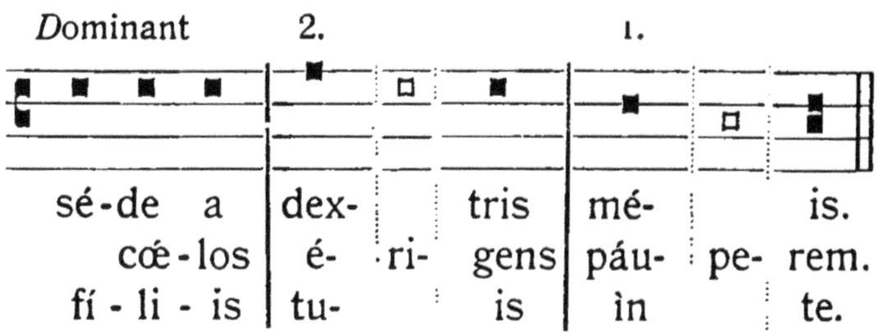

N. B. The second syllable of a word accented on the antepenultimate and falling to a cadence accent is called a "secondary syllable". It is shown in our examples under a white or open note. The secondary syllables are sung at the pitch of the note *following* them (see p. 60, Tone 1); if this note falls the secondary syllable also falls; if it rises the syllable also rises. Only with the finals à of Tone 3 (see pp. 63, 64 *seq.*) and a, ç (with cedilla) of Tone 7 (see p. 68) is the secondary syllable sung at the pitch of the preceding accentuated note.

Many *cadences* with *one* accent have *notes of preparation,* i. e., one or more notes or groups are inserted between the dominant and cadence accent. These preparation notes are treated, like the notes of the intonation, without regard to the verbal accent. If there is only one preparation note the syllable before the cadence accent is set to it; if there are two, then the two syllables preceding the accent, going back.

Thus *a* indicates the first preparation note (or notes), *b,* the second, *c,* the third:

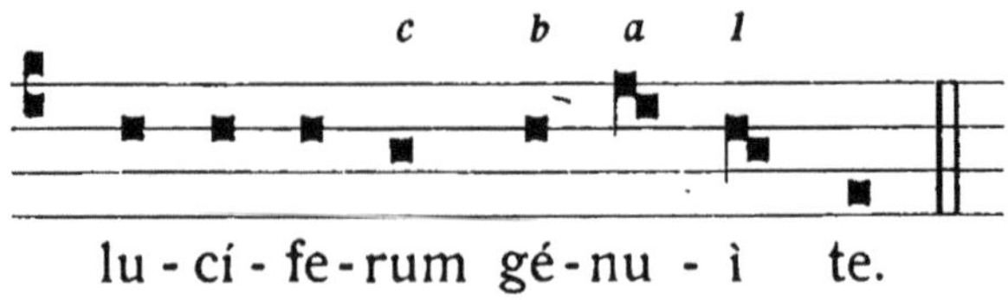

The psalm-tones have, with the exception of Tones 2, 5, 6, different *finals.*

These different finals are indicated in the Solesmes books at the beginning of the antiphon, after the indication of the tone, by the following letters:

A B C D E F G
a b c d e f g
(la si do re mi fa sol)

If the last note of the *final* cadence is the same as the *final* of the mode, the capitals are used; in all other cases, the small letters; if formulæ of the same mode close on the same tone the letters are modified slighty, e. g.: à, ç, *J*, italic *E* (see below); besides, at the end of the antiphon the final to be used is shown in notes, under which are the letters E u o u a e, i. e., the vowels of the words *sæculorum, Amen,* e. g.:

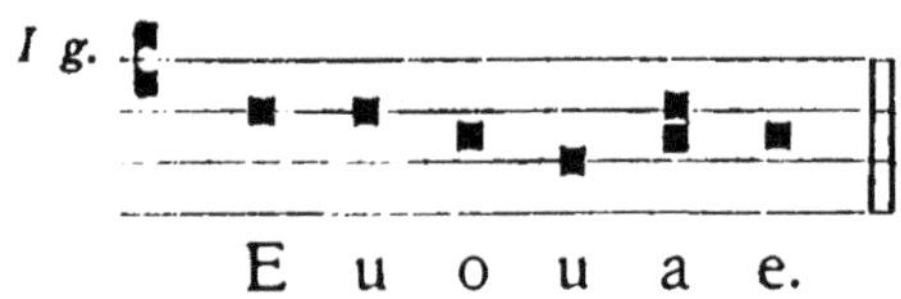

B) On Practising the Psalm Tones.[1])

81. *First Tone.*[2]) Intonation; 1 note and 1 podatus; mediation, 2 accents; final, 1 accent and 2 preparation notes; number of finals, 6; dominant (with which all the verses begin except the first), *la.*

1) Since the difficulty of pointing increases as more accents and preparation notes occur, it is desirable for instructional purposes to take the tones in the following order: 2, 8, 5, 6, 7, 1, 3, 4, P.

In colleges and schools the teacher may write on a blackboard the first verse of a psalm, or at least a half-verse, in columns (2 | 1) and with the preparation notes (c, b, a) as shown below, and thereupon the pupils can write the other verses in their proper columns, and afterwards sing the whole psalm through. Of course the simplest way is to sing them from printed formulæ such as those provided by the Solesmes Benedictines.

2) To show as many different cases as possible the second half of the verse is taken from various psalms, excepting in the first example.

I.

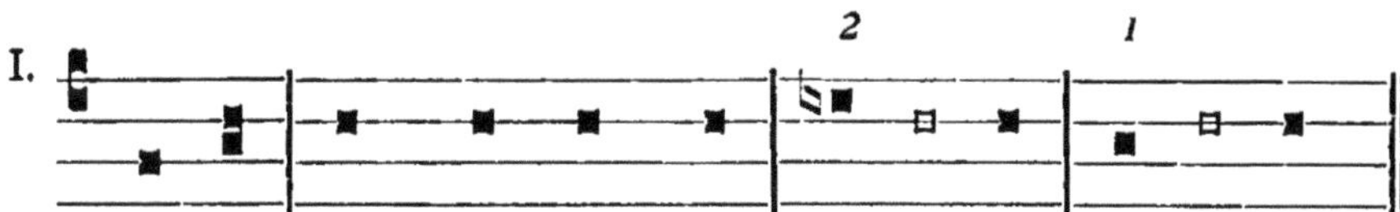

Di-xit | Dó - mi - nus | Dó-mi-no | me - o:
Ma - gna | ó-pe-ra | Dó-mi-ni:
in splendó - ri- | bùs san- | ctó - rum:
in his quæ | di-cta sunt | dè te:
Magní- | fi - cat: (The first verse not having sufficient syllables there is no mediation)
Et ex | -ul - tá-vit | spí - ri-tus | me - us:

II.

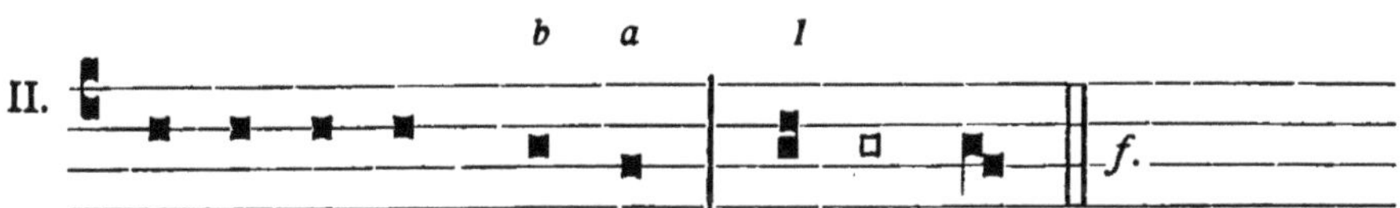

se-de a dex-tris | me - is.
stér-co-re é - ri-gens | páu-pe - rem.
lu-cí-fe-rum gé-nu- | ì te.
con-for-tá - ti sunt | sú-per me.
á-ni-ma me - a | Dó-mi - num.
sa-lu - tá - ri | me - o.

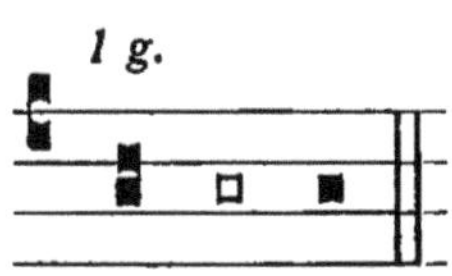

Dó-mi-num.

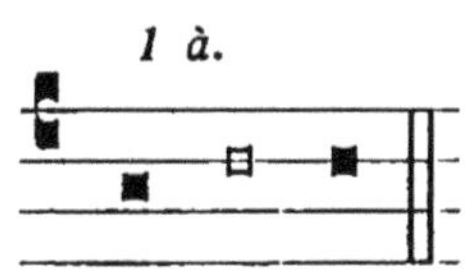

Dó-mi-num.

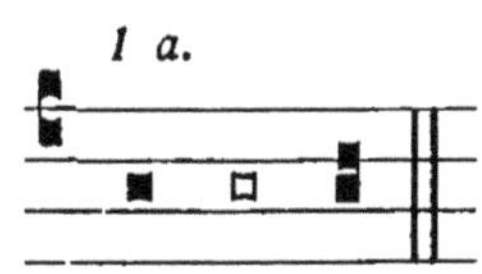

Dó-mi-num.

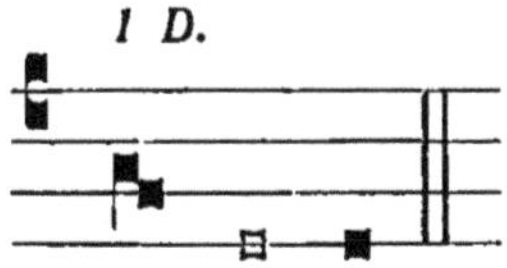

Dó-mi-num.

Dó-mi-num.

On great festivals the *Magnificat,* Tone I, has the following solemn mediation with *one* accent and 3 preparation notes (or groups). In this case if the verbal accent is on the antepenultimate *(progénies)* the group *(clivis)* does not fall to it as at other times, but an accentuated note is inserted before this group, to which the verbal accent is then set:

In this case the final cadence also gains a note:

82. *Second Tone.* Intonation, 3 separated notes; mediation, 1 accent; final, 1 accent with 1 preparation note; dominant, *fa.*

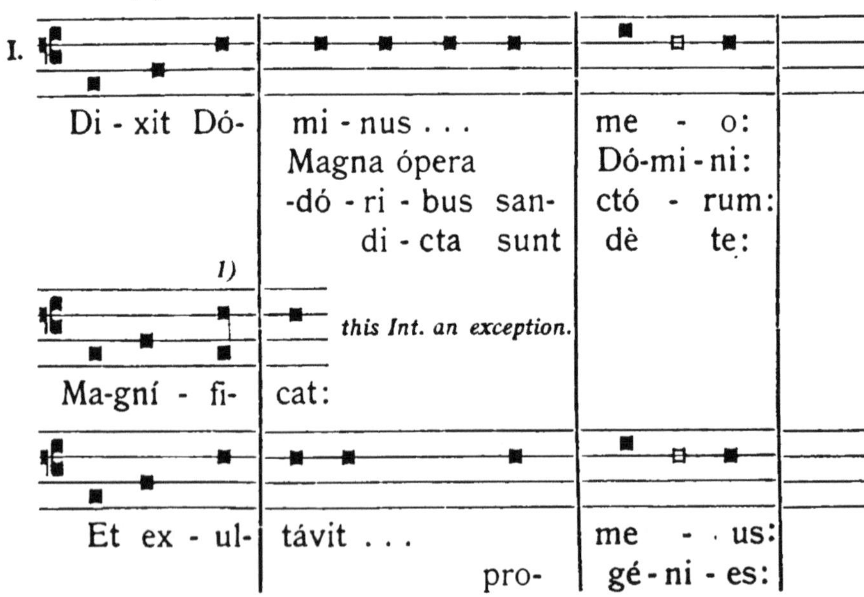

1) Cf. in the Graduale the Introit-verse for the Saturday after the 4th Sunday in Lent: *Attendite.*

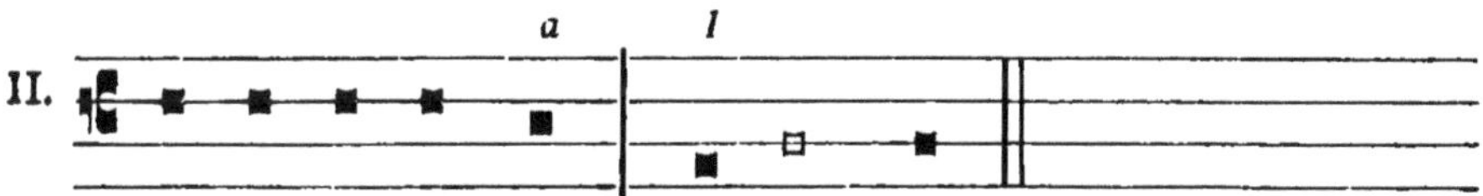

se-de a dex-tris | me - is.
é-ri-gens | páu-pe - rem.
gé-nu- | ì te.
con-for-tá-ti sunt | sú-per me.
á-ni-ma me - a | Dó-mi - num.
tá - ri | me - o.

On feasts the mediation of the *Magnificat* has 3 preparation notes (or groups):

Tones 2 and 8.

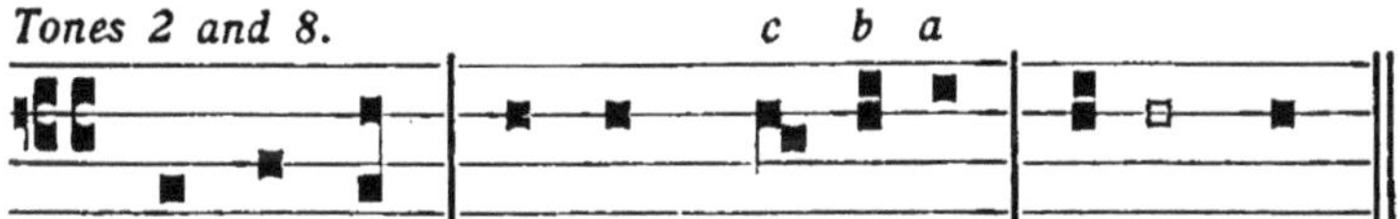

Ma-gní - fi - | cat:
Et ex-ul- | tá-vit spí - ri-tus | me - us:
po-tens est:

83. *Third Tone.* Intonation, 1 note and 1 *podatus*; mediation, 2 accents; for the first accent, if the verbal accent is on the antepenultimate, what was said on pp. 61, 62 holds good. Compare the psalm-tone for the introit-verse on the feast of SS. Peter and Paul, and on the vigil of an apostle *(cognovisti me, malitia).* Final, 1 accent; number of finals, 5: à, c with 1, a, g, E with 2 preparation notes (or group); dominant, *do.*

I.

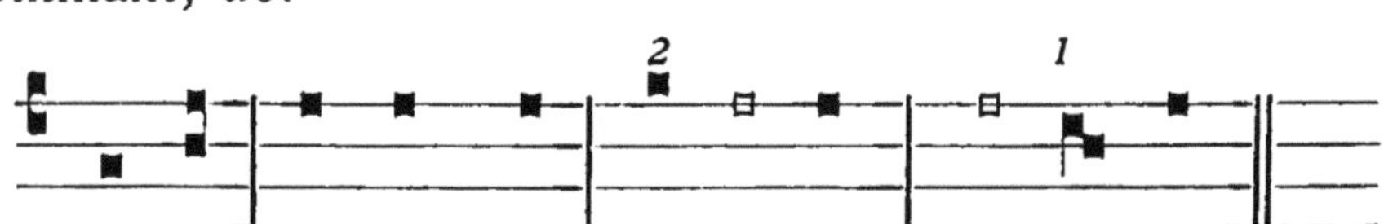

Di-xit | Dó-mi - nus | Dó-mi-no | me - o:
Ma-gna | ó-pe-ra | Dó-mi - ni:
-dó - ri- | bùs san- | ctó - rum:
his quæ | di-cta sunt | mi - hi:
Magní - | fi - cat:
Et ex- | ul-tá - vit | spí - ri - tus | me- us:

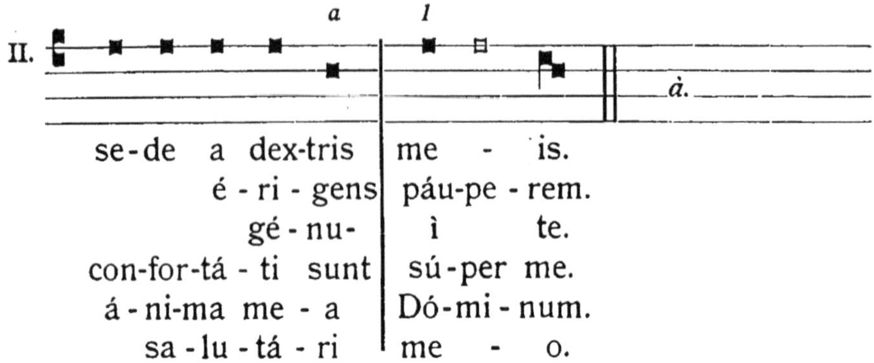

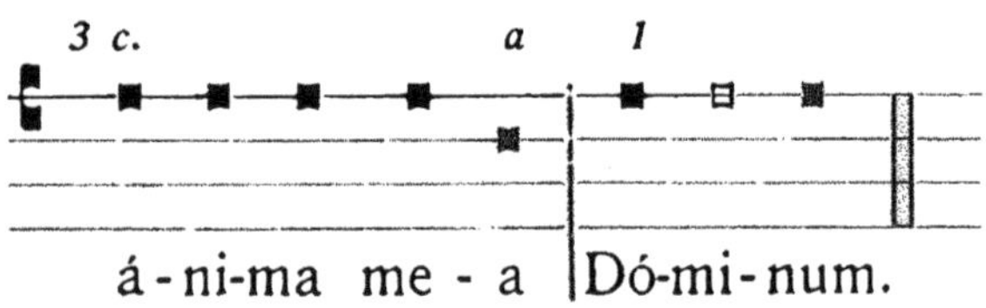

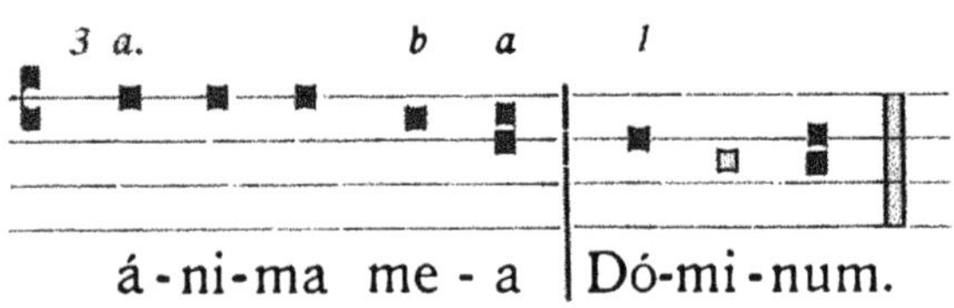

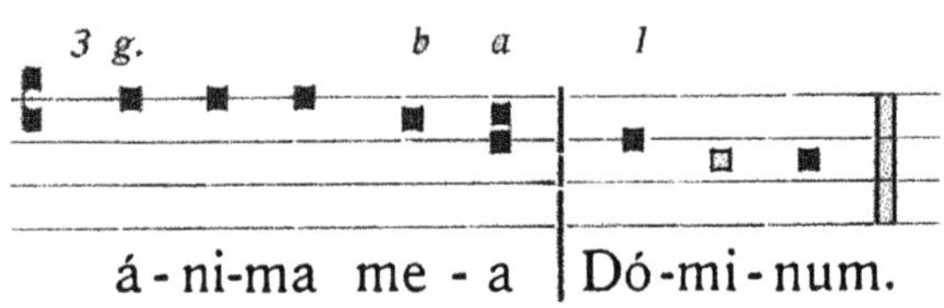

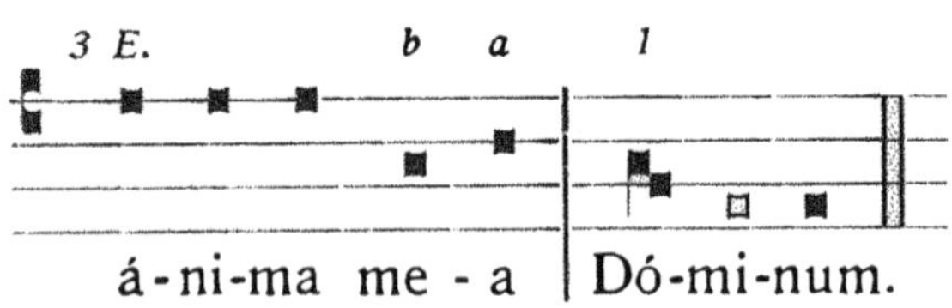

84. *Fourth Tone.* Intonation, 1 note and 1 *podatus;* mediation, 1 accent and 2 preparation notes; final, 1 accent with 3 preparation notes (or groups); finals, 4: E, Ẹ, a, g (the last one is without preparation); dominant, *la.*

I.

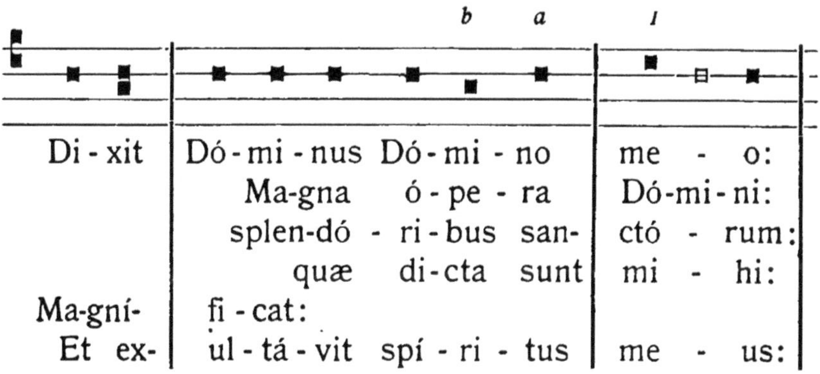
b a 1
Di-xit Dó-mi-nus Dó-mi-no me - o:
Ma-gna ó-pe-ra Dó-mi-ni:
splen-dó - ri-bus san- ctó - rum:
quæ di-cta sunt mi - hi:
Ma-gní- fi-cat:
Et ex- ul-tá-vit spí-ri-tus me - us:

II.

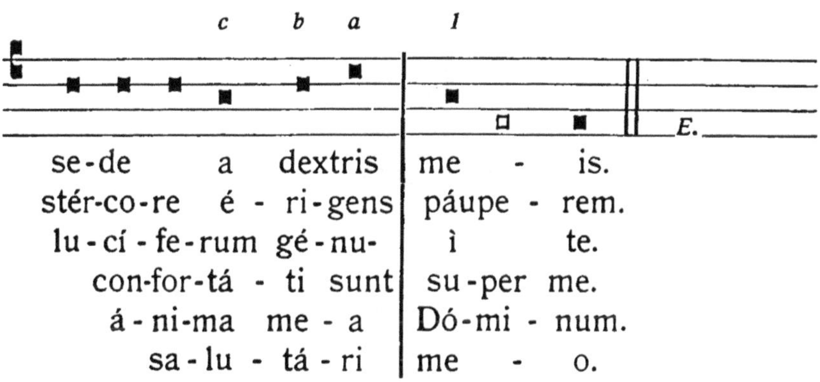
c b a 1
E.
se-de a dextris me - is.
stér-co-re é - ri-gens páupe - rem.
lu-cí-fe-rum gé-nu- ì te.
con-for-tá - ti sunt su-per me.
á-ni-ma me - a Dó-mi - num.
sa-lu - tá-ri me - o.

4 a.

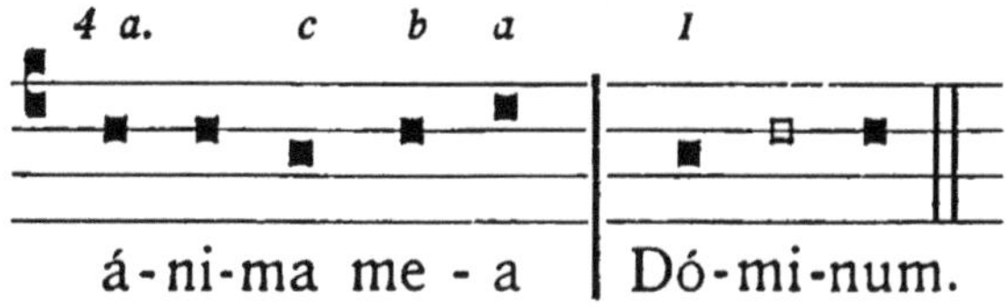
c b a 1
á-ni-ma me - a Dó-mi-num.

4 E

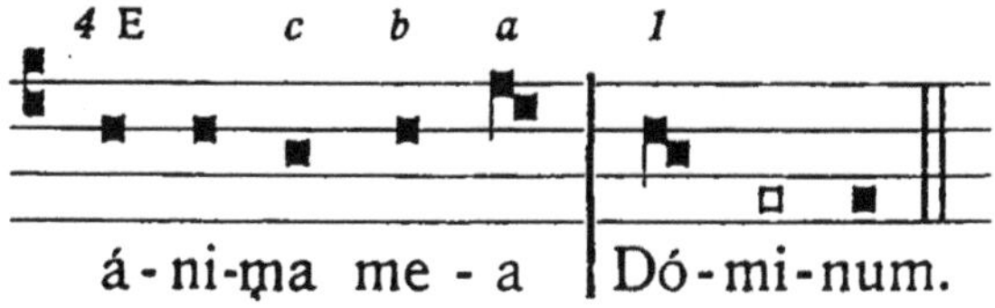
c b a 1
á-ni-ma me - a Dó-mi-num.

4 g.

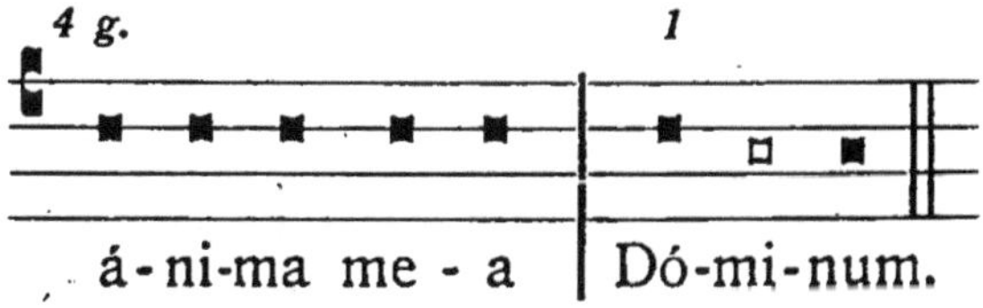
1
á-ni-ma me - a Dó-mi-num.

When the antiphon preceding the psalm is transposed, the psalm-tone has the following notation and finals:

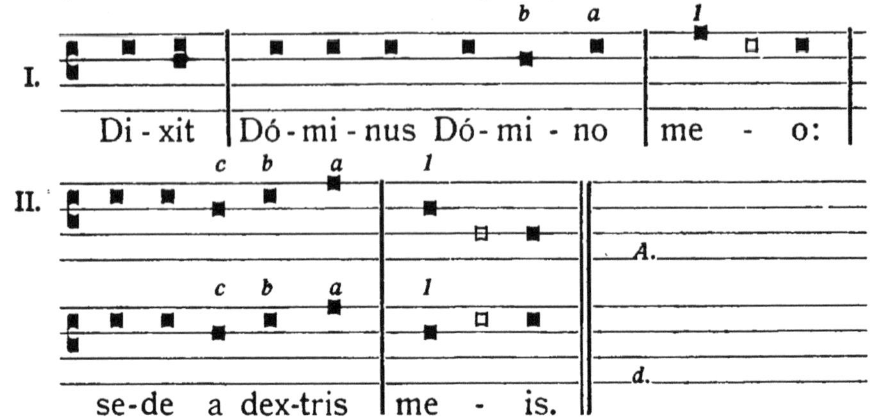

85. *Fifth Tone.* Intonation, 3 separated notes; mediation, 1 accent; final, 2 accents; dominant, *do.*

86. *Sixth Tone.* Intonation, 1 note and 1 *podatus*; mediation, 1 accent with 1 preparation note; final, 1 accent with 2 preparation notes (or groups); dominant, *la.*

I.

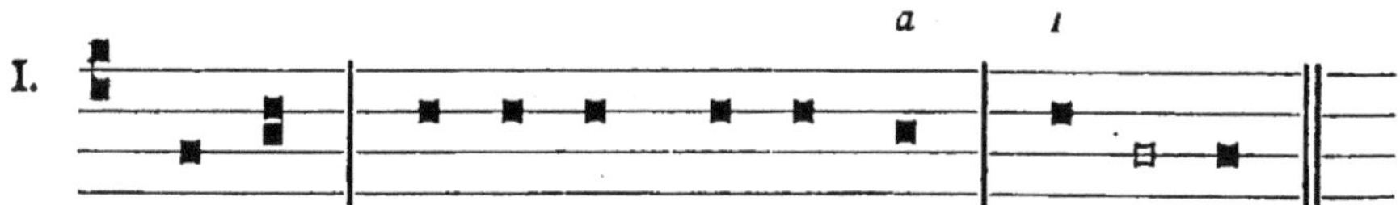

Di-xit | Dó-mi-nus Dó-mi-no | me - o:
Magna ó-pe-ra | Dó-mi-ni:
splendó - ri-bus san- | ctó - rum:
quæ di-cta sunt | mi - hi:
Ma-gní- | fi-cat:
Et ex- | ul-tá-vit spí-ri-tus | me - us:

II.

se-de a dextris | me - is.
é - ri-gens | páupe - rem.
lucí-fe-rum gé-nu- | ì te.
con-for-tá - ti sunt | sú-per me.
á-ni-ma me-a | Dó-mi - num.
sa-lu - tá-ri | me - o.

87. *Seventh Tone.* Intonation, 2 groups; mediation and final, 2 accents, no preparation note; finals 5, a, b, c, ç, d; dominant, *re.*

I.

Di - xit | Dó-mi - nus | Dó-mi-no | me - o:
Ma-gna | ó-pe-ra | Dó-mi-ni:
splen-dó - ri- | bùs san- | ctó - rum:
in his quæ | di-cta sunt | mi - hi:

The intonation begins with a *torculus* for all the verses.

Ma-gní- | fi-cat:
Et ex- | ul-tá - vit | spí-ri-tus | me - us:

II.

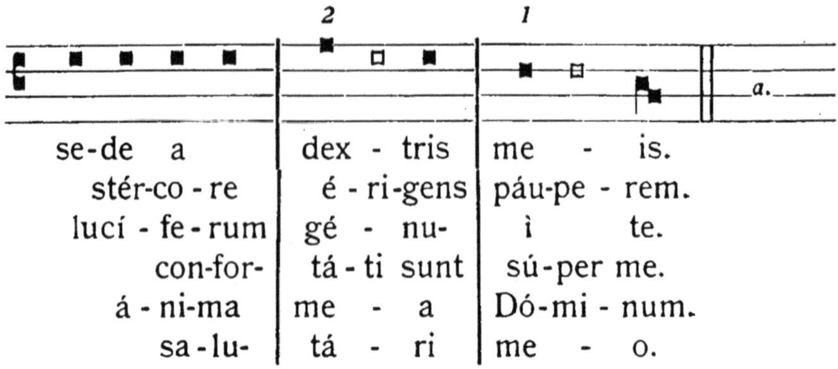

7 b.

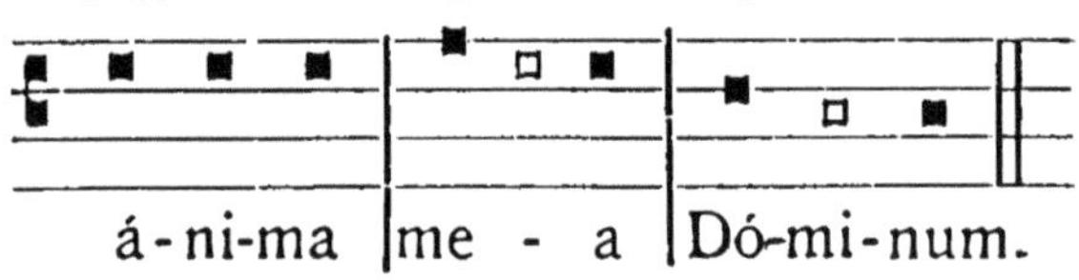

7 c.

7 ç.

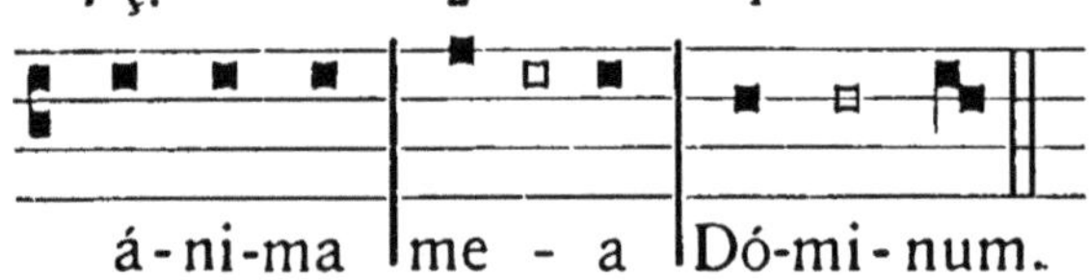

7 d.

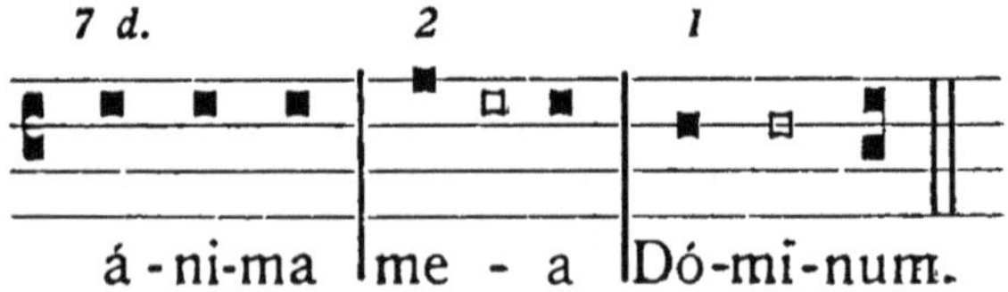

88. *Eighth Tone.* Intonation, 3 separated notes; mediation, 1 accent (as in Tone 2); final, 1 accent with 2 preparation notes; number of finals 2, G, c; dominant, *do*.

I. 

Di-xit Dó- | mi-nus Dó-mi-no | me - o:
Magna ó-pe-ra | Dó-mi-ni:
splendó - ri-bus san- | ctó - rum:
di-cta sunt | dè te:

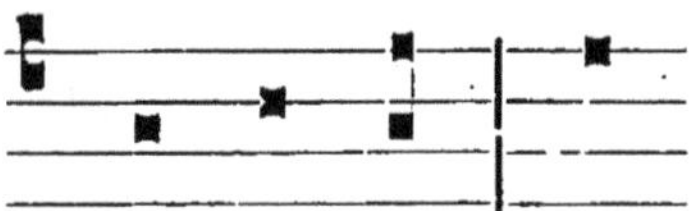

Exception, *cf.* Tone 2.

Ma-gní - fi- | cat:

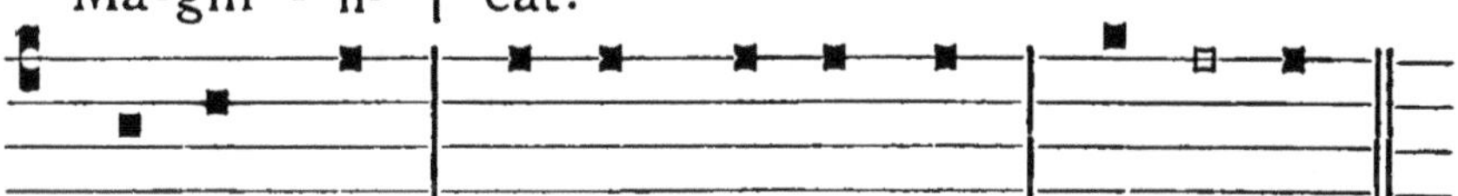

Et ex - ul- | tá-vit spí-ri-tus | me - us:
pro- | gé-ni-es:

II. 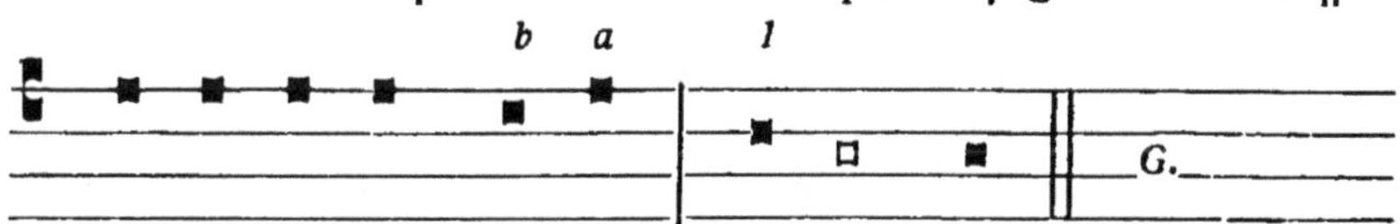

se-de a dextris | me - - is.
stér-co-re é - ri-gens | páu-pe - rem.
lu-cí-fe-rum gé-nu- | ì te.
con-for-tá - ti sunt | sú-per me.
á-ni-ma me-a | Dó-mi - num.
sa-lu - tá-ri | me - - o.

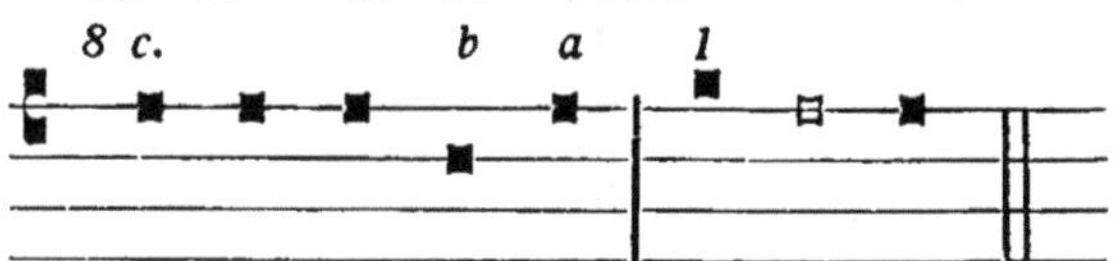

á-ni-ma me-a | Dó-mi-num.

The solemn form for the *Magnificat*, as for Tone 2, see p. 63.

89. *Tonus peregrinus.* Intonation, *podatus* and 1 note; mediation, 1 accent with 3 preparation notes; final, 1 accent with 1 preparation note. The secondary syllable in the final is sung at the pitch of the *preceding* accent-note.

I.

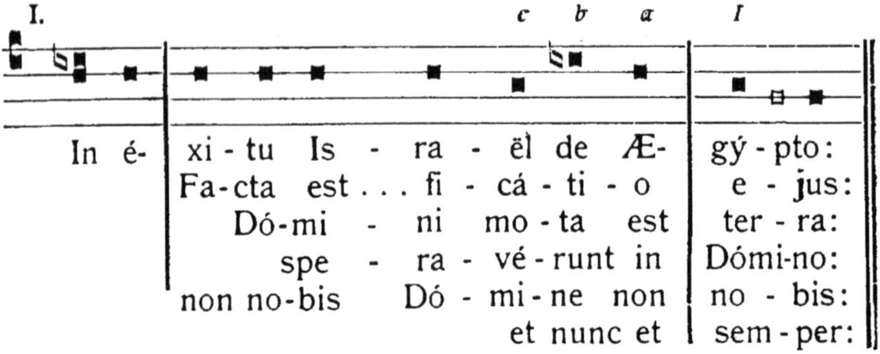

II.

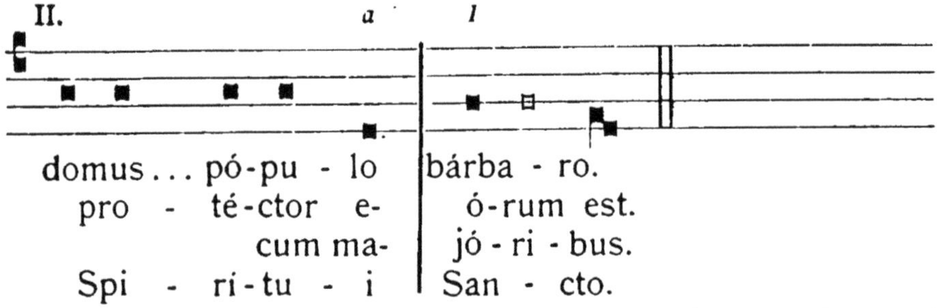

90. In many places the *Mediatio correpta,* i. e., a shortened mediation, is employed if in the middle of the verse before the * an indeclinable Hebrew word or a Latin monosyllable occurs. In this case a note of the mediation is omitted either *a)* in the middle or *b)* at the close, and the last 3 syllables are set to this shortened cadence.

a) In Tones 1, 3, 7:

1.

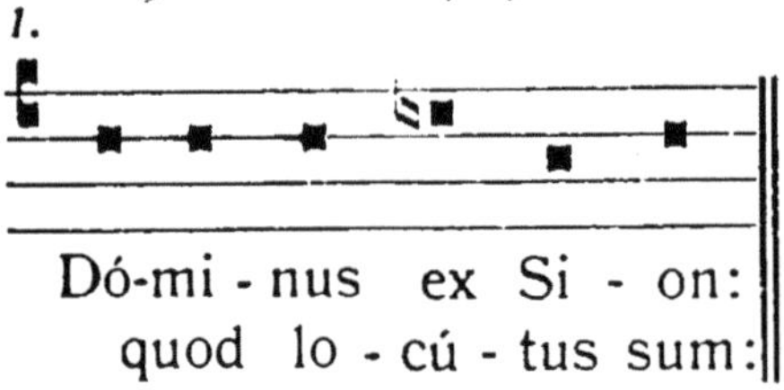

3.

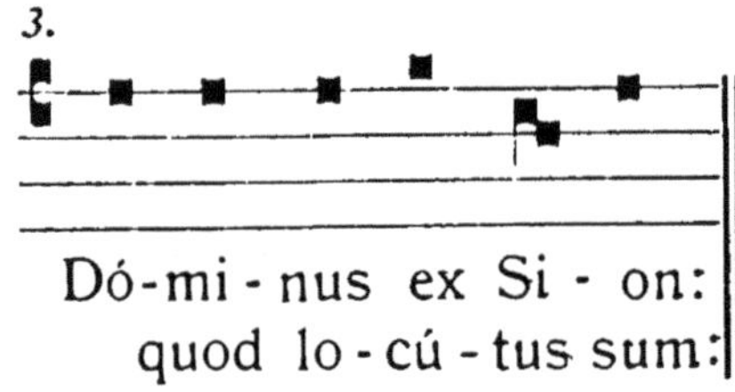

7.

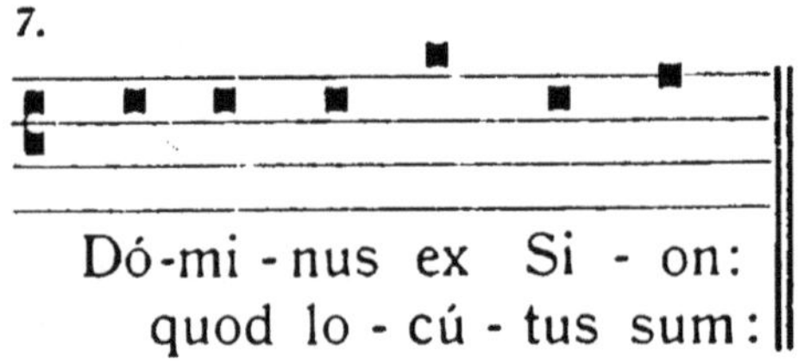

In Tone 1 the note *la* is omitted; in Tones 3 and 7 the note *do.*

Similarly with the *Tonus peregrinus,* only the fourth last syllable falls a whole tone:

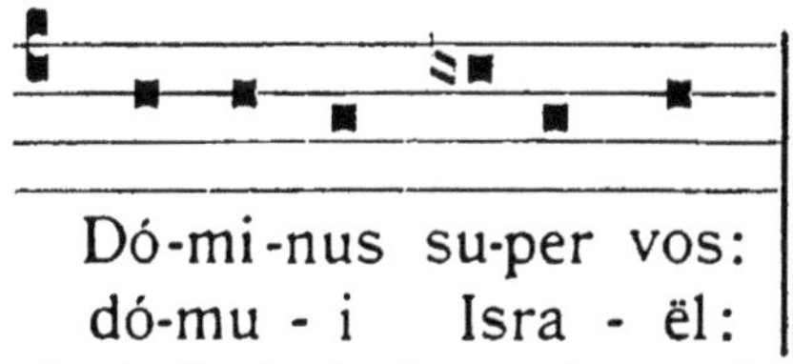

b) In Tones 2, 4, 5, 6, 8 the cadence should be formed as if *yet another* monosyllable were to follow the Hebrew word or Latin monosyllable; e. g.:

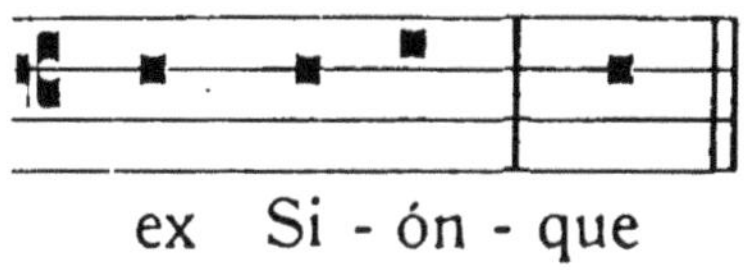

5, 8, 2.

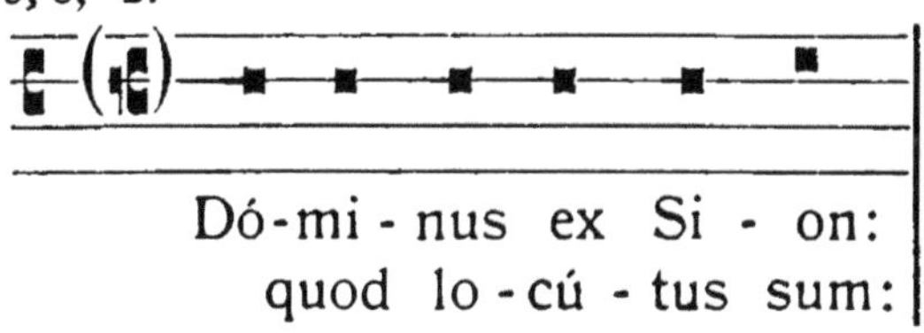

4.

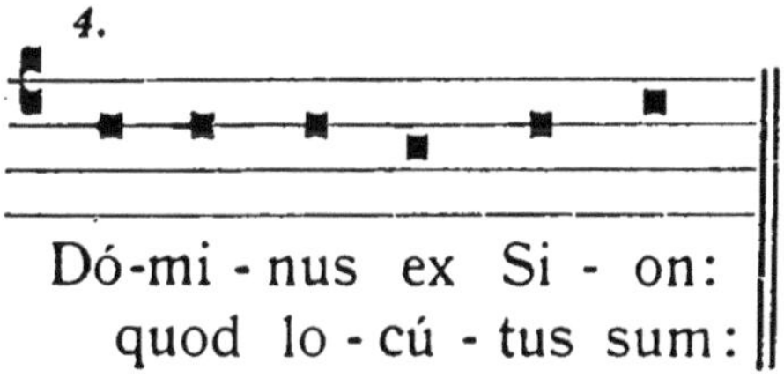

6.

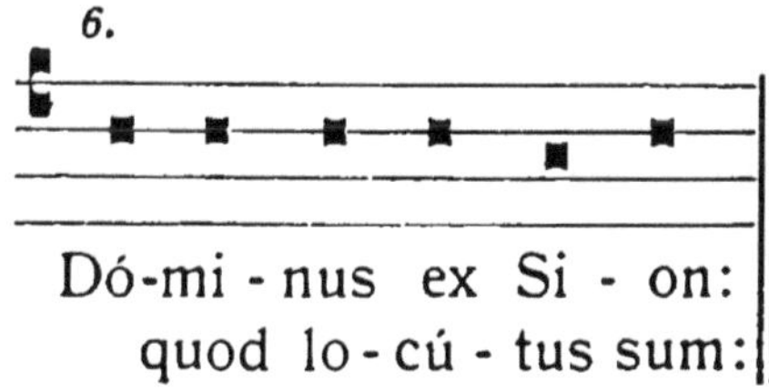

C) On Rendering the Psalms.

91. Upon the *Intonation* depends to a great extent the good or bad rendering of the whole psalm, and it must therefore be as clear and distinct as possible, attention being paid to tone, *tempo* (not too hurried) and rhythm.

In order to acquire a uniform, rhythmically correct method of psalmody, take care to mark the accents well, and to enunciate the syllables clearly and distinctly neither passing over the principal accents too hastily, nor lingering too long over them. Always avoid *staccato* which gives each syllable the same strength of tone; and also avoid making a little pause after each syllable. Do not omit to employ secondary accents where necessary:

in médio inimicórum tuórum. A uniform pronunciation (*fílius, suávis,* trisyllabic, not half the choir pronouncing *fil-yus, svávis,* dissyllabic) is indispensable.

92. Now, important as the verbal accents are, still more important is their subordination to the musical accents of the cadences which indicate the culminating point of the psalmody:

Dixit Dóminus Dómino meo: sede a dextris meis.

or if the cadence has 2 accents:

Dixit Dóminus Dómino meo: sede a dextris meis.

Hence it would be incongruous to give preponderance to any one of the other accents; this would spoil the form of the psalmody and open the way for individual caprice (one would accentuate thus, *Confitebor,* the other, *tibi,* another *in toto).* Equally incorrect would it be to lengthen a syllable: *in die iræ suæ.*

Go on quietly, but without any interruption, towards the cadence accents. Only when a half-verse is very long should breath be again taken at a place marked in many books with an obelisk (†). Do this without sustaining the previous note:

Me-mó-ri-am fe-cit mi-ra-bí-li-um su-ó-rum † mi-sé-ri-cors

In the monastic Office this denotes a fall *(flex)* according to the mode, in Tones 1, 4, 6, 7 a whole tone below the dominant *(sol, do),* in Tones 2, 3, 5, 8, a minor third below the dominant *(re, la).*

It does not sound at all well when the last syllable of the cadence is shouted out: *Domino me-o.* A soft, gentle dying away of the note is likewise in plain chant an absolute necessity.

93. Between the half-verses there should be a pause sufficiently long to allow a word of five syllables to be recited in the rhythm of the psalmody. The pause, like any other (cf. pp. 49 *seq.)*, must be prepared by a slight prolongation, therefore in accordance with the explanation in No. 70. *a)*:

The verses should be separated in the same way, only here the pause should be shorter by 3 beats; the prolongation as above (cf. No. 70, *a* and *b).* The same applies at the repetition of the Antiphon:

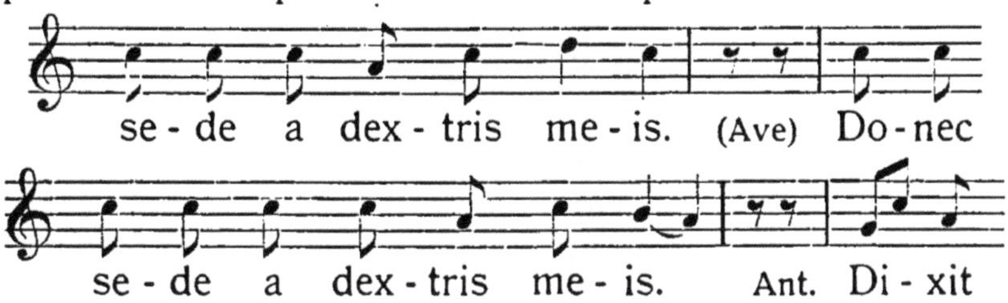

This prolongation and pause prevent overlapping, i. e., one choir not allowing the other time to sing the verse quite to the end.

94. As regards the pitch of the dominant, *a* or *b flat* is suitable on ordinary days, and *b flat* or *b natural* for festivals or at the *Magnificat* sometimes, with due regard to personal (whether boys are included or otherwise in the choir) and local circumstances. Sometimes a choir sings with a pure intonation when a high dominant is employed, whilst with its usual one it is apt to flatten.

D) Secondary Accents in the Cadences.

95. Since it is not always easy to perceive whether a *secondary accent* is to be used in a cadence (the principal accents are shown in the liturgical books for trisyllables, and dissyllables are accented on the first syllable), we here give for the Vesper psalms the secondary accents which fall to the cadence accents. If the cadence accent has only *one* accent of course the second subsidiary accent is not required, and therefore we do not include psalms whose cadences have not a secondary accent:

	1st half-verse. 2	1	2nd half-Verse. 2	1
Ps. 109.	*D*ominùs	ex Si on	gé-	nuì te
	splendóribus	sanctó-rum	ordi-nèm	Melchí-sedech
	et nùnc	et sém-per		
Ps. 110.	et nùnc	et sém-per	Veritas èt	ju-dí-cium
	(thus for all	psalms)	et àe-	qui-tá-te
Ps. 111.	suos ìn	ju-dí-cio	benè-	di-cé-tur
	confirmátum èst	cor é-jus	non còm-	mo-vé-bitur
	fremet èt	ta-bé-scet	mala nòn	ti-mé-bit
			exaltabitùr	in gló-ria
Ps. 112.	bè-	ne-dí-ctum	cœlo ét	in tèr-ra
	àd	oc-cá-sum		
	cùm	prin-cí-pibus	steri-lèm	in dó-mo
Ps. 113.	dè	Æ-gy-pto	èst	retrór-sum
	ùt	a-rí-etes	nòn	Vidé-bunt
	quòd	fu-gí-sti	ò-	do-rá-bunt
	Dominè	non nó-bis	cùm	ma-jó-ribus
	nòn	loquén-tur	ìn	in-fér-num
	èt	non aú-dient		
	àm-	bu-lá-bunt	vòs	a Dó-mino
Ps. 114.	*R*equi-èm	æ-tér-nam		
Ps. 115.	quòd	lo-cú-tus sum	in-	vo-cá-bo
Ps. 116.			ìn	æ-tér-num
Ps. 121.	ìn	ju-dí-cio	ìn	id-í-psum
	sùnt	Je-rú-salem	dili-gén-	ti-bùs te
			pá-	cem dè te

Psalm	1st half-verse. 2	1	2nd half-verse. 2	1
Ps 125.	gaudiò	os nó- strum	còn-	so-lá- ti
	face-rè	nobís- cum	exultà-	ti-ó- ne
	seminànt	in lá- crimis	facerè	cum é- is
	exultà-	ti-ó- ne		
Ps. 126.	cì-	vi-tá- tem	èx-	cus-só- rum
Ps. 129.	àd	te Dó- mine	sù-	sti-né- bit
	ìn-	ten-dén- tes	sustinuì	te Dó- mine
	propiti-á-	ti-ò est	Isra-èl	in Dó- mino
	misè-	ri-cór- dia		
Ps. 131.	bè-	ne-dí- cam		
	sà-	lu-tà- ri		
	confù-	si-ó- ne		
Ps. 137.	vocávero tè	ex-aú- di me	nè	de-spí- cias
	vivì-	fi-cá- bis me	retrí-	buet prò me
Ps. 138.	cò-	gno-ví- sti me	invè-	sti-gá- sti
	praè-	vi-dí- sti	pote-rò	ad é- am
	èt	an-tí- qua	decli-ná-	te à me
	còn-	cul-cá- bunt me	tà-	be-scé- bam
	(both columns 1st half-verse)			
	illù-	mi-ná- bitur	pèc-	ca-tó- res
	ma-gnì-	fi-cá- tus es	cogi-tà-	ti-ó- ne
	ìn	oc-cúl- to	iniqui-tá- tis	in mè est
	multi-plì-	ca-bún- tur		
Ps. 139.	pèc-	ca-tó- ris	é-	ri-pè me
	mé-	us ès tu		
	circui-tùs	e-ó- rum		
Ps. 140.				àd te
Ps. 141.	Domi-nùm	clamá- vi	co-gnó-	sce-rèt me
	àm-	bu-lá- bam		
	èt	vi-dé- bam	àd	te Dó- mine
	fú-	ga à me	persequén-	ti-bùs me

	1st half-verse.		2nd half-verse.	
	2	1	´ 2	1
Ps. 144.		mé-us rex		
		(both columns 2nd half-verse)		
	òp-	por-tú-no	nòn	est fí-nis
	bene-dì-	cti-ó-ne	pro-nùn-	ti-á-bunt
	vè-	ri-tá-te	è-	xul-tá-bunt
			gene-rà-	ti-ó-nem
Ps. 147.	nà-	ti-ó-ni	sù-	sti-né-bit
Magnificat.	in	pro-gé-nies	gene-rà-	ti-ó-nes.

Chapter IX.

The Antiphons.

96. The antiphons are short refrains, mostly sentences taken from holy Scripture, giving as an introduction to the psalm the particular point for meditation which the Church considers appropriate to it.

The mode of the antiphon is always the same as the tone of the psalm connected therewith. It is remarkable that the *tristropha* is scarcely ever employed in the antiphons, the *pressus,* seldom.

One and the same melody is often used for different texts; in fact one can trace back the majority of the old antiphons to 47 such typical melodies, as Gevaert has shown in his *Mélopée antique,* pp. 227 *seq.* Hence even choirs that are not very well trained can sing them without much difficulty.

97. *Divisions of the Antiphons.*[1]) For the effective rendering of the antiphons the division into fore and after phrases is of importance. This is effected according to the structure of the melody (in the fore-phrase the melody ascends, in the after-phrase it descends), as well as according to the division indicated by the text itself.

The accent over the rhythmical accents shows in the following examples the point where the melodic development reaches its culminating point, and where consequently the singer must pay special attention to expression.

1) Cf. *Pal. mus.* VII. pp. 268 *seq.*

a) *Antiphons with 2 Members:*

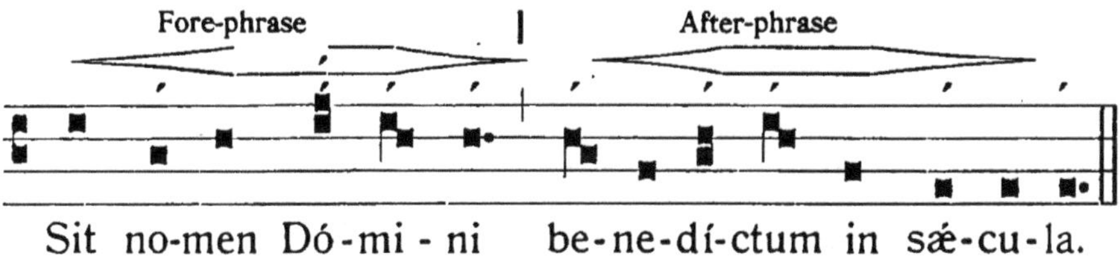

b) *Antiphons with 3 Members:*

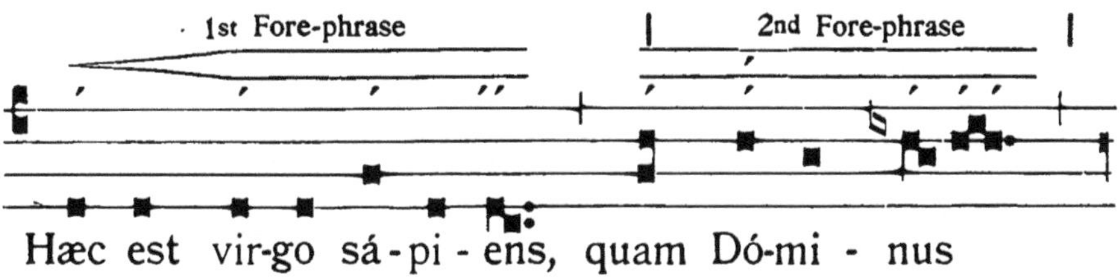

Sing the notes over (Domi-)**nus** without undue stress, quietly and strictly *legato*.

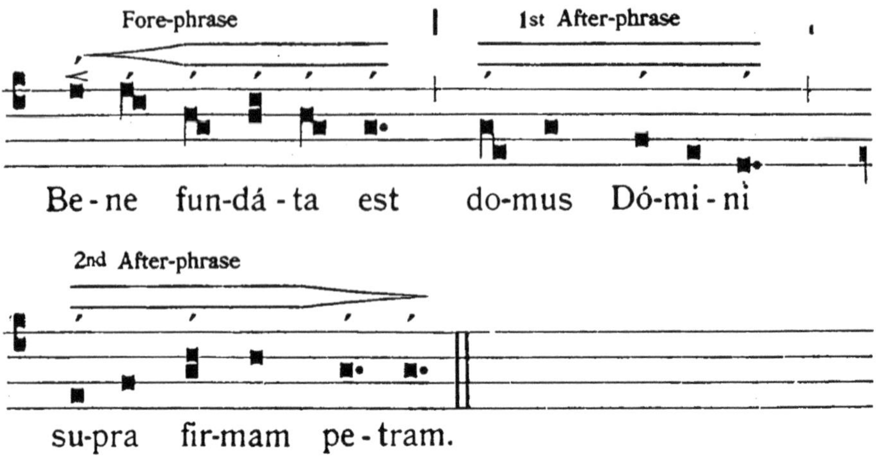

c) *Antiphons with 4 Members:*

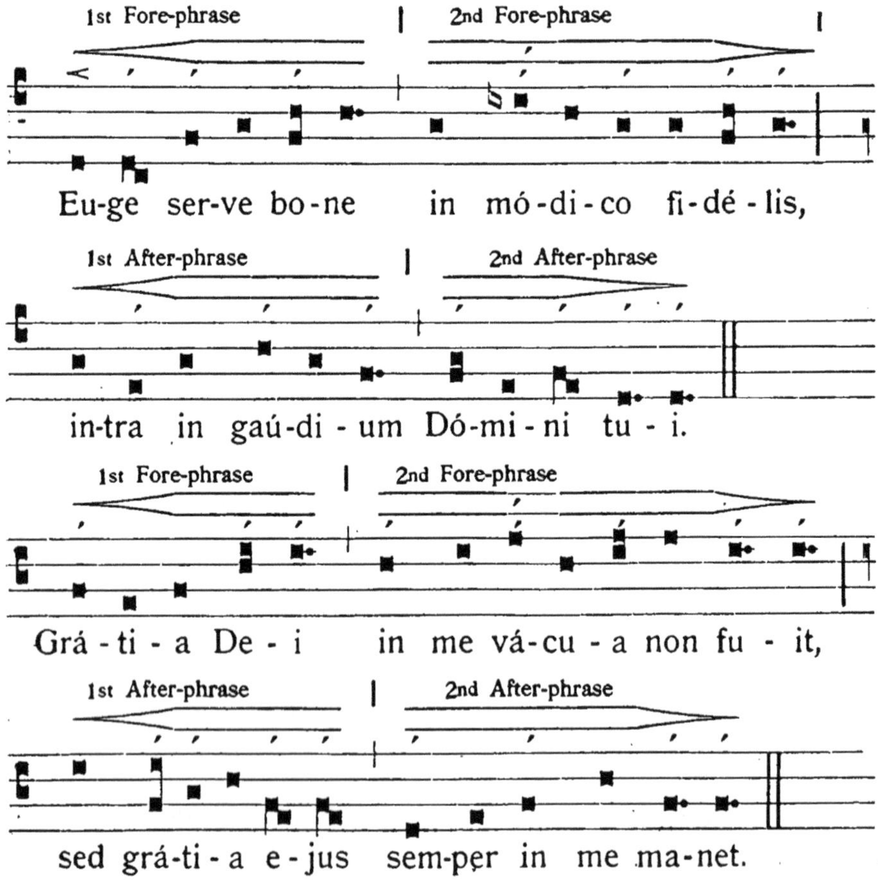

The above typical melody occurs more than 80 times in the Antiphonary.

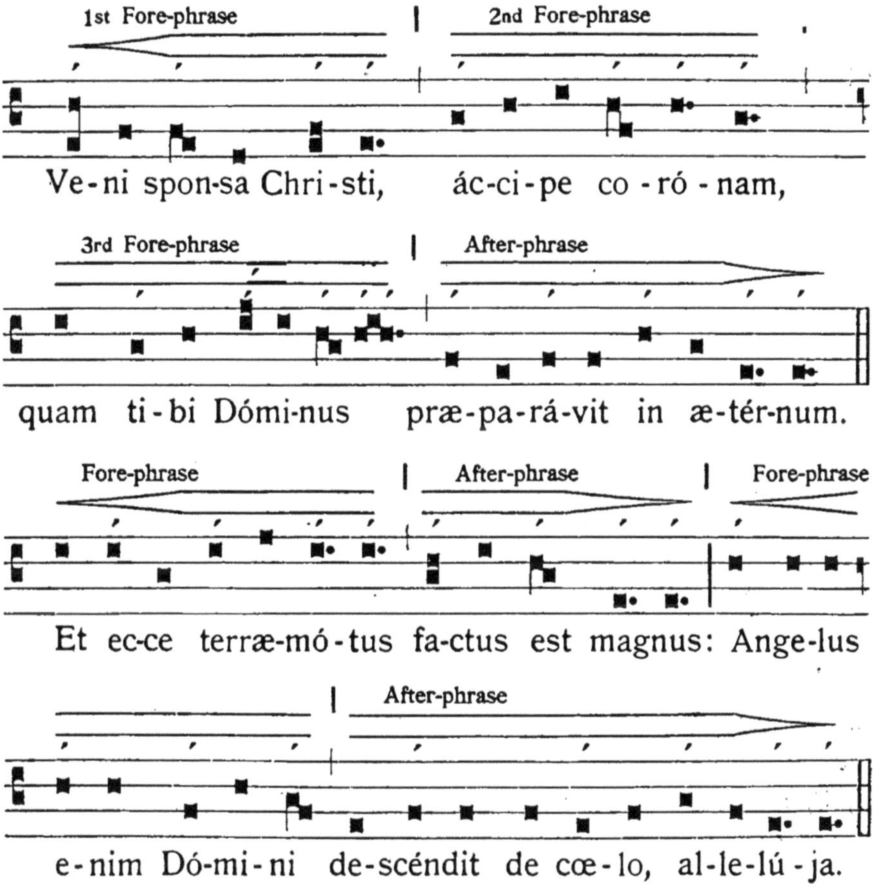

d) *Antiphons without developed Divisions:*

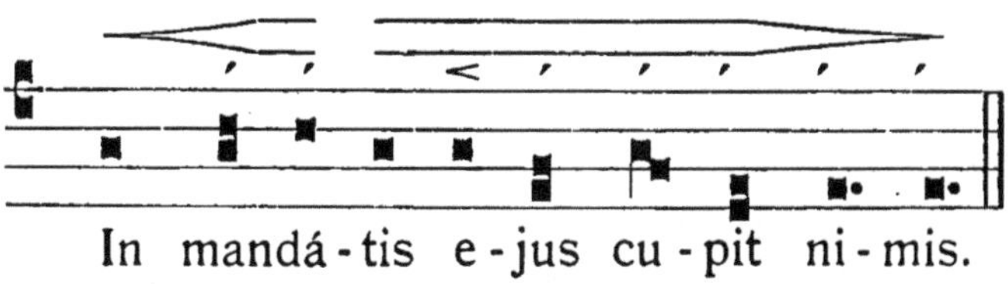

The longer *Magnificat*-antiphons have sometimes several members (4—6) in different relations to each other. Compare antiphons of the 2nd Vespers for Christmas, New Year, Epiphany, Ascension, and so on.

98. The number of notes in the members of many antiphons being alike, or almost alike, a beautiful proportion arises which the listener should be made aware of by the mode of rendering, i. e., length of the pauses, degree of loudness of each of the members, proportionate *tempo*.

Sometimes the melodic proportion depends upon that of the number of syllables, as in the following examples:[1])

Euge serve bone	6 Syllables,	8 Notes.
in modico fidelis	7 „	8 „
intra in gaudium	6 „	6 „
Domini tui	5 „	7 „
Tu es pastor ovium	7 Syllables,	9 Notes.
princeps Apostolorum	7 „	14 „
tibi traditæ sunt	6 „	9 „
claves regni cœlorum	7 „	12 „
Sacerdos et Pontifex	7 Syllables,	13 Notes.
et virtutum opifex	7 „	9 „
pastor bone in populo	8 „	13 „
ora pro nobis Dominum	8 „	12 „

Sometimes the melody extends its motives in order to lengthen a short division to suit the text and thus make the proportion symmetrical. Compare the antiphon *Bene omnia fecit* (p. 83) the 3 members of which have 7, 8, 5 syllables, for which 12, 13, 10 notes are given. Notice particularly *et mutos.*

99. *The musical Expression of the Antiphons.* Although many antiphons have only typical melodies, yet they all possess to an extent worth noticing characteristics that often enable them to express various sentiments with dramatic vividness.

The following melody commences energetically, as if, calling to mind the great deeds and struggles of Christ's first messengers, victory were certain (2nd V. Com. of apostles, Lib. us. p. 587):

---

1) Compare Pothier: *Les Mélodies grégoriennes* (Desclée, Tournai) p. 169, and Gontier, *Méthode,* p. 108.

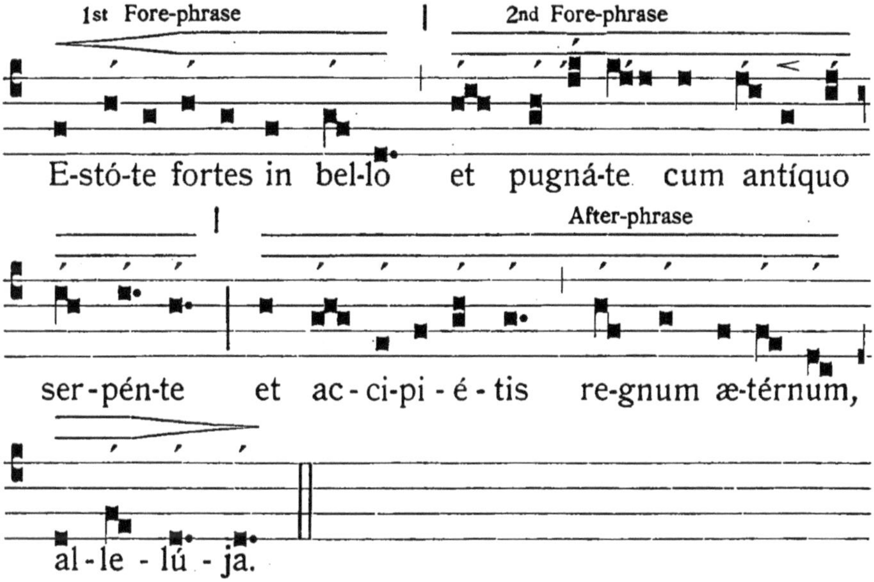

The sad remembrance of the fruitless labours of the past night seems to influence the following melody until it expresses the sudden resolve *(in verbo suo)*, in recognition of the power of the Messias, to labour anew:

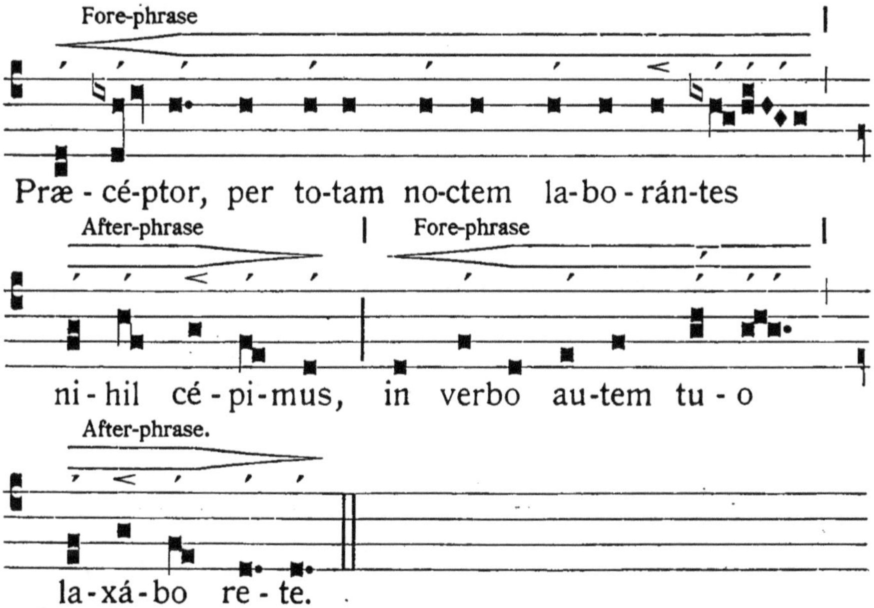

Magnificat-antiphon for the 4th Sunday after Pentecost (Lib. us. p. 511).

The striking way in which plain chant can express joy and sorrow may be gathered from the following melodies:

Feast of the Nativity of St. John the Baptist (Lib. us. p. 873).

Notice the melodic relation of the phrases *hic est enim* and *inter natos;* both are only expansions of the motive over *Puer;* in the same way *plus quam* and *(Jo)anne Bapt.*

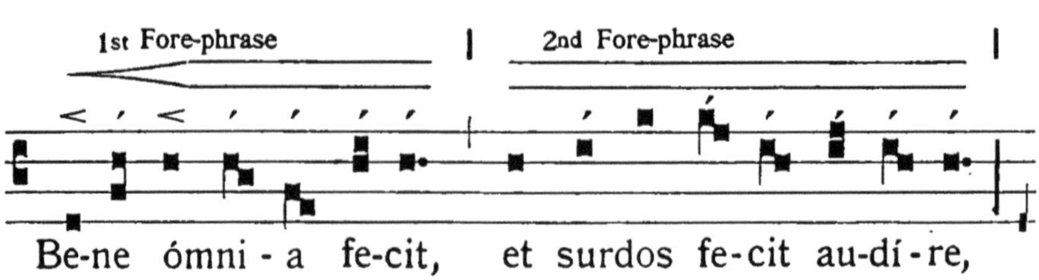

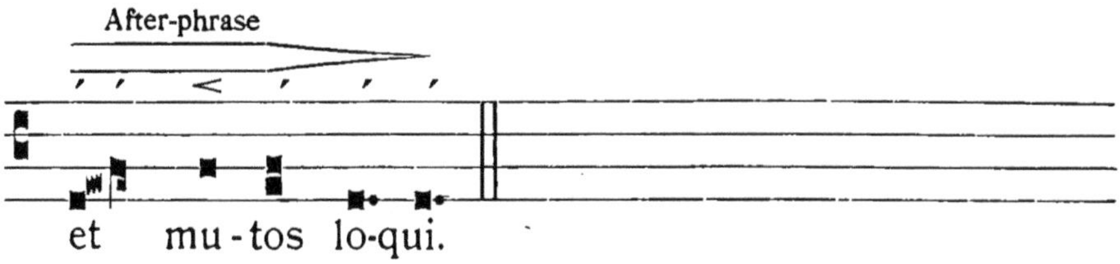

Magnificat-ant. on 11th Sunday after Pent. (Lib. us. p. 536).

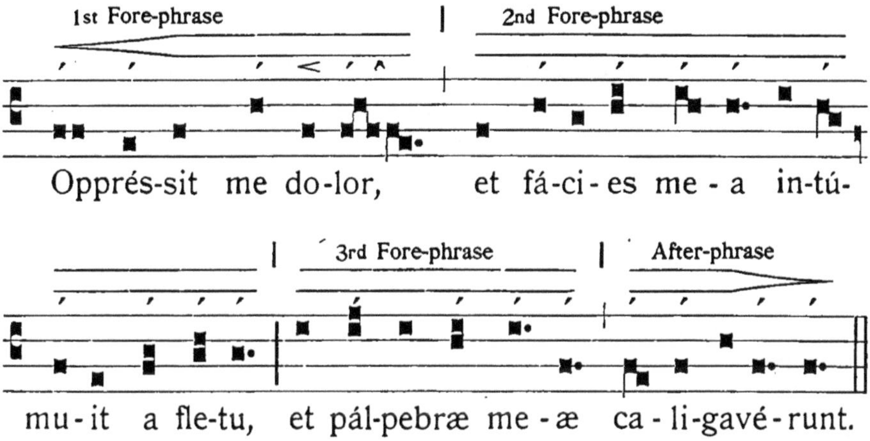

Magnificat-ant. on feast of 7 *D*olours (Lib. us. p. 978).

In conclusion we append yet another example showing how the melody is able to bring before our minds the awe and wonder expressed in the words:

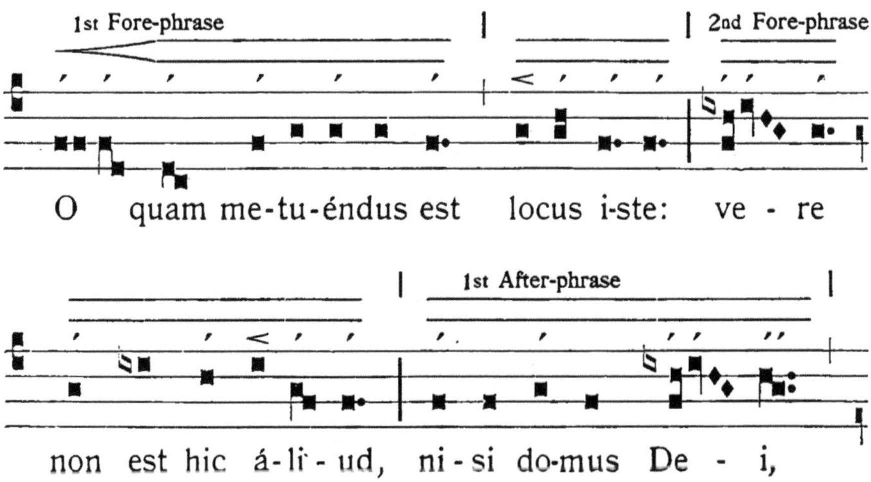

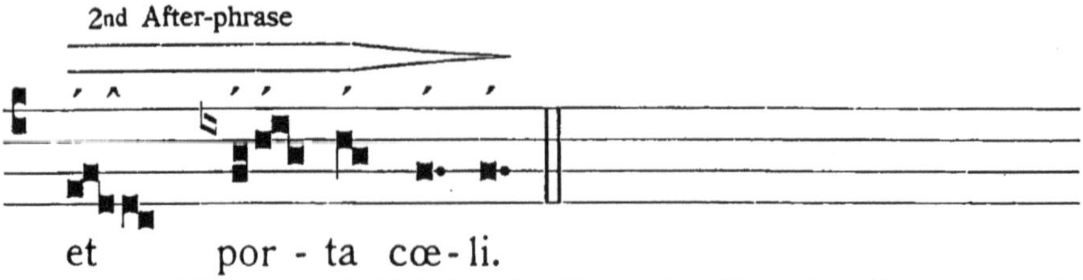

Magnificat-ant., 2nd V. for the Ded. of a Church (Lib. us. p. 693).

100. *On selecting the Pitch of the Dominant.*

To secure uniformity in the psalmody and maintenance of the pitch it is advisable to intone antiphons and psalms in the different modes at one and the same absolute pitch *(a, b* ♭, seldom *b* ♮*)*.

If, e. g., the first antiphon is in Mode II., the next one in Mode I., the others in Mode IV., keep to *a* or *b* ♭ as the common dominant, from which the cantor, if he has to intone without the organ, can easily strike the final and from this the initial note of the next antiphon.

This necessitates for the antiphons on *Corpus Christi* the following transpositions:

101. *At the beginning of Vespers* the priest intones:

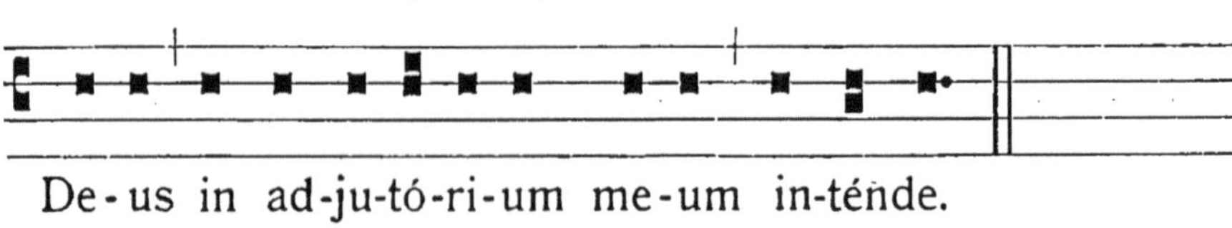

1) The two first notes give final and dominant of the particular Tone; the third note the initial note of the antiphon.

Choir:

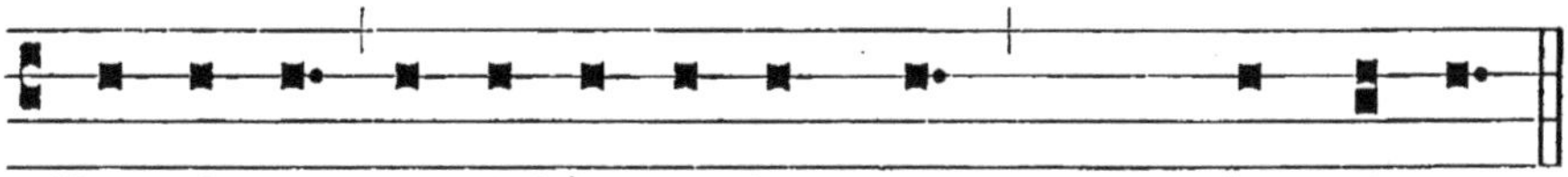

Dó-mi-ne ad àd-ju-vándum me fe-stí-na.
Gló-ri-a Patri et Fílio | et Spiritu-i Sancto.
Sicut erat in princípio et nunc et semper |
et in sæcula sæculó-rum. Amen.

Then:

or

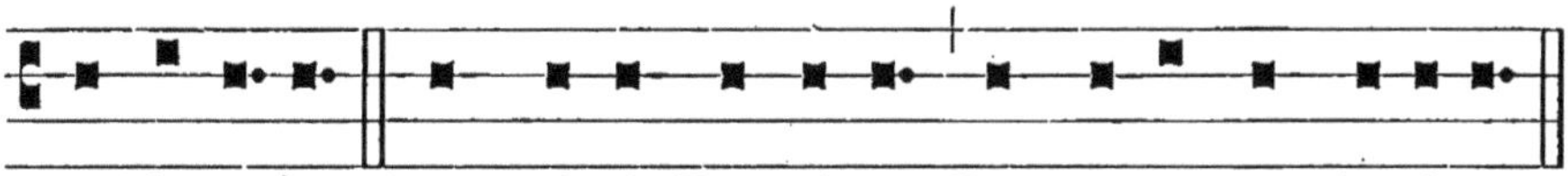

Al-le-lú-ja Láus ti-bi Dó-mi-ne Réx æ-térnæ gló-ri-æ.

Laus tibi Domine is sung from Septuagesima to Easter in lieu of *Alleluja*. In ferial Vespers *Deus in adj.* is sung on a monotone, but on the syllable *to* in *adjutorium* the voice rises a whole tone; likewise at *le* in *Alleluja*.

Chapter X.

The Hymns.

102. Hymns[1] are songs in praise of God and the saints, composed in verse, and consisting of several strophes sung by alternate choirs; they conclude with the praise of the Blessed Trinity (doxology).

Hymns came to the West through St. Hilary of Poitiers († 366), and were much cultivated by St. Ambrose[2] († 397) and widely spread through the rule of St. Benedict († 543), who prescribed a special hymn for each hour of the day *(Hora)*.

As regards the *musical rhythm* hymns may be divided into 3 classes:

---

1) On their historical development, authorship, metre, rhythm, and on the revision under Urban VIII., which was not always satisfactory, and the literature of hymns, see Herder's *Kirchenlexikon* and particularly *Geschichte des Breviers* by Dom Bäumer, O. S. B., translated into French by Dom Biron (Paris, Letzouzey et Ané 1905).

2) Cf. Rev. G. M. Dreves, S. J.: *Aurelius Ambrosius* (Freiburg, Herder, 1893).

103. a) Hymns in which the accents, that is to say, the *rhythm of the measure of the verse (metrical accent),* determine the *rhythm of the chant.* The verbal accent then agrees frequently with the metrical accent, but must sometimes give way to it. If the melody be elaborate, then of course more accents are to be employed than are given by the measure; the metrical accents retain meanwhile their importance, except in the rare instance in which a syllable provided with a *torculus* follows a syllable with the metrical accent (see below *creasti*). Cf. also Chap. VII. N°. 62.

To these belong:

I. The hymns in *Iambic* measure (Iambus = ⏑ ´–);

a) A strophe with 4 verses or lines, each of 8 syllables:

On the Epiphany (Lib. us. p. 199).

The principal accents in each line are on the second and sixth syllable.

The pauses after the first and third lines should be as short as possible; when you come to them let a slight prolongation of the last syllable suffice without taking breath. After the second line a suitable pause should be made.

Notice in this hymn and also in the one below, *Veni Creator,* the upward movement from the first to the third line.

As the metrical accent predominates, the rule given on p. 50 does not apply in passages like *Herodes Déum* (not *De - um*).

Moreover, as regards hymns in which the metrical construction comes out prominently, the *clivis* and *podatus* receive no accent of their own on the unaccentuated syllable, if the preceding syllable has a metrical accent and one or three notes:

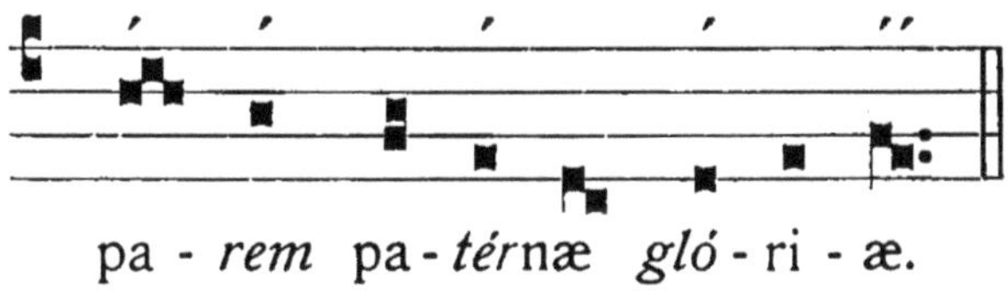

On the Ascension (Lib. us. p. 455).

On Whitsunday (Lib. us. p. 467).

The four lines of a strophe can as regards their melody be in the following relation to each other: A B A B (*Lucis Creator optime,*

Sunday Vespers), A B C A *(Jesu Redemptor omnium,* Vespers for Christmas), A A C A *(Jam sol recedit igneus,* Vespers for Trinity Sunday), A B C *D (Placare Christe servulis,* Vespers for All Saints).

β) A strophe with 6 lines of 8 syllables:

1. Cœ-*lé*-stis *urbs* Je-*rú*-sa-lem 2. Be-*á*-ta *pa*-cis
5. Spon*sǽ*-que *rí* - tu *cín*ge-ris 6. Mil-le *án*ge-*ló*-rum

ví-si-o, 3. Quæ *cél*-sa *de* vi-*vén*-ti-bus 4. Sa-*xis*
míl-li-bus.

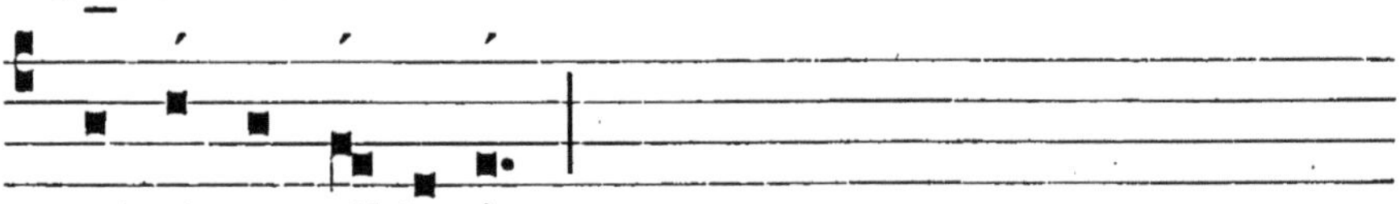

ad *á*stra *tól*-le-ris,

On the feast of the Ded. of a Church (Lib. us. p. 691).

Make only three well marked pauses, not six.

γ) A strophe with 4 lines of 12 syllables:

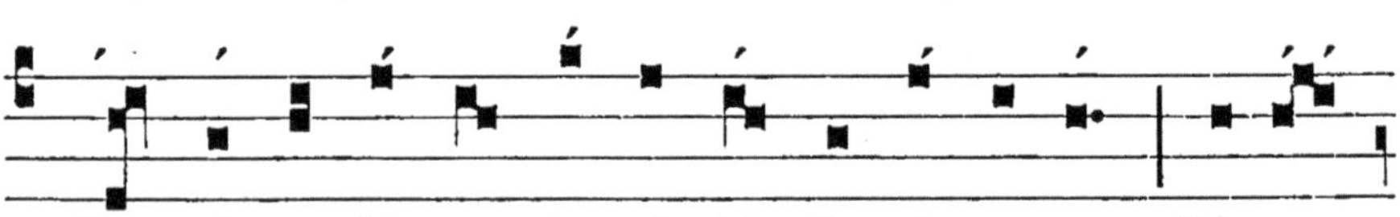

De-*có*-ra *lúx* æ-*ter*-ni-*tá*-tis, *áu*-re-am Di-*em*

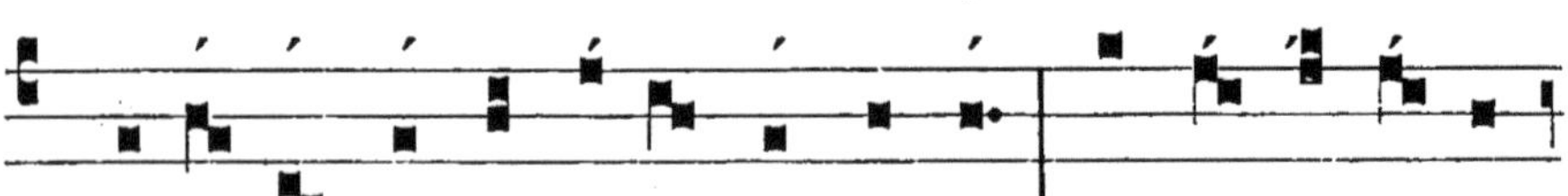

be-*á*-tis *ir*-ri-*gá*-vit *í*-gni-bus, A-*po*-sto-*ló*-rum

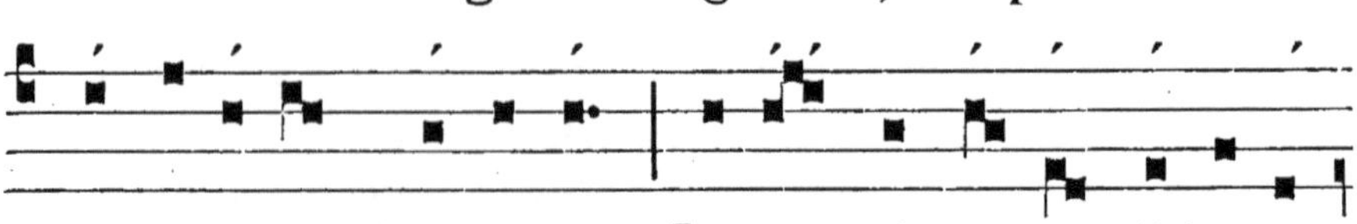

quæ co-*ró*-nat *Prín*-ci-pes, Re-*ís*que in *á*stra *lí*-be-*ram*

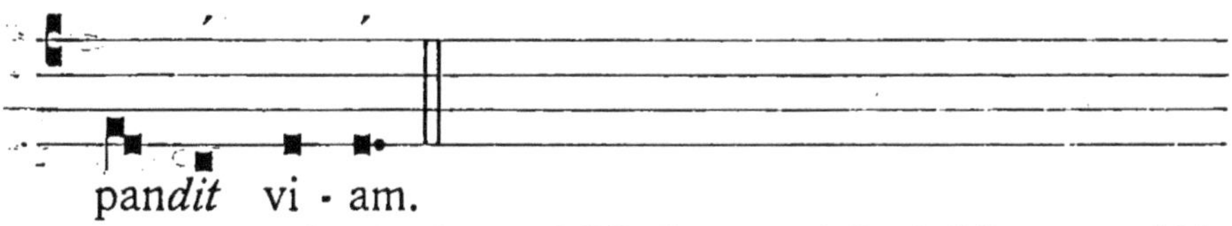

On the feast of SS. Peter and Paul (Lib. us. p. 883).

II. The hymns in *Trochaic* measure *(trochæus* = ´ ‿):

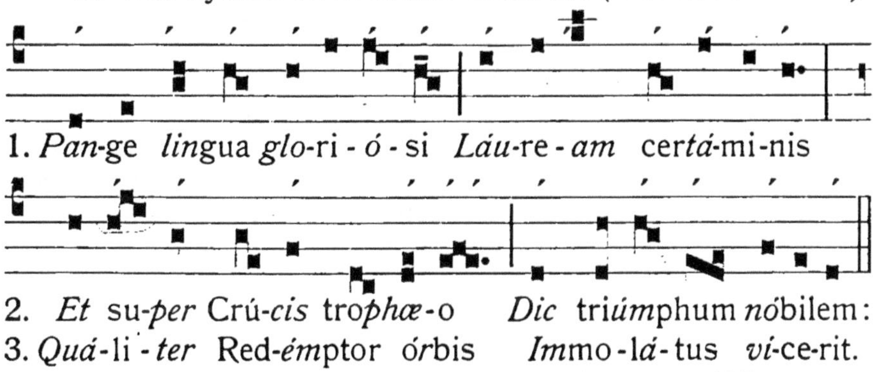

Hymn at the Adoration of the Cross (Lib. us. p. 361).

The hymns *Stabat mater* and *Ave maris stella* are also in Trochaic measure.

104. b) Hymns in which the *verbal accent preponderates* and the metrical accent only makes itself noticeable in certain places (particularly in the fourth line and when a line closes with a word accentuated on the penultimate.)

To these belong hymns in the *Asclepiadic* measure. The strophe consists of four lines, the first three of which have the following metre:

Te Joseph celebrent agmina cœlitum

The fourth line has: Casto fœdere Virgini

The rhythm of this fourth line is maintained in the melody:

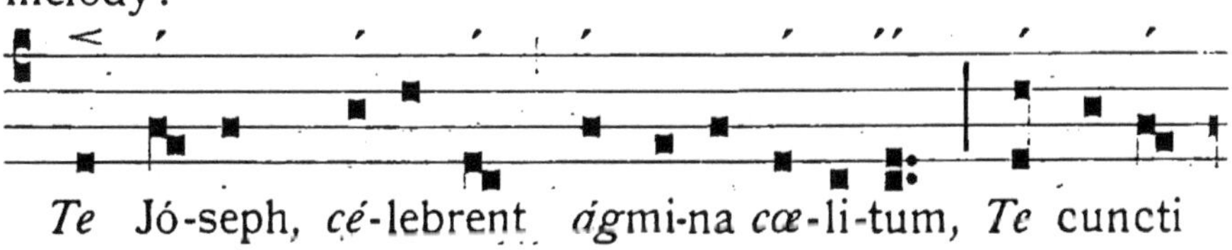

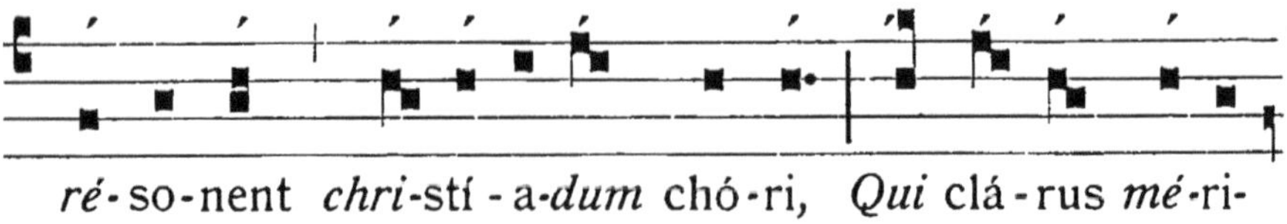

On the feast of St. Joseph (Lib. us. p. 790).

Notice in the second line *christiadum chóri;* and in the hymn *Sanctorum meritis* (com. of many martyrs) and in the hymn *Festivis resonent* (feast of the Precious Blood) the following:

105. c) Hymns in which attention is paid to the *verbal accent only.*

The rhythm of measured time is of course to be avoided.

To this class belong hymns in the *Sapphic* measure. This measure consists in ecclesiastical hymnody of four lines, of which the first three have this metre:

Iste Confessor Domini colentes

The fourth: Scandere sedes.

In the Calendar the abbreviations *mut. 3. Vers.* or *M. S.* indicate that in the first strophe of this hymn *supremos laudis honores* is to be sung instead of *beatas scandere sedes.*

106. *Elision.* If a word ends with a vowel or the consonant *m,* and the following word begins with a vowel or the consonant *h,* the vowel (also the *m*) of the first word is omitted (elided). Therefore, e. g., in the hymn for the feast of the Sacred Heart: *ille abstulerat, marisque et, illa amoris, percussum ad, regnumque in omne est.*

When there are two short syllables for a long one, the first can be treated as a consonant *(i* before vowels = *j),* or the note-value can be divided over two half units:

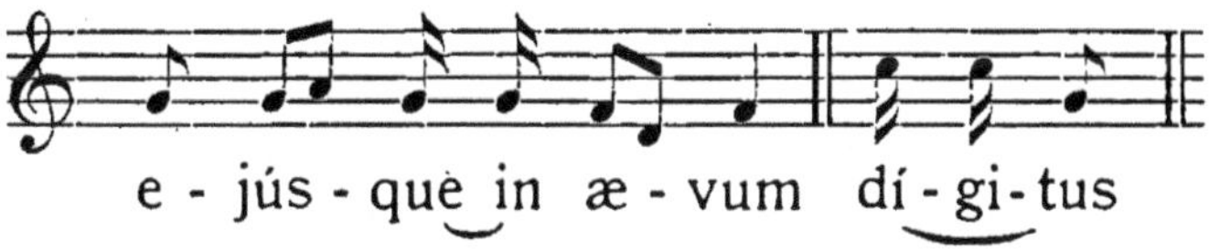

107. The following formulæ are used for *Amen* at the end of hymns according to their mode:

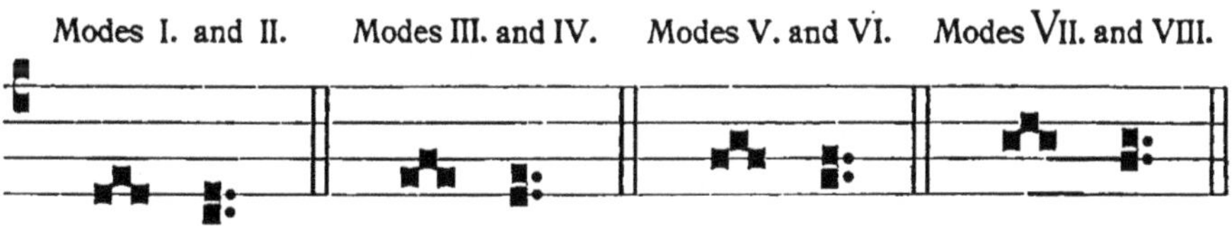

The *torculus* should be sung in the *tempo* of the whole melody; the *podatus* with sustained final.

Liturgical rules for hymns see p. 12. The last strophe of hymns is sometimes sung to different words according to the season.

108. *Recitation.* According to liturgical rule the strophes which are not sung should be recited. As regards hymns referred to under a) the recitation should be entirely according to the measure of the verse, but the syllables with the metrical accent are not lengthened contrary to the classical metre. Hymns under b) are usually recited as if the rhythm ⏗ ⏑ ⏑ repeated itself four times in each of the three first lines, and only the fourth line is recited in accordance with the metrical accents. The recitation of hymns under c) is influenced by the verbal accent only.

109. To the hymn are appended *versicle* and *response.* They generally have the following melody:

℣. No-tum fe-cit Dó-mi-nus àl-le-lú-ja.
℟. Sà - lu - tá-re su-um àl-le-lú-ja.

But in Vespers for the Dead (and at Matins on the three last days of Holy Week):

Au-dí - vi vo-cem de cœ-lo di-cén-tem mi-hi.
Beá-ti mór-tu - i qui in Dó-mi-no mori-ún-tur.

Or according to others:

Au - dí - vi vo-cem de cœ - lo di - cén-tem mi-hi.

The formula for the commemorations and after the concluding antiphons of the B. V. M. is:

O-ra pro no-bis san-cta De - i Gé - ni-trix.
Ut digni èfficiámur pròmissiónibus Chri - sti.

See "Secondary Syllable" p. 59.

A versicle ending with a Hebrew word or with a monosyllable can be sung as follows by those who do not use the *mediatio correpta* in psalmody:

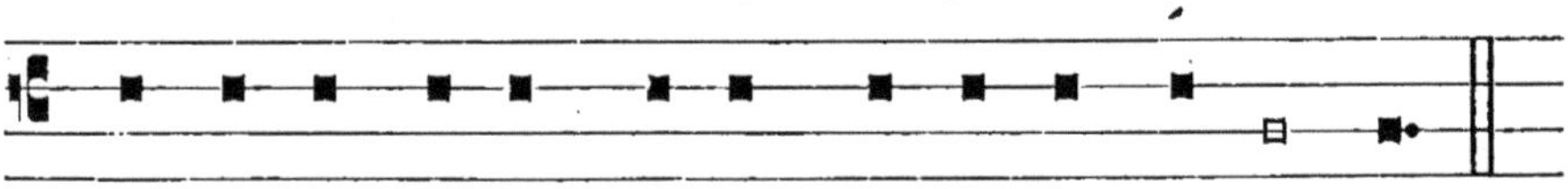

Ange - lis su - is De - us mandá - vit de te.
sú-per nos.
Jerú - sa - lem.

By others thus:

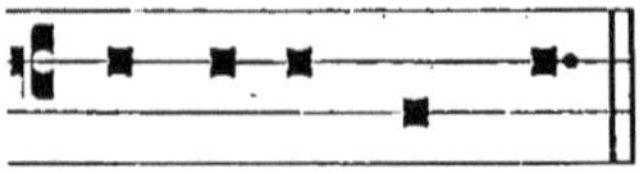

mandá-vit de te.
su - per nos.
Jerú - sa - lem.

but always:

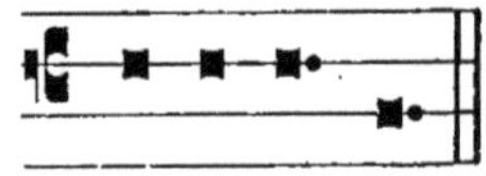

al-le-lú - ja.

Chapter XI.
The Ordinary Mass Chants.

a) Kyrie eleison.

110. *Kyrie eleison* is sung after the Introit.

In former times it was probably the beginning of a litany sung before High-Mass, as on Holy Saturday and Whitsun Eve. Since the 9th century each invocation is repeated thrice in honour of the most holy Trinity.

111. *Construction of the Melodies.*[1]) The *Kyries* of Masses I., II., IV., VIII., XIII., XIV., XVII. have the form *α)* *Kyrie* a a a, *β)* *Christe* b b b, *γ)* *Kyrie* c c c̄, i. e., the first three *Kyries* are alike, also the three *Christes;* the three last *Kyries* differ from a and b, and the last of all generally has a climax effected by repeating a motive of the *Kyrie,* and this must be marked by a *crescendo.*

The other *Kyries* have the form:

Mass III. and (VI.):	*α)* a b a, *β)* c db c, *γ)* e f ē;
V.:	*α)* a a a, *β)* b b ḃ, *γ)* a a a;
IX. and X.:	*α)* a b a, *β)* c d c, *γ)* e d ē;
XV.:	*α)* a b a, *β)* c d c, *γ)* e f g;
XVI. and XVIII.:	*α)* a a a, *β)* b b b, *γ)* a a c;
XI. and XII.:	*α)* a a a, *β)* b b b, *γ)* a a ab;

a a cb (XI.), in which the melody of the *Christe* is repeated a fifth below.

The nine-fold *eleison* in Masses II., III., VII., VIII., XI., XVII.[2]) is exactly the same; in the remaining Masses two melodies are used, seldom three.

In Masses I., III., IV., VI., VIII., IX., X., XII., (XIII.) the melody for *Christe* is sweet and tranquil, whilst in

1) In the following remarks Kyrie I., Kyrie II., etc., indicates the melodies of Mass I., II., etc., in the Vatican edition of the *Ordinarium Missæ;* the same as regards Gloria I., II., etc.

2) Cf. Wagner: *Einführung in die gregorian. Melodien* (Freiburg, Switzerland Universitätsbuchhandlung, 1895).

Masses V., XI., (XVI.), XVIII. the *Christe* is precisely the part where the climax of the melody is reached. In Masses II., VII., XIII., XIV., XVII., there is a marked upward tendency from the first melody to the last.

Thus there is considerable variety in the melodies, and each must be well studied if its characteristics are to be properly brought out.

In most of the Masses one of the *Kyrie* melodies (usually the first) is employed for *Ite* and *Benedicamus*.

112. If the *Kyrie* is sung *nine* times it should be rendered by two choirs in this way:

First choir	*Second choir*
1st Kyrie	2nd Kyrie
3rd Kyrie	1st Christe
2nd Christe	3rd Christe
1st Kyrie	2nd Kyrie

3rd Kyrie, both choirs together (at least for *eleison*).

If it cannot be sung nine times, the portions assigned above to the second choir can be *recited.* This is desirable for weak choirs, especially with *Kyries* in the form a b a, c d c, e f g (e).

In reference to the *pitch for the recitation,* recite the Kyries a) in Modes I., V., VIII. at the pitch of their finals *(re, fa, sol),* e. g.:

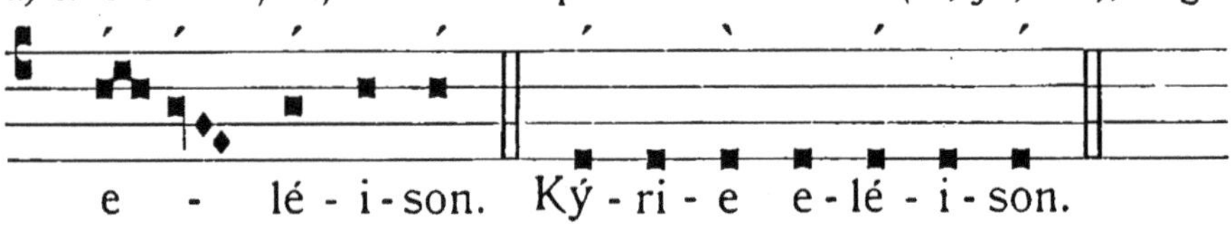

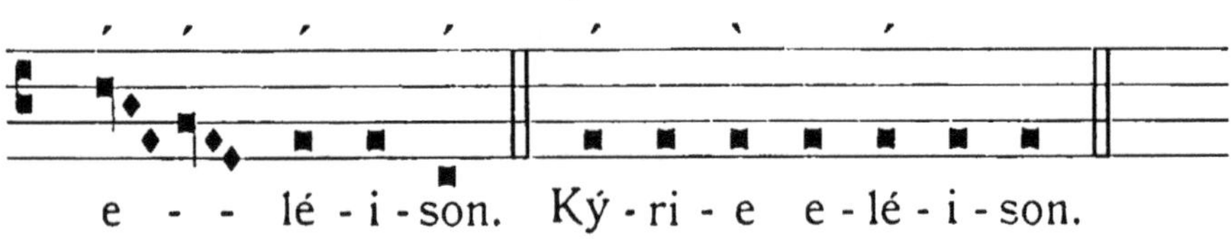

b) Those in Mode IV. at the pitch of the final, or better, a third below the same:

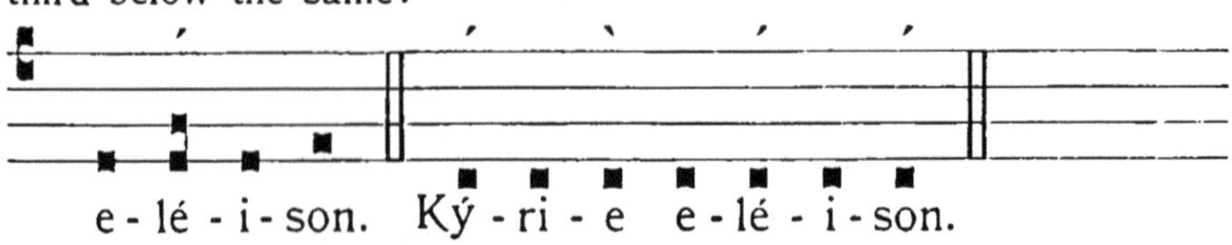

c) Those in Mode III. a third above the final.

113. Most of the *Kyries* have *certain appellations* from the *tropus* (trope)[1]) which was set to these melodies. A trope is an interpolation in the liturgical text, varying as to length; they sang, for instance, between *Kyrie* and *eleison* thus (Mass II.):

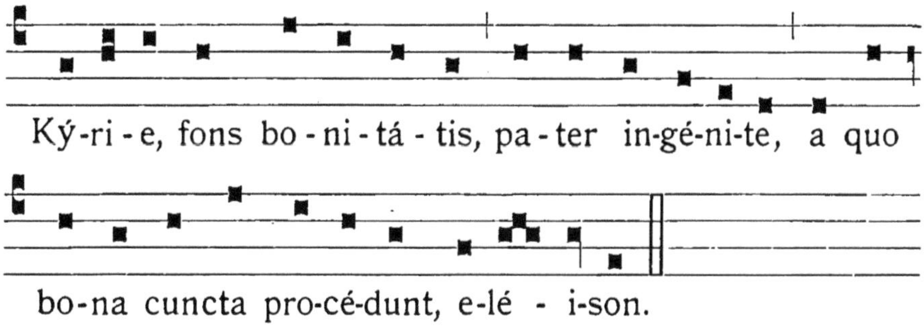

Gloria, Sanctus, Agnus, Ite, Introitus, etc., also had tropes of this kind.

The monk Tutilo of St. Gall was the author of many of them.

b) Gloria.

114. This is intoned by the priest, on the appointed days, after the *Kyrie eleison.*[2])

This hymn (song of the angels, also "greater doxology" = praise of the Blessed Trinity, in contradistinction to the "lesser doxology", the *Gloria Patri* at the end of psalms) probably came in the fifth century from the Greek Church to Rome where it was originally sung only at Christmas. Pope Symmachus († 514) extended the use thereof to feasts of our Lord and of the martyrs, but only for the Pope's Mass. Priests up to the ninth century were only allowed to sing it at Easter. Since the eleventh century it has been in general use.

The most ancient melody for the *Gloria* is the one in Mass XV. in the *Ordin. Missæ.*

115. Most of the *melodies of the "Gloria"* can be divided into four parts: (1) to *gloriam tuam,* (2) from *Domine Deus — Filius Patris,* (3) from *qui tollis — mi-*

1) Cf. *Rassegna Gregoriana* (Rome, Desclée 1904) Nos. 11 and 12. — Kienle, *Choral Sch.,* p. 119. — Reiners: *Die Tropen, Prosen und Präfationsgesänge* (Luxemburg, Hary, 1884) — in particular Gautier: *Les Tropes* (Paris, Paimé—Picard 1886, and Frere: *The Winchester Troper* (London, Harrison 1894) with splendid facsimiles.

2) Intonations see pp. 119 *seq.*

serere nobis, (4) from *quoniam* — *Amen.* Each part has a different characteristic; cf. Masses III., IV., XII., XIV. In each part the phrases are very closely connected and they usually have an upward tendency, e. g., *Gloria* of Mass XII., first part:

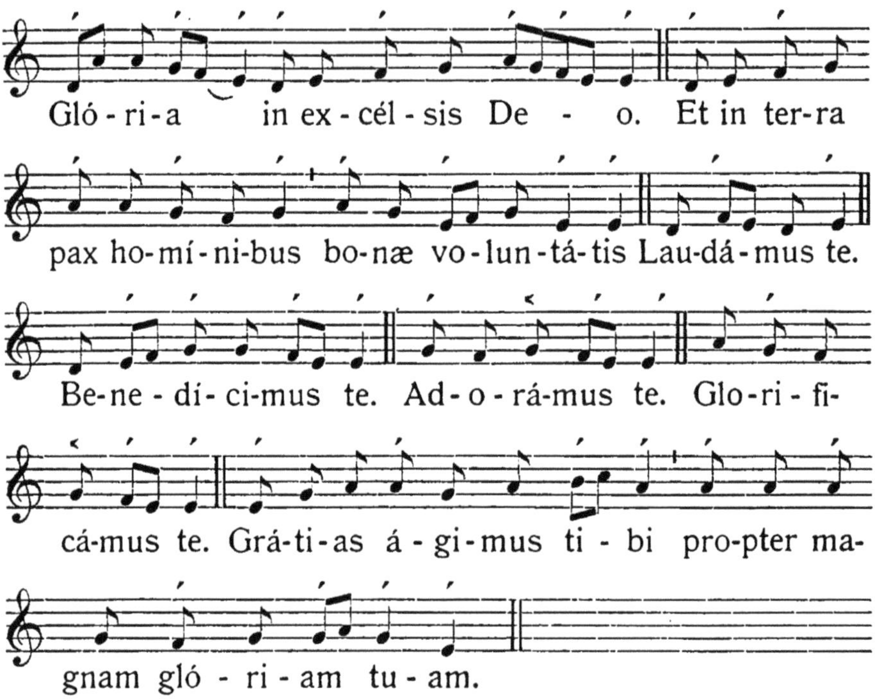

The same in Masses I., II., III., (IV.), VI., IX.

Of course the whole effect would be spoiled by too long a pause between the sentences.

Gloria, Mass IV., second part:

The same in Masses III., VI., VII., XII., XIII.

Gloria, Mass I., third part:

The same in Masses (II.), III., (IV.), VI., IX., X., XIV.

Gloria, Mass I., fourth part:

The same in Masses IV., VI., VII., IX., (X.), XIII.

In some cases owing to the construction of the melody a somewhat different division should be made. Thus in the *Gloria* of Masses II., VI., XIII. a longer pause would be desirable after *Glorificamus te.* In Masses II., III., XII., (XIV.) the culminating point in the music is before *Cum Sancto Spiritu.* The concluding sentence therefore must be commenced *largo* and with a good, full tone of voice, well brought out.

In Mass XV. the similarity of the melodic construction to that of the psalms is evident. Hence the melodies require to be rendered in a brisk, flowing manner:

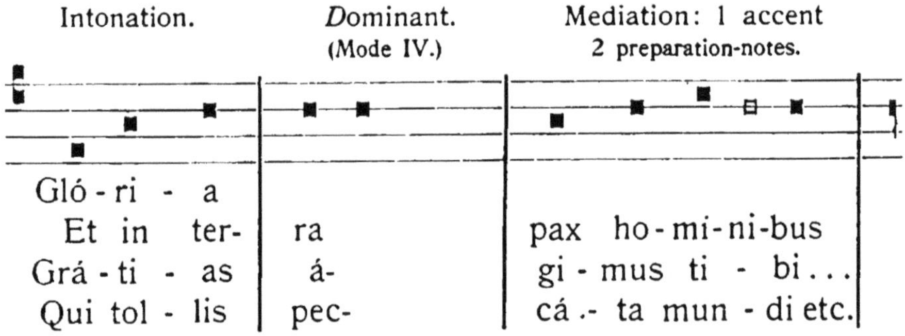

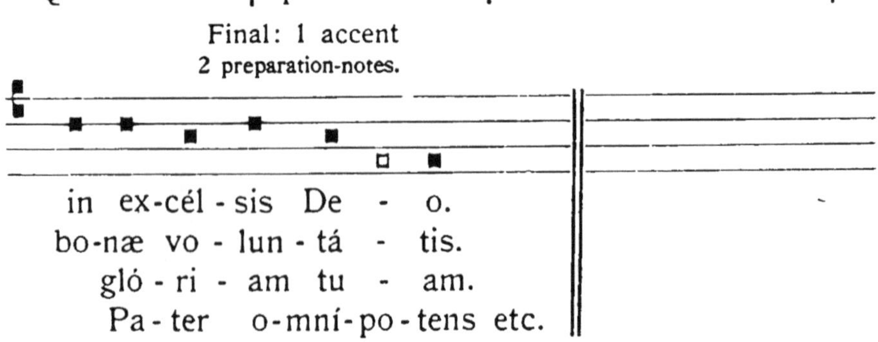

The short sentences, e. g., *Laudamus te,* simply make use of the final cadence.

The same applies to the *Gloria* of Mass XI., though rather more freely expressed:

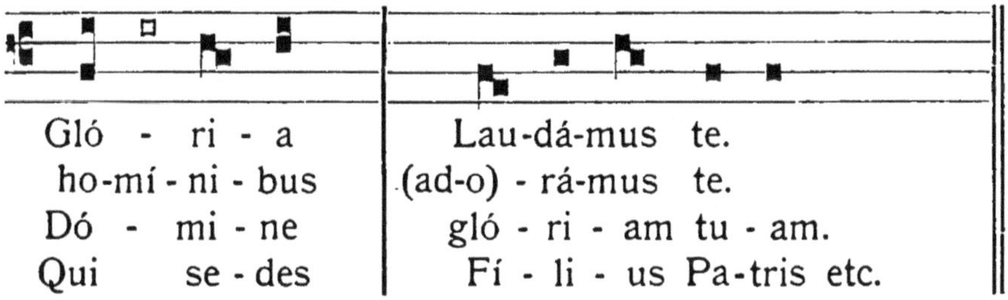

The closing sentence *Cum Sancto Spiritu* is very brilliant and spirited.

Almost the only melodies in Mass V. are the three following:

116. If the whole of the *Gloria* cannot be sung, every alternate sentence should be recited. Of course the melody loses a great deal thereby, as the passages are so closely related to each other. The words at which an inclination of the head is enjoined *must be sung,* viz., *Adoramus te; Gratias agimus tibi,* etc.; *Domine Fili Unigenite, Jesu Christe; Qui tollis peccata mundi, suscipe deprecationem nostram.*

If the *Gloria* is to be sung it is usually indicated in the Calendar by the abbreviation *Gl.* or *Glor.;* if not, or if we find therein *sine* (without) *Gl.,* it is omitted.

c) Credo.

117. After the Gospel the priest intones the *Credo* if prescribed for the day.

It is of Greek origin and came from Spain (introduced by the Council of Toledo 589) to Franconia and thence to Rome, and at the express wish of St. Henry II., Emperor, it was permanently adopted for the liturgy by Pope Benedict VIII. († 1024).

118. The simple melody repeated for each sentence as in psalmody is admirably suited for the solemn words, summarising as they do the most precious truths of our belief in God the Father, Son, and Holy Ghost, and their Divine Work, a humble confession of our faith, wherein each sentence is of equal importance.

Dom Molitor rightly remarks:[1]) "The attempt frequently made to portray the various articles of the *Credo* is altogether wrong . . . From a liturgical point of view it is a joyous, unrestrained confession of the Church, a loving submission full of faith, as between Bride and Bridegroom, an echo of the words of God Incarnate: *Ego cognosco Patrem* — "I know the Father". *Caritas omnia credit* — "Charity", says the Apostle, "believeth all things". Why, then, all this fuss and straining after effect in music? The agonies of the crucifixion, the glory of the resurrection, the terrors of the last day, ought not to be brought before the faithful thus dramatically. It is a misapprehension of liturgical requirements and of the Church's intention."

119. The *Credo* should therefore be sung in the spirit of thankfulness and child-like submission. Owing to its simple melody it can easily be mastered by the whole congregation, and when sung by a large body of the devout faithful it cannot fail to produce a truly grand effect.

There is nothing to be said against the custom of rendering *Et incarnatus est* more slowly and *piano*. But at *Crucifixus* the *tempo* should be as before.

---

1) Frankf. Broschüren, p. 180.

According to liturgical rule the *whole* of the *Credo* must be *sung,* recitation not being allowed.

The Calendar indicates when the *Credo* is to be sung, thus: *Cr.* or *Credo.*

d) Sanctus and Benedictus.

120. The *Sanctus* comes immediately after the last word of the preface, and it is desirable that it should be at once intoned by the cantors without any organ prelude. It is one of the most ancient parts of holy Mass.

The melody of Mass XVIII. is one of the very oldest, the natural continuation of the melody of the preface.

121. The *Sanctus* melodies are so constructed that the ascent of the melody generally reaches its culminating point at *Pleni sunt cœli.* An exception is the *Sanctus* in Mass III., with its splendid, vigorous opening.

The *Benedictus* according to the liturgical rules is not to be sung until *after*[1]) the Elevation, except in cases where an authorised custom to the contrary exists. It is either quite the same as *Pleni sunt cœli* with the *Hosanna* following it (cf. Masses [I.], II., [IV.], XII.), or for the greater part the same (as in Masses V., VII., VIII., [XI.], XIV., XV., [XVI.], XVII.). Masses VI., IX., XIII., form, however, exceptions to this.

When the *Sanctus* has been intoned the full choir can continue it; a small portion of the choir then sings *Pleni sunt cœli,* and finally all unite in *Hosanna.* The *Benedictus* is intoned by the cantor and continued by the full choir.

Since these chants occupy the time immediately before the sublime moment of the consecration, and since

---

1) As however in the typical edition of the *Kyriale Vaticanum* the *Benedictus* is united to the *Sanctus* without any observation or separation by a double bar, the proposal, unanimously adopted by the Pontifical Commission on Gregorian Chant, 1904, that the *Benedictus,* so far as time allows, may be joined to the *Sanctus* before the Elevation, has probably received the approbation of the Roman authorities.

they express the choir's welcome to, and adoration of, the Saviour, they should be sung with lively faith and fervent love.

e) Agnus Dei.

122. The *Agnus Dei* is sung immediately after the *Et cum spiritu tuo* with which the choir responds to the priest's *Pax Domini.*

Originally sung or omitted *ad lib.*, it was at length prescribed by Pope St. Sergius (687—702).

123. The melodies in Masses X., XII.—XVI. have the form which we will indicate by the letters a b a, i. e., the second *Agnus* is different from the first and third; the same with regard to Masses II., IV., VIII., but in these the *miserere* and *dona* are always alike. The melodies in Masses I., V., VI., XVIII. have the form a a a; to these may be added Masses (IV.) and XVII. in which only the word *Agnus* is differently treated the second time; in Mass VII. the form is a a b, and in Mass XI., a b c.

Text and melody require a devotional but sometimes an energetic and vigorous rendering; compare Masses I., III., V., VII., XI., XV.

Concerning *Asperges me* and *Vidi aquam* see p. 105.

Chapter XII.

The Variable Mass Chants.

124. To the variable Mass chants (the Proper), i. e., those chants which have different words according to the season or feast, belong: *Introitus, Graduale, Alleluja, Tractus, Sequentia, Offertorium, Communio.*

125. *They differ from one another:*

a) In their *melodic peculiarity,* which is disclosed in the best melodies of the Gregorian tradition, e. g., when there are two melodies with the same text, let us say, for a *Graduale* and *Communio.*

Typical melodies which are numerous in antiphons out of Mass are seldom found in the antiphonal Mass chants (mostly more elaborate), viz., *Introitus, Offertorium, Communio.*

On the other hand, for some Graduals and Allelujas typical melodies are employed.

b) *In the Preference for certain Modes:*

The *Introitus,* preferably Modes I. and III., less frequently Modes V. and VI.

The *Graduale,* chiefly Modes VI. and V., less frequently Modes IV. and VIII.

The *Alleluja,* mostly Modes I. and VIII., seldom Modes V. and VI.

The *Offertorium,* nearly always Modes II., IV. and VIII., seldom Modes V. and VI.

The *Communio,* preferably Modes I. and VIII., less frequently Modes III. and IV.

The *Tractus* is written in Modes II. and VIII., more frequently in the latter.

a) Introitus (Entrance).

126. The *Introitus* (Introit) is intoned by a cantor, on feasts by several cantors, when the priest commences Mass at the foot of the altar with the sign of the Cross.

It consists of an antiphon, psalm-verse, *Gloria Patri,* etc., after which the antiphon is repeated.

Formerly a whole psalm was sung; in remembrance thereof the psalm-verse in the *Missale* and *Graduale* to this day is not indicated with ℣. *(versus),* but with Ps. *(psalmus).* — The Introit was already in use under Pope St. Celestine I. (422—432).

127. The *Introit* has generally 2 to 3 parts, seldom 4, and these should be made apparent by suitable pauses. The pauses *within* one part must never be equal to the pause between one and the other part, as otherwise the general outline of the melody would be broken up into disconnected portions. The division of the text, discernible from the punctuation (mostly a colon), and the division of the melody, coincide usually, but not always.

Examples:

Introit for the 4th Sunday of Advent:

Part I. *Roráte cóeli désupèr et núbes plúant justum:*
Part II. *àperiátur térra, et gérminet Sàlvatórem.*

Introit for the 3rd Mass on Christmas Day:

Part I. *Púer nátus est nóbis, et filius dátus est nóbis:*
Part II. *cujus impérium super húmerum éjus:*
Part III. *et vocábitur nómen éjus: mágni consilii ángelus.*

The division of the antiphons given in Chapter IX. can easily be applied to the melodies of the Introit, as they also have antiphonal characteristics.

128. Note carefully the effect of the Introits for the 2nd Sunday of Advent *(Populus Sion),* 4th Sunday of Advent *(Rorate);* 2nd and 3rd Masses for Christmas Day *(Lux fulgebit* and *Puer);* 4th Sunday in Lent *(Lætare);* Purification *(Suscepimus)*; 5th Sunday after Easter (*Vocem jucunditatis,* very cleverly adapted for the text *Gaudens gaudebo* on the feast of the Imm. Conception); the Ascension *(Viri Galilæi);* and very particularly the dramatical chants for Sexagesima Sunday *(Exsurge);* Palm Sunday (*Domine,* with the impressive cry for help, *adspice)* and Whitsunday *(Spiritus Domini),* and you will then acknowledge how true is the remark made by Dom Kienle (*Choral-Schule* p. 113): "The Introit makes a splendid opening, announcing as it does with its elaborate and spirited melodies the grandeur of the coming mysteries. The movement should be rapid and *full of life and vigour.*"

But *sweet and tranquil melodies* are not wanting, e. g., see 3rd Sunday of Advent *(Gaudete),* Quinquagesima Sunday *(Esto mihi),* Maundy Thursday *(Nos autem),* Low Sunday *(Quasi modo);* compare very particularly the striking melody for *Hodie scietis* on the Vigil of the Nativity.

129. As the Introit chants rarely exceed the compass of an octave and are of a tranquil, solemn character, presenting no great difficulties, they are admirably adapted for full choir.

The mode of rendering is as follows:

Should the choir be a small one and capable of singing it through twice, it is better for the whole choir to continue it after the intonation. Cantors then sing the first half of the psalm-verse; full choir, the second, cantors, *Gloria Patri,* etc.; full choir, *Sicut erat;* the full choir now commences the melody anew, including the intonation, the *tempo* being quicker than before.

If the Introit can be sung *once only,* after the intonation the full choir continues, and *Sicut erat* being concluded the text is recited on the final, or in Mode I. on *fa* (better than *re*), in Mode VII. on *do* (better than *sol*).

From Passion Sunday to Easter (exclusively) the *Gloria* is omitted after the psalm-verse, as in all *R*equiem Masses.

There is no Introit on Holy Saturday and Whitsun Eve.

Asperges and *Vidi aquam* are rendered in the same way as the Introit.

b) **Graduale** (Song of Degrees).

130. The *Gradual* follows the Epistle or Lesson.

It consists of two verses mostly taken from the psalms, and it is one of the very ancient chants.

It has this appellation because it was sung on the steps of the *Ambo* (pulpit), from which the deacon afterwards announced the gospel. In earlier times it had another distinguishing mark, as whilst it was being sung neither the priest nor his assistants proceeded with the liturgical ceremonies but listened to the singing.

The Graduals are veritable masterpieces in the way of melody. Hence it is necessary to make a special study of the mode of rendering them.

If a well-trained voice, the proper management of the breath, strict *legato,* round and full notes freely brought out, are indispensable for singing well, this is particularly the case with regard to the Gradual chants. Therefore untrained singers would do well to *recite* them. After at ime such might try the first verse, which is usually simpler, e. g., *Christus factus est* on Holy Thursday, *Ecce sacerdos magnus* from the Mass *Statuit* (for a confessor and bishop), or *Diffusa est* from the Mass *Cognovi* (for widows). Then melodies in Mode II. could be attempted, e. g. *Justus* from the Mass *Os justi* (for a confessor not a bishop), as this one often occurs, generally with unimportant alterations.

131. This melody, as the Solesmes Benedictines have shown,[1]) is constructed similarly to that for the psalms. Compare the Graduals *Justus, Requiem, Nimis honorati* (feast of St. Matthias, etc.), *Angelis suis* (1st Sunday in Lent and Holy Guardian Angels).

The first verse has 4 parts:

Part 1.

Intonation.	*D*ominant, simple or florid.	Cadence with or without Neuma.
Ju-	stus ut palma flo-	ré-bit
Ré-	quiem æ-	tér-nam
Ni-	mis hono-	rá-ti sunt
An-	gelis	su-is

Part 2.

sicut ce-	drus Lí-	ba-ni
	do-na eis	Dó-mi-ne
a-	míci tui	De-us
*D*eus man-	dá-vit de	te

Part 3.

mul-	tipli-	cá-bi-tur
et	lux per-	pé-tu-a
ni-	mis confor-	tá-tus est
ut	custódi-	ànt te

Part 4.

in do-	mo	Dó-mini.
lú-	ceat	é-is.
princi-	pátus e-	ó-rum.
in ó-	mnibus viis	tuis.

The second verse is constructed in the same way.

132. To give some idea of the *richness* and *beauty* of the Gradual melodies we here give some specimens in Mode V., which is employed about 70 times in the *Liber Gradualis.* They can serve as vocal exercises.

The second verse has amongst others the following *Intonations:*[2])

---

1) *Pal. mus.* III., pp. 36 *seq.*

2) Cf. Gastoué: *Cours théorique et pratique de* Plain-chant *Romain grégorien* (Paris, Bureaux de la Schola Cantorum, 1904) pp. 46 *seq.*

Feast of St. Stephen, like the one for the 2nd Mass on Christmas Day.

N.B. The 𝅘𝅥 is to be rendered *decresc.*

3rd Mass for Christmas Day.

Assumption, also Holy Innocents.

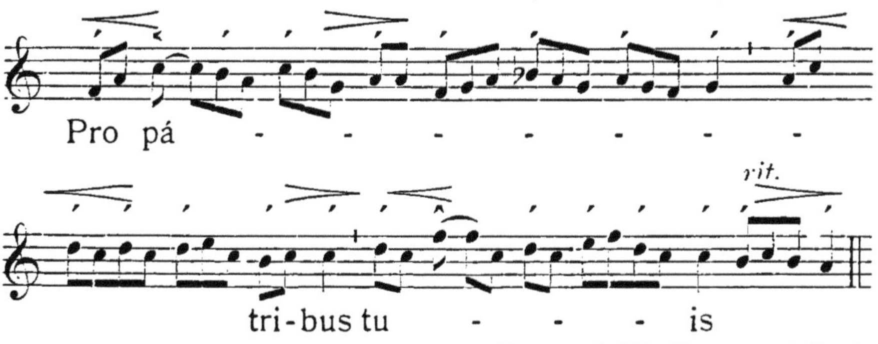

Feast of SS. Peter and Paul.

Generally at the *close of the first half-verse* we find the following melodies:

2nd Mass Christmas Day.

Feast of St. Stephen.

From the Mass *Cognovi;* one of the finest ascents in the music that plain chant has produced.

The following are specimens of *closing melodies:*

Feast of SS. Peter and Paul.

3rd Mass Christmas Day; also on the Assumption.

From the Mass *Cognovi.*

Feast of the Epiphany.

These and similar motives give great elegance, swing and variety to the Graduals.

133. The first verse of the Gradual, after being intoned by one or two singers can be sung by a small, trained choir: it is best for the second verse to be sung by 2 or 4 cantors only.

In many places the custom has grown up (where it does not exist, for the sake of unity in the rhythm do not introduce it) of allowing the entire choir to sing the last word of the second verse, indicated by * or ‖ ; where this is the case take good care when the choir joins in with the cantors to maintain the rate of movement and not to drag it.

If in Graduals, Mode V., different clefs are used for the two verses, do not make any modulation after the first verse, as otherwise the rise intended in the melody of the second verse would be much interfered with. Therefore take both verses at the same pitch (cf. *Christus factus est,* Grad. for Holy Thursday).

From Low Sunday to Trinity Sunday instead of the Gradual an *Alleluja* is sung. Holy Saturday has likewise no Gradual.

Alleluja.

134. To the *Gradual* is appended, excepting from *Septuagesima* to Easter, the *Alleluja* (Hebrew for "Praise God").

To give expression to this invitation to praise God, a melody *(júbilus, jubilátio,* also *neuma* and *sequéntia)* of a particularly joyous and animated character is appended to the *Alleluja. Alleluja* and *Neuma* form of themselves a splendid song of praise; both also make an effective framework to the verse (usually taken from the psalms) in the same style.

The Alleluja melodies are included among the oldest chants of the Church. Scarcely anything is known about the composers of the various melodies.

135. The *Alleluja* is intoned by one or two singers, the choir repeats the *Intonation* and sings the *Neuma,* whereupon the cantors sing the verse, of which the last word, or the last word but one, from * or ‖ is sung by the choir which then continues the *Neuma* melody to the end. The cantors thereupon repeat the *Intonation* and the choir the *Neuma.* This is done when the *Alleluja* is sung after the Gradual and holds good from Trinity Sunday to Septuagesima and during Easter week.

From Low Sunday to Trinity Sunday two *Allelujas* are sung in the following manner:

The first is sung as explained above. The last word having been sung by the choir, the cantors intone the second *Alleluja;* the choir adds at once the *Neuma.* From the versicle onwards all is done as explained above for the *Alleluja* after the Gradual.

136. The *numerous notes* of the *Neuma* have often been objected to. But let us hear *St. Augustine:* "He who exults needs no words.[1]) Our speech is moreover unworthy of God; but if speech can be of no avail, and yet some kind of speech is necessary, what remains but to let our hearts break forth into accents of joy and jubilation without words, thus not limiting our boundless joy to empty words."[2])

The numerous notes of the *Neuma* are not thrust in anyhow, regardless of plan.

It is precisely from these melodies that one perceives in what a masterly manner plain chant weaves together simple motives by means of repetitions, inversions, extensions and various connections of the parts.

The members of the *Neuma* divided by pauses or the *mora vocis* can be in the following relation[3]) to one another:

AA¹ (= extended form of A), AB, AAB, ABA, ABC, AAA, AA¹B¹B, ABACA.

137. In the *verse* of the *Alleluja* the motives of the *Alleluja* and its *Neuma* often recur. Compare *Alleluja* and *Neuma* of the Mass *In virtute* (Common of a martyr not a bishop) with its verse *Posuisti* (on the feast of the Stigmata of St. Francis the same melody occurs):

I. II. = A + B + C.

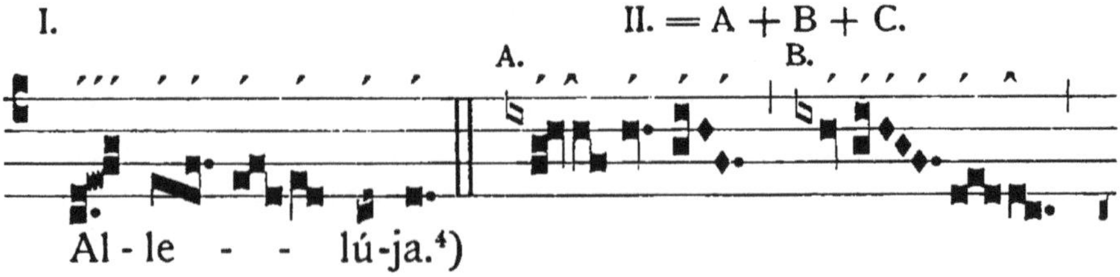

1) Migne, l. c. 37, 1272. 2) L. c. 36, 283. 3) Cf. Wagner: l. c. p. 218 *seq.*
4) Lib. us. p. 602.

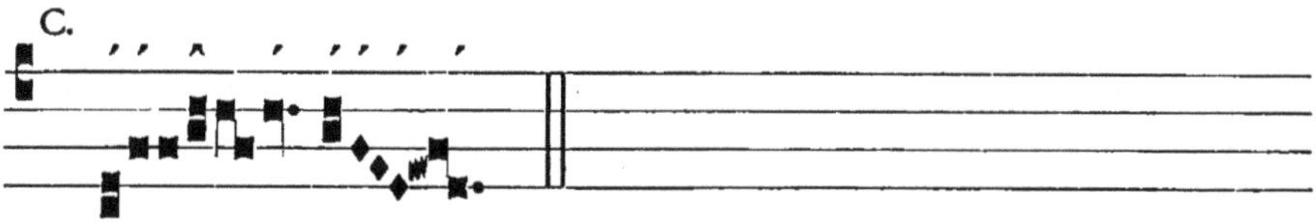

Posuisti = I, *Domine* = A + B + 1st part of I, *ejus* = extended B, *coronam* = C + B with repetition, *de lapide* = A, *pretioso* = I + II.

Although this chant does not exceed the compass of an octave, it is nevertheless very melodious and varied.

For other examples see feast of St. Thomas, M., 2nd Sunday after Easter (2nd All.), Easter Monday, 4th Sunday after Easter (2nd All.), Sunday in Oct. of Ascension (2nd All.), 18th Sunday after Pentecost, feast of St. Agatha, Visitation B. V. M., Octave of SS. Peter and Paul, particularly 5th Sunday after Easter (2nd All.).

The Alleluja of the 4th Sunday after Pentecost employs for the words *Qui sedes super thronum* the melody which is used in the Gradual: *Clamaverunt* (Mass *Salus autem,* Com. of many martyrs) for the words *(Domi-)nus his, qui tribulato sunt corde* — certainly an isolated case.

138. *Typical melodies* for Alleluja and verse are found:

a) In Mode VIII.:

α) on the 1st Sunday of Advent, *β)* in the 1st Mass for Christmas Day, *γ)* on the Ascension (2nd All.), *δ)* on the feast of St. Lucy, etc.

Part 1.	Part 2.
α) Ostende nobis *D*omine	*α)* misericordiam tuam
*β) D*ominus dixit ad me	*β)* filius meus es tu
*γ) D*ominus in Sina in sancto	*γ)* ascendens in altum
*δ) D*iffusa est gratia	*δ)* in labiis tuis
Part 3.	**Part 4.**
α) et salutare tuum	*α)* da nobis.
β) ego hodie	*β)* genui te.
γ) captivam duxit	*γ)* captivitatem.
δ) propterea benedixit te *D*eus	*δ)* in æternum.

Neuma scheme for the Alleluja, AB,

Neuma scheme for the final word of the verse, ABCC; this typical melody is the one most frequently employed; *another* typical melody in Mode VIII. occurs on the Vigil of the Nativity, on Ember Saturday at Whitsuntide, on Trinity Sunday, on the feast of SS. Philip and James.

Neuma scheme A A[1] B[1] B;

b) In Mode I.: on the Friday and Saturday (3rd All.) of the Whitsuntide Ember Days, feast of St. Andrew, Purification, in the Mass *Os justi* (Com. of abbots).

Neuma scheme A A[1] B C D;

c) In Mode II.: 3rd Mass for Christmas Day, feast of St. Stephen, St. John the Evang.; St. John the Bapt. (cf. also the 1st All. for the 3rd Sunday after Easter), etc.;

(Concerning the psalmodic construction of this melody with its 4 parts, each of which has intonation, dominant and cadence [the cadences of Parts 1 and 3 are alike], see Pal. mus. III., pp. 54 *seq.*)

Neuma scheme A A[1];

d) In Mode IV: 3rd Sunday of Advent, Ascension, Pentecost (1st All.), feast of the holy Guardian Angels;

Neuma scheme A A[1];

e) In Mode V.: Assumption, feast of St. Bartholomew, in the Mass *Salus autem* (Com. of many martyrs), feast of the Dedic. of a church (2nd All. for Paschal time);

(It is interesting to compare this melody in Mode V. with that in Mode VIII. on Easter Monday.)

Neuma scheme A B C;

f) In Mode VII.: Corpus Christi, feast of St. Laurence, Transfiguration, Appar. of St. Michael (2nd All. for Paschal time), feast of the most holy Rosary.

Besides these typical melodies there are a considerable number of *original* melodies remarkable for their swinging motion and vivacity.

The *Alleluja* on Holy Saturday has, as pointed out by Wagner *(Einführung,* p. 25), the intervals of *Per omnia sæcula sæculorum* and *dignum et justum est* at the preface.

139. Among the most beautiful *Alleluja* melodies are included those for the Circumcision, Easter Sunday, Easter Monday, Pentecost *(Veni Sancte Spiritus),* Corpus Christi (see above), Assumption (see above), All Saints, and from the Common those in the Masses *In virtute, In medio* and for the feast of the Dedic. of a church.

When the choir has once overcome its antipathy to "so many notes" (the choirmaster must analyse the construction of the melody), and when it has grasped the rhythm (the choirmaster must clearly explain the rhythmical value of each group of notes) then all will soon appreciate these exquisite musical lyrics.

d) Tractus.

140. The *Tractus* (Tract) is sung from Septuagesima to Easter and on certain penitential days in place of the *Alleluja*.

It consists of several verses of a psalm (sometimes a whole psalm or a portion of a Biblical canticle) which are sung to an elaborate psalm-tone. Whilst formerly an antiphon was inserted between the psalm-verses, now the Tract runs uninterruptedly. The derivation of the word is not clear *(tractus* from *trahere* = to draw, *tractim* = in a drawn way).

141. Only *two* Modes are used for the melodies, II. and VIII., the latter occurring more frequently than the former.

Each verse can be sung by two cantors in turn, or the whole choir can sing one verse (preferably the last one); in many places the choir sings only the last word of the verse indicated by *.

Here are some examples of the Tractus. Notice particularly the brilliant closes shown on the next page. Speed and expression go on increasing:

1) Melodies from Lib. us. p. 599.

Close of the preceding melody *Beatus vir*:

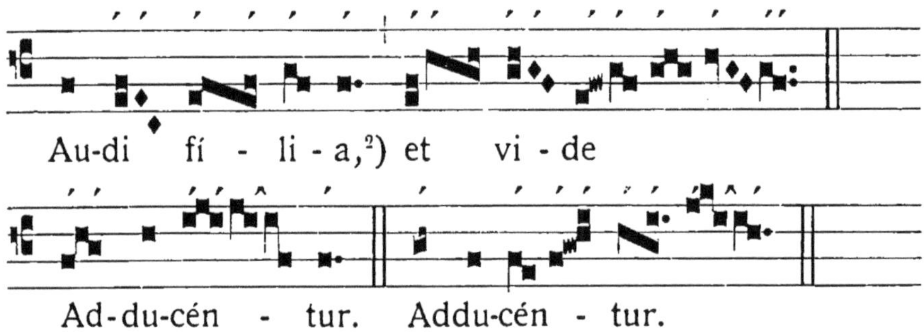

Close:

e) Sequentia.

142. Some feasts are distinguished by a Sequence sung immediately before the Gospel.

It consists of several verses, which generally run in couplets. It is sung by alternate choirs.

The Sequences (also *Prosæ* = Proses) arose from the practice of setting words to the notes of the *Alleluja-Neuma*. Masters in

1) Melody from Lib. us. p. 233. 2) Melodies from Lib. us. p. 677.

the art were Blessed Notker the Stammerer[1]) and Adam of St. Victor. Of the numerous Sequences of the middle ages only the five following have been retained:

143. *The Sequence for Easter,* "Victimæ paschali" wherein some details of the history of the resurrection of Christ are dramatically narrated.

Author, Wipo, a Burgundian, c. 1048.

The melody is imbued with a spirit of triumphal joy. The faith of the Church, at all times triumphantly announcing the victory over suffering and death, is expressed in the jubilant *scimus Christum surrexisse* in a manner as elevating as it is consoling. This passage should be sung with emphasis and solemnity; *tempo* moderate, not dragged.

144. *The Sequence for Pentecost,* "Veni Sancte Spiritus". Here the human heart, conscious of its poverty, in devout and earnest strains humbly begs for the seven gifts of the Holy Ghost.

The authorship is claimed for Innocent III. (1216), King Robert of France (1031), Hermann Contractus (the Lame) of Reichenau (1054).

The strophes are double ones. The melody of the first double strophe is tranquil. The next two become more forcible, whilst the two following are calm and rather peaceful. Both of the concluding verses are vigorous and vehement like the flaring up of the fiery tongues and the rushing of the mighty wind on the Day of Pentecost.

Do not lengthen the accentuated syllables, as otherwise an unpleasant $^6/_8$ time is unavoidable.

145. *The Sequence for Corpus Christi,* "Lauda Sion". "How majestically this sublime poem opens! What a clear and striking exposition of the Church's faith! What a splendid close to this magnificent prayer to the divine Shepherd who nourishes His sheep with His own Flesh, allowing us to be his companions at table, in joyful expectation of the eternal Day when we shall be His joint-heirs!"[2])

---

1) Schubiger: *Sängerschule* pp. 39—59 and part 2 pp. 6—39 (Melodies); J. Werner: *Notkers Sequenzen* (Aarau, Sauerländer 1901).)

2) Guéranger: *Institut. liturg.* I. 334.

The author of this Sequence is St. Thomas of Aquin (1274); the melody was composed by Adam of St. Victor.[1])

In passages like *in hymnis et canticis* take care that a ♯ does not slip in at *fa*. At Beuron abbey the whole Sequence is sung through in 6 m. 2 s.

146. *The Sequence for the two Feasts of the Seven Dolours, "Stabat Mater"*, a hymn full of tender compassion for the Mother of Sorrows, united with earnest prayer for the fruits of redemption.

The author of it is Jacopone da Todi, O. F. M. (1306). We should first of all ponder over the text and then the mode of rendering the melody[2]) will come of itself.

147. *The Sequence in the Mass for the Dead, "Dies iræ:"* Striking descriptions of the Day of Judgment, alternating with humble appeals for ourselves (strophes 7—17) and our departed brethren (strophes 18—19).

The author of it is Thomas of Celano, O. F. M. (1250).

At Beuron abbey the entire Sequence is sung through in 5 m. 33 s.

Always give those who do not understand Latin an English translation, and this should of itself be a preventive against a mechanical, meaningless mode of rendering this Sequence which is so frequently used.

148. The whole of the Sequences must be sung or at least recited.

As regards the *Dies iræ* the Bishop of St. Brieuc, in reply to his request for a dispensation from singing it, was informed by the Cong. of S. Rites on Aug. 12, 1854, that the singers might omit some strophes. But this decision is not included in the new edition of the *Decreta authentica* S. R. C. (Rome, Printing Office of Propaganda, 1898—1900.)

f) **Offertorium** (Song of Oblation).

149. The *Offertorium* follows the *Oremus* of the priest after the Gospel or after the *Credo*.

It consists now of an antiphon set to elaborate melodies.

---

1) Misset et Aubry: *Les proses d'Adam de S. Victor (Paris, Welter 1900) pp. 260 seq.: "Laudes crucis attollamus."*

2) Cf. C. H. Bitter: Eine Studie zum *Stabat Mater* (Leipzig, Seitz, 1883.)

Formerly several verses of a psalm were added to the antiphon, between which it was wholly or partially repeated. A remnant of the old plan is seen in the Offertory of the Requiem Mass at *Hostias* and the repetition *Quam olim*. The Offertory can be traced to the time of St. Augustine in Africa (431).

150. The Offertory melodies are generally of a grand character, but owing to the numerous melismas and bold passages full of motion they are less suitable for large choirs. Differing from the elaborate *Alleluja* and Gradual chants, the Offertory melodies should be more sustained and the *tempo* slower. Compare the Offertories for Christmas, Easter, Pentecost, etc. Unlike many Graduals, the Offertory melodies have not a tendency to typical forms, but are almost always original.

Really typical melodies employed for different texts are unknown for the Offertory. A melody is, it is true, sometimes sung with *one* other text (cf. the Offertories for Pentecost and Corpus Christi), but for a melody to be made use of for *three* different texts is quite an exception. Cf. the Offertories for Easter Monday, the Assumption; and the Offertory of the Mass *Lætabitur* (com. of a martyr not a bishop).

151. Veritable gems among the Offertories are the following: 1st Sunday of Advent, *Ad te levavi* (how confident the *non erubescam);* Vigil of Christmas, *Tollite portas* (how glorious the *æternales);* the 3rd Mass for Christmas Day (how expressive *Tu fundasti);* feast of the Holy Innocents, *Anima nostra* (cf. the Gradual with the same text); Palm Sunday, *Improperium* (what a climax at *et non fuit* and *et non inveni);* Tuesday in Holy Week, *Custodi me* (how impressive *de manu peccatoris* and what a grand close *eripe me);* 20th Sunday after Pentecost, *Super flumina* (notice the dying away of *Babylonis* and *Sion* and the repetition of the plaintive motive at *Sion),* then from the Common the Offertories of the Masses for an abbot, *Desiderium* (with the elaborate *pretioso*), and for a virgin not a martyr, *Filiæ regum.* Dom Kienle says of this latter *(Choral Sch.* p. 141): "Certainly a most beautiful Offertory in Mode III., adorned with all the splendour and richness of the East, a bridal song full of devotion and heavenly bliss."

The following Offertories deserve special mention: 16th Sunday after Pentecost, *Domine,* and 23rd Sunday after Pentecost, *De pro-*

fundis, which at the close repeat the text and melody at the commencement *(Domine in auxilium meum respice,* and *De profundis clamavi ad te Domine),* producing splendid effects. The *Domine convertere* (2nd Sunday after Pentecost) displays a charming simplicity, quite incomparable.

If some few melodies appear to lack development, do not forget that the verse now sung was only a preparation for a second or third verse elaborately treated, like the first verse in many Graduals.

Holy Saturday has no Offertory.

g) Communio.

152. This is intoned by the cantor when the priest has received the Precious Blood.

It consists of an antiphon.

The *Communio* belongs to the most ancient chants of the Church. Formerly it was sung in connection with a psalm (particularly the 33rd [1]). A reminiscence of the ancient practice is preserved for us in the *Requiem Mass,* wherein the *Communio* is provided with a verse, *Requiem æternam,* after which a portion of the antiphon is repeated *(cum sanctis tuis).*

153. *Melodies of this class* may undoubtedly be included among those that exhibit the greatest variety throughout the whole of the *Graduale:*

a) As regards their external form:

In addition to chants which are almost syllabic in their character and differ in nothing from ordinary antiphons (cf. the *Communio* on the Transfiguration and on the Saturday of the second week in Lent, etc.), there are many that surpass the Introit melodies as regards elaboration (cf. Introit and *Communio* of the Mass *Lætabitur,* of the Mass *Protexisti,* of the Mass *Sancti tui* — com. of one martyr and of many martyrs), and not a few that can bear comparison with Offertory melodies (cf. Offertory and *Communio* of the 1st Sunday in Lent, of the Monday in Passion Week, of the Sunday within the octave of Corpus Christi). The text, it is true, is generally considerably shorter.

---

1) *Pal. mus.* VI. 22.

β) As regards their *expression,* and, one might say, their *dramatical effect.*

Sing the melodies for the 3rd Sunday of Advent *Dicite* (particularly *pusillanimes confortamini);* the 2nd Mass for Christmas Day *Exsulta* (particularly *lauda filia);* the 3rd Mass for Christmas *Viderunt* (particularly *salutare);* feast of the Holy Innocents *Vox in Rama* (with its plaintive character); Passion Sunday *Hoc corpus* (very deep and earnest); Pentecost *Facta est* (vehement like the rushing of the wind); 21st Sunday after Pentecost *In salutari tuo* (with its entreating tone, almost tempestuous); com. of a martyr in Paschal time *Lætabitur* (a resounding song of jubilation), etc.

The following are of special interest:

α) The Communio *Quinque prudentes* from the Mass *Dilexisti.* Further see pp. 180 *seq.*

β) The melody of the Communio for Wednesday in the fourth week in Lent *Lutum fecit,* childlike in its simplicity; with its short phrases it portrays most vividly the happiness of the man born blind but now healed, who can with difficulty express his exuberant joy.

γ) A contrast to this antiphon is the Communio *Videns Dominus* for the Friday of the fourth week in Lent. The first little phrase could scarcely be simpler, and yet it puts us at once in sympathy with the sisters of Lazarus who are weeping for their dead brother. Our Lord also "wept", and the major third following the previous tranquil passage expresses in an unmistakable way the importance of this event. Quite dramatic is the *Lazarus, come forth!* and the melody on *prodiit* impresses upon one the greatness of this miracle.

Chapter XIII.

The Chants and Intonations of the Priest.

a) Intonations of the Gloria and Credo.

154.

1. 

II.
Gló-ri - a in ex-cél-sis De - o.
III.
Gló - ri - a in ex-cél - sis De - o.
IV.
Gló - ri - a in ex-cél-sis De - o.
V.
Gló-ri - a in ex - cél - sis De-o.
VI.
Gló - ri - a in ex - cél - sis De-o.
VII.
Gló-ri - a in ex - cél - sis De - o.
VIII.
Gló-ri - a in ex-cél-sis De-o.
IX.
Gló - ri - a in ex - cél - sis De - o.
X.
Gló-ri - a in ex-cél-sis De - o.
XI.
Gló - ri - a in ex-cél-sis De-o.
XII.
Gló - ri - a in ex-cél-sis De - o.

XIII. 

XIV. 

XV. 

155.

I. II. IV. 

III. 

b) The Prayers.

156. Three forms are used for chanting the prayers:

a) The *solemn form (tonus festivus vel solemnis)* divides the prayer into three parts by means of a cadence with one accent and two preparation notes (see Psalmody, pp. 59 *seq.)* and an inflexion, generally in the second part, on the last syllable, in dactylic words on the penultimate.

The cadence is indicated in the Missal by : or ; , seldom merely , . The inflexion by ; or , .

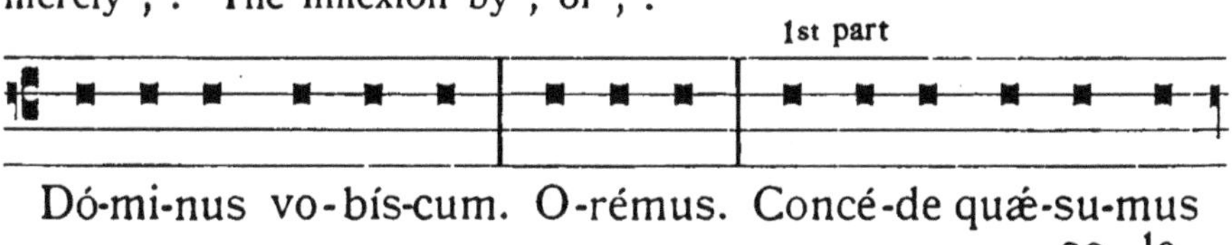

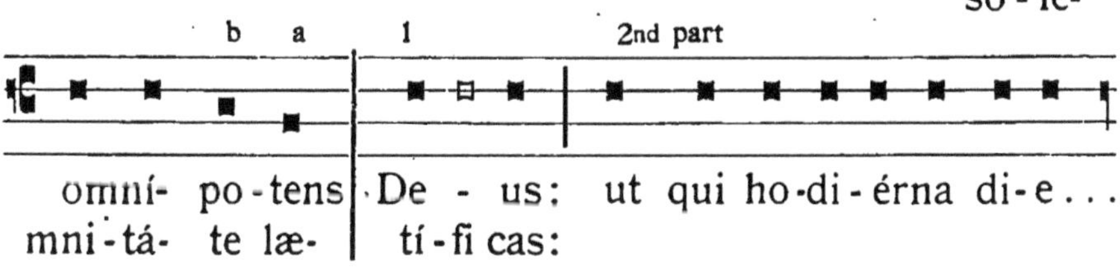

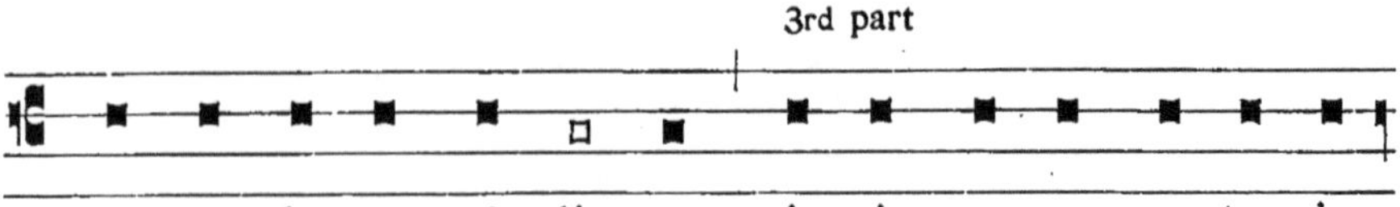

a-scen-dís-se cré-di-mus; ip-si quoque men-te in non ha-bé - mus;

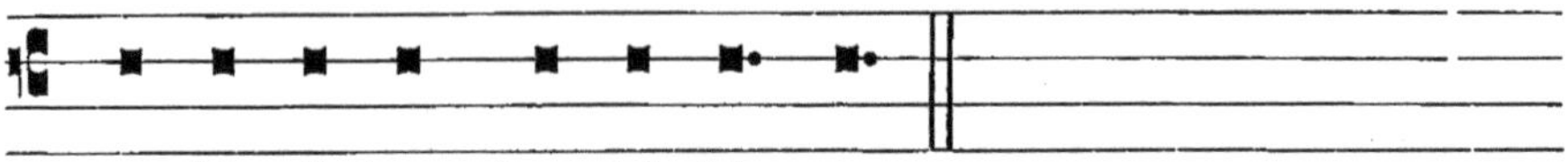

cœ́-lé-sti-bus ha-bi-té-mus.

For the preparation notes and secondary syllables the same rules apply as for psalmody.

The *conclusio* has likewise three parts, but the inflexion of a semitone occurs at the end of the first part (*tuum)* and the cadence at the end of the second part *(Sancti Deus):*

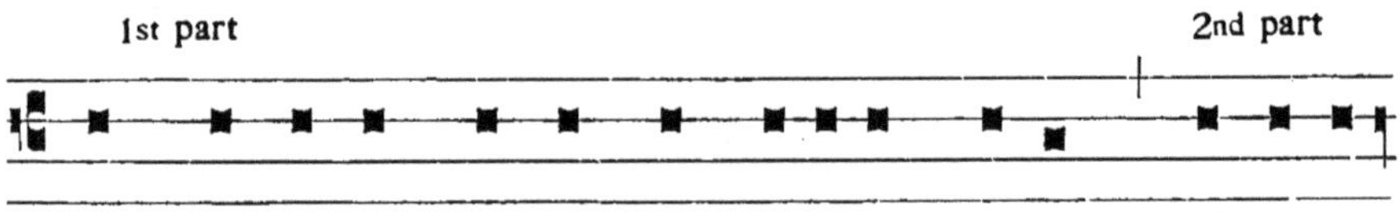

Per Dó-mi-num n. J. Chr. Fí-li-um tu-um, qui te-cum

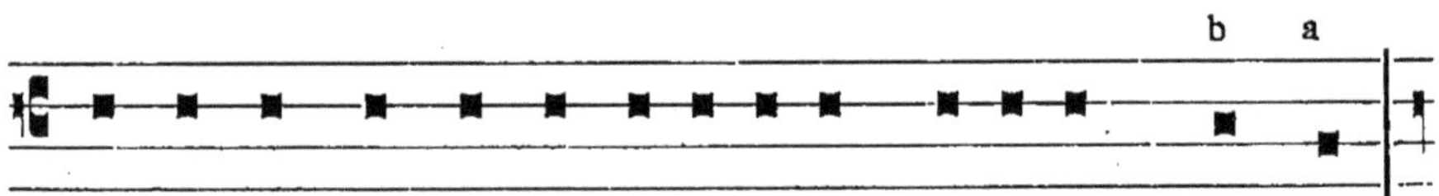

vi-vit et re-gnat in u-ni-tá-te Spí-ri-tus San-cti

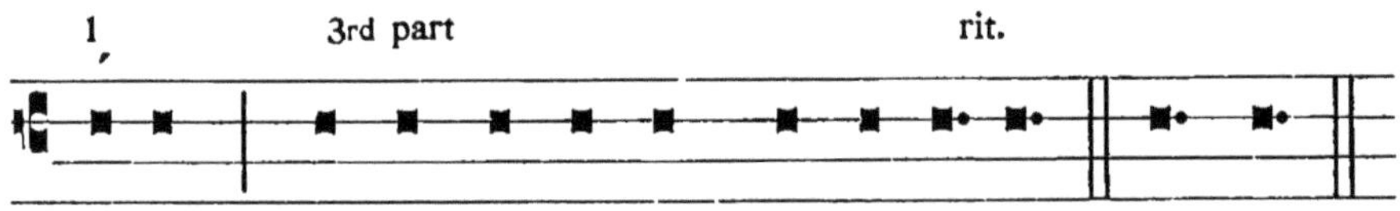

Dé-us: per ó-mni-a sǽc. sæ-cu-ló-rum. A-men.

If it is a short prayer the inflexion of a semitone is omitted.

The prayers are sung in this solemn form on doubles and semidoubles at Mass and Vespers.

157. *β)* The *simple form (tonus simplex ferialis)* is without any inflexion. The three parts are made distinct by pauses with a suitable (short) *ritardando.*

Thus for Mass and Vespers if they are not *ritu dupl.* or *semi-dupl.;* and always for the *Missa* et *Vesp. Defunctorum,* even *ritu duplici.*

158. *γ)* The *semi-solemn form (tonus ferialis)* is like the simple one, but on the last syllable (in dactylic words also on the penultimate) of the last word and of the *conclusio (nostrum* or *sæculorum)* an inflexion of a minor third below is made:

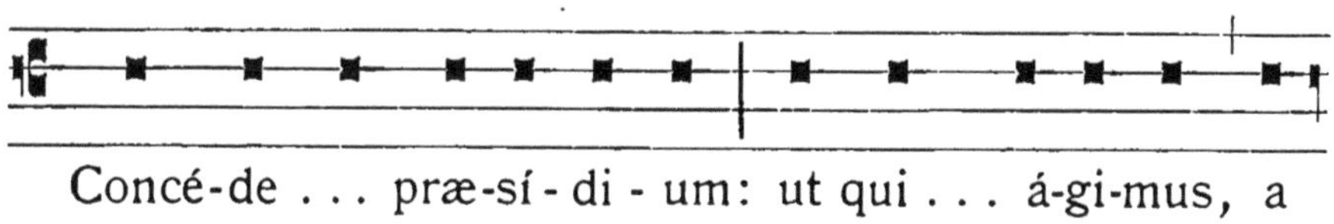

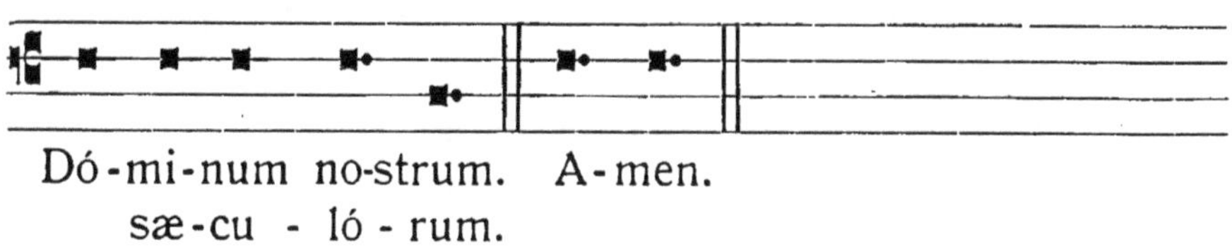

Always thus if the short *conclusio (per Christum* or *per eumdem Christum* or *qui vivis,* etc.) is prescribed.

We may also mention:

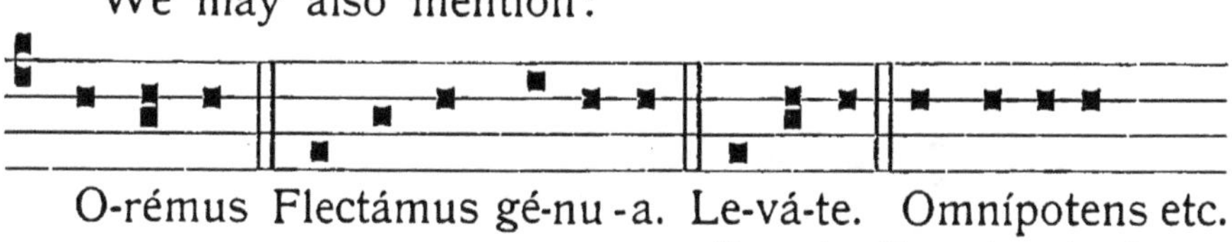

according to the simple form.

Concerning the tone for the prayers on Good Friday see p. 128.

c) The Epistle and Lessons.

159. The *Epistle* is sung on *one* note. But before an interrogation at the last syllable (or the last monosyllable) the voice falls a semitone below, rising again by a *podatus* to the reciting note, and the *penultimate* (in dactylic words also the antepenultimate) likewise falls a semitone. (If there is a monosyllable at the end of the interrogative sentence the *last* rule is not observed):

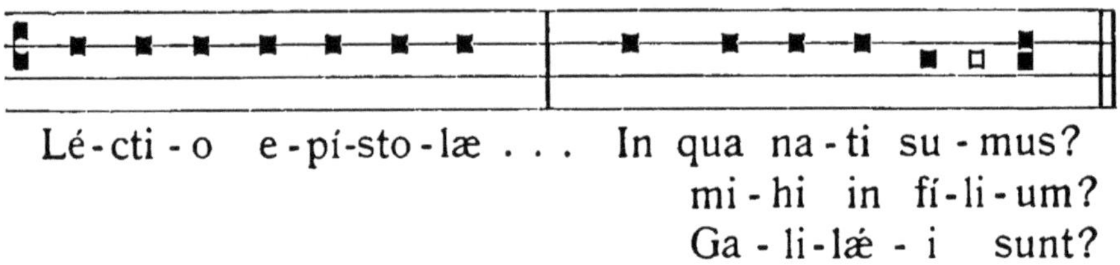

In many places at an interrogation they sing some of the syllables before the last verbal accent a semitone lower, and the syllable immediately preceding the last accent a whole tone below the semitone:

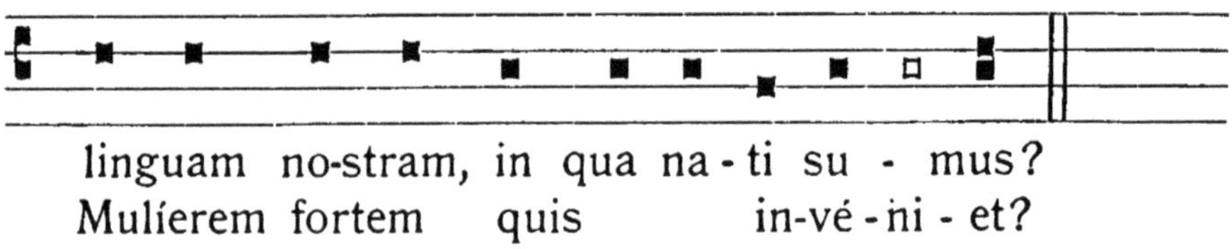

160. In the *Lessons (Prophecies)* the interrogation is treated as in the Epistle, and the syllable (or syllables) after the last verbal accent in *each* sentence is sung a fifth below·

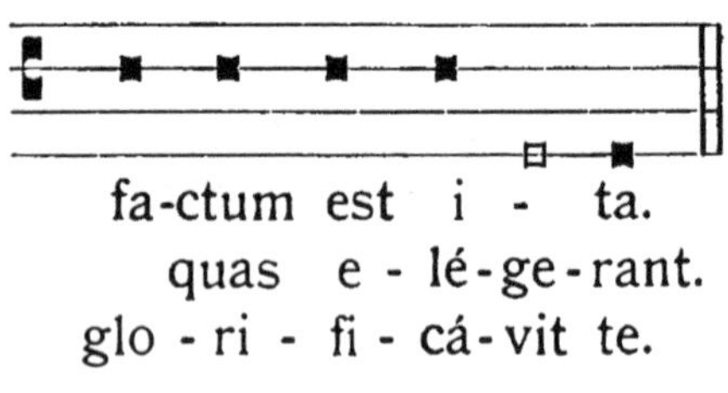

If the sentence closes with a monosyllable or a Hebrew word, it is sung in the following way by those who use the *mediatio correpta:*

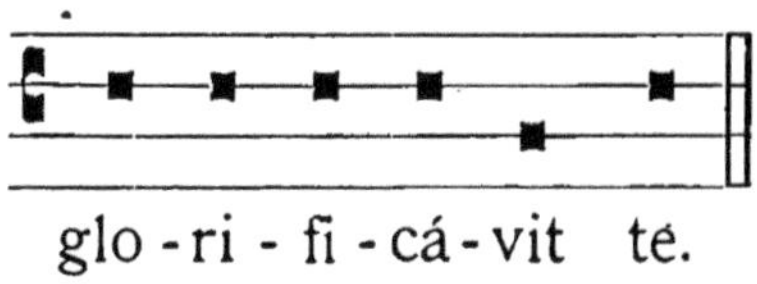

The final sentence of the Lessons which occur at Mass is recited *without* any inflexion whatever.

161. The *Little Chapter in the Office* is recited on a monotone; the interrogation is treated as in the Epistle, and at the end there is the following cadence:

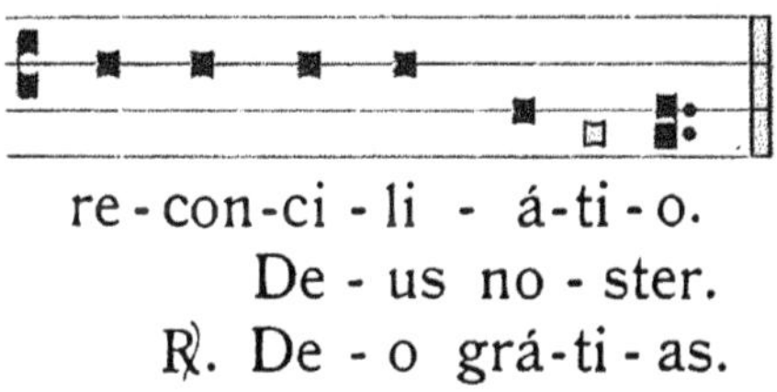

The cadence is sung in the following way by those who use the *mediatio correpta*, should the last word be Hebrew or a monosyllable:

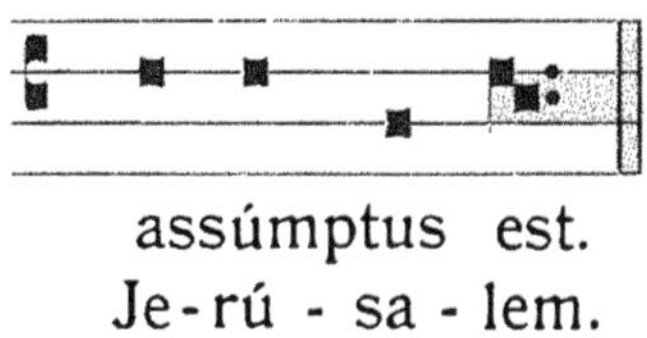

In many places they sing the Little Chapter with the *flex* (see p. 72), and mediation and final in this way:

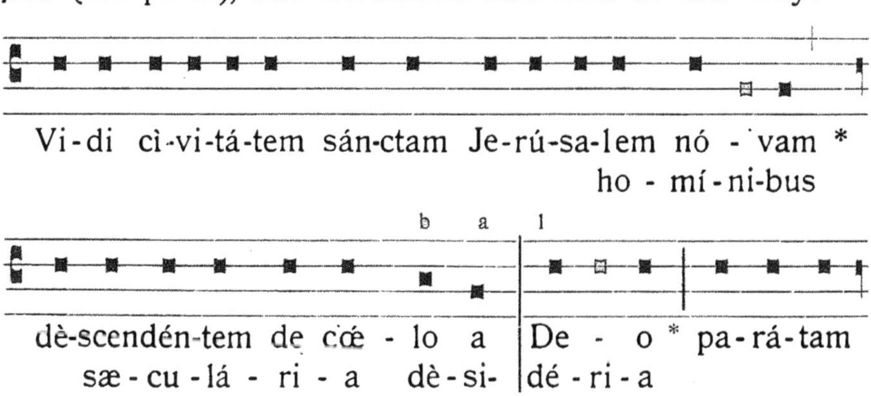

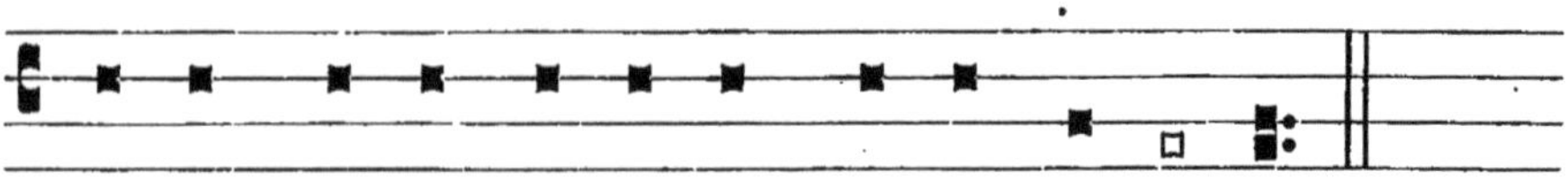

síc-ut spónsam or-ná-tam ví-ro sú - o.
hoc sǽ-cu-lo.

d) The Gospel.

162. The Gospel has *Dominus vobiscum,* etc., as at the collect, on a monotone, at the interrogation a modulation as in the Epistle, at the full stop a cadence with one accent and two preparation notes:

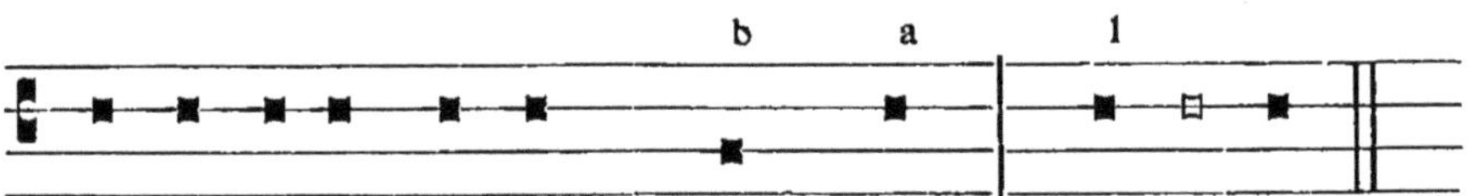

Sequén-ti-a etc. se-	cún - dum	Lú - cam.
se-cún-	dum Mat-	thǽ - um.
Gló - ri - a	ti - bi	Dó-mi-ne.
ad-ver-sá-	ri - i	vé - stri.
vé-	ni - o	àd vos.
qui-	a pec-	cá-trix est.
lampá-	di - bus	su - is.

At the conclusion there is a cadence with two accents, to be sung with a moderate *ritardando:*

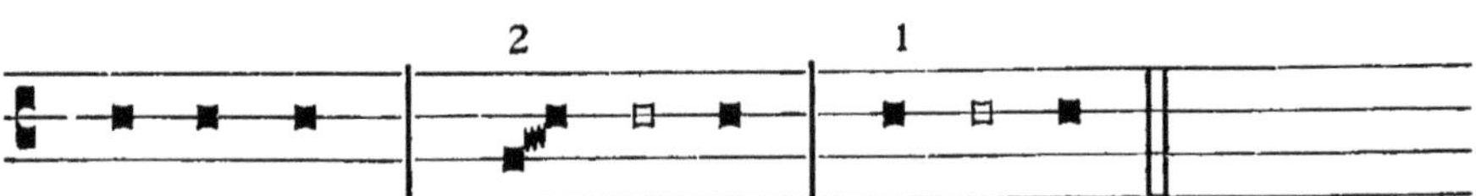

ve-nit in	nó - mi-ne	Dó-mi-ni.
gaú-di - um	Dó - mi-ni	tú - i.
æ - tér-nam	pos - si-	dé - bit.
mi - hi	Pá - ter sic	fá-ci - o.
vi - vet	ìn æ-	tér - num.

Some begin this cadence at the last accent but two:

| vi - vet | in æ-térnum.

c) Preface and Pater Noster.

163. Both are constructed like the psalms (the *Pater noster* is rather more free) and are introduced by an antiphonal chant between priest and choir. They have the solemn tone *(cantus solemnis* or *festivus),* used on doubles and semidoubles, and the simple or ferial tone *(cantus ferialis),* used on other days.

The *solemn tone* has a short intonation:

(and so has the simple tone), a middle cadence with two accents and a final cadence with one accent and three preparation notes (or groups):

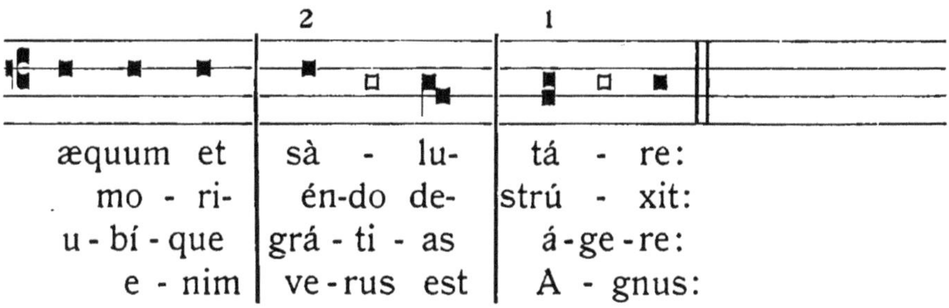

The *simple tone* for the preface has a middle cadence with one accent and two preparation notes.

Compare the tone used for the prayers on Good Friday:

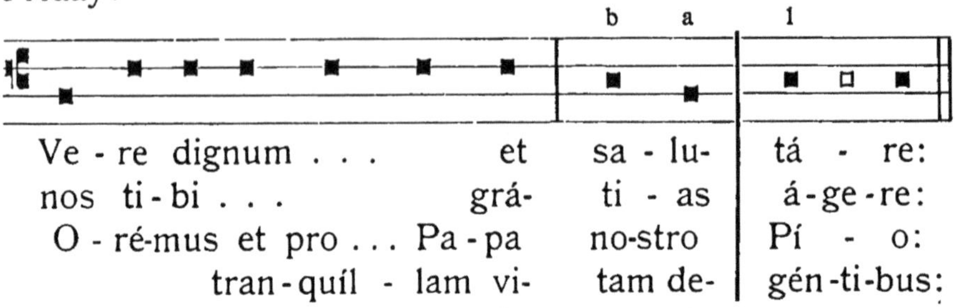

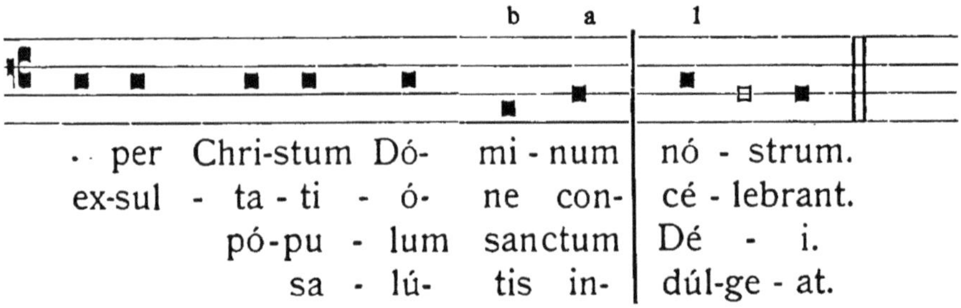

The *solemn tone for Pater noster* has a middle cadence with one accent and two preparation notes, and a final cadence with one accent and three preparation notes (or groups).

The simple form approximates to that for the preface:

Compare the final cadence of the solemn preface.

Solemn Form for the Preface.

164.

165. Simple Form for the Preface.

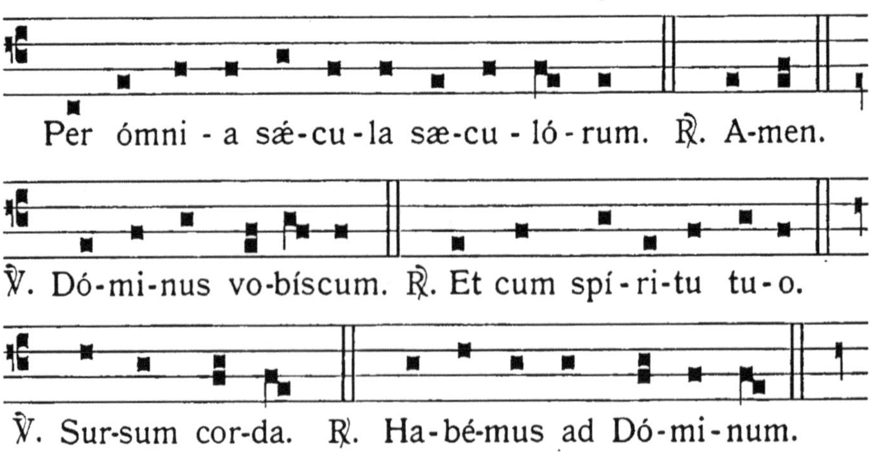

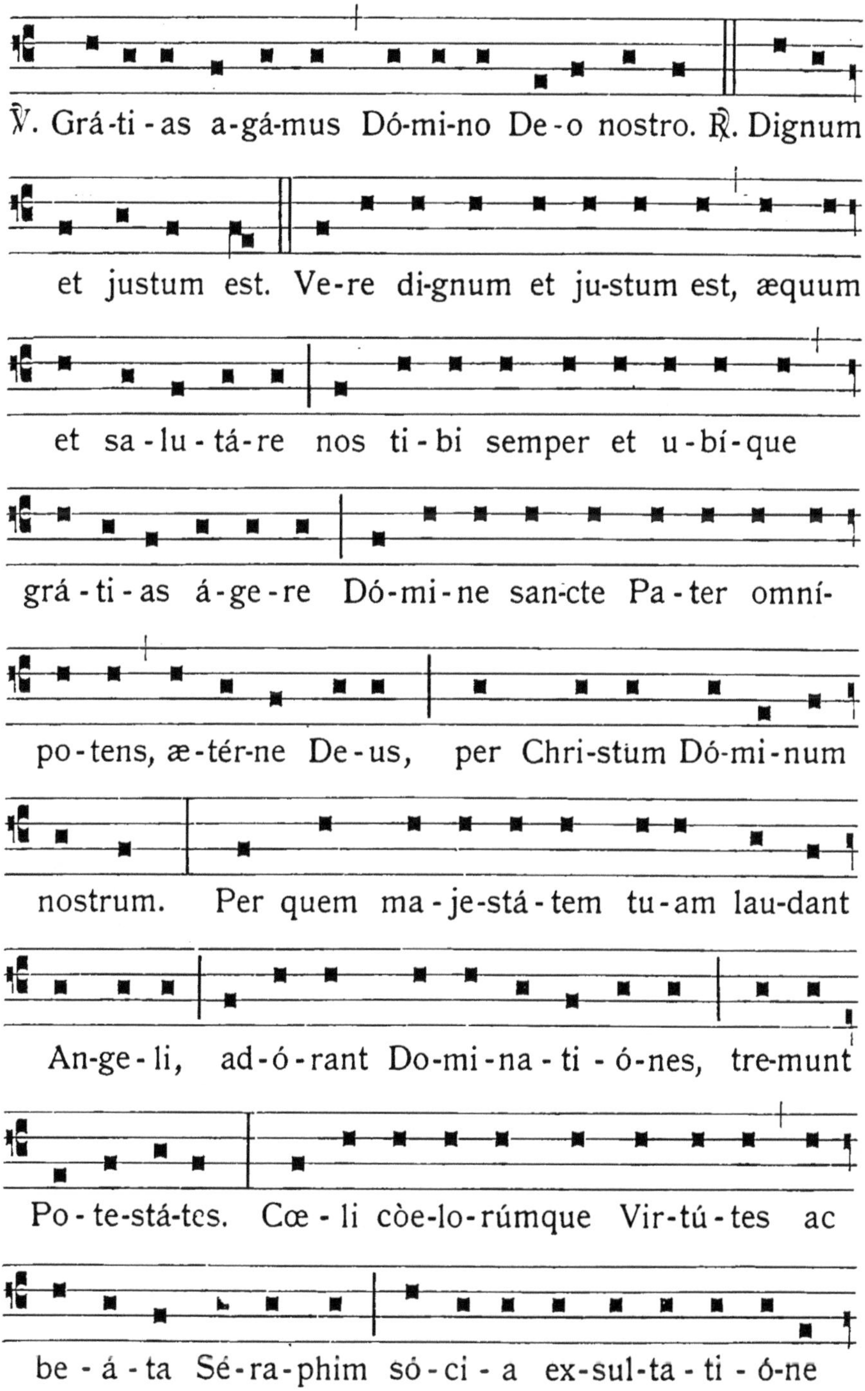
℣. Grá-ti-as a-gá-mus Dó-mi-no De-o nostro. ℟. Dignum
et justum est. Ve-re di-gnum et ju-stum est, æquum
et sa-lu-tá-re nos ti-bi semper et u-bí-que
grá-ti-as á-ge-re Dó-mi-ne san-cte Pa-ter omní-
po-tens, æ-tér-ne De-us, per Chri-stum Dó-mi-num
nostrum. Per quem ma-je-stá-tem tu-am lau-dant
An-ge-li, ad-ó-rant Do-mi-na-ti-ó-nes, tre-munt
Po-te-stá-tes. Cœ-li còe-lo-rúmque Vir-tú-tes ac
be-á-ta Sé-ra-phim só-ci-a ex-sul-ta-ti-ó-ne

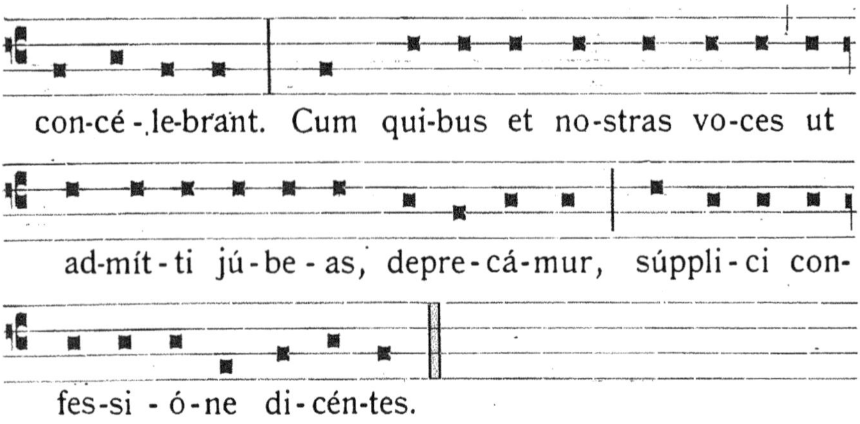

Solemn Form for Pater noster.

166.

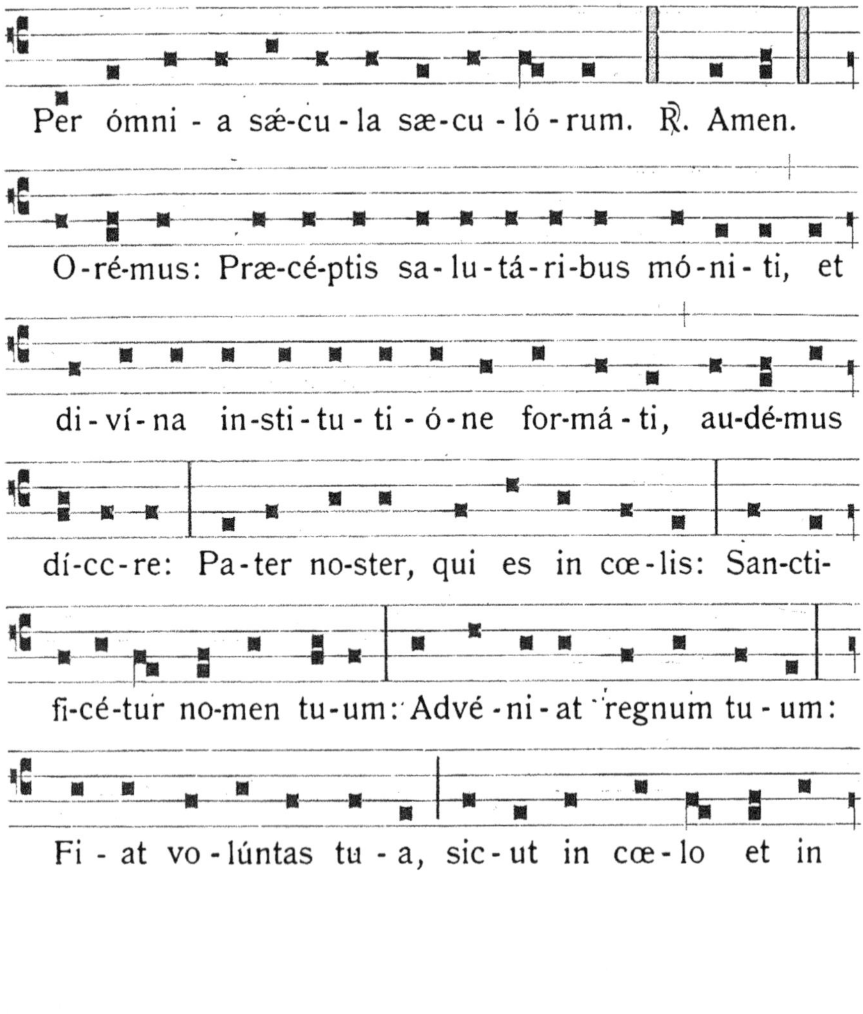

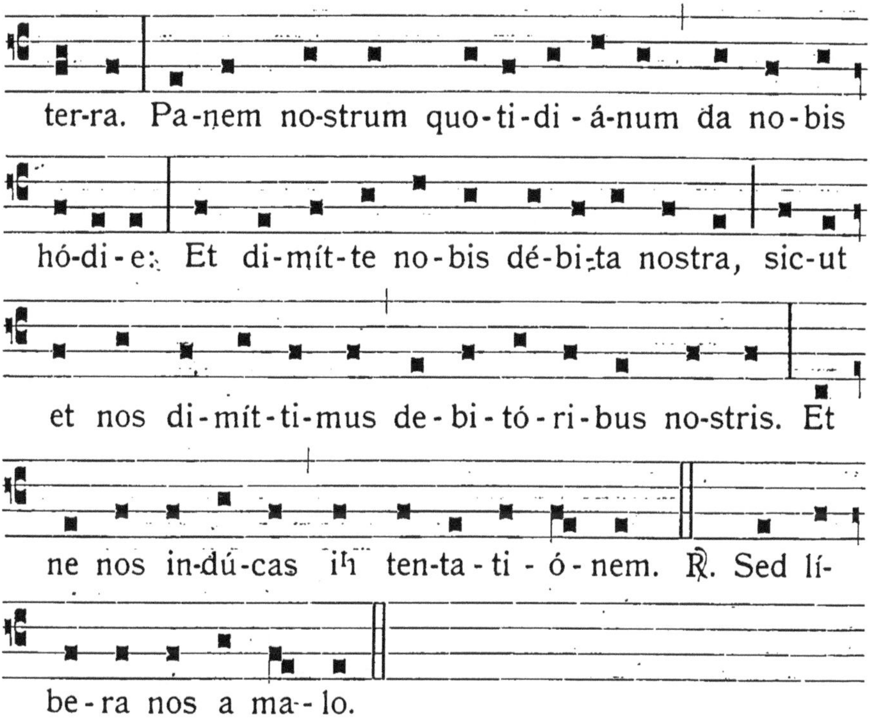

Simple Form for Pater noster.

167.

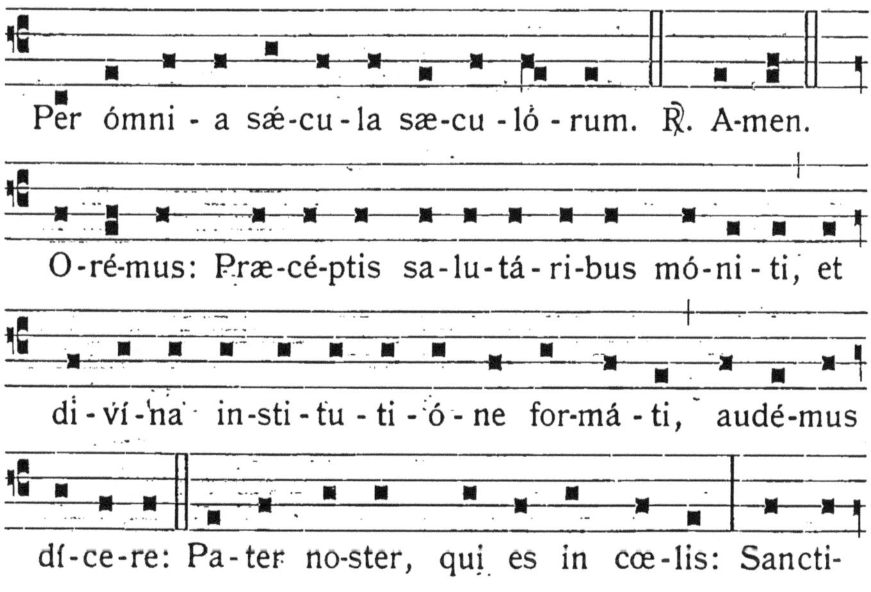

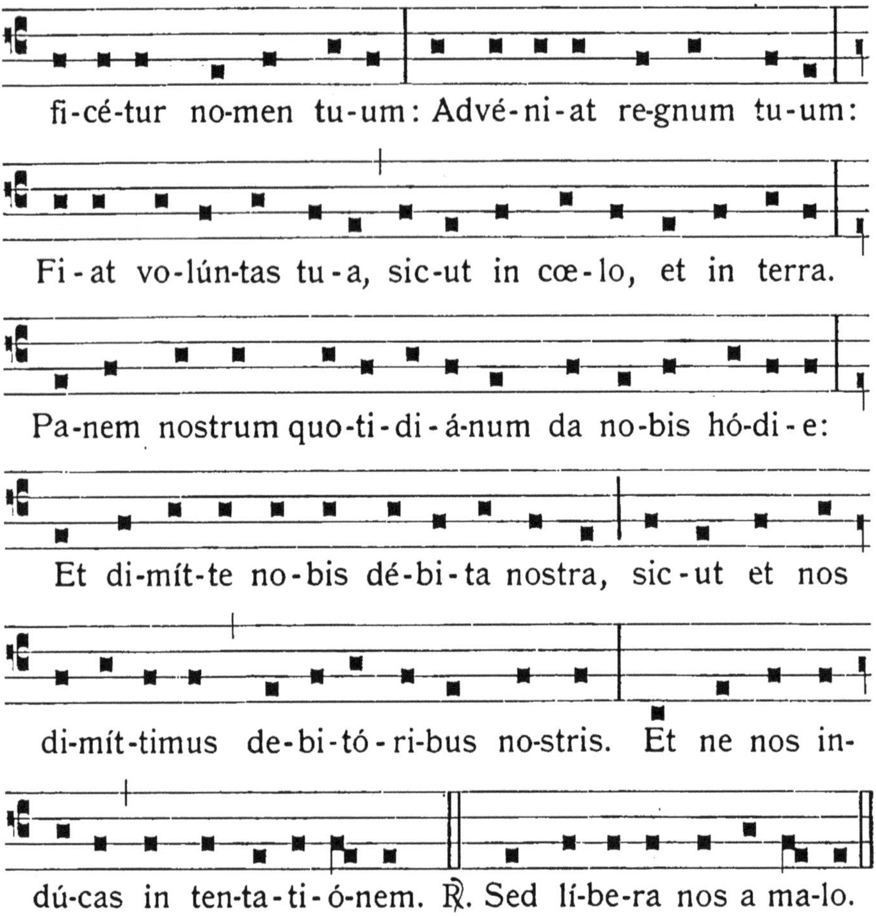

168. Do not sing

not

but

not

(too many pauses)

but

not

but

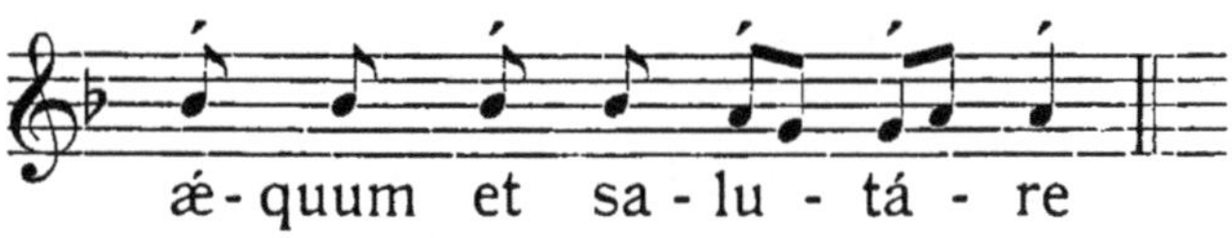

not

but

not

but

not 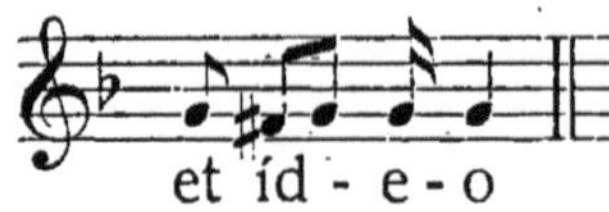

but 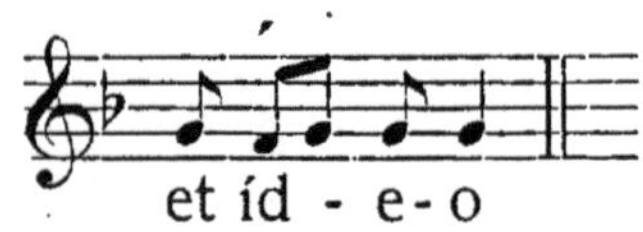

not 

but 

169. The Preface and Pater noster should be sung in a sustained tone of voice, therefore not too quickly, particularly as regards the simple forms. The declamation of the text should be as beautiful and tuneful as possible, attention being paid to the secondary accents, and unnecessary pauses avoided. Sublimity and dignity, a spirit of joy and inward devotion should be the distinguishing marks of the priest's chants as the moment approaches when the sacrificial action will transport him to the mystical *Sancta Sanctorum,* the Holy of Holies of the New Covenant.

"If the priest in the name of the Christian people, and in union with the intercession of our Lord in the Holy Eucharist, raises his voice in order that it may be heard before the throne of God, then it is surely worth his while to learn to sing these heavenly prayers as well as he can." (Kienle, *Ch. Sch.* p. 92.)

f) Ite and Benedicamus at High Mass and Benedicamus at Vespers.

170. I.

Be-ne-di-cá-mus Dó - - - mi-no.
II.
I - te
mis - - sa est.
Be-ne-di-cá-mus Dó - - - - -
etc.
- - mi - no.
IV.
I-te missa est.
Be-ne-di-cá - mus Dó - - - mino.
etc.
V.
I - te
mis-sa est.
VI.
I - te mis-sa est.

VII.
I - te
mis-sa est.
VIII.
I - te
mis - sa est.
etc.
Be-ne-di-cá-mus Dó - - - mi-no.
IX.
I - te mis - sa est.
Be - ne-di-cá-mus Dó - - mi-no.
XI.
I - te mis - - sa est.
Be-ne-di-cá-mus Dó - - mi - no.
XII.
I - te mis - sa est.

171. For Vespers.

172. **g) Other Intonations.**

173. Concluding Antiphons of the B. V. M.

174. For Good Friday.

Holy Saturday.

175. At Burials.

High School.

Chapter XIV.

Liturgy and Plain Chant.

176. Our liturgy is, as Dom Guéranger once said in a letter to Arch-abbot Maurus Wolter, of Beuron, *the very centre of Christianity.*

This is perfectly true, for the liturgy unfolds to our gaze the *highest truths of our holy religion* in a form easily understood by the people, and in a most comprehensive and admirable manner. The *far-reaching benefits* of the Christian revelation are vividly and constantly *mirrored* in it, and by it souls are ever and effectively born again in the bloodless sacrifice of Christ, no less than in the fruits thereof, to wit, the Holy Eucharist, the sacraments and the common prayer of the Church. All this is the one great, solemn act of Divine worship in the Church of Christ.

In the sacred liturgy *heaven and earth are united,* and the *saints join together in celebrating their glorious feasts* where Christ, the Head, calls his members to the mystical tabernacle of the covenant, in order to allow his divine and human life to flow out to them from the holy place of sacrifice, being one with them and in them.

In the liturgy a *great act of God is performed,* and at the same time the highest thing that created beings are able to conceive and to accomplish in honour of the Almighty. The liturgy is in truth *opus Dei,* the *one grand continuation of God's work* in the Eucharistic order, wherein the marvels of creation, redemption and sanctification are repeated day by day in harmonious concord; and it is the one great thing that the *creature* owes his

God, and can offer to his God, *in gratitude* for all this. In the performance of the liturgy the *most excellent supernatural virtues of faith, hope and charity* are exercised, and are united with their source and end, God, the eternal truth and goodness, in adoration, praise and thanksgiving, acts which claim the highest rank in the faculties of a created being.

177. Moreover, the Catholic liturgy is a *symbolical representation of the supernatural effects of grace, and it aids us in obtaining these graces by prayer and the power of the sacraments.* But more than this. Our liturgy is a *constant "vitæ individua communio"*, an inseparable, uninterrupted *communing of Christ with His bride;* His visit by grace and His tarrying with us — a thrice blessed union, like unto the familiar intercourse of the Master with His disciples in the days of his sojourn on earth, and in many respects closer and more effective.

178. The liturgy when rightly interpreted in its widest sense is the means by which the Church lives in union with Christ — the closest possible union for the whole Church militant; by means of it she is ever being born again; it is the richest source of the purest spiritual joy whereby the heart is inflamed with the ardour of divine love, and human life is changed into supernatural life.

179. Such a liturgy deserves of itself a liturgical art, above all a liturgical *chant* wherein the ardent feelings of the bride of Christ can find their natural expression at the moment when she is permitted to repose on the Heart of her Beloved, and wherein the divine and human love of this Heart, and all that His bride the holy Church desires to say in His praise and in declaration of her boundless love in return, finds its true echo; wherein also the laments and petitions of all and every one of the faithful ascend to the throne of mercy.

180. The liturgical chant is therefore necessarily an *antiphonal chant;* Christ's voice answers the Church, the voices of individuals, as representatives of Christ and of the people, answer a mighty choir composed of the great mass of people. Even if there were no prototype for this in the Jewish temple service or in the worship in heaven as revealed to the seer in Patmos, nevertheless our liturgy from its very nature would have led to antiphonal chant.

181. Praying and singing are essential to the liturgy, and consequently the choir, and even the people, should cooperate, and the proper place for the choir is near the altar with those who serve at the altar. Hence a clerical habit was worn by the singers when exercising their office, and they joined in many of the ceremonies with the clergy, as is still the case to this day in many monasteries. The position of our mixed choirs in an organ gallery (usually over the entrance to the church) has tended considerably to weaken the consciousness of this intimate connection, thus hindering the proper appreciation of liturgical chant, nay, of liturgy itself.

182. If the Catholic liturgy is in reality an *act of Christ and of the whole Church,* the liturgical chant can only fulfil its object entirely when it is connected as closely as possible with this act, when it interprets the various texts in accordance with the thoughts and sentiments that move Christ and His Church in their united action, and from them produces a tone-picture. The liturgical chant, no less than the liturgical prayer, must be an act of the Communion of Saints, the official, solemn homage paid by the Church to her Saviour, an outcome of her consciousness of intimate communion of heart and soul with Christ. That in no way hinders personal feeling and expression, but it requires composer and singer to give themselves fully and entirely to the liturgy of the Church, really *living* with the Church and her liturgy.

183. Like the first and the last end of all the external acts of God, the *main object* of the liturgy is the *honour and glory of God.* That which our Saviour said of His works at the close of His life: *Ego clarificavi te super terram,* "I have glorified thee on the earth" (John 17, 4), holds good of His life and work in the holy Eucharist and likewise of the entire liturgy of His Church. Hence the conception of *divine praise* was of old almost identical with that of liturgy and sacrifice, and in this sense St. Benedict says in his holy Rule, that High School for the service of God, cap. 16: *Ergo his temporibus referamus laudes Creatori nostro super judicia justitiæ suæ,* "in these holy hours let us offer praises to our Creator on account of the judgments of His justice." And this with good reason. For all things by which God has revealed His greatness, justice and power, call upon us to adore Him, to praise and to thank Him.

How thoroughly in accordance with the spirit of the Church is the union of praise and prayer in the *Gloria* of the Mass: *Gratias agimus tibi propter magnam gloriam tuam: Domine Deus, Rex cœlestis . . . . miserere nobis; Domine Deus . . . . suscipe.* And then comes immediately the reason in this lifting-up of the heart in praise: *Quoniam tu solus sanctus, tu solus Dominus, tu solus Altissimus.* There can be no better incentive to prayer for grace and forgiveness than the greatness and sublimity of God. Because God is God and because the utmost we can do is to adore and praise His Godhead, offering hymns and thanksgivings, we know that we shall be heard and that our redemption is certain. This is the Church's view of prayer and of her liturgy. Even when she intercedes for the dead, when she desires to direct the Eye of God to the needs of her children and thus move the Heart of God to exercise clemency and mercy, she offers praise, as, e. g., in the *Requiem: Te decet hymnus Deus in Sion, et tibi reddetur votum in Jerusalem.* That is the true spirit of Christianity. For God is great and at all times worthy of adoration, and whether He rewards or punishes, whether He gives life or takes it, His goodness is not lessened. The sufferings of this time are often the surest proofs of His love, for which a soul steadfast in faith must be grateful. *Deus exultatio cordis mei.* Hence God must be the delight of our heart, and whenever we think of Him it should be a feast-day in the soul, a festal joy; and a reflection of the eternal Easter morn should illuminate our interior and attune us to the praise of the Almighty.

184. Thus it is with the singers in choir, called to the praise of the Most High, to a participation in the Church's sacrifice of praise, in the festal train of the heavenly Bridegroom, when He descends from His eternal throne upon the altar, in order graciously to devote Himself to us, to sacrifice with us, to live in us. Therefore from the altar the singer must expect the chief incentive for his work. The altar and the wonders that are there accomplished should influence and guide him when rendering the liturgical chant.

185. When the singer has by degrees made himself familiar with the spirit of the liturgy, and with its feasts and seasons, when he has learnt to understand its language and signs, and has entirely adopted its sentiments and intentions, it will no longer be difficult for him to come to a right understanding in regard to the liturgical melodies. Much of what he has been accustomed to will with the knowledge he has acquired of liturgical requirements appear in a new light, and other things at first thought strange or apparently unjustifiable will now be comprehended for more solid reasons. Above all, the task which the liturgical chant has to perform will come to be fully understood, and this task is no other than to serve the liturgy and its objects, and by its means to edify the people and to glorify God alone.

186. *The Gregorian Chant is the liturgical Chant of the Church.* "This chant adapts itself to the liturgy better than any composition in the modern style. Its melodies are just the right length, neither too short nor too meagre for solemn functions in a cathedral, neither too long nor impracticable in less favourable circumstances. Moreover, it gives the text without repetition or mutilation of the words, and omits none of them. Every syllable is enunciated by the whole choir at the same time. Though another system may be allowed or may often be necessary in polyphonic works, yet the simple style of plain chant deserves the preference having regard to the delivery of the words." [1]) Next to its spiritual relation to the liturgy it was these external advantages which have made it the special *protégé* of the ecclesiastical authorities, and for centuries the favourite of the Christian people. The Church has repeatedly recognised it as her own,[2]) and by this she declares that these traditional melodies fully satisfy the requirements of her liturgy, and that what inwardly moves her in the solemn hour when she celebrates the sacred mysteries, and what she desires to express in song is well expressed in those melodies. Moreover, these unison chants best maintain the close connection with the chants of the officiating priest, they admirably symbolise the one-mindedness of the congregation, and by their tranquil, almost ethereal, strains, guide the mind gently but firmly to the altar.

187. As the liturgical song, plain chant is *prayer and action,* as liturgical prayer and as liturgical action it must be understood and rendered by the singer.

---

1) Dom Molitor: Frankf. Brosch., pp. 178 *seq*.
2) Cf. the *Motu proprio* of Pius X., 22 Nov., 1903.

188. As indicated above, this relation to the liturgy explains why the Gregorian chant differs, for example, so much from popular hymnody. In this connection a comparison between the best known *Christmas hymns* and the *plain chant melodies* for the Christmas Midnight Mass may be instructive:

Let us take as examples the familiar hymns, *In dulci jubilo,* "Zu Bethlehem geboren, Schönstes Kindlein" (Born in Bethlehem, O sweetest Babe), which are undoubtedly beautiful specimens of German popular hymnody, and which never fail to attract one owing to their devotional style and child-like simplicity. Here text and melody have quite different characteristics from the chants in the *Graduale.* The thoughts and sentiments of the composer and of those who sing those hymns are different; they think with delight of the Babe of Bethlehem; they wish to rival the angels by making music and singing a cradle-song to the new-born King; to rejoice His infantile heart, to play with him as one plays with the little ones, to show Him their love, and to draw a smile from His rosy lips. Hence these hymns express the happiness, the delight, the tears, of a child, and in their way they have succeeded admirably in doing this. The same may also be said of the French *noëls* however much they may differ in their character from the German hymns.[1]) But now for the plain chant melodies of the Christmas Mass: *Dominus dixit ad me: Filius meus es tu: ego hodie genui te.* Here our Lord utters the first word; it is a message from the eternal Son of God, who took flesh for us, the Lord of glory, yet lying in the crib in all the poverty and helplessness of a little child. God the Father spoke the one eternal Word, He spoke it in Him and to Him: Thou art my Son, begotten by me, equal in power, in the brightness of glory and in all perfections, my most perfect image, surrounded by my paternal love. This day, this glorious day for all eternity, have I begotten thee, this day my fatherly love has given thee to the world as its Redeemer and King; this day I give thee the boundaries of the world and all that it contains, and appoint thee Judge over all that is created. That is like turning one's eyes toward eternity, toward the mystery of the Godhead, toward the Heart of the heavenly Father, a contemplation so sublime, so illuminating, that other thoughts are out of the question, and the soul struck with amazement, and in adoration before this abyss of

1) These remarks also apply to certain English hymns and carols. Trsl.

divine perfection and beauty, is a witness of this mystical life, this endless giving and receiving, being and being begotten. And this divine joy, this sea of light, breaks upon the dark earth, disguised under a weak human form, and illuminates it like the day-blush of a sun still hidden from us. Now what else can the Church do in view of this? Must she not adore Him and forgetting all else humbly thank Him who wishes to be all in all? Thus begins the Introit of the first Christmas Mass, the first greeting of Emanuel, the first revelation of the divine childhood that is to enlighten us, the forsaken descendants of Adam, and consequently so much simplicity, so much joy, such as is only known to perfect innocence. Would it be possible to speak of anything so sublime, or to express it in song, more worthily and at the same time more simply? There is something in this melody which seems to aid us in contemplating the mystery of the eternal Sonship, fully comprehended by God alone, and the effect would be lost if a more elaborate melody were employed with the resources that can be offered by musical art.

The popular hymn and this Introit reflect the infantile sweetness and perfect innocence of the new-born Saviour and King. In the former it is sought to express pleasing ideas concerning His humanity; in the latter, sublime thoughts concerning His divinity, and the melodic forms employed are well adapted for these purposes. Of course both views are right, but for the liturgy one prefers the conception so happily expressed in the Introit.

Text and melody of the other chants for this day follow the lead given in the Introit of the Midnight Mass. For the Christmas liturgy — as shown by these chants, as well as by the antiphons for both Vespers, the responsories at Matins, the thoughts for the octave (New Year) and the Epiphany — is not so much the humble crib at Bethlehem as the eternal generation of the Son from the Father, the central point from which all emotions of the heart and soul receive their impulse, their life.

189. If we compare, moreover, the texts and melodies of the other cycles of feasts with the popular hymns for the same periods, a divergence similar to that pointed out with regard to the Christmas chants will be perceived.

The solemn season of Lent inspired poets to write hymns on the passion and of a penitential character. The wounds of Jesus Christ, His bitter passion and death, form the subjects of private and of congregational devotions through the whole of Lent, whilst the liturgy opens Passiontide proper only 14 days before Easter, and concludes the mysteries of His last sufferings in the short space of a few days. Of course we must not forget that the remembrance of the Redeemer's death and of our redemption thereby from sin and death is effectually renewed in every Mass, and applied to our souls by the repetition of the sacrifice in an unbloody way. In fact every Mass has hidden within it the whole continuity of His life from His birth to His suffering end and glorious resurrection. Thus the Church was fully justified in giving opportunities throughout the course of the ecclesiastical year for the closer consideration of the various phases of this life, and she has made use of the first five weeks of Lent to bring before us the most important points in the struggle between the Messias and the chosen people. *Circumdederunt me dolores mortis* — thus *Septuagesima* Sunday[1]) shows us our Saviour hunted to death, in the midst of desolation, calumny and disgrace, at the zenith of His labours, which indeed had gained Him a great many submissive, docile disciples, but at the same time many powerful, malicious enemies and blasphemers. Now this mental struggle goes on through the quiet time of the 40 days' fast until the triumph of Palm Sunday leads to the decision. Hoping and loving, forgiving and forgetting, our Saviour endures the blackest ingratitude and all the suffering that follows him at every step and turn; louder and louder resounds His prophecy concerning His cross and passion, His betrayal and death, a sign that His Heart, agonised by horror of the approaching night of suffering, had become, in the tumult of the streets as well as in His intercourse with His beloved ones, the chosen place for vehement struggles which were soon outwardly manifested on the Mount of Olives.

Such emotions of the soul of course demand language and music different from those required to express the feelings of a pious penitent contemplating the sacred wounds, even if these hymns were not for use in connection with the eucharistic sacrifice. Justifiable as are the ideas that pervade hymns of this kind and many polyphonic motets, ancient and modern, the musical treatment of these events and deeds must nevertheless be different for liturgical purposes.

190. Lastly, liturgical and extra-liturgical prayers and melodies differ, in so far as the former faithfully reflect in

1) Cf. remarks on p. 176 concerning the chants for High Mass on Palm Sunday.

themselves the spirit of the liturgy, because as regards the liturgical prayers and melodies, the thoughts, words and actions are Christ's, conceived, spoken, sung and carried out in accordance with His spirit and intentions. With good reason, therefore, one can assert that the more Christ's sentiments are expressed, the more the liturgical prayers and melodies will be instinct with the liturgical spirit.

This is why the Introit for Easter, apparently so simple, is such a good example of an eminently liturgical plain chant melody, and therefore it is worth while to add it to the examples already given. The victory of Christ is the victory of the spirit, of His spiritual superiority ("mirabilis facta est *scientia tua* ex me"), of His divine power, the sources of which are in the inseparable union with God, in His divine Sonship *(adhuc tecum sum);* and here one thinks chiefly of the great day, whose sun has for ever risen for the humanity of Christ, of the glorification of the human nature, which has now obtained the full possession of all those good things that can render a human being happy. Christ's humanity has found in God its object, its rest, its own happiness, fully and entirely, and to day the Risen One enters upon this life as the first-born of countless brethren, in the glorious robe of unending merit. Before such an horizon even the shadows of the last days of the passion vanish away. Only the *adhuc tecum*, the closest union with God fills the soul with the euphony of indescribable harmony, with indescribable jubilation, surrounds it with supernatural brightness, buries it in the abyss of divine peace, divine glory and happiness. *Resurrexi.*[1]) So far as tones can express these things, is not the melody of this Easter Introit exceedingly impressive, breathing inward peace and joy?

191. Considerations of this kind are not needed in order to appreciate every plain chant melody. And yet a little experience will convince a person that only a clear comprehension of the spirit of the liturgy and its modes of expression can enable him to appreciate the liturgical chant fully, and hence it is the indispensable duty of the choirmaster thoroughly to familiarise himself

1) Cf. Vivell on this Introit in the Greg. Rundschau, 1904, pp. 62 *seq.*

with the essentials of the liturgy, its structure, the predominating thoughts for the seasons and feasts, in order that he may be in a position to instruct his singers in a satisfactory manner. He will thereby not only awaken their interest in the sacred chant, but at the same time prevent in the surest way a mechanical performance, and this will gradually lead up to an improved method more in accordance with liturgical and artistic requirements.

192. If it is an art, and sometimes a very great art, to pray rightly, i. e., in spirit and in truth, it is all the more so as regards singing in spirit and in truth. If this could be attained to a greater extent, then through the liturgical chant there would again be realised in many that which the Arch-abbot M. Wolter[1]) says of the enthusiastic early Christians:

"If the canonical hours together with the sacrifice constituted the apostolic divine worship, the daily routine of the first Christians, it must unhesitatingly be asserted that these first-born children of the Church, strengthened their souls with psalmody and hymnody for the mighty struggles of martyrdom. *Officium* and *Sacrificium,* i. e., Holy Scripture and the liturgy — these two consecrated vessels filled by the Holy Ghost and set up in the sanctuary of the New Covenant, yielded to those happy disciples of the apostles the sole substance of their spiritual nourishment. Out of them with joy they drew the heavenly manna that strengthened and refreshed their heroic souls on their pilgrimage through the desert to the promised land. What the fiery tongues of the Holy Ghost had spoken in the apostles quivered anew, in the holy chants of the canonical hours and of Mass, on the tongues of the baptized, so that the Church, the bride of Jesus Christ, offered to her heavenly Bridegroom a full, worthy, undivided, undiminished praise; and thus the whole Church, not alone the sacrificing priesthood, resembled a mighty harp of David, on whose golden strings the finger of God, the Holy Ghost, wondrously played to the praise of the Most High and of the Lamb."

1) Gertrudenbuch (Regensburg, Manz, 6th ed. 1902) pp. XII. *seq.*

Chapter XV.

The Artistic Value of Plain Chant.

193. We shall here speak of plain chant in its widest sense, including therefore psalmody and recitative. We have in the first place to call attention to the *melodic forms* in plain chant and then to explain the *capability of expression* possessed by its melodies. We shall claim an artistic value for plain chant in so far as its melodies, constructed in accordance with certain well considered rules, and its musical form, are calculated to satisfy and please the educated hearer.

A. Theory of Form.

It deals with:

I. The Structure, and
II. The Development of the Melody.

I. The Structure of Plain Chant Melody.

194. As a unison and liturgical chant in free rhythm, plain chant has only the forms possible without the aid of time and harmony, and which do not interfere with the object aimed at by the liturgy, and with the comparatively rapid course of the liturgical offices.

a) Melodic Forms.

195. The form of plain chant most frequently used is *antiphonal-chant of various kinds, as psalmody, antiphony* and *responsory* (including Introit, Gradual, and Offertory), and this is often made *more animated and effective* by the employment of *solo* and *chorus.*

196. We meet with antiphonal chant in its simplest form in *psalmody,* wherein as a rule two choirs of equal strength answer each other, repeating one and the same melody to different texts. In this form the half-close and close have a special melodic formula, whilst the middle parts are each time on a monotone. As a matter of course the artistic value cannot be in the single verse of a psalm for itself alone, but only in the *psalm as a well-ordered whole, with its closely connected but varied divisions.* Practically therefore the effect depends upon both sides performing their task in a satisfactory manner, i. e., the second choir must take up the chant from the first choir briskly, but quietly and with precision, and in the same *tempo,* and if possible with the same tone-colour and degree of force (this likewise holds good as regards the alternate employment of upper and lower voices), so that the chanting of both may proceed uninterruptedly and vigorously, thus keeping the parts firmly connected together and producing an animated and striking effect, a figure of devotion and recollection, of manly vigour and fraternal unity. Psalmody as employed in the liturgy of to-day requires a *choral effect* from its very nature. This is the pith of the matter, the chief point, the principal factor by means of which the desired effect is produced. All that is opposed to a good and thoroughly satisfactory choral effect, all that hinders or spoils the even flow of the melody (as, e. g., undue haste, over-loudness of some of the voices, exaggerated pathos, etc.) ruins psalmody.

The same fully applies to the *recitation* of the psalms (and hymns).

197. In *antiphony* the alternate chants have an extended form in which the melodies, usually short ones, introduce and close the psalm; formerly they interrupted it, and they do so now in some cases, e. g., in the *Invitatorium,* and in the *Nunc dimittis (Lumen)* on the Purification. Antiphony also furnishes a kind of refrain in order to remind the singer of the principal thought — generally a short summary suitable for the feast — so that he may be influenced by it, and rejoice in it, keeping it before him while singing the psalm and the whole office.

The antiphon enlivens the psalmody, gives it a fresh impulse, opens new points for consideration, makes the divisions more distinct and solemn.

198. We also meet in plain chant the *refrain* proper, for instance, in the splendidly vigorous hymn *Gloria laus* to whose jubilant strains the Messias enters into His city, and in the grandly conceived *Pange lingua* (refrain *Crux fidelis,* and *Dulce lignum),* the magnificent hymn on the miraculous wood of the Cross. This form is closely related to that for responsories, only in the latter the repetition is not always at regular intervals.

This kind of refrain differs from the *Invitatorium* in that the text as well as the melody has the same form as the strophes, and in *Gloria laus* the whole is always repeated, whilst the *Invitatorium* is repeated alternately with its second half *(venite adoremus).*

199. The *responsory* begins with a sentence of some length to which one or more short sentences are appended; these are repeated after the parenthesis following them, and sometimes the *whole,* with the exception of the parentheses, is begun anew and again sung through. The *Libera* after the Requiem Mass offers a well known example; to a less extent the Offertory of the same Mass.

The *responsory* exhibits a considerably more extended range than antiphony. Its melody is chiefly melismatic and requires to be rendered in a flowing style, usually with an accelerated rate of movement, with the exception of Offertories. It is important to start the parentheses briskly, so that out of the various divisions a *tout ensemble* may be formed that loses nothing in the way of *force and energy but steadily gains in these respects.*

200. Among the antiphonal chants we must also include the melodies of the *Ordinarium Missæ,* the *Alleluja* of the Mass and the Sequences. The latter are, as a rule, so constructed that a second choir repeats the melody of the first to other words, forming in a way its echo. Concerning the chants of the *Ordinarium Missæ* see above pp. 93 *seq.*, and below pp. 194, 195; concerning the *Alleluja* pp. 109 *seq.*

201. It must be allowed that plain chant by means of alternate choirs is able to apportion its melodies in a very simple and effective manner, and that this contrivance is constantly made use of with the best results. In this alone plain chant has the advantage over popular hymnody, which is seldom constructed on the antiphonal plan. Besides this, by the entry of different choirs the chant receives the character of the liturgical action, and is thus enabled to attract the attention of singers and hearers more easily and for a longer time. The choir appears in this way not as a unit but — what is more important and, æsthetically considered, of greater value — as a union, a *voluntary joining of parts to a whole,* and this adds not a little to the impression. There is a mutual giving and receiving, an exchange of thoughts and sentiments. Involuntarily the hearer is attracted by this, takes part in the action of the choir, and soon recognises in the antiphonal melodies voices from his own interior, songs in which his own soul expresses itself. In so far as many of these chants, easier than polyphony, are admissible for large choruses, the effect of the antiphonal chant will be greater in its simplicity than that of the alternate choruses artistically developed in the more modern 8 and 16 part compositions. Through the Tridentine reform of the Missal, and to a certain extent previously, many of the melodies, e. g., those for the Offertory and partly also those for the *Communio,* have been reduced owing to considerable abbreviations of the text. That might have been a relief for many, but as regards the artistic structure of the melodies these abbreviations — although the main part of the melodies was at first left undisturbed — meant a reduction which could but injure the original design and spoil the artistic effect.

b) Construction of Periods.

202. The *perfect symmetry* of the parts, necessary for the construction of periods in the later classical music, is wanting in plain chant, if by this we understand a perfectly equal expansion. Only a few hymns with syllabic melodies exhibit this strictly symmetrical construction, and in these cases it is only the text and melody that made it possible. Yet even in these simple hymns there are some exceptions in which one or more superfluous notes are to be found.

203. *Plain chant forms the free period* for the most part by closely adhering to the division of the text, and periods of this kind are not wanting even in short chants. Generally we find 2—4 such periods in a melody, seldom more. The close of each division is usually denoted in our books by a colon in the text. Thus, e. g., in the Introit for the Epiphany the first period comprises the first half of the text: *Ecce advenit dominator Dominus:* (here a colon). This is followed by the closing sentence (as the 2nd period) *et regnum in manu ejus, et potestas, et imperium.* Moreover, the first sentence is subdivided into two parts *(ecce advenit — dominator Dominus),* the closing sentence into three *(et regnum in manu ejus — et potestas — et imperium).* Here therefore the closing sentence has the preponderance. In this the melodic concatenation of the divisions is very beautifully effected by making the close of the first part and the beginning of the second answer each other with the progression of a fourth, *do-fa,* so that the second principal sentence takes up the last motive of the first, and the closing sentence introduces itself in like manner by repeating on *et* the motive of the last division but one.

But the musical division does not always exactly follow that of the liturgical text. Thus in the Introit *Statuit (Commune unius Martyris Pont.* and *Commune Conf. Pont.)* the first period closes with *pacis.* Elsewhere the melody exhibits more divisions than the text. The reverse is the case in the Introit *Terribilis* (Dedic. of a church), wherein the musical period does not close till after *hic domus Dei est et porta cœli.* In the simple melody for *Alma Redemptoris,* the period, in accordance with the division of the text, but not with the sense of the words, is closed at *succurre cadenti,* where accordingly a slight pause should be made.

204. In Gregorian chant more importance is attached to the symmetry of the *musical contents*, or to that of the various divisions, than to external symmetry. Not infrequently, for instance, *a climax in the fore-phrase finds its suitable resolution in the after-phrase, or a tranquil preparation in the fore-phrase its culminating point in the after-phrase.* Here we call attention to the analyses of antiphons given in Chap. IX. We possess moreover excellent examples of this kind of symmetry in several *Alleluja* melodies, in which the *Jubilus* or *Neuma* shows in a certain way the musical inversion or the musical resolution of the fore-phrase. Observe the following melodies from this point of view:

For further examples of this kind see the *Alleluja* on the feast of St. Marius (19. Jan.), on that of St. Ignatius (1. Febr.), on the 3rd Sunday of Advent, Whit-Tuesday, 7th Sunday after Pentecost, etc. The *Alleluja* on the feast of St. Agnes contains an interesting development of this form of resolution, the *Neuma* repeating the striking motive of the fore-phrase:

1) Dom. I. Adv. Lib. us. p. 103. 2) Dom. II. Adv. Lib. us. p. 109.

Concerning the development of the motives of the fore-phrase see below p. 170.

205. In yet another respect symmetry in many plain chant melodies is unmistakeable, though effected with a certain freedom, namely in the *equalisation of the members according to the height attained by the melody.* This equalisation is effected by *parallelism* or by *inversion.*

To the former we may assign the Introit *Statuit* (fore-phrase and after-phrase: rise and fall); to the latter, such as the Introit *Sapientiam* (fore-phrase, mean height + rise; after-phrase, rise + mean height, and fall), and *Me exspectaverunt* and *Nos autem* (both with the relation 1 + 4 low position or mean height, 2 + 2 rise). Moreover, the above mentioned melodies for *Alleluja* give examples of such inversions. The antiphon at the *Magnificat* of the second Vespers on the Epiphany (with the relation 1 + 5, 2 + 4, in the middle 3) shows a similar plan, and here by means of the melodic repetition at the third *hodie* a good contrast to the second *hodie* is obtained.

206. More frequently the symmetry of the members is made more apparent at the end of the various parts by certain formulæ, one might call them *rhyme-endings,* whereby the close is rounded off and the entry of the next part better prepared.

We have a striking example of this in the *Communio* for All Saints, wherein the phrases close in the following manner:

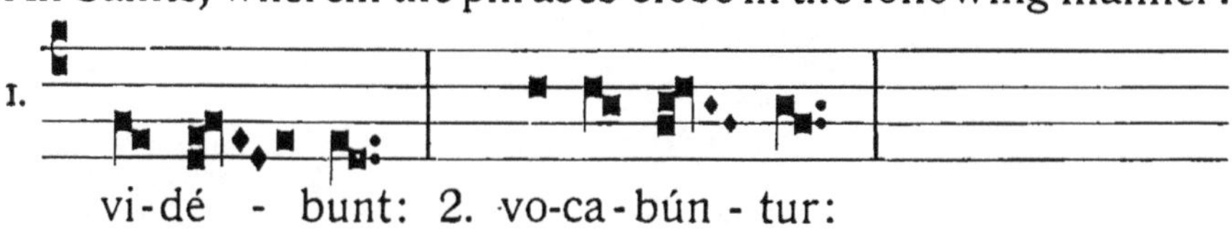

1) Lib. us. p. 742.

or *Alma Redemptoris*, the period, in accordance division of the text, but not with the sense of the words, is closed at *succurre cadenti*, where accordingly a slight pause should be made.

In Gregorian chant more importance is attached to the symmetry of the *musical contents*, or to that of the divisions, than to external symmetry. Not infrequently, for instance, *a climax in the fore-phrase finds its resolution in the after-phrase, or a preparation in the fore-phrase its culminating point in the after-phrase.* Here we call attention to the examples of sub-phrases given in Chap. IX. We possess very excellent examples of this kind of symmetry in several *Alleluja* melodies, in which the *Jubilus* or *Neuma* shows in a certain way the musical inversion or reciprocal resolution of the fore-phrase. Observe the following melodies from this point of view:

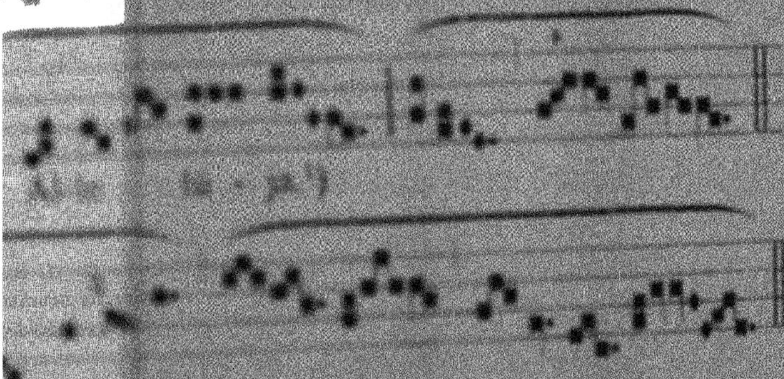

For further examples of this kind see the *Alleluja* on the feast of St. Marius (19. Jan.), on that of St. Ignatius, on the 3rd Sunday of Advent, Whit-Tuesday, after Pentecost, etc. The *Alleluja* on the Sunday after Pentecost, etc. The *Alleluja* on the contains an interesting development the *Neuma* repeating the str of the fore-phrase:

Concerning the developmentof the motives of the fore-phrase see below p. 170.

205. In yet another respect smmetry in many plain chant melodies is unmistakeable,though effected with a certain freedom, namely in the *equlisation of the members* according to the *height attainedby the melody*. This equalisation is effected by *parallesm* or by *inversion*.

To the former we may assignhe Introit *Statuit* (fore-phrase and after-phrase: rise and ıll); to the latter, such as the Introit *Sapientiam* (fore-phrse, mean height + rise; after-phrase, rise + mean height, ad fall), and *Me exspectaverunt* and *Nos autem* (both wit the relation 1 + 4 low position or mean height, 2 + 2 risc. Moreover, the above mentioned melodies for *Alleluja* ive examples of such inversions. The antiphon at the *Mgnificat* of the second Vespers on the Epiphany (with thcrelation 1 + 5, 2 + 4, in the middle 3) shows a similar pan, and here by means of the melodic repetition at the tird *hodie* a good contrast to the second *hodie* is obtaied.

206. More frequently the symmetry of the members is made more apparent at the ed of the various parts by certain formulæ, one might cd them *rhyme-endings,* whereby the close is rounded of and the entry of the next part better prepared.

We have a striking example of ıis in the *Communio* for All Saints, wherein the phrases closen

1) Lib. us. p. 742.

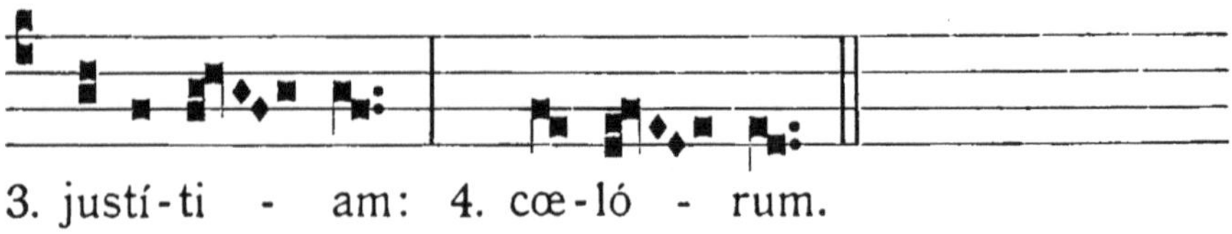

Also in the Offertory *Diffusa est* from the Mass *Cognovi,* wherein the three phrases have the following closes:

Compare moreover in the Introit for the first Sunday in Advent the parallelism *animam meam* (first fore-phrase), *erubescam* (second fore-phrase), and *confundentur* (after-phrase); in *Asperges* the closes on *et mundabor* and *dealbabor,* in the Introit of the *Requiem* Mass, on *Domine* and *eis.* More extended formulæ, e. g., in the Introit for the Epiphany:

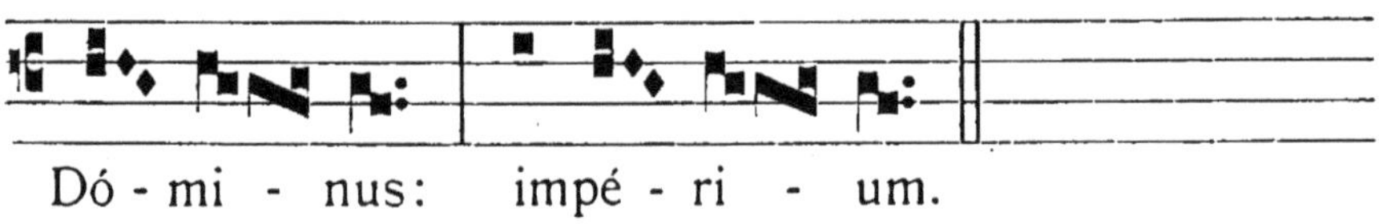

In the Introit for the second Sunday of Advent the three members close alike on *gentes, suæ* and *vestri,* but the middle one ends on the fifth. The formula at the close of the fore and after-phrase of the Introit, Mode VIII, as on Whitsunday and very often in Paschal time and on other occasions, being more frequently used is better known:

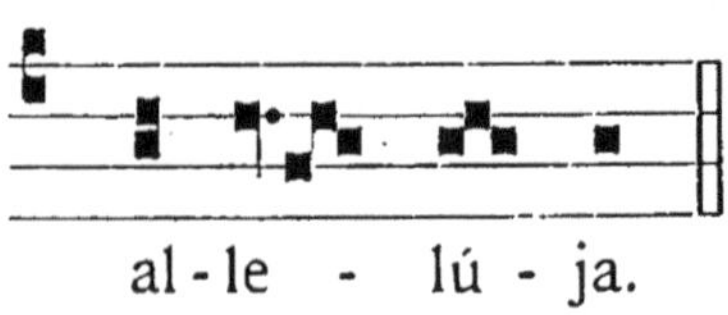

Still more extended is the parallelism in the Easter Introit:

Fore-phrase.

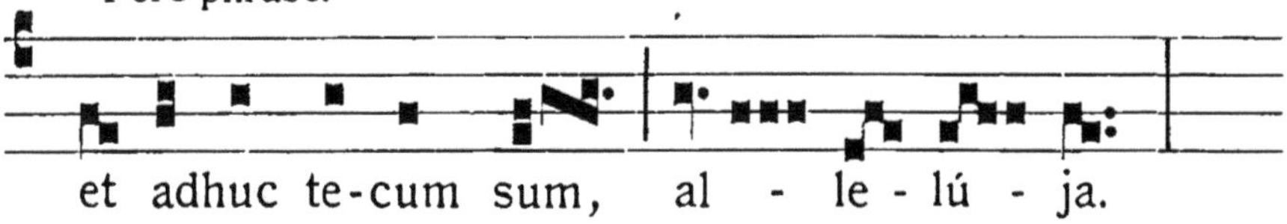

Closing-phrase.

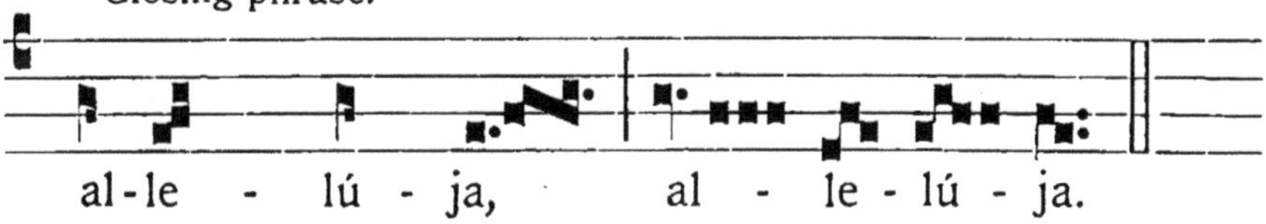

Examples from the *Kyriale* are given above pp. 93 *seq.* and 95 *seq.*

In the *Communio* of the Christmas Midnight Mass we possess a pleasing example wherein the parallelism is formed in the two outer and inner members (1 : 4, 2 : 3) in a simple but attractive manner:

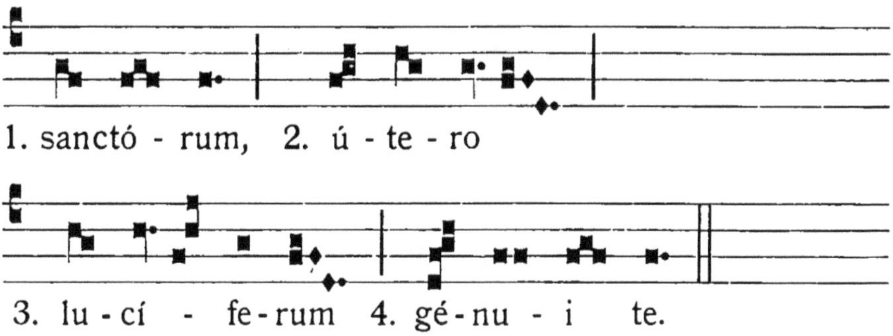

II. Inner Development.

207. Plain chant chiefly makes use of the following means:

a) Repetition,
b) Imitation, or working of a short or more extended motive,
c) Climax,
d) Contrary motion,
e) Purely rhythmic Imitation.

a) Repetition.

208. We have already seen above (pp. 159 *seq.*) how plain chant repeats certain melodic formulæ in order to make the final cadence more prominent. We find this repetition employed in another way with a view to give energy to the movement, and thus to enliven it. The different ways in which this device is carried out are as follows:

1. The repetition of a *motive or of part of a melody that has just appeared, and then its further development,* often as the resolution at the same time of a previous point of rest:

Alleluja-Neuma Dom. IV. Adv.

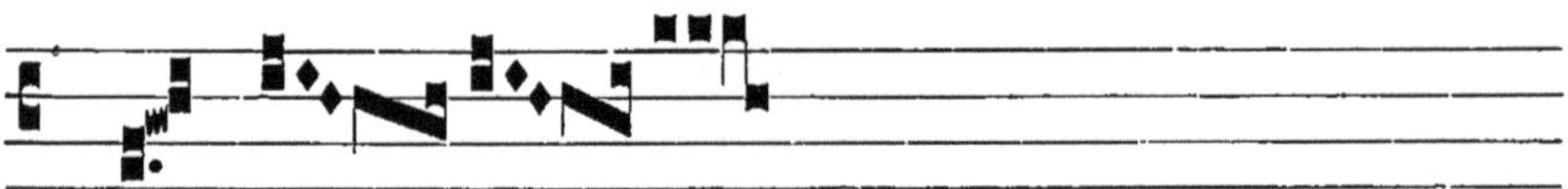

re-gna. Gradual on feast of the St. Cæcilia.

Neuma from the 2nd *Alleluja* Dom. post Ascens.

cla-mor *Alleluja* on the feast of St. Agnes.

With a slight change:

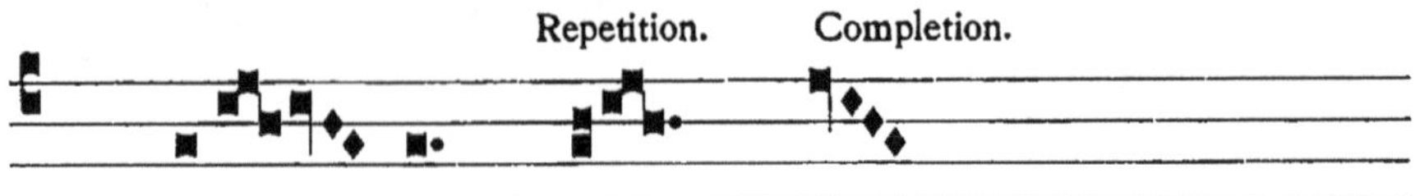

Alle-lú - - ja. *Alleluja,* Assumption.

Among the most beautiful passages of this kind may assuredly be reckoned the free repetition in the verse of the Pentecost Alleluja *Veni Sancte* (at *et tui amoris*), also in the Offertory, Missa vot. B. M. V., *Beata es Virgo* (on *Virgo* and *permanes)*, the *Neuma* of the Alleluja *Post partum Virgo* from the same Mass, *Tu es Sacerdos* from the Mass *Sacerdotes tui, Opportebat* (3rd Sunday after Easter).

2. *The return to a previous motive which is further developed:*

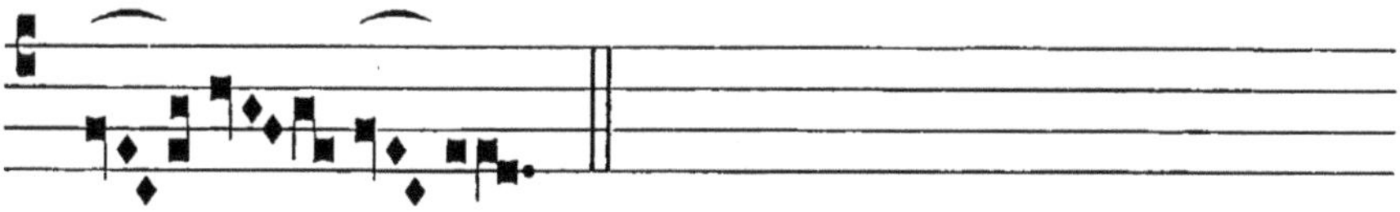

Neuma from the 1st *Alleluja* Dom. post Ascens.

3. *The mere repetition of a motive or part of a melody without further development:*

Alleluja-Neuma for the 18th Sunday after Pentecost.

G*radual* for the 3rd Sunday after Epiphany.

4. *Repetition transposed:*

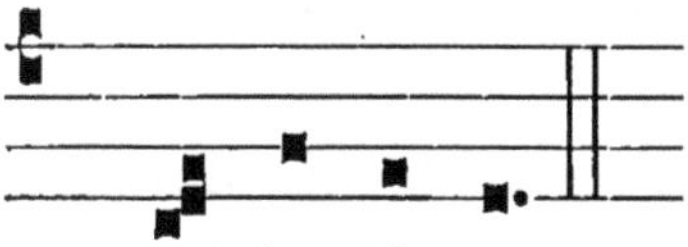

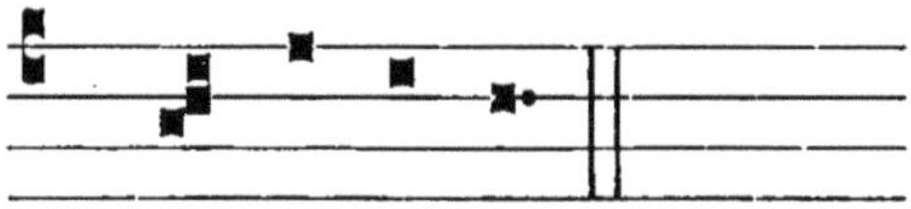

Mass XVII.

Mass XI.

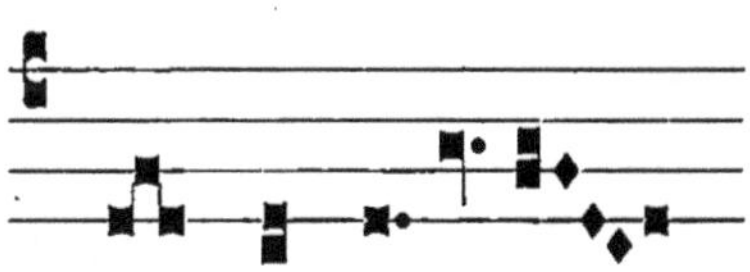

Mass XI.

Two phrases are used three times with slight variants in the melodious *Magnificat*-antiphon for the 2nd Vespers of St. Andrew after a short introduction, and a third phrase twice.

Introduction: Cum pervenisset beatus Andreas ad locum ubi crux parata erat,

Middle sentences:

Melodic member 1:	exclamavit et dixit: securus et gaudens ita et tu exultans
2:	O bona crux, venio ad te, suscipias me
3:	diu desiderata, discipulum ejus,
Conclusion:	qui pependit in te.

209. *Extended repetitions* are contained in the Gradual *Tecum principium* for Christmas (Midnight Mass). Compare the melodies of

V. 1. in splendoribus sanctorum
ante luciferum genui te.

V. 2. donec ponam inimicos tuos
scabellum pedum tuorum.

Yet only very few hearers and only a few singers would notice off-hand that whole passages agree with each other note for note, and that the repetitions take place at once. Both sentences are differently introduced, and thus one feels the repetition as an imitation or extension of the first member.

What plain chant can at times effect with this simple repetition of certain formulæ and skilful grouping is shown, e. g., in the *Alleluja* for All Saints. It contains the following repetitions:

a) 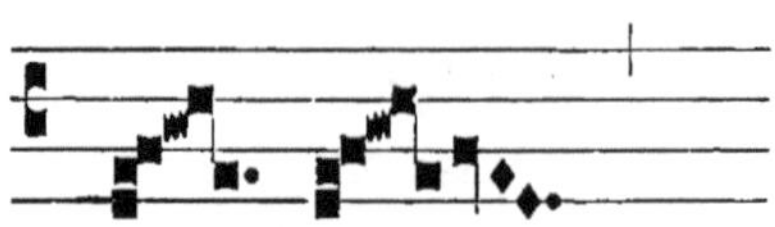 In the *Neuma*.

b)

c)

d)

The whole melody, which with its brilliant melismas must be included among the most beautiful and expressive chants, is built up by means of the skilful repetition of four members, to which only small combinations of notes are added (first middle member and close in the *Neuma* and the bold rise at *omnes:* a major chord with a major seventh immediately above it).

Here the reader may be briefly reminded of the numerous repetitions in the melodies of the *Ordinarium Missæ* (especially *Kyrie* and *Gloria),* and in those of the *Alleluja* and the verse pertaining thereto. Compare what has been said about this on pp. 93 *seq.* and 95 *seq.*

Repetitions of this kind are certainly as justifiable as any imitations in modern music, though, strictly speaking, they ought not to be reckoned among them. They give connecting points, recall to the memory what has gone before, place it in a new light and initiate new motives and melodies. They give the hearer time to collect himself, to follow the development leisurely and enjoyably, they deepen the impression, and they not only help him to appreciate the whole melody, but they induce him to appropriate the motive to himself and to view it as the expression of his own thoughts and sentiments.

b) Imitation in the strict Sense.

210. Imitation is very frequently made use of in plain chant. The following are the forms mostly employed:

1) Imitation in *direct* motion (seldom):

α) to a slight extent:

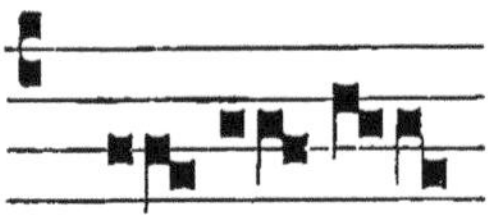

Alleluja-Verse, Missa vot. B. M. V.

Alleluja-Verse for the 1st Sunday of Advent.

Alleluja-Neuma for Whit Monday.

On different syllables of the text:

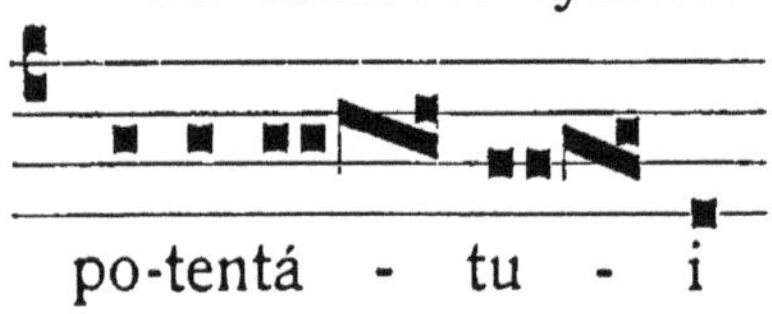

Offertory for the 22nd Sunday after Pentecost.

β) to a greater extent:

il - li

Gradual *Ecce Sacerdos,* Mass *Statuit.*

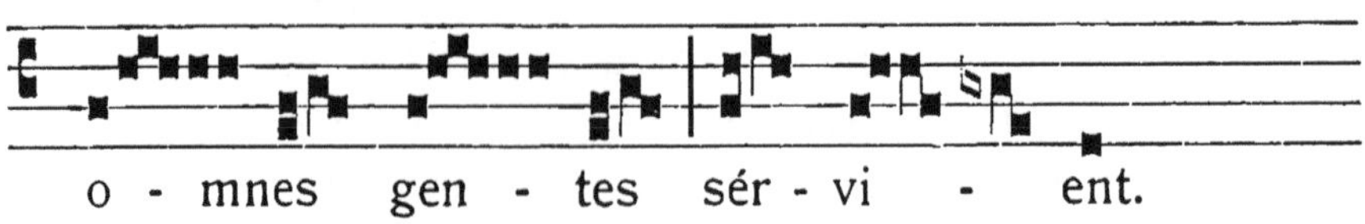

Offertory on the Epiphany.

Alleluja-Verse, Missa vot. B. M. V.

Compare above p. 53: *Domino.*

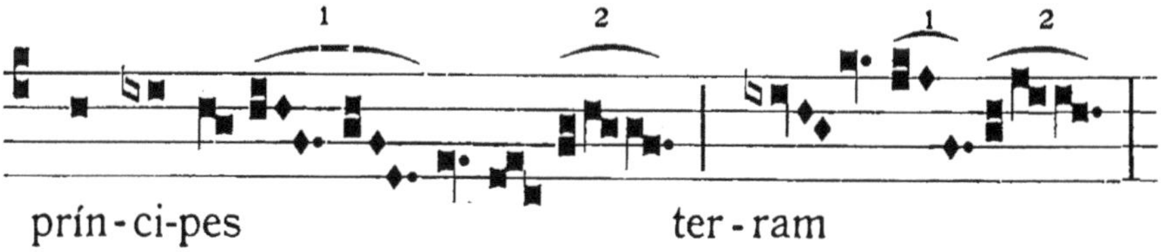

Gradual Co*nstitues,* Missa vot. Apost.

An expressive imitation begins in the Offertory of the Requiem Mass with the verse *Hostias et preces.* Compare with this the close of the fore-phrase *ejus.*

2) Imitation in *contrary* motion (seldom):

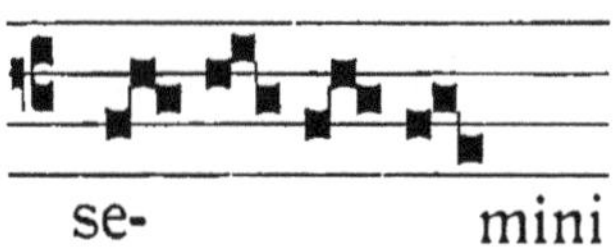

From the *Offertory* of the *R*equiem Mass.

3) Imitation with *prolongation,* as:

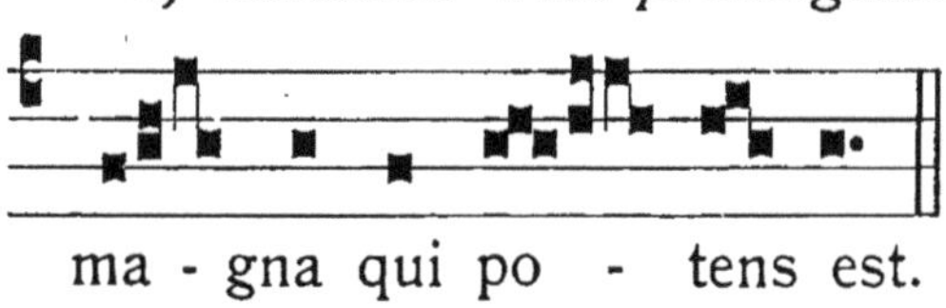

Communio Immac. Conc. B. M. V.

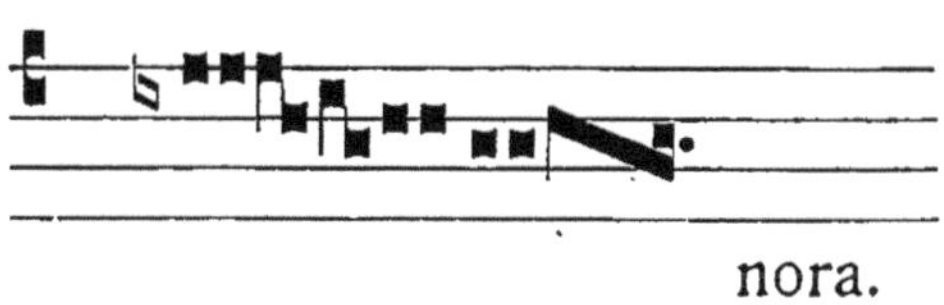

From the *Alleluja*-Verse Dom. IV. Adv.

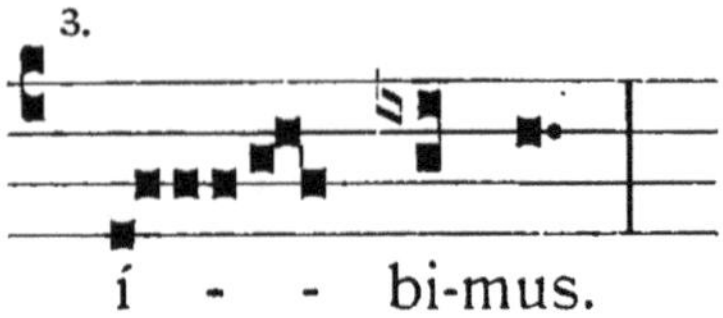

Alleluja Dom. II. Adv.

or *abbreviation,* as:

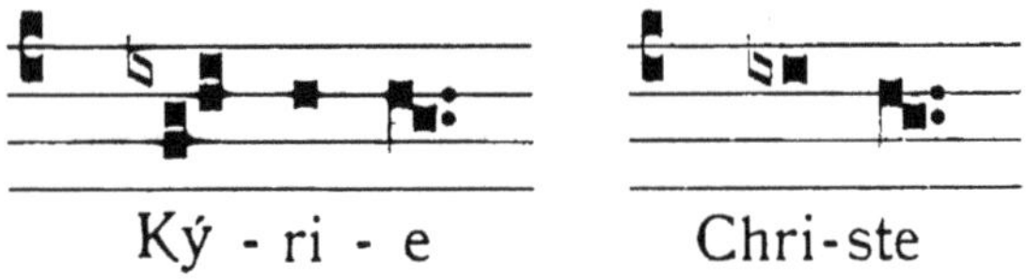

From the *R*equiem Mass.

Sanctus and *Benedictus,* No. III Cantus ad lib.

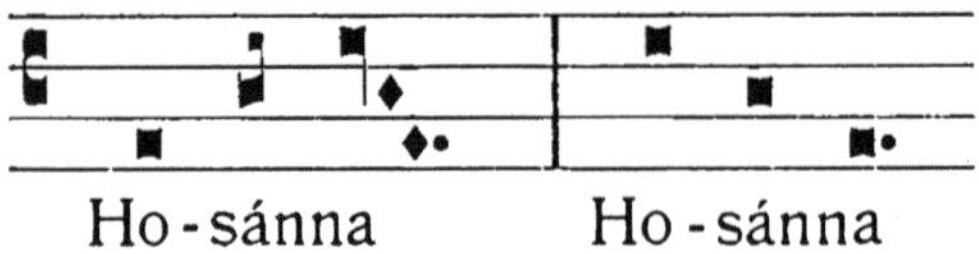

The same *Sanctus* contains an abbreviation and prolongation:

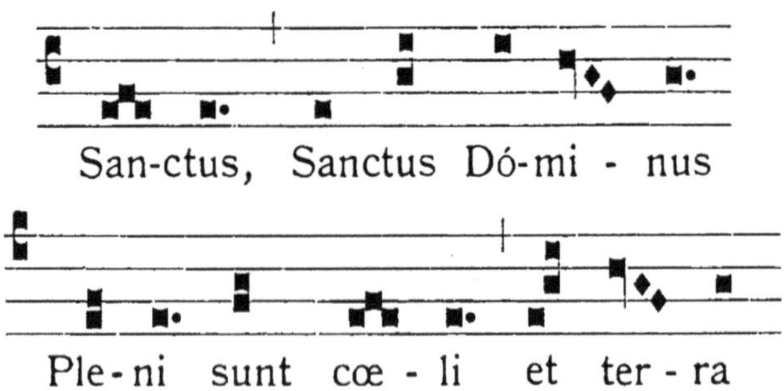

4) The following passage may serve as a specimen of purely melodic imitation:

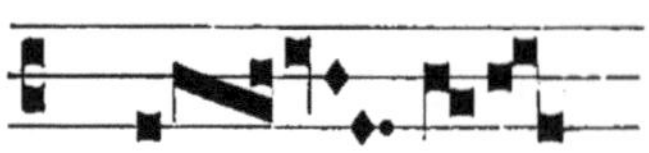

2nd Gradual Verse, Dom. II. Adv.

211. Plain chant frequently obtains an effect similar to imitation by the melody leaving out a tone, generally a sustained one *(do* or *fa* usually), at equal or unequal intervals, in order to return to it again. It plays round the one tone whereby it is made more noticeable in the melody:

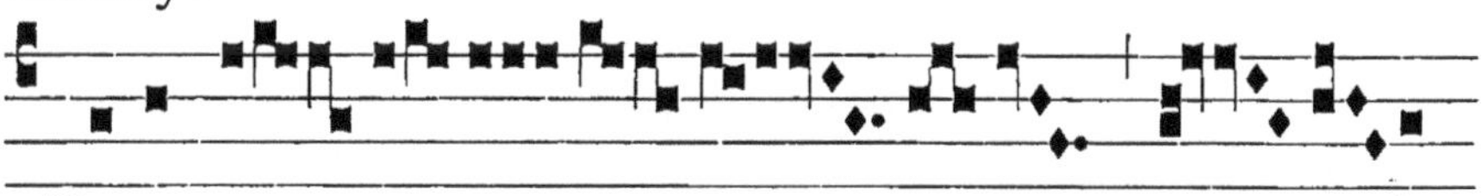

De-us so- lus.

Tract, Missa vot. SS. Trinit.

Sometimes a strict imitation or repetition is united with this:

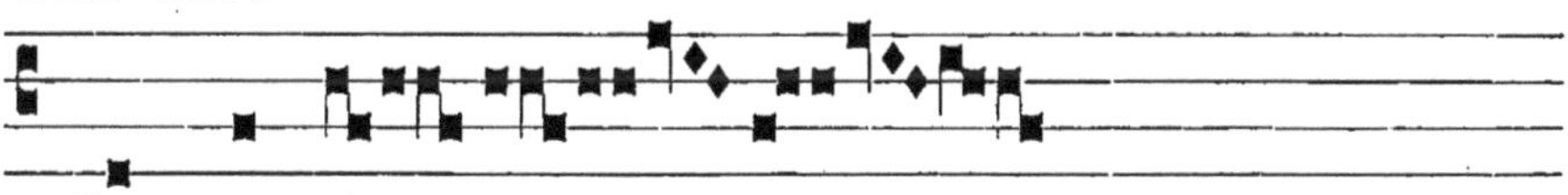

Con-gre-gá- te

Gradual, Dom. II. Adv.

In rendering such passages the tone in question is usually to be kept lightly sustained, unless a *pressus* is developed out of it.

Thus ensues a charmingly playful kind of seeking and losing, a striving after something and then forsaking it, by which the resolution at the end — often effected with the help of a wider interval — is made prominent, as shown in the following passage:

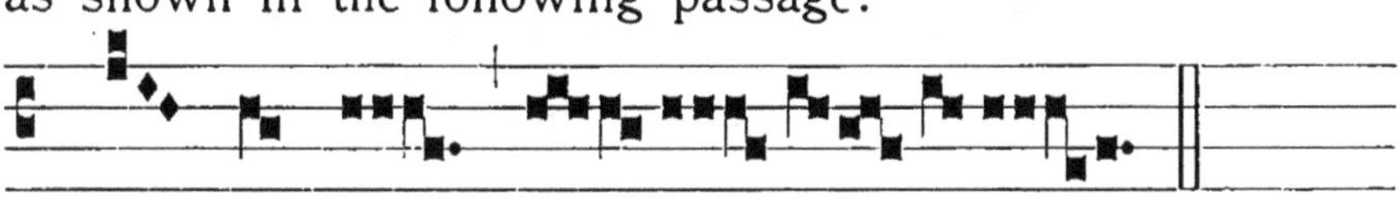

gló - ri - æ. *Offertory* for the Vigil of the Nativ.

Here the third, minor second, and again a third, find their resolution in the fourth. Similarly in the 2nd Gradual verse, Dom. III. p. Epiph. (twice a third, then a fourth):

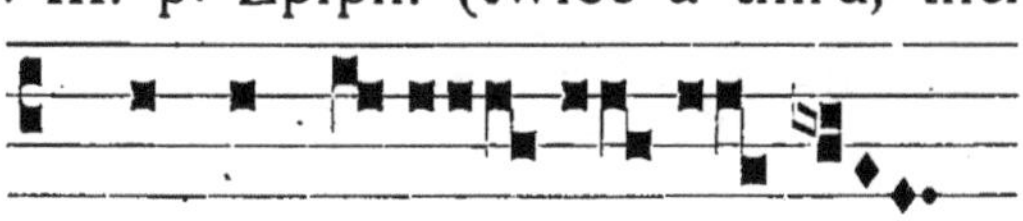

Dó-mi-nus

A kind of inversion of this formula, showing a preparation by means of suspense, is found in forms like these:

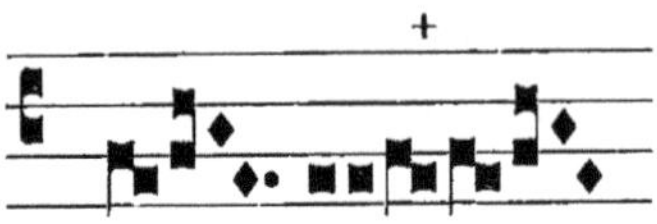

Alleluja-Neuma for the Vigil of the Nativity.

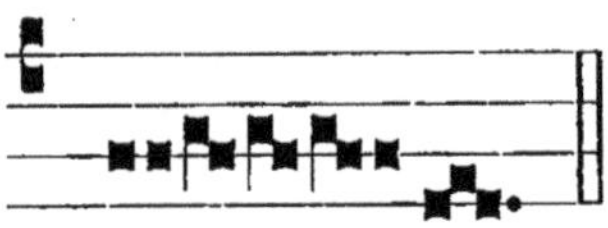

Close of the Ist Gradual verse *Sacerdotes* (Com. Conf. Pont.)

In many Graduals the second phrase is built up on a motive borrowed from the first phrase, or at all events it introduces itself with such a one. In the Gradual *Os justi* (Com. Doctorum) the phrase over the opening words of the verse *Lex Dei* is from the one over *et lingua,* the closing melisma over *supplantabuntur* being a repetition of the close over *ejus* in the fore-phrase, so that the verse may be considered to be an extended, free variation of the melody for *et lingua ejus.* Similarly, the intonation of the second *Agnus Dei* in Mass XVI. is a repetition of the *qui tollis peccata* of the first intonation.

c) **The climax** as a natural and effective Principle.

212. We here give the *Magnificat*-antiphon for the 2nd Vespers of Christmas with the *hodie* four times repeated:

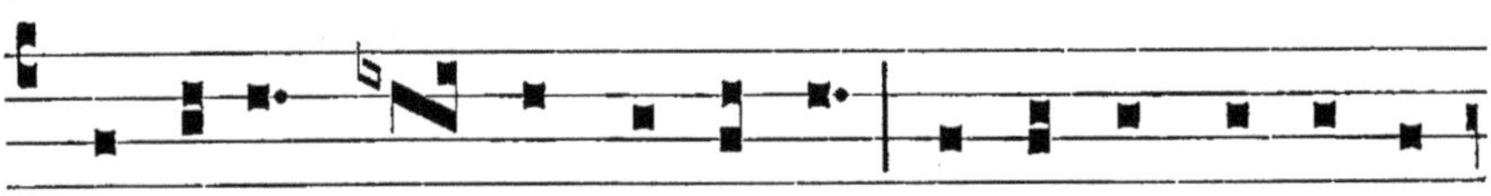

Hó-di-e Chri-stus na-tus est, hó-di - e Sal-vá-tor

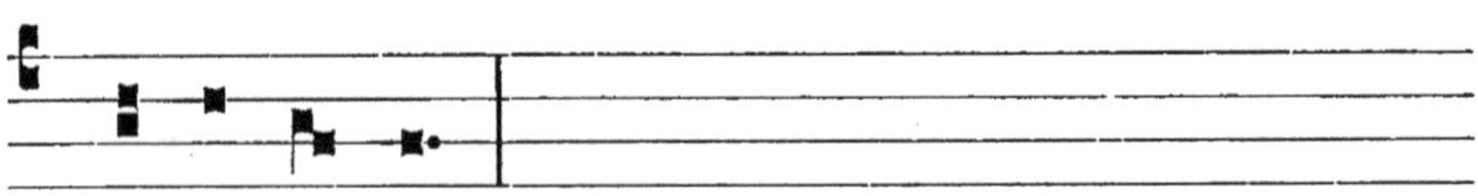

appá-ru - it:

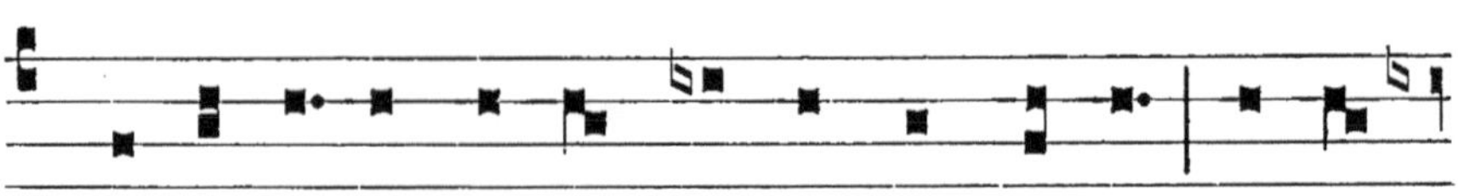

hó-di-e in ter-ra ca-nunt An-ge-li, læ-tán-

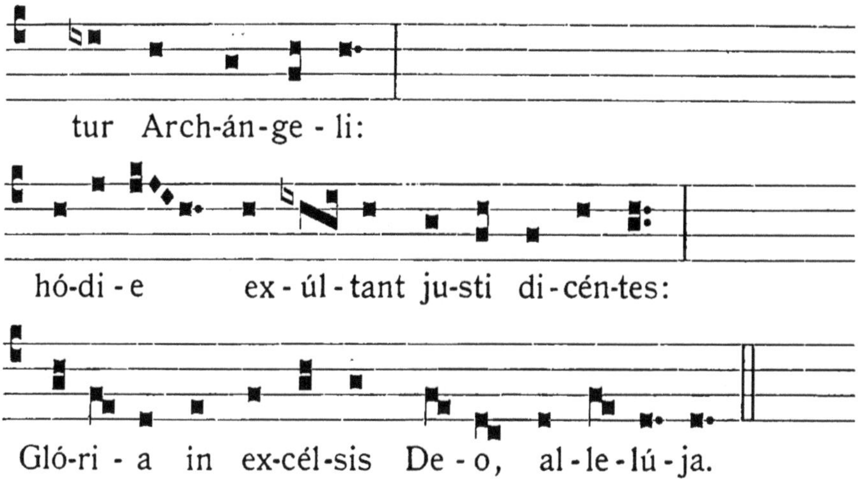

Here then the fourth *hodie* with is bold spring corresponds to the second *hodie* which is in a lower position, and the repetition of the first member at the third *hodie,* and again at *lætantur Archangeli,* makes the entry of this climax more effective.

Worthy of mention is likewise the grandly constructed *Communio* for the feast of All Saints with its brilliant climax at the third *beati,* which also gains in force and expression by the recurrence of the movement at the second *beati.* It should be noticed at the same time that the melody for the second sentence at the beginning rises a third to *fa,* so that this third repetition mounts up triumphantly from the third (in the major chord up to the major seventh), and not like the second from the fundamental tone.

By means of such climaxes the movement grows, the parts are kept in proper relation to one another, and are well connected together, so that the hearer is able to grasp and appreciate the whole melody.

In the cases mentioned the *repetition* of certain *words (hodie . . . hodie . . .,* or *beati . . . beati,* etc., is of assistance, the relation to one another of the thoughts being thereby impressed upon one. Where this fails, the repetition of melodic or rhythmic motives gives us a substitute.

Cf. the last *Kyrie* in Masses II., III., IV., VI., (VII.), VIII., IX., X., XIII., (XIV.), XVII., and the *Gloria* melodies pp. 95 *seq.*

d) Contrary Motion.

213. It occurs frequently in the *Kyriale.* See, e. g., the relation of *Kyrie* and *Christe* in Masses I., III., VI., VIII., IX., X., XIV., etc. Contrary motion of the same kind is also met with sometimes in the *Agnus Dei,* Mass II.:

in the *Sanctus,* Mass III.:

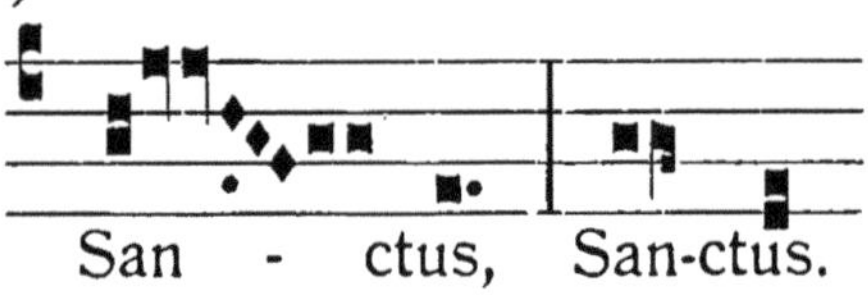

In hymns we also find contrary motion or resolution in some of the members.

e) Purely rhythmic Imitation.

214. This means that certain rhythmical motives are repeated, the intervals or melodic element not being similar or the same. This kind of imitation gives the melody a uniform character which makes all the more impression on the hearer inasmuch as he is seldom aware of it.

Thus one remarks, e. g., that in the Gradual *Propter veritatem* (Assumpt. B. M. V.) the following rhythmical motive

is frequently utilised, and, as shown in the scheme appended, in a free way as regards the melody:

Here the two introductory notes are omitted in one case, whilst the motive is all along rhythmically unaltered in the main, but progresses melodically sometimes in similar, sometimes in contrary motion.

We find motives like this more or less constantly in other melodies and also in the above mentioned Gradual.

B. Musical Contents.

215. Plain chant is not only an art on account of the excellence of the forms employed in its construction and the development of its melodies, but quite as much on account of its **capability of musical expression,** rendered possible by the ample means it possesses, therefore on account of the musical contents of the chants.

216. To understand this thoroughly we must bear in mind that plain chant is liturgical prayer and liturgical chant, and has no desire to be anything else; hence its value can only be estimated from this point of view.

a) As liturgical prayer and as liturgical chant the melodies must exactly suit the liturgical offices, and not delay them to any considerable extent; it must be subordinate to them; for liturgical music must always appear as only a part of a grand whole, and as a means to attain a higher object.

b) Owing to this close relation to the liturgy, plain chant must breathe the spirit of the liturgy if it is not to violate the unity and truth of the liturgical action or to endanger it.

217. From this the following conclusions may be drawn:

a) The liturgical chant is no more a private prayer than holy Mass and the Divine Office are private devotions.

That which plain chant has to express, to represent to us, cannot possibly be a personal matter in the sense of an unrestrained subjectiveness.

b) The melodies must never lose themselves in descriptive details and word-painting, for such things are neither required by the liturgy nor possible in the time available within the liturgy. Since the chants are only means to an end and parts of a higher action — here the action of the priest appointed by the Church and acting in the name of Christ, therefore the action of Christ Himself — the music must be in reality an outcome of this action, of Christ's eucharistic prayer and work; it must only accompany and illustrate, producing an effect upon the worshipper in accordance with this standpoint;

c) All inclinations, sentiments and thoughts must in liturgical chant emanate from the liturgy and its eucharistic centre. They must be eminently Christian, worthy of Christ and of His Most Sacred Heart. Hence there must be nothing purely natural, purely human. The liturgical life — the same applies to the Christian life — is a day whose sun never sets, though it may be hidden by dark clouds — there is no pain for which there is no soothing balm, no sorrow for which there is no palm of victory and most sweet consolation. We must at all times be with the Church, with Christ, "dwelling in heaven", whose light fills our life here upon earth and even penetrates to its darkest nights. Joy and thanksgiving; therefore *Alleluja* was the prayer of the apostles, of the first Christians, and it is the prayer of all who "live godly" in Christ, and this is best done when choir and people are present at the liturgical offices and cooperate therewith.

218. The liturgical chant must differ from merely religious music, and particularly from profane music, even more than the liturgical vestments differ from our ordinary garb. Consequently in forming an opinion as to the effect of Gregorian chant we must not apply the same standard as that employed in criticising profane or religious music. That would be unjust and untruthful.

The characteristics of these melodies are such as best suit the narrower sphere of the religious life, and more particularly the liturgical life.

Though outwardly limited yet they are in another respect the most important that human art has to deal with.

Inward, personal feeling, true to life, is here as much necessary as in any other art, if not more so, but it will always exhibit its specialities, i. e., clearness and purity of style; above all, heartfelt joy in gratitude for the wonderful works of God, for His goodness, His gracious presence, as brought before us by the liturgy.

Here also is appreciation of joy and sorrow, but it is not excessive joy, nor sorrow without consolation; it is not contention and strife, nor fretful questioning and seeking after this or that, for all these difficulties are solved in Christ, the centre of the liturgy; all these human differences cease to be heard in the harmony of the eucharistic prayer of praise and thanksgiving, in the sublime, divine praise of the most High, wherein Alpha and Omega are *one* thought, *one* word.

Let us now consider some **characteristic melodies.**

219. *Palm Sunday.* The loud Hosannas with which the Galileans, bearing palms and olive branches, welcomed the Messias and in triumphal procession escorted Him to the royal city, to Sion, to the citadel of God, have died away: *Hosanna in excelsis. Gloria laus et honor tibi sit, Rex, Christe, Redemptor.* — Now silence reigns around. The multitudes have departed. The noise in the streets has ceased. The populous city is at rest. *Our Saviour is alone* — alone with His thoughts and memories, with His hopes and cares. The joy caused by this festal triumph is now succeeded by the apprehension of terrible suffering. The Redeemer sees in spirit his adversaries, how, full of malice, they contrive plots, how they evoke a storm, how, in short, they strive their utmost to undo at once all that has been achieved by labours extending over years. The thought of the terrible death awaiting Him is again presented before His eyes — the excruciating torture, the humiliations, the insults. They are dark shadows, sad forebodings of that evening in the Garden of Olives, forebodings of that night on which He was to suffer still more, to keep silence, to atone, to shed His blood, — forebodings of that impenetrable darkness that would oppress His Heart when dying on the Cross. With such apprehensions the Introit begins — Christ's prayer to the Father: "O Lord, remove not thy help to a distance", for the gigantic struggle is at hand, the decisive hour approaches. Look therefore "towards my defence, deliver me from the lion's mouth, and my lowness" from the power of these bloodthirsty persecutors. A prayer therefore from a sorrowful, deeply oppressed Heart, a cry of anguish from the innermost soul, an entreaty "with a strong cry and tears" (Hebr. 5, 7). The dignity of a king and the solemn earnestness of a high-priest are expressed in this melody, but we also hear the lament of one who is hurried to his death, and the horror which the sight of the danger awakens in His soul. Therefore "look upon me, O God" with a look of Thy omnipotence, with an eye full of compassion for Thine Anointed, Thy Messenger, Thy Son:

Strike with the right hand, save me, set me free.

Save me, Thy beloved Son, Thy First-born. How impressively this *me* mounts up. The chant presently dies away full of humility, hope and peace, until the verse, like a fresh outburst of suppressed fear and agonizing pain, begins with the vehement lament: "O God, my God, look upon me, why hast Thou forsaken me?" Again this thought of death on the Cross, to which His life's path leads without the possibility of diverging from it or turning back. With striking impressiveness, therefore, our Saviour sings in the Offertory: "My heart hath expected reproach and misery:"

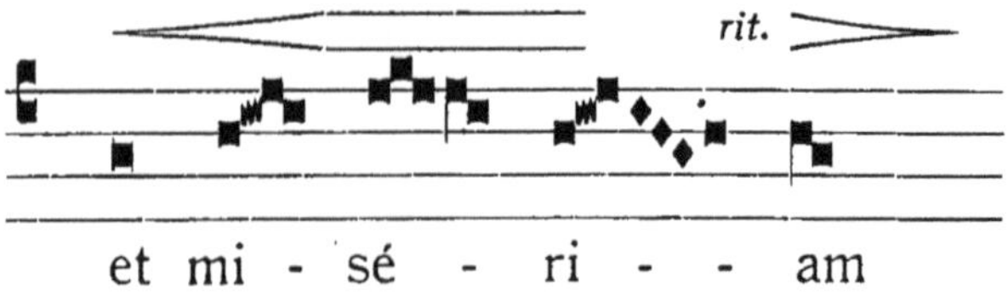

Et miseriam! — as the reward for so much love this misery in His Heart! Beating only for others, It feels this awful void and abandonment. Hence this word — a reproachful lament, a sigh; but what an accusation in these reproaches: '"I looked for one that would grieve together with me, and there was none." What a bitter disappointment is expressed in this short *et non fuit!* What is not denied to the poorest, what accompanies the most miserable criminal to his death, a little sincere compassion in his dire need — this is not accorded to me! How this cry of anguish is wrung from His Sacred Heart!

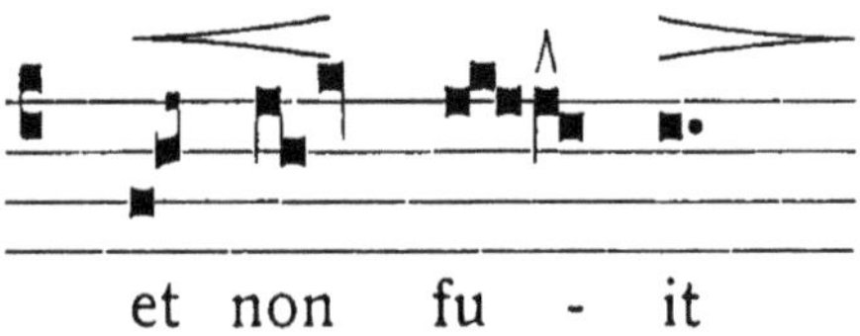

And the Heart so much in need of consolation sought one who would say a loving word, who would deign to give Him a friendly look — but no ray of light penetrated to this night of suffering. "I sought for one and I found none" — with greater vehemence — amidst all this affliction His Heart is almost breaking — He utters the painful words *non inveni* — this also I found not. The melody very suitably is an extension of the above *et non fuit:*

What they gave me — gall for my food, vinegar for my thirst — is mockery and insult, deliberate cruelty. Oh, this burning thirst of our Blessed Saviour, who was so grievously misunderstood!

The word *aceto* (vinegar) at the conclusion dies away sadly. Only a final welling-up of the agony and, lo, peace and resignation return to the soul. Hence the *Communio* begins in a hopeful, trusting tone with the sweet word "Father", which is not heard in the Introit:

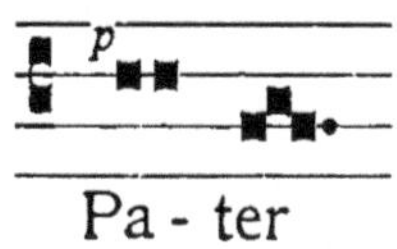

A longing gaze at the Father "of mercies, and God of all consolation:" "Father, if this chalice may not pass away, and I must drink it" — if I must drain this bitter chalice of suffering — and the thought makes Him shudder —

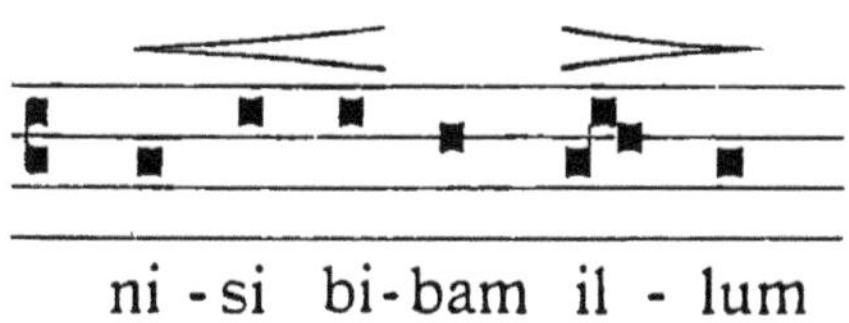

if Thy fatherly will must be accomplished in me, Thy will be done to Thine honour and for the salvation of the world! *Fiat* — no matter how painful the sacrifice may be — however much it may be against nature —

Expressing this firm resolve, the strains of the *Communio* at High Mass on Palm Sunday die away. The victory that the Galileans celebrated so enthusiastically that morning must first be won by the shedding of His blood even unto death. The Great Week has begun. Our Saviour has taken the first step for the accomplishment of the will of His Father, as His obedient Son. In spirit He has already taken the chalice, however terrible the reality may be. He has made the sacrifice. *Fiat* — for it is the will of God.

220. A tone-poem of quite a different character from the above, but scarcely less grand and dramatic in its conception, is the *Communio* "Quinque prudentes Virgines" from the 1st Mass for Virgins only.

In the quiet style of a narrative — it is a parable we are about to hear, a parable indeed which represents the history of all the elect — the singer begins with these simple words: "The five wise virgins took" for the night-watch "oil in their vessels with the lamps", to meet the bridegroom. The melody begins quietly and smoothly, so that the listener is involuntarily kept in suspense. All this is only a preliminary — the situation. Then all at once — "at midnight a cry was made" — there is excitement. The signal. The desired one approaches — the melody grows, expectation and surprise being portrayed throughout this chant:

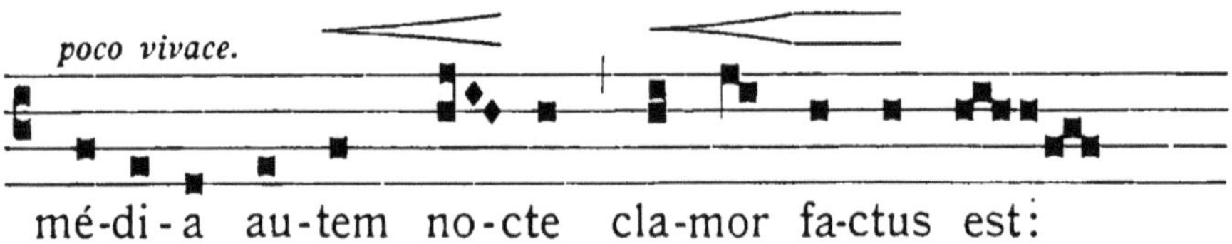

It is indeed the Bridegroom. There is no longer any doubt. O happy expectation! *Ecce sponsus!* Behold he cometh to conduct thee to thy eternal home. — The melody returns to the vigorous phrase at *media autem nocte.* But now it resounds more impressively, more joyfully: *Ecce sponsus!*

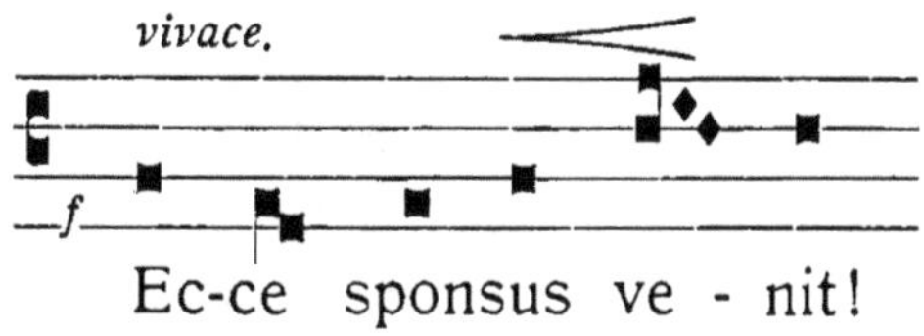

This *venit* is now a blessed reality, it is no dream. The joy of my soul is there; he will stoop to my lowness, he will be mine own. Joyously the melody announces: *venit! exite!* "Go ye forth to meet Christ our Lord". That is an overpowering jubilation, not an entreaty nor a command; it is joy beyond measure. "Go ye forth, for now is the time to hasten without delay to meet Christ our Lord on the wings of love:"

Like a flash of lightning this *exite* illuminates the night. In a very suitable manner the melody here reaches its culminating point as regards range as well as expression and emphasis; therefore it should be sung with full force. Pause slightly on the last syllable of the word (at *te),* so that the wide intervals *fa do la* may not be taken too hastily. At *Christo* the melody is again more meditative. The singer, imitating the virgins, will endeavour to realise beforehand what this word *Christus* means for the soul. Here therefore the *tempo* should be somewhat slackened. The *pressus* with emphasis. *Domino* softly dying away.

221. *Very short chants* are often made effective and *really dramatic* by means of vivid passages which must be viewed more as exclamations. In the following ex-

ample Christ speaks to his disciples who gratefully respond to each sentence with a joyful *Alleluja:*

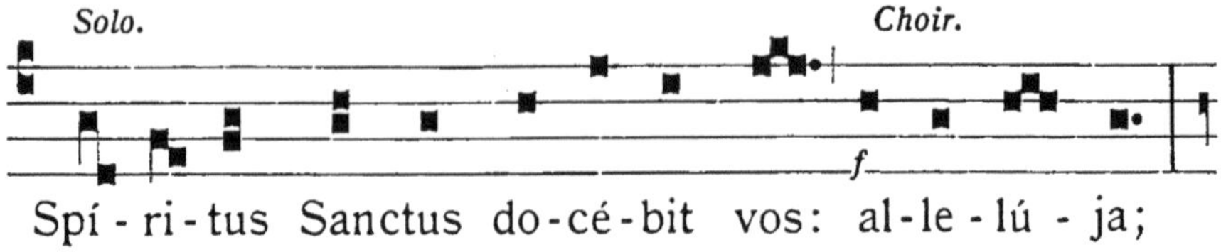

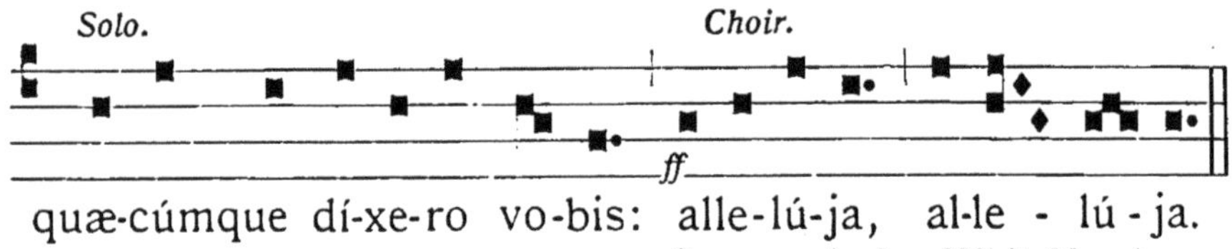

Communio for Whit Monday.

Solo melodies tranquil. Entry of the chorus precise, in joyous astonishment, of one mind, with strong accentuation. Similarly the *Communio* all through the octave of Pentecost.

222. The Mass for the feast of the Immaculate Conception possesses in its Offertory a sweet melody, a song to Mary, with all the grace of an expressive lyric. — *Ave Maria!* How these words ought to elevate the mind to-day, for we celebrate the day on which the Creator's greeting called into existence the soul of Mary and adorned it with a spotless royal robe. And with what rapture must God have contemplated this pure soul on whom He would hereafter bestow the most sublime dignity, crowning it with a diadem of the choicest virtues and of exquisite loveliness. And with what joy must God's mercy and justice have greeted this rosy morn as it flooded the heavens with its first rays, a sign that the darkness was vanishing at the approach of the sun of redemption. Therefore we also greet thee, O gracious Mother, at the moment when thy pure soul and body began an eternity full of grace and mercy, full of power and blessedness, full of a mother's work. Hence we poor children of Eve exclaim:

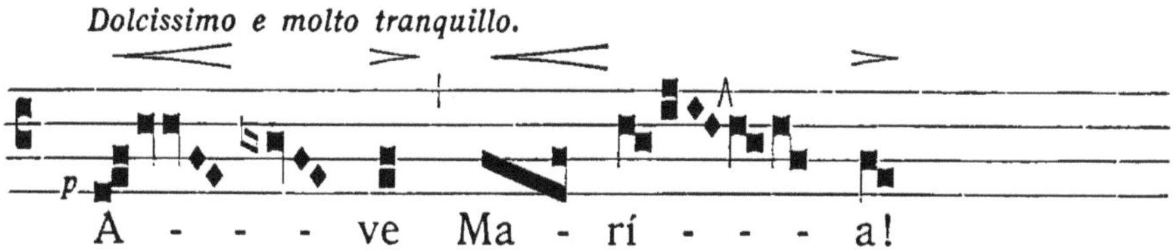

The *crescendo* here always soft and smooth, but expressive. The whole devoutly, tenderly, like children greeting their mother.

Then this *gratia plena!* The melody must have a vigorous motion, like rolling billows, as if the singer were contemplating the boundless ocean of grace in Mary's soul. How majestic, but yet how sweet and gentle, must it all be when we think of the grace bestowed on Mary! This passage is almost dreamy:

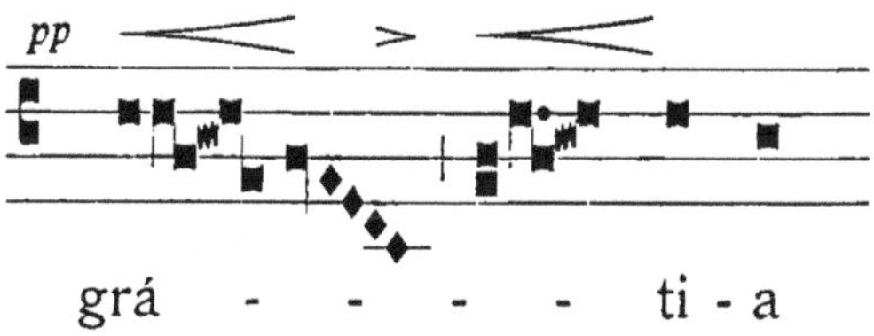

but at *plena* the melody bursts forth triumphantly:

Further on take care that *Dominus tecum* is sung *piano,* for these words must here be dealt with as a mystical allusion to Mary's dignity as Mother of God, already bestowed upon her in her Conception. Then comes the brilliant *benedicta tu!* Thou art the promised one, chosen from among all the daughters of Eve to be the mother of all the living, of all the children of God, to bear in thy chaste womb the Son of God, the Saviour of the world. Praised indeed be the hour of thy Conception, praised be thou thyself, O immaculate Queen!

223. The melodies to which we have referred are particularly well adapted for portraying grand and sublime ideas, but we must at least call attention to the no less striking tone-pictures in miniature, so simple and joyous, as we have them in the Introit *Hodie scietis* and *Quasi modo geniti infantes,* and many others.

Then we must not forget the splendid sequences for Easter, Pentecost and *Corpus Christi,* and many proses such as the melodious *Inviolata.* They all belong to the rich treasury of the Gregorian chant, and exhibit its capability of producing artistic forms, united with a wonderful power of expression.

224. A choirmaster should certainly not undervalue such studies as will enable him to ascertain the characteristics of the various melodies, otherwise he will never be able to grasp them in a satisfactory manner. If he does study them he will stimulate both himself and his choir. The practices, pleasantly interspersed with such explanations as may be necessary, will tire the singers less, help them to appreciate Gregorian art, and induce them to do their best to render the chants devotionally and with the proper expression.

Chapter XVI.

Mode of Rendering.

A. The Necessity for a good Rendering.

225. The *rendering* imparts to the music its *proper expression*; it is its life and soul, its reality; from it the melody receives its colouring, its light and shade, its warmth and movement.

The rendering is not the music as a matter of course. The object of it is to produce the true effect of the music. The rendering does not as a matter of course give the true import of the melody, but it can enhance it and make it more effective.

The rendering is often of more importance to the hearer than that which is performed. Thus also in every-day life we notice the tone of voice which a person uses when speaking to us more than the actual words — whether he wishes to be hearty or cool towards us, impressive, or reproachful. The tone of voice tells us in such cases more than the words; it gives us the individual; it reveals his disposition and intentions.

226. The *less prepared* the hearer is and the *less intelligent* he is, the more important is the rendering. And again, the more holy and sublime the object which the melody should have in view, the greater must be the singer's effort to attain this object by means of a satisfactory performance. Now the Gregorian chant in our churches is heard by persons in every rank of life and of varied intellectual capacity, and for all these it should be an interpreter of the liturgical offices, the liturgical prayer, in which they pour out their hearts and by which they are lifted up to God.

227. Further, the *higher the artistic value,* the artistic form, of the melody, the more must the singer endeavour by means of an intelligent rendering to convey to the hearer the impression desired by the composer.

Now Gregorian possesses rich treasures in the way of deeply impressive chants, which must be reckoned among the finest ever produced, wherein the Christian spirit of prayer reveals itself in such a convincing way that the heart, glowing with the love of God, finds in them the expression of its feelings when the spoken word no longer suffices.

228. Plain chant takes its *text* chiefly from the *Word of God* itself, which it discloses to the worshipper by means of its chaste melodies.

229. Finally, the *arch-enemy* of plain chant, and that which has long robbed it of its good name, is the bad mode of rendering. Precisely for this reason the above remarks are by no means unnecessary, for painful facts show that where plain chant is used faults frequently occur that would not be tolerated for a moment with any other music (shouting, singing anyhow, in a mechanical way, without the least expression, knocking things about noisily), even if they are not extolled as correct principles (taking descending passages too rapidly, defects in the phrasing and so on).

Hence, a good mode of rendering is decisive for the future of plain chant. It is only by satisfactory renderings that the restoration of the Gregorian chant can be completed.

B. Preliminaries.

I. Study Text and Melody.

230. a) The text is, as a rule, the best key to the comprehension of the melody.

Therefore it is desirable that the meaning of the text should be explained to those who do not understand Latin, sufficiently at all events to enable them to grasp the leading ideas and to give expression to them. But the meaning of the text is only made quite clear when considered in conjunction with the liturgy, the particular season or feast. Accordingly, for a perfect rendering of plain chant a thorough knowledge of the liturgy, at all events on the part of the choirmaster, is absolutely necessary.

In the first Mass on Christmas Day the *Alleluja* will not sound as it did when the same melody was sung on the 1st Sunday of Advent; it will make quite a different impression upon me.

The melody of the 4th antiphon on the feast of the Dedication of a church, *Bene fundata est,* will be sung more firmly with this text, I might almost say more massively, than on the feast of the Annunciation when the same melody was sung to the words *Ecce ancilla Domini,* spoken by the B. Virgin. Concerning this latter antiphon Gevaert says *(Mel.* p. 153): "The *cantilene,* which to the end need to be sung *piano,* express with charming *näiveté* the profound awe of the Blessed Virgin on receiving God's message."

On Holy Thursday the text of the Offertory runs: "The right hand of the Lord hath wrought strength, the right hand of the Lord hath exalted me: I shall not die but live, and shall declare the works of the Lord." The text of itself is easy to understand, but quite a new light is thrown upon it when one considers why it is used on Holy Thursday. On that day the *penitent sinners* were received into the Church again. With what feelings of joy and gratitude will they and their mother the Church say these words at the moment of their reunion! In the *mouth of Christ* the words refer to His mission as the Messias; Christ, the sign of contradiction, set by the justice of God for the salvation and for the fall of many, Christ, the chosen of God, appointed to be the Judge of the world, elevated to God's throne, is about to suffer death, whose portals He passes in power and majesty. Suffering and death are his victory; unending glory, his reward. Christ dies not, but wins in death eternal life for Himself and the whole world. Christ dies not, but continues to live in the holy Eucharist, fitting us all for the life wherein He is all in all, a personal hymn of glory for the mighty works of God.

On the feast of the Holy Innocents the Church calls to mind with the deepest sympathy the tears of the poor mothers of Bethlehem, and a soft echo of the cries of the little ones seems to pervade the melodies of the Introit and Tract, and particularly the melody of the *Communio (Vox in Rama)*, so full of woe. The Church however does not forget the glory of the youthful martyrs. Hence the joy, the jubilation, that resounds in the Gradual and Offertory.

231. b) *Next to the Text, diligently and carefully study the Melody;*

For the melody is also speech which not infrequently elucidates the text in an admirable manner, and makes the meaning thereof more apparent.

The singer having now received sufficient preliminary instruction in theory and practice (see "Preparatory School" and "Normal School") he may begin to practise new melodies, first studying their *structure* (cf. above, pp. 153 *seqq.)*, and endeavouring to understand thoroughly the *divisions* in general and the *relationship of the various parts to each other.* In this way he will lay the foundation for an intelligent mode of rendering. Then the *climaxes* of the melody are of importance. Where did the composer wish to place the most emphasis? Such passages must be prepared, effectively introduced, and sung with an increasing degree of force. They not infrequently receive their resolution in a *decrescendo.*

What the accent is for the syllables of a word, what the word is for the sentence, the climax is for the various rhythmical members, the various accents of the neums; each passage must be dealt with accordingly, whether increasing or decreasing in force. If this is not done the melody is broken up into small portions, meaning nothing.

This climax is found sometimes in the middle of a phrase, sometimes it is prepared by only a few accents. The ascending melody, occasionally a piling up of the *pressus,* the frequent repetition of the same neums (compare the 2nd verse in the Gradual *Specie tua,* at *mansuetudinem,* see p, 108), and other devices for an upward movement, usually allow it to be easily recognised. The more energetic the upward movement, and the bolder the melody, the more the *crescendo* must be made effective. If, on the other hand, the melody is simple, if its intervals move within narrow limits, take all the more care to avoid exaggeration or affectation.

The rise to the climax no more excludes a transient *decrescendo* than the diminution of the force after it is reached excludes a *crescendo* at some passages, only one must not lose sight of the tendency towards the climax.

232. When the foundations have been firmly laid the difficulty is over as regards the simple chants, and the singer will be in a position to sing them satisfactorily.

The elaborate melodies with their repetitions and imitations will however require to be studied. It is of importance that passages of this kind should be as closely connected as possible, and that unity should be preserved, so that the chant may be presented to the hearer as a *well-arranged whole.* A carefully delivered, smooth *crescendo* or *decrescendo* will be constantly required.

Repetitions more especially must never be given in quite a uniform style; moreover, they should seldom be treated as mere echo effects, as they often lead to a climax.

If anywhere, good taste and refined feeling are here all in all, theory and rules of no account. One person may view a melody in this way, another in another way, and thus the expression will vary accordingly. A slight difference of opinion often has a considerable effect on the dynamical treatment. In general, with due regard to the object of plain chant, "too much" is decidedly worse than "too little", though, as a matter of fact, more toning down of the melody would generally be desirable. It is by no means impossible to sing plain chant without any variation as to *tempo* and degree of force. But the more one desires to produce with it a really musical and artistic effect, the more necessary it is to increase and decrease the force of the tone in a suitable manner. Many passages without this are almost unintelligible. Compare the passage for *in conspectu* in the Offertory for the 22nd Sunday after Pentecost.

As a matter of course, dynamics in general are of more importance for solo melodies than for chants sung by a large choir or by the people.

233. Now let us try with the aid of some examples to show how plain chant melody of itself presses for dynamical treatment.

The first *Kyrie* in Mass III. is characterised by the motives, *podatus* + *climacus* (twice); whereupon another motive answers with *clivis* + *climacus:*

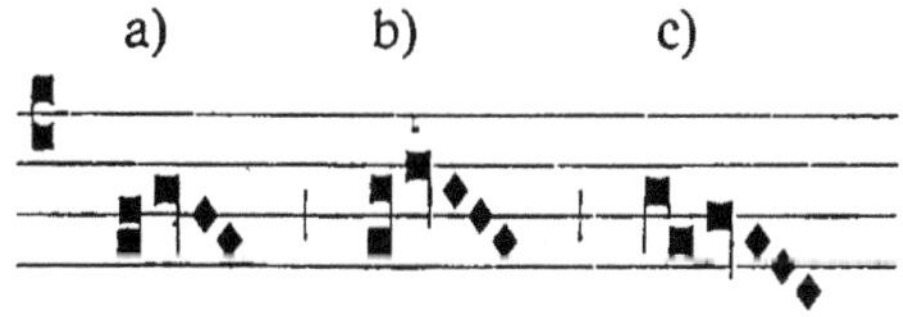

Here b) is doubtless an ascent from a), and c) the resolution. But the motives show increase and decrease of the tone:

This decreasing of the tone is of course only possible in slow time and must always be moderate.

On the syllable *ri (Kyrie)* and on the word *eleison* there is an emphasis which makes the whole passage impressive. Here the *tempo,* to suit the character of this melody, can only be *sostenuto quasi lento.* The *Kyrie* after the *Christe* requires a marked acceleration of the *tempo.*

We will therefore sing it something like this:

Begin softly, expressing your feelings as a humble petitioner, but full of confidence; slightly accelerate at *eleison,* then accentuate well, finally letting the last tone die away *pianissimo.*

In the *Christe* rather more force on the two *pressus:*

Here again the same moderate movement, and in rising to the second *pressus* (from *g* to *c)* do not hurry.

The third *Kyrie* with more animation. The melody is here further developed, but soon returns to its previous manner, an effective plan with a repeated supplication:

All must be made more impressive in this final repetition, which receives good points of support in the *pressus.* The repetition should perhaps be started rather more softly. After the * * accelerate the *tempo,* and increase the strength of the tone; take *eleison* energetically, letting the final syllable die away gently.

This *Kyrie* is a model of a prayer of supplication clothed in melody. The singer *prays;* he is not yet tranquilised; he seeks something that he does not yet possess; his soul hungers and thirsts for it. And yet a peace of the soul that cannot be disturbed seems to pervade this melody, a consciousness that the supplication will not be in vain, that he is speaking to a loving Father; that he has had the happiness of raising his eyes and heart to God.

II. Pray whilst you sing.

234. *a)* That which the composers of plain chant felt when praying and contemplating the truths of our holy faith, they expressed in their chants. Prayer is therefore the key to their comprehension.

b) The preface says: "With the angels and archangels, with the thrones and dominations, and with all the troop of the heavenly army, we sing a hymn to Thy glory". What a sublime prototype of devotion and unanimous joy *(socia exsultatione)* for our song, what an incentive to sing the praises of God, if not with angelic voices, yet so far as possible with angelically pure hearts!

c) Plain chant undoubtedly serves in the first place to glorify God. But God, who knows the thoughts of our hearts, can take no pleasure in mere lip-service.

d) In the second place, it serves to edify the people. Only what comes from the heart speaks to the heart, and only what is inspired and ennobled by the spirit of prayer can awaken devotion and promote edification. Therefore pray whilst you sing.

235. Opposed to the prayerful character of plain chant is:

α) Straining after Effect. Do not show off the short and less important passages in a noticeable, affected way, thereby losing the general effect; not all double notes are to be sung with <, nor all the accentuated notes with >; after a *f* or even a *ff* do not sing *p* unexpectedly; when the *tempo* is lively do not all at once begin a sentimental *largo,* and so on.

β) A dull, heavy Style of Execution. This is made worse when there are too many minor chords in the accompaniment. *Joy* is the fundamental characteristic of the *liturgical prayer;* hence in the *liturgical chant* bright, pleasant effects![1])

C. Means in Detail.

236. *The Choice of the Tempo* is *of the utmost Importance.*

"If you wish to summarise everything on which the satisfactory production of a piece of music depends as regards the director, you may say truly that it lies in this, that he must always give the right *tempo;* for the choice thereof tells us at once whether he has understood the composition or not."[2])

What influences the Choice of the Tempo?

1) The character of the melody, the text and the feast;

2) The number of singers;

3) The character of their voices;

4) The acoustics of the church.

---

1) Cf. Dr. Sauter: *Der liturgische Choral,* pp. 58 *seqq.*

2) Richard Wagner: *Ges. Ausgabe* (Leipzig, Fritsch, 1873 *seqq.)* Vol. 8, p. 341.

In general, Gradual, *Alleluja* and Tract require a lively *tempo*, whilst the Introit must be more solemn, the Offertory tranquil, the *Communio* sometimes animated, sometimes less so.

The *Alleluja* with its *Neuma* requires a firm, fluent movement. Press on here, especially at the repetition and *Neuma*, accelerating the *tempo*. It should be a jubilant exclamation. The verse should be started, as a rule, rather more quietly.

In starting the verse in the Gradual the *tempo* should almost always be slightly accelerated.

The *antiphons* are often made more solemn by singing them rather slowly. But do not drawl. Even when *ppp* and when singing slowly the melody must always flow along lightly and briskly. Many like to sing the *Magnificat*-antiphon slower, but even here it is best to make the *tempo* dependent upon the above mentioned circumstances. (1—4).

At processions the *tempo* must be considerably slower, for it may be that only short melodies with pauses have to be sung. The pauses at these processions should be more frequent.

For ordinary purposes the metronome rate should be ♪ (▪ ▪ ♦) = M. M. 120 to 140; for psalms 130—150 will not be too high a rate.

What Franz Kullack[1]) said, though exaggerating considerably, in regard to musical productions applies also to plain chant generally: "Ten degrees too quick is better than irritating everyone by being too slow."

237. So soon as the melody develops into *antiphonal chant* a rather accelerated *tempo* is in place.

---

1) *Der Vortrag in der Musik am Ende des 19. Jahrhunderts.* (Leipzig, Leuckart, 1898) p. 27.

The antiphonal choir should give more *life* and *action*. Hence the entry of the voices must be precise, brisk, energetic, each choir answering the other promptly. It must be like throwing a ball from one side to the other. That by no means prevents a slackening of the *tempo* at the right place. But this *più moderato* must not degenerate into a drawl.

The same applies to the responsorial chants, especially if the verse is sung by a cantor, and more so to the Tract, and to *Benedictus es* (Ember Saturday, Pentecost), and, above all, to the *Gloria* and *Credo* of the Mass. Here the movement must be brisk, becoming quicker towards the end.

At the *Gloria* of the Mass two choirs can sing the sentences in turn, or the following plan can be adopted:

Introduction: Full choir: Et in terra pax hominibus bonæ voluntatis.

Antiphonally:

1st Half-choir (or upper voices):
Laudamus te.
2nd " " Benedicimus te.
1st " " Adoramus te.
2nd " " Glorificamus te.

Full choir: Gratias agimus tibi propter magnam gloriam tuam.

Middle part: (tempo mostly slower):

2nd Half-choir: Domine Deus, rex cœlestis, Deus Pater omnipotens.
1st " " Domine Fili unigenite, Jesu Christe.
2nd " " Domine Deus, Agnus Dei, Filius Patris.
1st " " Qui tollis peccata mundi, miserere nobis.
2nd " " Qui tollis peccata mundi, suscipe deprecationem nostram.

Full choir: Qui sedes ad dexteram Patris, miserere nobis.

Close (tempo primo, poco a poco più mosso):

1st Half-choir: Quoniam tu solus sanctus.
2nd „ „ Tu solus Dominus.
1st „ „ Tu solus Altissimus, Jesu Christe.
2nd „ „ Cum Sancto Spiritu.
Full choir: In gloria Dei Patris. Amen.

Distributed in this way more variety in the colouring and force of the tone is obtained. The full choir falls in and with its volume of sound closes the three parts in a marked and emphatic manner. For the half-choirs lighter movement, prompt entry; in the first and second parts the repetitions *qui tollis* and *tu solus* very impressively; the same as regards *Adoramus, Benedicimus, Glorificamus,* until the full choir breaks in with its jubilant *Gratias agimus Tibi propter magnam gloriam tuam.* In contrast to this the middle part should be rather slower. Think how the leader of the heavenly choir approaches the Blessed Trinity, prostrates himself and begins: *Domine, Pater omnipotens;* how in the same way another comes forward with a profound obeisance and addresses God the Son: *Domine Fili,* etc. Press on at the last part, make it imposing, keeping back the *ritardando* to the very last so that instead of dying away it may sound full and majestic to the end.

238. For the *opening phrases* a *definite p* or *pp* (therefore without any hesitation or delay) is desirable, and this for the commencement of the intonation proper as well as for the continuation by the choir. At all events a hard, vehement attack of the tones is not beautiful and makes any increase in the force difficult if not impossible.

The *first note of all* should be rather sustained. This is an old rule founded on the necessity of indicating to those in church the commencement of the singing, and also with a view to start with a good tone of voice, to make a basis on the sustained tone.

A *hurried*, unsteady intonation spoils the whole phrase. Therefore it is very necessary not to be flurried or impatient. The cantor does well to allow the organ-note to have its full effect on the ear, so that he may get the pitch exactly (which is of the utmost importance in rapid modulation), find himself at home in the new melodic position, and sing perfectly in tune.

239. *After the intonation* the choir must start at once in the *full tempo.* From the very first there must be a clear understanding as regards the *tempo.* It does not do to try and get it afterwards in the course of the piece by increasing or decreasing the rate of movement. Therefore practise until the choir has acquired the *feeling for the right tempo for a melody,* and only sings it in the right *tempo, and this from the first to the last note.* This is all the more important for the choir as here the momentary influence of the choirmaster is with difficulty exercised, and consequently the inspiration that in polyphonic music unites all the elements together is wanting, if not entirely, at least to a great extent.

Moreover, when the cantor has finished his intonation with a slight *ritardando* the choir after a very short pause should start off at the full rate of movement, but quietly and with moderation.

Drawling at the beginning always makes a bad impression and often effects the very reverse of that which is desired. Instead of leading up to a climax it is a hindrance, a burden, crippling the movement just when it needs an impulse.

Hence at the *Gradual* and *Alleluja* it is better to let the cantor sing the *Neuma* in full *tempo* rather than allow the choir to drawl it.

240. *Pauses* in the course of the melody are to be avoided as much as possible. Each pause must have its justification either in the construction of the melody (division) or in the real need of the singer.

When there is a pause, it must be made with precision, and be maintained for the proper time, and the voices must then instantly start again, all together. Only in this way can it have a supporting and strengthening effect on the movement.

If more pauses are necessary than are denoted in the choral books, it is as well to mark them with a pencil. This helps to keep the voices together and is useful at the practices and for subsequent renderings in church.

241. Moreover it is very desirable to put in *marks of expression*. If this is not done it is difficult to ensure a uniform mode of rendering, and singers who do not know Latin can otherwise scarcely attain to an intelligent rendering.

At the beginning of the piece the character of the movement may be indicated: devotionally, delicately, briskly, energetically, with vivacity, or *largo, mosso, con moto,* etc.; then in the course of it the degree of force, *p, mf, f, cresc., decresc.,* or *accelerando* and *ritardando,* to indicate the rhythm more precisely; at many passages *espressivo,* and so forth.

It is by no means "modernising plain chant" to apply to it a system adopted as a matter of course for all other musical performances, and the disuse of which in their case would be blamed. If the preacher in the pulpit must take pains to acquire a good and *impressive* delivery, no less so the singer in choir. Marks of expression help this. Only they must not be too numerous. Colour, but nothing coloured, and always be true.

242. A *crescendo* or *decrescendo* constantly lasts throughout a rather long phrase, and this means a development or resolution. Here the movement should be beautifully even and well balanced.

Moreover, *short groups* not unfrequently need *light and shade.*

Thus with the *quilisma* a *crescendo,* introduced according to circumstances with *pp, p* or *mf,* comes naturally.

In the same way formulæ such as  produce a good effect with a moderate *crescendo* and *decrescendo.*

Ascending passages which end as above in a *pressus* require a stronger *crescendo:*

Kyrie from Mass XIV. *Alleluja-Neuma,* 2nd Sunday of Adv.

In passages like 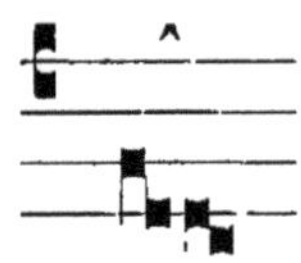 the first note must not be made too short. Here it is better for an idea to be too long than too short.

Sometimes wide intervals (fourth, fifth) must be sung slower in order to get the proper effect. But the *ritardando* must not be extended too far, and owing to it the *tempo* for the whole of the following phrase must not be dragged. Passages like the intonations of the Introits *Gaudeamus, Justus* (17th Sunday after Pentecost), or like the *Christe* of Mass XI., and *Rex cœlestis, Qui sedes, Tu solus Altissimus Jesu Christe* in the *Gloria* of Mass IX. and the *Christe* in *Kyrie* I. ad libitum, *Domine Deus, Qui sedes* and *Cum Sancto Spiritu* of the Easter Mass, the second *Sanctus* of Mass II., the wide intervals in the *Gloria* of the same Mass and in *Dies iræ,* and similar passages, are to be practised till the choir can sing them without difficulty and fluently.

243. Of immense importance for a satisfactory rendering is the *legato*. This is often spoilt owing to the tone over the vowels being cut off and the consonants held (sung) too long. The consonants must be as short as possible (Nr. 29, pp. 19 *seq.)*. Words like *semper intende,* etc., easily cause the fault just mentioned.

244 If in the more elaborate *chants* syllabic passages occur, it is necessary to get the right balance as regards movement and volume of sound.

245. Do not introduce the *formation of a close* too soon, in order that half of the phrase or thereabouts may not appear to be a close. Therefore maintain the *tempo* (or increase it) until the closing cadence really begins.

246. The final note of a neum may often serve as a preparation or transition tone to the following note or as an up-beat, for this binds the groups more closely together and facilitates and enlivens the execution:

Here care must be taken that

a) The accent is *not* displaced, but kept in its usual position, and that

b) The final note which is drawn to the following group retains its full time-value and is not shortened.

It would be wrong therefore to sing example 1 like this:

247. When studying plain chant it is quite right to pay attention to details. But in *rendering the chants in church* it is the *"tout ensemble" that is decisive, the melody as a whole.* Therefore each melody must be grasped and rendered as a whole. This cannot be too often insisted upon. If it be otherwise we offer the hearer mere scraps; we place a puzzle before him which he has neither time nor inclination to solve in church.

248. Always choose a *suitable pitch.* For Vespers the common dominant for psalms and antiphons should be *a* or *b* ♭, on higher feasts *b* ♮. For the other chants the plan of giving the same pitch for each piece in a certain mode (e. g., for all Introit melodies in Mode I., *d,* for all Graduals in Mode V. *f)* is *not to be commended.* The pitch should be determined according to the *range* of each piece ($\overline{e}$ occurring once or twice can easily be managed by most choirs); according to the position of the climaxes, which generally require a good volume of sound; according to the character of the piece; according to the condition of the singers (take into consideration whether they have been singing a good deal); according to the acoustics of the church; according to the character of the feast (the Introit *Spiritus Domini* with the fundamental tone *f* would not sound particularly solemn on Whitsunday) and so forth.

It is best to sing the chants in the *Ordinarium Missæ* always at the same pitch, by which means flattening is often prevented. When two chants follow each other immediately (e. g., *Introit* and *Kyrie)*, they must of course be harmoniously connected.

The rule according to which plain chant notes are of themselves of *equal value*, has naturally no influence on the *tempo* and its increase and decrease.

Chapter XVII.

Organ Accompaniment.

249. *What advantages are derived from an accompaniment for plain chant?* Answer: A good organ accompaniment has the following advantages:

a) It can support the voices, make the singing more uniform, conceal many faults (singing flat or too sharp), modify others (coarseness, voices out of tune), not forgetting that the organist can greatly facilitate the intonation of the chants.

b) It can help singers and hearers to appreciate plain chant melody. It can enhance the artistic effect provided that the harmony selected is in keeping with the spirit of the chant, that the organ is not played too loud for the singers, and that the whole accompaniment is kept in subordination to the chant.

On the other hand, an obtrusive, noisy, heavy organ accompaniment is a very great hindrance, for it drowns the voices and induces shouting; it prevents the voices from moving freely, obscures the rhythmic and melodic tone-picture, disfigures the melody and deprives it of its expression.

250. A *written* or *printed* organ accompaniment is a makeshift, but in most cases a necessary makeshift.

A printed accompaniment is a makeshift inasmuch as it can only take into consideration circumstances such as ordinarily prevail in choirs, therefore a moderate number of singers and moderate capabilities, whilst almost on every occasion other circumstances arise — it may be that the singers are not in such good form as usual, or less numerous, or they may dislike this or that chant; they may be inclined to flatten, to hurry or to drawl; or perhaps the pitch must be altered owing to climatic and other influences, or on account of the feast, or the *Ordinarium Missæ*, or the harmonised Mass that may be selected.

251. A *free accompaniment* straight away from the unison melody enables the organist to help the choir in passages where help is needed, and at the same time to remain in the background when such help is not needed. Moreover, more attention can then be paid to the acoustics of the building, and to the character and degree of loudness of the stops. All this is even of more importance when the organist has to accompany only *one or two singers*. Very little experience is required to convince anyone that each singer has his peculiarities, certain ways; some feel exertion more than others; some can sing better when the notes are in a certain position; others produce in one register a full, mellow tone, and in another a poor quality of tone, or in many passages their voices are flat or too sharp. Such peculiarities, though by no means advantageous, must nevertheless be taken into consideration, and can be more effectively dealt with by means of a free accompaniment, as it enables one to vary the position of the chords (soprano or tenor position) and to employ unison, harmony in two, three, four or more parts, close or extended position, *crescendo* or *decrescendo* (swell-organ). In addition to this, if the organist accompanies from the Gregorian notes he has, like the singers, a graphic picture of the melody before him. The accompanist ought not to undervalue this point.

He knows also that the simple melody facilitates transposition and helps him to keep his choir well in hand.

In view of such advantages it is hardly worth remarking that a not particularly suitable chord is selected, or one causing hidden consecutive fifths or octaves, as will happen now and then to the most experienced organist. A skilful player will know how to conceal little frailties of this kind and not reproach himself or anyone else for committing them.

However, in *by far the most cases* a carefully arranged organ accompaniment is not only to be recommended, but an absolute *necessity*.

This is but too true. A good organ accompaniment, improvised, presupposes many things, facility in harmonising, thorough appreciation of the melody, a rapid glance at the phrases, good taste, skill as regards execution and transposition. The traditional melodies require as a rule a lively *tempo*, and sometimes present problems that require a good deal of thought on the part of very experienced musicians.

252. *Conditions necessary for a good Organ Accompaniment:*

I. Choice of the harmony.

II. Necessary attention to the rhythmic progression of the melody.

III. Discreet execution.

253. I. As regards the *harmony* it is desirable that it should be:

a) Strictly diatonic.

Nevertheless a ♯ or a ♭ foreign to the scale is not such a great misfortune, but the general effect is purer, more chaste, when only diatonic harmony is employed. Moreover, it amply suffices. If modulation is admitted, the harmony in such rare cases must make the change according to the modal system.

b) In general, the *triad* suffices with its *inversions.*

The use of the *major seventh* may unhesitatingly be allowed, for very beautiful effects can be obtained with it.

The *minor seventh* should seldom be used with the major triad; in particular avoid anything sentimental. In the middle parts it will scarcely have a disturbing effect; in the soprano, however, it is seldom satisfactory.

In certain circumstances the minor seventh may be used over the diminished triad, even in the soprano:

c) It is not at all necessary for the plain chant accompaniment to be in the strict style of composition, still less in the style of the polyphonists of the 16th century (Palestrina style).

On the contrary, the organist may make use of all such liberties as are in accordance with the spirit of the melody, or are not opposed to it, and which produce a good musical effect. Here cultivated musical taste, or we may simply say, artistic taste, is decisive. In selecting his chords a professional musician will apply his subjective feeling, and in doing so will allow himself many liberties and things out of the common, yet always remain artistic. His accompaniment will then form with the melody a whole with which it ever coincides, or rather, from which it receives its inspiration.

Here is the border-land between school and art. Those who have not the talent must be content to conform to rule, allowing others to have their freedom, their inspiration, their art.

d) Among the usual liberties allowed in a plain chant accompaniment we include the resolution of the major seventh upwards, and the unprepared entry (by a skip) of the major seventh or of the chord of the 6th and 4th, and the like.

e) If the melody begins with the tonic the harmony can commence with the chord of the tonic. There are however not sufficient reasons for insisting upon this as a general rule. On the contrary, another chord may answer the purpose equally well, and perhaps better. Neither is it necessary that half-closes on the tonic should always take the chord of the tonic. But the close of a period requires a corresponding point of rest in the harmony, and the commencement of new melodic members a noticeable change of harmony when possible.

The harmony must *always accompany;* therefore when the melody pauses, progresses, presses onward or lingers, the harmony must do the same.

f) In general, *bright, clear, pleasing harmonies* are preferable. The radiant sunniness of the melody should be reflected in the harmony.

The Gregorian melody is free, and therefore it cannot tolerate a dry, learned accompaniment. The melody is a song expressing deep feelings, and the accompaniment should do justice to it. Only a thorough connoisseur of Gregorian melody, a man of refined taste, and at the same time a skilful harmonist, can produce a perfect plain chant accompaniment.

254. II. The *rhythmic progression* of the melody is another matter of great importance, especially as regards the manner in which the *harmonies are connected or changed.*

Concerning this Dr. Mathias says:[1]) "In plain chant accompaniment the chord should not be changed on lightly sustained tones of the melody." That is perfectly right, generally speaking, and for ordinary cases cannot be too much insisted upon. Nevertheless, a great deal depends upon circumstances, for instance, whether the organist is obliged to lead or support the voices, and with what stops, and in what degree of loudness *(f* or *mf, p, pp, ppp)* the accompaniment is being played; whether the change occurs as the resolution of a point of rest in the harmony, or only as a transition, and, lastly, in what *tempo* and in what degree of loudness the chant is being rendered. Further, it is not immaterial whether the new chord for the succeeding notes of the melody is tied or not.

In the following examples

the rhythmic progression of the melody at a) is in no way hindered by the harmony, whilst at b) the change of chord severs the neums and alters their rhythm.

1) *Die Choralbegleitung* (Regensburg, F. Pustet, 1905) pp. 37 *seq.*

255. The influence which a change of chords exercises on a light and effective accentuation of the melody is naturally a very different matter, in proportion as this change is more or less marked. Let us hear what Dr. Mathias says concerning this, in his *brochure* above referred to (pp. 39 *seq.*):

"1. The slightest change in the harmony, as also the weakest harmonic accentuation and pressure, ought to be effected by the motion of a *middle part within the chord that has been already struck.*

2. A stronger accent and a greater pressure means the motion of *more of the middle parts* within the limits indicated, or a *skip of an octave* in the bass.

3. More plastic is the effect of the *progression of the bass* within one and the same harmony (apart from the skip of an octave already mentioned), as in this way the chord concerned is "lifted off its hinges", and receives a new significance.

4. A distinct *departure* from the preceding harmony means a greater change, in the first place merely in the *middle parts.*

5. Then in the bass, and this *as far as possible by a stepwise progression* to a closely related harmony, namely to that of the dominant, subdominant or of the three parallel keys.

6. The change in the harmony is much more considerable when *all the parts* move at the *same time;*

7. And when they move *by skips* it is always more marked.

8. But the accentuating effect is greatly *increased* by the immediate succession of *less closely related chords.*

9. If the changes in the harmony referred to in Nos 7 and 8 are viewed as decidedly emphatic and "heavy" then the effect of dissonances must be described in general as "harsh" and "piercing" (suspensions, anticipations). This however only holds good in cases where the dissonating tone is in the upper part, therefore in the plain chant melody, or in the bass. In the middle parts the suspension at least blunts or dipserses the effect of the change instead of emphasising it, since the suspension in this case brings about a closer connection between the preceding and succeeding harmony, allowing the change to take place gradually and spreading it over a wider area. The dissonance in the upper part is "harsh" because it produces its effect in a very obtrusive manner."

If however the accompaniment to the chorus or to a solo is *pp, ppp,* then the effect of the dissonant tones, even in an outer part, is different. They not infrequently impart a kind of mysteriousness or dreaminess to the melody.

256. Dr. Mathias's remarks in his work above mentioned concerning the change of harmony with reference to the rhythmic progression of the melody are summarised in the following paragraphs:

1. The *change of harmony* should as a rule only be made on the *first* notes of the groups of two or three notes, and should occur on the *sustained* tones of the melody. Yet as regards groups of three members the three notes can be provided with light harmonies, especially if they are accentuated or bear new syllables.

2. The *difference in the melodic points of support* may whenever possible be indicated by *suitable changes* in the harmony, *heavy or light.*

3. *Suitable harmonic forms* should be employed for the *various melodic figures.*

4. The *organic connection* of the melodic figures can be made evident by suitable *progressions of the parts* in the accompaniment, particularly as regards the *bass.*

5. The melodic *divisions* must be reflected in suitable harmonic cadences.

257. It is not only in accordance with the usual custom, but it is most desirable in view of the characteristics of the Gregorian chant, when the accompaniment simply follows the melody and therefore never appears as complete in itself. Now and then this may be all very well, particularly when accompanying a few voices singing low notes. More caution however is necessary if the organ overtops the melody. But here too *a priori* one can scarcely define with anything like precision what is beautiful, what suits the character of the melody, or what is opposed to it.

258. Concerning the *execution* of the accompaniment there is in reality little to say beyond what is, properly speaking, a matter of course.

The accompaniment ought so far as possible to subordinate itself to the chant, unless the organist is obliged to lead the choir. When the singers pause the organist must do the same; he must not be in advance of them; still less should he invariably give out the intonation. That can be tolerated in extreme cases but can never be recommended as desirable. It savours too much of the whipping-up process. At pauses the organ can entirely cease, or a note can be sustained, or the chord can be held down in the lower octave *p*, etc. As regards registration, soft stops (not too keenly toned) are to be recommended. Solo and choir should be accompanied in the middle position or in the lower octave, as required in each case, and as may best suit the *timbre* of the voices. With the *Ordinarium Missæ* and the psalms a pleasant change is made in this way. If you are playing in the tenor octave a soft 4-feet stop sometimes produces a very good effect (for solo, *ppp*). Use the swell-organ discreetly, the pedal for choral effects, but without stops that make the touch heavy; for solo a 16-feet *pp* stop may be coupled from the manual to the pedal. The *harmony* for the chorus should as a rule be in four parts.

A skilful organist will, however, vary his accompaniment both for solo and chorus, sometimes holding out a note and sometimes employing 2, 3 or 5 part harmonies. No hard and fast rules can be given for this. Here all depends upon art, good taste, and readiness in grasping what is needed for the moment.

If the choir is inclined to *flatten*, a slight strengthening of the bass is generally better than a sharp 4-feet stop in the manual. The advantage of this is that it produces the effect quietly. Only in case of need draw the 4-feet stop on the manual. If the choir is fatigued or not disposed to sing, the intonation should be, say, a minor or major second higher. This will be better than an intonation on a lower note. Many singers raise the tone from habit, perhaps as the result of excitement or of overstraining themselves, or it may be from inability to manage the voice, or from a defective ear. In such cases endeavour, but of course very discreetly, to draw the singer's attention to the fault, but meanwhile do not let the organ lag behind! Rather than do so it is better to omit the soprano part from the accompaniment altogether, and at pauses to hold out quite softly the lower parts only. Then give the singer the note just a little beforehand so that he may start in tune. If all this has no effect it is best for the organ to be silent.

If the choir drags, the closing chords should be quickly cut off, or there should be more movement in the pedal, or such harmonies should be used as will tend to rouse the singers.

Harmonies like this:

will urge them on. A slight *staccato* in the bass will be of still further assistance in this direction.

A sudden *change of pitch* makes it difficult to intone properly and is often the cause of flattening. For example, if the priest sings *Oremus* before the Offertory on *a* the organist must not immediately begin the Offertory (e. g., *In virtute, e♭-f-a♭*) on *a*♭; a short cadence is necessary so that the singers may at once feel at home in the new position.

259. *Preludes, interludes, and postludes* should be in proper relation to the plain chant melody. It is therefore important that they should have characteristics in common. Where this fails all contrapuntal devices and the well-meant efforts of the strict purist can only be disturbing or tedious. The organist to whom God has given the talent for developing Gregorian motives in an interesting and artistic manner, will, of course, most closely approach the ideal. But the motive must not be so altered that no one is able to detect the Gregorian melody therein. In the ancient chants there is no lack of interesting melodic and rhythmic themes. The organist who understands his art and appreciates plain chant will without any difficulty be able to select something suitable. A motive is not the whole of the melody, and still less can this be said of the initial notes; consequently a prelude on a plain chant motive is by no means always a prelude to the particular melody.

Why during the priest's Communion should a postlude on the *miserere* or *dona nobis* from the *Agnus Dei* not be so desirable as a prelude to the *Postcommunio,* since in view of what is going on at the altar motives from the *Agnus Dei* are generally more appropriate? — A modulation following immediately after the chant, unless introduced in a very skilful and unostentatious manner, is always rather too pronounced. If time allows, it is best to remain, for a few moments at least, in the mode of the preceding melody.

260. *Bistropha* and *tristropha* are often treated more successfully with the third and fifth. In this way the notes are supported and carried on more easily. In other cases, it is true, one is almost compelled to take the octave.

Passages like this 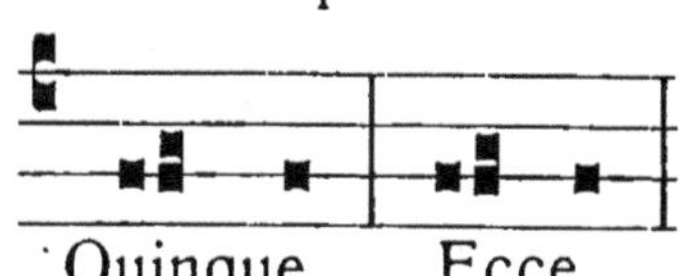

are generally harmonised thus:

But perhaps the reader prefers the following harmony:

Similarly the following passages:

or

The examples which we shall now give by no means lay claim to have hit upon everything that is possible or right as regards choice of harmony and marks of expression. A different conception of the melody must naturally result in a different choice of harmony.

Introitus "Lætare".

Fourth Sunday in Lent.

Joyously, and with animation and energy.

quasi piano
cum læ-tí - ti - a, qui in tri-stí - ti-
rit.
- - a fu - - í - - stis:
f p
ut ex-sul-té - tis, et sa-ti-é -
f
- mi - - ni ab u - bé - ri-bus

*)
con - so - la - ti - ó - nis ve-
rit.
- - stræ.
*) or
con-so - la - ti - ó - nis
ve - stræ.
rit.

Offertorium "Assumpta".

The Assumption.

Very devoutly and quietly.

quietly
dán - - - - tes be-ne-dí-
molto cresc.
- - - - cunt Dó - -
f
- - - mi-num, al - le - -
rit.
- - - lú - ja.
ppp

Communio "Quod dico vobis".

From the Mass *Salus* (3rd Com. plur. Mart.)

Graduale "Propter veritatem".

The Assumption.

V. Choir. *Molto sostenuto.*

pp
mf a tempo.
et de - dú - cet te mi-
mf
- ra - bí - li - ter déx - -
f.
p rit. pp
- - te - ra tu - a.

Solo.
dolcissimo.
pp
Au-di fí - - - - - - - - - - - - - li - a, et vi - de, et
ppp
cresc. molto.
poco rit.
mf
pp
vivo.
f
mf
a tempo

in - clí - na au - rem tu - am:
mf
qui - a con - cu - pí-
vit Rex spé - -

ci - em tu - am.
morendo
pp
morendo
Choir. Allegro energico.
f
Al - le - lú - - ja a -

Solo più tranquillo
p
As - súm - pta est
p
Ma - rí - a in cœ-

pp
mf
f
lum: gau - - - det ex - ér-
- ci - - tus An - ge - ló -
- - - - rum.

Here, however, hints and suggestions encroach so much upon what is purely a personal matter, that a

---

1) *Note.* The choir begins solemnly and slowly, in a soft rather suppressed tone of voice. The accompaniment never so loud as the singing and in exact agreement with the melodic movement. The *Alleluja* with great energy, brilliantly. *Assumpta,* again quietly at first; later on develop brilliantly. — The bars help one to get a general idea of the chant and they show the most important points of rest (immediately after the bar). Groups of three notes should not be played as triplets, but must be viewed as three quavers. If the accompaniment is played on a piano the pedal must be judiciously used. — Notice the striking imitation at the end of the first example on the third syllable of *consolationis* (p. 215)   with the resolution  A similar passage in the Offertory *Assumpta* (p. 217) on *Dominum* 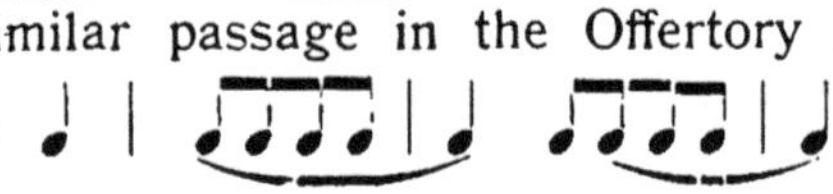 and on the second syllable of the *Alleluia*  More free, but on that account not less interesting, are the imitations in the Gradual *Propter veritatem,* e. g., at *Rex*   and at *tuam*  and 

"School" cannot venture to do more than just indicate. Personal views and personal preferences in regard to plain chant are justifiable and necessary, and may lighten the task. In truth, what organist or singer who takes a personal interest in plain chant will always have quite the same ideas? We conclude our "School" with this thought:

There are many things to learn that cannot be taught by a "School", for

Art is boundless — and
Of its study there is no end.

Appendix I.

A Short History of Gregorian Chant.

261. Church music is as old as the Church, and the choral chant, as regards some of its melodies, undoubtedly originated in the first centuries of the Christian era.[1]) As to the influence of Hebrew and Greek music very little information of a reliable nature has been obtained. The liturgical chant is called *par excellence* "Gregorian Chant" because, according to tradition, Pope St. Gregory the Great (590—604) collected into one uniform whole the various chants of the liturgy (e. g., Introit, Gradual, etc.), and arranged and codified them on a definite plan.

The Roman church possessed chants systematically arranged *before* the time of St. Gregory the Great. A Frankish monk[2]) mentions in the 8th century Popes St. Damasus, St. Leo, St. Gelasius, St. Symmacus, St. John I. and Boniface II., as having laboured on behalf of the chant. Moreover, St. Ambrose (397) is known as the "Father of ecclesiastical music", and the Milanese chant is called after his name "Ambrosian".[3]) How far this chant (see below p. 239) can be traced to St. Ambrose has not been determined, and in view of the fact that there are no MSS. bearing on the subject of an earlier date than the 11th century, it cannot be determined. According to Kienle *(Choralschule,* p. 126)[4]) it is "based on the same principles as Gregorian; we find the same musical system, the same modes, the melodies are built up with the same little figures, and there is the same freedom as regards rhythm. Both elaborate and simple melodies are employed, but the elaborate ones are often more elaborate, and the simple ones still simpler, than the Gregorian. The theory of form is the same, but the character is appreciably different."

---

1) Cf. Leitner: *Der gottesdienstliche Volksgesang im jüdischen und christlichen Altertum* (Freiburg, Herder, 1906).

2) Migne: *Patrologia Latina* (Paris), 138, 1347.

3) *Ambrosiana, Scritti varii* (Milano, Cogliati, 1897): IX. Mocquereau, *Chant ambrosien.* See also above, p. 4.

4) French edition: *Théorie et pratique du chant grégorien* (Tournai, Desclée).

It is certain that *antiphonal* chant[1]) was in use at Milan through the influence of St. Ambrose, as also the singing of *hymns.*[2]) Whether the melodies of the hymns of St. Ambrose (about 18) were also composed by him, or whether before his time they existed as folk-songs cannot with certainty be ascertained.

262. a) What Evidence have we in Proof of St. Gregory's Work of Organisation in Connection with the Chant of the Church?[3])

I. α) *Egbert,* Bishop of York (732—766) writes in his *D*ialogue *De institutione catholica*: "We . . . observe the fasts as our teacher and master, blessed Gregory, ordained in *his Antiphonarium* and *Missale* which he sent to us by our teacher, blessed Augustine." (Migne, *Patrologia Latina,* 89, 441).

But what proof is this of St. Gregory's *musical* labours?

β) The second Council of Cloveshoe[4]) (747) ordains that the "feast days of the Lord shall as regards baptism, masses and *chant (in cantilenæ modo)* . . . . be performed according to the book serving as a pattern which we received from the *R*oman Church."

According to this the above mentioned *Antiphonarium* certainly contained the chant in some kind of notation, and therefore St. Gregory transplanted to England a definite system for liturgical chant, and must in consequence have been in possession of it himself.

γ) *Acca,* Bishop of Hexham (740) appealed to the cantor Maban "who had had at Canterbury singing-masters trained by scholars of *blessed Pope Gregory;*"[5]) moreover, *Putta,* who was consecrated Bishop of *R*ochester about the year 669 writes that "he has to thank the scholars of blessed Pope Gregory for his knowledge of the *R*oman chant *(modulandi more Romanorum)".*[6])

δ) St. Bede the Venerable calls the deacon *James,* who from the year 625 was the companion of St. Paulinus, Bishop of York, a "master

1) Migne, l. c., 32, 770.

2) L. c. 14, 31 and 16, 1017.

3) Cf. Morin O. S. B.: *Les véritables origines du Chant Grégorien* (Maredsous, 2nd ed., 1904), German by P. Thomas Elsäßer (Paderborn, Schöningh 1892); Brambach: *Gregorianisch* (Leipzig, Spirgatis, 2nd ed., 1901). Leclercq, O. S. B. in the *Dictionaire d'Archéologie Chrétienne* (Paris 1905), *l'Antiphonale dit Grégorien,* columns 2443 seqq. (with copious references to the literature appertaining thereto).

4) Mansi: *Ampl. Coll. Conc.* 12 *col.*, 399, cap. 13; Hefele: *Konziliengeschichte* (Herder, Freiburg), 2nd ed., 1877, 3rd vol., p. 564.

5) Beda: *Hist. eccles.* Migne, l. c. 95, 270.

6) L. c 95, 175.

in ecclesiastical song according to the method of the *R*omans or Canturians"[1]) (there was a singing-school in Canterbury founded by *R*ome, hence this "or").

The tradition therefore can be traced in England down to a few decades after the death of St. Gregory.

II. In regard to Italy we have no evidence dating from the 7th century, nevertheless it can be proved that the chief portions of the choral melodies were already systematically arranged at the beginning of the 7th century (St. Gregory died in 604), for:

a) The text set to the old melodies is from the *Itala,* i. e., the most ancient Latin translation of the Bible. Now, according to the testimony of St. Isidore of Seville in the first half of the 7th century, the *Itala* version had been *supplanted* by the Vulgate, St. Jerome's translation of the Bible. If the chants had originated *after* 600 it is inexplicable why they did not follow the new text of the *Vulgate* then in use, instead of the out-of-date *Itala.*[2])

b) The texts for Masses, the date of which is subsequent to 600, were not set to original melodies (cf., e. g., the Thursdays in Lent for which an office was first compiled by Gregory II.;[3]) therefore the collection of Mass chants was considered to be closed after 600.

III. *a) Pope Hadrian I.* (772—795) wrote an introduction (prologue) to St. Gregory's Antiphonary which was sung in the Mass of the 1st Sunday of Advent. It runs thus:

"Gregory . . . . occupied the highest place of honour to which he had a (kind of) right *(unde genus ducit)* . . . he composed this book of chants *(hunc libellum musicæ artis composuit)*[4]) for the use of the singing-school throughout the ecclesiastical year: *Ad te levavi*", etc.

The words *unde genus ducit* can only apply to St. Gregory as he alone had a Pope amongst his ancestors, namely, Felix IV.

---

1) Migne, l. c. 95, 116.

2) Cf. *Revue Bénédictine* (Maredsous, 1890) p. 321, and Wagner: *Ursprung und Entwicklung der lit. Gesangsformen*, pp. 210 *seqq.*, in his *Einführung in die gregorian. Melodien* (Freiburg, Switzerland, Universitätsbuchhandlung, 1895, 2nd ed., 3 vols). French edition: *Origine et développement du chant liturgique jusqu' à fin du moyen-âge* (Tournai, Desclée).

3) *Liber Pontificalis,* ed. Duchesne (Paris, Thorin, 1886), vol. I. p. 402.

4) Cf. *Musica sacra* of Milan, 1890, pp. 33 *seqq.*

According to others *unde genus ducit* merely means that Gregory, a Roman *by birth,* had attained to the highest dignity in his native city; therefore these verses could be applied both to Gregory the Great and Gregory II. (who was also a Roman *by birth).*

But then the two first verses of the prologue "had been previously inscribed on the ivory diptychon[1]) at Monza above the figure of St. Gregory the Great in *relievo,* and it is all the more certain that they refer to him and not to one of his successors since he himself sent the diptychon to Queen Theodelinda, and the inscription, though not actually in consequence of this event, was in all probability engraved thereon not so very long afterwards." Dr. Ebner: *Kirchenmusikalisches Jahrbuch,* 1892, pp. 101 *seqq.)*

β) Walafrid Strabo (807—849) says:

"It is related *(traditur)* how blessed Gregory regulated the order of the masses and consecrations (the *Sacramentarium* and *Pontificale)* and how he arranged the greater part of the liturgical chants as retained to the present day, being the most suitable. The inscription which is at the beginning of the *Antiphonarium* indicates this."[2])

γ) Leo IV. (847—855) writes to the Abbot Honoratus *inter alia:*

"The same holy Pope Gregory, this great servant of God, renowned preacher and shepherd, full of wisdom, who laboured zealously for the salvation of man, composed with great labour and musical skill the chants which are sung in our church and elsewhere. By this means he would influence the heart of man more effectually, rousing them and enlivening them; and in truth the sound of his sweet melodies has not only allured spiritual men to the Church, but has even drawn those who are not so cultivated or sensitive."[3])

In this document the expression *dulcedo Gregoriani carminis,* the sweetness of the *Gregorian chant,* is used.

δ) John the Deacon (c. 872) writes in the 2nd book, 6th chapter, of his life of St. Gregory:

"He arranged for the singers a most useful collection, the *Antiphonarius Cento* (= different parts put together). He likewise

1) Diptychon, a tablet with two leaves (later more), on which from the 4th century onwards were written the names of persons connected with a church, especially benefactors.

2) Migne, l. c. 114, 948.

3 See *Neues Archiv* (Hanover 1880), p. 389.

instituted a singing-school which still cultivates the sacred chant of the Holy Roman Church according to the rules drawn up by him .... to this day is shown near the Lateran the couch from which in his illness he gave instruction in singing; the rod also with which he chastised the boys, and the Antiphonary are there, and are venerated as relics."[1])

The *liber Antiphonarius* in early times contained Introits, Offertories, Communios and Antiphons, whilst the *Cantatorium* contained the solo chants (e. g., Graduals).

b) Diffusion and Period of Perfection. (From St. Gregory to the Beginning of the 13th Century.).

263. The Roman chant was brought to England in the year 597 by St. Augustine and his companions who had been sent thither by St. Gregory. An influential singing-school was established at Canterbury by St. Augustine. To the names above mentioned we should add St. Benedict Biscop (690), who brought the Cantor John from Rome, and St. Wilfrid (709). The school of York is also worthy of notice.

The Roman chant came to *Franconia* and *Germany* through the efforts of king Pepin to whom, in compliance with his request, Pope Paul I. (757—767) lent Simeon, the cantor next in rank to the *Primicerius* of the Roman school, for some time. The *singing-school at Metz* founded by St. Chrodegang (it flourished down to the 12th century), and likewise the schools at Rouen and Soissons, became of great importance. Decisive, however, for the introduction of the Roman chant were the stringent ordinances of Charlemagne (768—814), who sent two clerics to Rome to learn the chant, and obtained Roman singers; then the extraordinary activity of the *Singing-school of St. Gall,*[2]) and the less important school subsequently founded at Reichenau.[3])

1) Migne, l. c. 75, 90.
2) Schubiger: *Sängerschule von St. Gallen* (Einsiedeln, Benziger, 1858).
3) Brambach: *Die Reichenauer Sängerschule* (Karlsruhe, 1888).

264. In these *schools* the utmost importance was attached to the *mode of rendering the chant,* and for theoretical and practical purposes the so-called Tonalia[1]) were made use of to assist in imparting the oral tradition. Here as elsewhere they began to produce new compositions, and they endeavoured to treat the chant scientifically.

The *compositions* down to 950 are thoroughly imbued with the same spirit as of old, whilst the productions from 950 to 1400, particularly towards the end of that period, are in part somewhat inferior to the earlier ones as regards simplicity (they had a liking for wide intervals), naturalness and warmth of feeling.

The number of melodies emanating from this period, and *still in use at the present time,* is not very considerable.

The *theoretical treatises*[2]) were chiefly based on the writings of the Greeks, whose theories they did not always successfully apply to the chant. Moreover, one constantly notices in them a want of perspicuity and precision in the expressions employed, and they frequently fail to give detailed hints as to the mode of rendering, so necessary for us in this period of restoration.

265. In addition to these works efforts had previously been made to *show the intervals more accurately in the notation,* for the neums were insufficient without the help of an experienced master. Indications were of course given in regard to the number of notes to be sung on a syllable, and as to when the melody should rise or fall. At first the notes were designated by the letters of the alphabet (see also p. 24).

Hucbald (930) noted the tetrachord D E F G with four signs (three of them not unlike our F). Lower or

1) Mathias: *Königshofen als Choralist* (Graz, "Styria", 1903).

2) Cf. W. Brambach: *Die Musikliteratur des Mittelalters* (500—1050), Leipzig, 1883. Kornmüller in the *K. M. Jahrbuch,* 1886—89.

higher tetrachords were represented by these signs reversed (Dasian notation). Then in the spaces between the six lines of his staff he wrote the syllables of the text, indicating at the commencement of the line a whole tone by a *t,* and a semitone by an *s.*

Hermann Contractus (the Lame), 11th century, showed by means of letters the distance of one tone from another (*e* = *equaliter,* the same height; *t,* whole tone; *s,* semitone; *ts,* tone and semitone, a minor third; *tt,* two whole tones, a major third; *d* = diatessaron, a fourth, etc., etc. Towards the end of the 10th century there are traces in Italy and Aquitaine of the *diastemata, diastema* = interval (neumatic notation), i. e., they fixed the intervals by showing the neums in a higher or lower position, and made this clearer by using *one* line (later on two or four); then they made the lines represent the distance of a third, the *fa* line being coloured red, the *do* line, yellow or green, and at length indicated the clefs (see pp. 22, 23) by means of letters. The notation attained this degree of perfection through *Guido of Arezzo* (1050?).

N. B. In the following lists N. denotes a chorister famed for his labours on behalf of the notation, C., a composer, Th., a theorist.

266. 9th century: *Alcuin,* Abbot of Tours, Th., 804; *Theodulf* of Orleans, C. *(Gloria, laus,* Palm-Sunday) 821, *Aurelian* of Reomé[1]), c. 850, *Remy* of Auxerre, Th.

10th century. *Ratpert* (singer), *Blessed Notker Balbulus* (the Stammerer), C. of sequences (over 50) which were, everywhere highly appreciated in the middle ages; Germany's "most famous chorister" (Kienle[2]), 912. *Tutilo,* C. of tropes, 915, Eccehard I. and Eccehard II., singers, all in St. Gall; further, *Regino,* Abbot of Prüm, C. and Th., 915; *Hucbald,* Belgian monk, C., Th., N. (see above) 930;

---

1) *Cäcilia,* Strasburg, 1904, pp. 95 *seqq.;* 1905, pp. 28 *seqq.*

2) *Kirchenlexikon,* Freiburg, Herder, "Sequenzen", pp. 159 *seqq.*

St. Odo of Clugny, C. N. (?), and Th. *(?)*, 940; *Letald,* French monk, C., c. 997.

11th century. *Notker Labeo* of St. Gall, Th., 1022; *Fulbert* of Chartres, C., 1029; *Berno* of Reichenau, C. and Th., 1048; *Hermann Contractus* (the Lame) of Reichenau, C. *(Alma Redemptoris, Salve Regina?),* N. and Th., 1054; *Wipo,* a native of Burgundy, C., *(Victimæ paschali,* see Sequence), c. 1048; *Pope St. Leo IX.,* C. *Gloria* (Cant. ad lib. I., *Kyriale),* 1054; *Wilhelm, Abbot of Hirschau,* Th., 1091; *Guido of Arezzo,*[1]) Th. (Micrologus = school of chant), N. (see above) c. 1050; *Theoger of Metz,* Th., c. 1080; *Aribo Scholasticus* of Freising, Th. 1078.

12th century. *St. Bernard, Abbot of Clairvaux,* C., Th.[2]), 1153, with the assistance of the Abbot Guido of Cherlieu (c. 1158) rearranged the choral books for the Cistercian order in which the compass of the chants was not unfrequently curtailed, and some of the more elaborate groups of notes were abbreviated, though in other respects everything was treated in a very conservative manner.

John Cotton, Th.,[3]) John de Garlandia, Th.; Adam de St. Victor in Paris, C. (Sequences[4]) about 50 of them certainly by him — see *Lauda Sion* p. 115), c. 1192; St. Hildegarde, C., 1179.

c) Decadence of the Ancient Melodies. From the 13th Century to 1850.

267. After the 13th century the domain wherein plain chant had alone been supreme was gradually encroached upon by polyphony. Some of the theorists endeavoured, for example, to treat *musica plana* and *musica mensura-*

1) Cf. *Cäcilienkalender,* 1876, p. 49. *K. M. Jahrbuch,* 1887, pp. 1 *seqq.;* 1890, pp. 95 *seqq.*

2) Cf. Kienle in the *Gregorius-Blatt* (Düsseldorf, Schwann), 1901, pp. 2 *seqq.* and 17 *seqq. K. M. Jahrbuch,* 1889, pp. 1 *seqq.*

3) Cf. *K. M. Jahrbuch,* 1888, pp. 1 *seqq.*

4) Edition by Misset—Aubry (Paris, Welter, 1905)

bilis in the same way, to the disadvantage of the mode of rendering the chant, whilst others were successful in keeping the two quite distinct. The plain chant compositions, particularly at a later period, were decidedly inferior; the melodies, it is true, were in the main still preserved intact to the end of the 16th century,[1] but from that time the desire to reform the chant, partly justifiable, became more and more marked, and this in the end meant the *abbreviation of the melodies,* even those which had their origin in the classical period of plain chant.

13th century. Walter of Odington, Th., Jerome of Moravia, Th., Franco of Cologne, Th., Elias Salomon, Th., Jacopone da Todi, C. *(Stabat mater).*

14th century. John of Muris, Th., Marchetti of Padua, Th., Engelbert of Admont, O. S. B., Th., 1331.

15th century. Adam of Fulda, O. S. B., Th., 1460, Tinctor,[2] Th. (treats of plain chant and mensural music).

16th century. Gafori in Milan, Th., 1522, Glareanus (Henry Loris of Glarus), Th., 1562.

17th century. The theorists: *Cardinal Bona,* 1674, *Jumilhac,* O. S. B., 1682, and the C. Dumont, 1684.

18th century. *Gerbert,* O. S. B., Abbot of St. Blase, 1793: *De cantu et musica sacra a prima ecclesiæ ætate,* etc., 2 vols.; *Scriptores ecclesiastici de musica,* 3 vols., (New edition: Graz, 1903).

The latter work was continued by Coussemaker (1876): *Scriptores ecclesiastici de musica mediævi,* (four 4to vols).

In France *Nivers* (c. 1700) published a plain chant edition prepared in accordance with his views. His *Graduale* and *Antiphonale* (both 1658), privileged by the king and approved of by the (plain chant-) composer Dumont

1) Molitor, *Choralwiegendrucke* (Ratisbon, Fr. Pustet) 1904, and *Unsere Lage* (Ratisbon, Fr. Pustet) 1904; English edition, *Our Position*, published by the same firm, 1904.

2) *K. M. Jahrbuch,* 1899, p. 69.

(1684), was widely diffused, and served as a model for the reformed edition of Rennes (1853). The editions of Digne and Dijon (both 1858) are in the same style.

268. In 1614—15 the so-called *Medicæan Gradual*[1]) appeared in the *Stamperia orientale* of Cardinal Medici in Rome, with many abbreviations of, and changes in, the ancient melodies. This edition was prepared by Anerio and Suriano, and for a long was ascribed to Palestrina to whom Pope Gregory XIII. had entrusted the revision (not the reform) of the choral books, necessitated by the new official edition of the Breviary and Missal.

Outside Italy the *Medicæan edition* was used in very few places, and was almost entirely forgotten until it again appeared in 1848 as the *Mechlin Gradual* with numerous alterations. It became of more importance when Pius IX., in his efforts on behalf of uniformity in the chant, after certain unimportant alterations and additions had been made therein, declared it to be the official edition.[2]) (It was however deprived of its official character in 1903). This edition was printed at *Ratisbon* by Herr F. Pustet, Printer to the Holy See (begun in 1871), and was widely diffused in Germany chiefly by means of the Society of St. Cæcilia, founded by Dr. Witt and approved of by the Holy See in 1870, with a view to the restoration of church music in accordance with liturgical requirements. The *Vesperale* which was subsequently published was based on the *Antiphonale* of Venice (1585) and on that of Antwerp (1611). Though these editions could not for a length of time satisfy all requirements, we must thankfully acknowledge that mainly owing to the efforts

---

1) Cf. Molitor: *Nachtridentinische Choralreform* (Leipzig, Leuckart) 2 vols., 1901—1902.

2) Ahle: *Die Choralausgabe der hl. Ritenkongregation* (Ratisbon, Fr. Pustet, 1895).

of Dr. Witt (1888)[1]) and Dr. Haberl, whose practical *Magister choralis* reached its twelfth edition in 1900, to say nothing of translations in several languages, the thoroughly unecclesiastical music formerly in vogue was ousted to a great extent and interest in the chant reawakened.

d) Revival of the Ancient (unabbreviated) Melodies.[2])

269. *Abbot Guéranger* of Solesmes (1875), the restorer of the liturgy in France, gave the impetus to this revival. His view of the matter, viz., that "if a considerable number of the most ancient MSS. in various countries agree with each other, then they contain the original version of the Gregorian chant," induced Father Lambillote, the French Jesuit (1855), to undertake extended journeys in order that by diligently studing the MSS. he might arrive at a decision in regard to the correct version of the chants. His lithographs of Codex 359 in the library of St. Gall are well worth attention. Unfortunately the melodies contained in his Gradual which appeared in 1856 are considerably *abbreviated* and *altered.* The Rheims-Cambrai Gradual, published since 1851 by *Lecoffre* of Paris, is not much better.

Father Dechevrens, S. J., who for many years (since 1861) has assiduously studied the theory of plain chant, arranges the ancient melodies according to the MSS., but has his own particular views as to the rendering, being of opinion that measured rhythm should be employed. So far the results arrived at are not satisfactory from a theoretical or practical point of view.

In Germany *Michael Hermesdorff* (1885) published in 1863 a Gradual for the Diocese of Treves, which for that

1) See *Dr. Franz Witt,* von Dr. A. Walter (Ratisbon, Fr. Pustet, 1889); also *Franz Witt*, by H. S. Butterfield, reprinted from the *Month* and included among the little biographies published by the Catholic Truth Society, London. Trsl.

2) Cf. Molitor in *Histor. polit. Blätter,* 1905, pp. 653 *seqq.*, 727 *seqq.*, 825 *seqq.*

time was a remarkable work, but the sources from which he obtained his material were certainly scanty.[1] The same holds good of the Cologne Gradual of 1865. Moreover, H. Oberhoffer (1885), Dom Schubiger, O. S. B. (1888), R. Schlecht (1891), Dr. Benedict Sauter, O. S. B. (particularly by means of his *Choral und Liturgie),* H. Böckeler (1899), Dom Ambros Kienle, O. S. B. (1905), later, Professor Dr. Wagner and Dom Raphael Molitor, O. S. B., by their zeal and energy succeeded in promoting the study of plain chant and the proper mode of rendering it.

In *England* for some decades the *Plainsong and Mediæval Musical Society* has devoted a great deal of attention to the chant, and, amongst other things, we have to thank it for the publication of the *Graduale Sarisburiense* (Salisbury).

In *France* the *Schola cantorum* with its *Tribune de St. Gervais* (Paris), under the direction of *Charles Bordes* and *Amadée Gastoué,* is actively at work on similar lines.

In *Italy* an effort has been made on behalf of the revival by the new edition of the *Antiphonarium Ambrosianum* (1889).

270. The merit for this revival of the Gregorian melodies chiefly belongs to the *Benedictines of Solesmes,* and especially to Dom Pothier, who as the result of arduous archæological and practical studies extending over 24 years, published in 1884 the *Liber Gradualis* (2nd ed., 1895), a book that must necessarily satisfy historians and especially æsthetics. As an introduction thereto he wrote his important work *Mélodies Grégoriennes* (1880). *Dom Mocquereau* founded in 1889 the monumental work entitled, *Paléographie musicale* (8 vols. have appeared),

1) A later edition (1875 and onwards), thoroughly revised, was never finished.

tho

ous

awa

d)

of t

His

of t

each

Gre

Jesu

that

deci

His

are w

tained

sidera

Gradu

not m

F.

1861)

arrange

has his

of opi

So far

theoreti

In

1863 a

time was a remarkable wo:k
he obtained his material w
same holds good of the Col
H. Oberhoffer (1885), Do
R. Schlecht (1891), Dr. B
cularly by means of his C
(1899), Dom Ambros Kie
fessor Dr. Wagner and
by their zeal and energy s
of plain chant and the pr

In *England* for s
Mediæval Musical Socie
attention to the chant.
have to thank it **for** th
Sarisburiense (Sali

In *France* the
St.
and *A*
lines.

In
revival
sianum

I.

Calendar.

nd Abbreviations in
ectorium, Ordo) for
ers, Organists and

nptio B. M. V., Assumption
he B. V. M.

B.

beatus, blessed.
V. = beatæ Mariæ Virgi-
of the B. V. M.

C.

— *campánum*, bell.
= *cantátur*, is sung.
= *cantóres*, cantors, or chanters.
= *capitulum*, Little Chapter
aft the psalms, see p. 11.
dra Petri, St. Peter's Chair
(fest of).
ss (cessant), ceases (cease).
in.= cinis, Ashes.
ircncisio, Circumcision.
l. =classis, class; *I. cl., II. cl.*,
1st 2nd class (feast of the).
œn Dñi. = Cœna Dómini,
Mandy Thursday.
com.= commemorátio; see p. 12.
Com= Commúne, the Common;
se p. 10.
Conptio, Conception B. V. M.
(8 Dec.).
C., C or *Conf. = Conféssor*, a
Cofessor.

which gives phototypical reproductions of the ancient MSS. with explanatory remarks, and treats of history, æsthetics and mode of execution on a broad scientific basis. He also made use of the voluminous material, obtained from original sources, for the revision of the Gradual of 1884 (1895), and this led to some corrections of minor importance.

Leo XIII. officially recognised the labours of the Benedictines in his Brief *Nos quidem* (17 May, 1901) to Abbot Delatte, of Solesmes. Pius X. "who has restored the Gregorian chant — *cantum gregorianum restauravit*" (Decree of the Cong. of S. Rites, 8 Jan. 1904), confided the new edition of the official choral books to the Benedictines of Solesmes, and gave directions through the Cardinal Secretary of State that it should be based on the Gradual published by them in 1895 (2nd edition). So far, the only portion of this *Editio Vaticana* that has appeared is the *Kyriale.*

Appendix II.

The Ecclesiastical Calendar.

Explanation of Latin Words and Abbreviations in the Ecclesiastical Calendar (Directorium, Ordo) for the Convenience of Choirmasters, Organists and Singers.

A.

a, ab, from; *a cap.* = *a capitulo,* from the Little Chapter onwards, see pp. 11, 12.

Abb. = *abbas,* Abbot.

Abs. = *absolútio,* Absolution (Requiem).

absque, without.

add. = *ádditur,* is added (e. g., *Allelúja).*

Adv. = *adventus,* Advent.

álias with date = the feast is to be found on the particular day.

a. l. = *aliquibus locis,* in some places.

alternátim, alternately.

Ang. = *ángelus,* angel.

ang. custódes, guardian angels.

Anniversárius, anniversary.

Anniv. Dedicatiónis Ecclesiæ, Anniversary of the *D*edication of a church.

Annuntiátio, Annunciation.

annus, year.

ante, before.

Ant. = *antiphóna.*

Ap.,(App.)=*Apóstolus,* an Apostle, *(Apóstoli,* the Apostles*).*

Arch. = *Archángelus,* Archangel.

Ascénsio, Ascension.

Assúmptio B. M. V., Assumption of the B. V. M.

B.

B. = *beátus,* blessed.

B. M. V. = *beátæ Maríæ Vírginis,* of the B. V. M.

C.

camp. = *campánum,* bell.

cant. = *cantátur,* is sung.

" = *cantóres,* cantors, or chanters.

cap. = *capítulum,* Little Chapter after the psalms, see p. 11.

Cáthedra Petri, St. Peter's Chair (feast of).

cessat (cessant), ceases (cease).

Cin. = *cinis,* Ashes.

Circumcisio, Circumcision.

Cl. = *classis,* class; *I. cl., II. cl.,* 1st, 2nd class (feast of the).

Cœna Dñi. = *Cœna Dómini,* Maundy Thursday.

com. = *commemorátio;* see p. 12.

Com. = *Commúne,* the Common; see p. 10.

Concéptio, Conception B. V. M. (8 Dec.).

C., Cf. or *Conf.* = *Conféssor,* a Confessor.

Cf. non P. = *Conféssor non Póntifex,* Confessor not a Bishop.
Cf. P. = *Conféssor Póntifex,* Confessor and Bishop.
conj. = *conjúngitur,* is joined, particularly in hymns.
Convérsio, Conversion.
Cor Jesu, Heart of Jesus.
coram expósito (SS. Sacramento), in presence of the Blessed Sacrament exposed.
Coróna (spinea), Crown of Thorns.
Corpus Christi, Feast of Corpus Christi.
Cr. = *Credo,* Creed.
Crux, Cross.
c. = *cum* with.

D.

de, of *(de seq.,* of the following feast); *(de eódem,* of the same).
Decollátio, Beheading (St. John B.).
Dedicátio, Dedic. of a Church.
def. = *defúnctus,* the deceased.
deinceps, thenceforth.
dic. = *dicitur (dicúntur),* is or are said.
dies, day, days.
distribútio, distribution.
D. E. = *Doctor Ecclésiæ,* Doctor of the Church.
Dolóres, Seven *D*olours B. V. M.
Dom. = *Domínica,* Sunday.
Dñs = *Dóminus,* (our Lord Jesus Christ).
duo, two.
dupl. = *duplex,* double (feast).

E.

Eccl. = *ecclésia,* church.
Epiphania, Feast of the Epiphany.
Ep. = *episcopus,* Bishop.
exaltátio, Exaltation of the Holy Cross.
exinde, from thenceforth
exspectátio, Expectation (of the Birth of our Lord).

F.

F. = *feria,* week-day.
Fest. = *festum,* feast.

G.

genufléxio, genuflection.
Gl. = *Glória.*

H.

Hébdomas major, Holy Week.
hon. or *in hon.* = *in honórem,* in honour.
Hym. = *hymnus,* hymn.

I.

Imac. = *immaculáta,* immaculate.
immediáte, immediately.
incipit (incipiunt), begins (begin)
inclinátio, inclination.
infra, within (e. g., the Octave).
Innoc. = *Innocéntes,* Holy Innocents.
integer, entire, the whole.
inter, between.
Intr. = *Intróitus,* Introit.
in utrisque Vesperis, in both 1st and 2nd Vespers.
Invéntio, the Finding (of the Holy Cross).

J.

júngitur, is joined.

L.

L. (Ll.) = *lectio (lectiónes),* lesson, lessons.
Lánceæ et Clavórum, of the Lance and Nails (feast).

Lib. = *Liber,* book.
Lit. = *Litania,* litany.
locus, a place; 2º *loco,* in the second place, in the place of.

M.

Magn. = *Magnificat.*
major, greater, *duplex majus,* (feast of the rank of a greater double).
M. V. = *Mariæ Virginis,* of the B. V. M.
M. = *martyr; Mm.* = *mártyrum,* of the Martyrs.
Matérnitas, Maternity.
M. S.; see p. 90.
M. = *Missa,* Mass.
mutátur, is changed.

N.

Nat. = *nativitas,* birth.
necnon, also.
Nomen, Name.
non, not; see *Cf. non* P.

O.

Oct. = *octáva,* Octave.
omittitur, is omitted.
omisso, being omitted.
Omnia, all.
Omnium Sanctórum, All Saints Day.
Or. = *orátio,* prayer.
Org. = *órganum,* organ.
org. silent, the organ not to be played.

P.

Pag. = *página,* page.
Palm., Dom. Palmárum, Palm Sunday.
Parascéve, Good Friday.
Partus, birth (see above *exspectátio).*
P. = *Pascha,* Easter; *paschális,* Paschal (in particular *T. P.* = *témpore paschali,* in Paschal time).
Pass. = *Pássio,* Passion; *Dom. Pass.* = *Domínica Passiónis,* Passion Sunday.
Patroc. = *Patrocínium,* Patronage.
Pent. or *Pentec.* = *Pentecóstes,* Pentecost.
permittitur, it is allowed.
Plaga, Wound.
plures (plúrimi), several (e. g., *plur. mártyrum,* feast of many martyrs).
P. or *Pont.* = *Póntifex,* Bishop (see above C. *Cf.).*
Pp. = *Papa,* Pope.
ppr. = *próprium,* proper; *ómnia ppr.,* all proper.
post, after.
præcédens, preceding; see p. 12.
Præf. = *Præfátio,* Preface.
Præsentátio, Presentation.
pretiosissimi sánguinis, of the most Precious Blood.
prohibétur, is forbidden.
Proph. = *Prophéta, prophetia,* a prophet or prophecy.
Propr. Diœc., Diocesan Proper, an Appendix to many liturgical books containing the feasts of saints celebrated in a particular diocese.
Ps. = *psalmi.*
pulsátur (org.) the organ is played.
pulsátur (camp. bell) is rung.
Purificátio B. M. V., Candlemas Day.
Puríssimi Cordis, feast of the most pure Heart of Mary.
Púritas, purity.

Q.

Quadr. = *quadragésima,* Lent.
quadragínta, forty.
quátuor., four.
quibúsdam locis, in some places.
Quinquagésima, Sunday before Ash Wednesday.

R.

rel. = *réliqua,* the rest, what remains.
reperitur, is found.
rep. = *repétitur,* is repeated.
℟. = *Responsórium,*
Resurréctio, Resurrection.
Rogatiónum Féria, Day in Rogation Week.

S.

Sabb. = *Sábbatum,* Saturday.
Sac. = *Sacérdos,* Priest.
s. (SS.) = *sanctus (sancti),* holy, saint (saints).
SS. Sacr. = *Sanctissimum Sacraméntum,* the Blessed Sacrament.
sd., sem. = *semidúplex,* semidouble feast.
secréto, silently, in secret.
Septuagésima, 3rd Sunday before Ash Wednesday.
seq. = *sequens,* the following (see p. 12).
Seq. = *Sequéntia,* sequence.
Sexagésima, 2nd Sunday before Ash Wednesday.
silet (silent), remains or remain silent.
simpl. = *simplex,* simple.
Sindon, Winding sheet.
Soc. = *sócii,* companions.
sol. = *Solémnis,* solemn.
Solémnitas, solemnity.
suffr. = *suffrágia;* suffrages, see p. 12.
súmitur, is taken.
Suppl. = *suppleméntum,* supplement.
supra, above.

T.

tacet, is silent.
T. P. see above, *Pascha.*
T. = *(témpore)* Pass., in Passiontide.
T. Quadr., in Lent.
Tenebræ, Matins and Lauds on the last three days of Holy Week.
ter, thrice.
Tr. = *Tract.*
Transfigurátio, Transfiguration.
Translátio, Translation.
Triduum sacrum, three last days of Holy Week.
Trínitas, Trinity.

U.

utérque, both (see above *in utrísque Vésperis).*
ut, as; *ut in I. Vesperis,* as in 1st Vespers.
ut in Festo, as on the feast.
ut heri, as yesterday.

V.

vacat, falls out, is wanting.
variátur, is changed.
Ven. = *Venerábilis,* venerable.
V. = *Virgo,* virgin.
℣. = *versus, versiculus.*
Vp. = *Vésperæ,* Vespers.
Vid. = *Vidua,* widow.
vide, see.
Vig. = *vigilia,* vigil.
vigínti, twenty.
Visitátio, Visitation.
Vúlnera, Wounds.

Examples from the (Freiburg) *Directorium: † † Fer. 6. Epiphania Domini dupl. 1. cl. cum Octava* (what follows is not of consequence to choirmasters, etc., until we come to) *M. c. Gl. Cr.*

Therefore on Friday (the 6th day from Sunday), the Epiphany, *duplex:* the entire antiphon must be sung before and after the psalm; 1st class with octave . . . Mass with *Gloria* and *Credo.*

Vp. 2dæ de eodem Festo = 2nd Vespers of the same feast without commemorations.

Dom. XXI. post Pentec. . . . . . . Festum Puritatis B. M. V. dupl. . . . . Inter Festa pro aliquib. loc. (Dom. 3. Octbr.) . . . . . M. c. Gl. . . Cr.,

21st Sunday after Pentecost . . . Feast of the Purity B. V. M.; *duplex* . . . . to be found under feasts for particular places, (3rd Sunday in Oct.): Mass with *Gloria* and *Credo.*

In 2. Vesp. com. seq. et S. Pirminii ac Dom. necnon Oct.

In the 2nd Vespers (all for the feast of the day) commemoration of St. Pirmin (Conf. and Bishop = *Ep. Cf.* or *Conf. Pont.,* as indicated in the Vespers for the Saturday); therefore *Magnificat*-antiphon, etc., from the 2nd Vespers of the *Commune Conf. Pont.;* then *Magnificat*-antiphon, etc., of the Sunday (21st after Pent.) and *Magnificat*-antiphon, etc., of the octave of all Saints (from the 2nd Vespers of the feast).

Appendix III.

Vocal Exercises.

General Remarks.

a) The Vocal Exercises are divided into two Courses, viz., Course A (First Step) for the attainment of accuracy in singing the intervals (striking the note) and the acquisition of a feeling for rhythm; and Course B (Second Step) for voice production and correct pronunciation.

b) The Exercises for Course A are to be solfa-ed (see No. 27, pp. 18, 19), that is to say, the name of each note is to be sung. To make this easier for the pupil at the commencement, in the first two Exercises for Lessons I. and II., and in some other places where it appeared desirable, the names are inserted under the notes. In all the other Exercises the pupil is to practise *naming* the notes therein correctly and fluently before singing them.

The Syllables and Words are placed under the Notes for Course B.

c) The name of each note when solfa-ed must be enunciated sharply and distinctly, the full sound of the vowel being held out to its proper length according to the value of the note; the articulation of the consonants passing to the next vowel must be very quick, but distinct. In this way vowels *and* consonants produce their proper effect, and the pupils acquire a good *legato* style and perfectly distinct utterance (see Nos. 28, 29, pp. 19, 20).

d) At first always sing *piano,* for this is the only method by which one can learn to equalise the voice, a matter of the utmost importance. Not until Course B is taken in hand should the Exercises be sung *mezzoforte; forte* exceptionally (see p. 251).

e) Course B begins after the 3rd Exercise for Lesson VIII„ see p. 279.

Directions in Detail for Course A.

Lessons I. and II. Intervals of a Second, Neums with 2 Notes.

Preliminary Instruction: 1) Clefs (see No. 36, p. 22);

2) Signs for pauses (see No. 38, pp. 23, 24);

3) Notes: *punctum* and *virga* (see Nos. 30—33, pp. 21, 22);

4) The simplest forms of neums with one accent and two notes; *clivis* and *pes* (see No. 52, p. 33);

5) The names of the notes: Guidonian syllables (see No. 34, p. 22).

Pitch. For high voices take *do* at the pitch of *f* (as if in F major); for low voices it should be *c.* This holds good throughout the Exercises whenever the *Fa Clef* is used.

Delivery. All notes are of equal length (see Nos. 39, 40, pp. 24—27). At first sing each note with *equal force* (but *softly);* then each time sing the first of the two notes with rather more force (as in $^2/_8$ time). It is desirable that the pupil should himself mark the rhythm by slight movements of the hand.

To accustom him to *sing the closes* correctly he should not be allowed to interrupt the rhythm, but should quietly go on beating time. It is only the last note that is to be held out, and this to the first beat of the following rhythmic group (the following bar); the second beat (the second and third in Lesson III.) marks a pause (silent pulse) and is made use of to take breath, and then at one in the next bar the following section is started. The close of the last section is to be sung in like manner without a *ritardando* or further prolongation of the last note. Example:

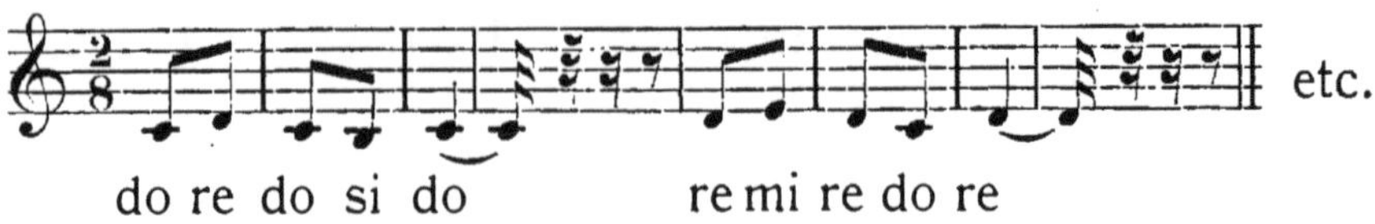

(see Nos. 69—71, pp. 49—52.)

Tempo rather slow[1], see M. M. 69 for the single note.

Lesson III. Intervals of a Second, Neums with three notes.

Preliminary Instruction. Neums with one accent and three notes: *Torculus; porrectus; climacus; scandicus;* (see No. 52, pp. 33, 34).

The *scandicus* is written in two ways, but the mode of delivery is the same; therefore and =

Pitch as in Lesson I.

Delivery. The first note of each group is accented as in $^3/_8$ time (see No. 54, pp. 37, 38).

Tempo as in Lesson I.

Lesson IV. Intervals of a Third.

Preliminary Instruction: 1) Further forms of neums with one accent:

a) *bistropha* and *bivirga* = (see No. 52 a), p. 33).

b) Two forms of the *pressus* = = (see No. 66, pp. 46—48).

2) Neums with four notes and two accents (see No. 52, pp. 34, 35).

Delivery. 1) To impress the interval of a third on the pupil's ear, he should strongly accentuate the first and last note of each group in Exercises 2 and 4, therefore *do* re *mi* (notes not to be too low); then in the proper rhythm, i. e., only accenting the first note of each group.

2. With a *torculus* (Exercises 5, 7) it is time to try to accentuate the second note. Do not forget that *the first note of each group is accented.*

3. Neums with 4 notes usually have the principal accent on the first note, and a weak secondary accent on the third one (as in $^4/_8$ time). See Nos. 54, 55, pp. 37, 38, and No. 61, pp. 41, 42.

Lesson V. Free Rhythm.

Preliminary Instruction: 1) *Do clef* on the fourth line (see No. 36, p. 22).

2) The altered semitone, ♮ (see No. 35, p. 22).

Pitch. For Exercises with the *Fa clef,* as in Lesson I.; with the *Do clef,* for a high voice *do* = *d,* for a low voice *do* = *a.*

Delivery. At first accentuate strongly, but little by little the accents should be moderated so that a soft, smooth glide may be attained, but always so that the rhythm can easily be recognised, a binary figure (rhythmic group of two notes) being clearly distinguished from a ternary figure (rhythmic group of three notes).

N. B. Ternary figures are *not* in the same relation to binary figures as triplets are to doublets in modern music (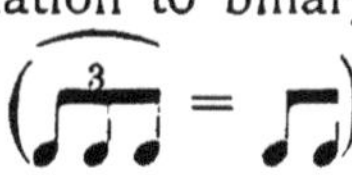). One group (a beat)  is *not* like the other , but one *note* is equal to the *other note* in time-value.

When there is a disposition to sing a ternary figure *after* a *binary figure* quicker, stop the pupil and let him sing the ternary a shade slower, taking particular care to accentuate the first note well, and to dwell upon it a little.

It is desirable later on to practise Exercises 1—4 more frequently, perhaps at the commencement of the Lesson. The free alternation of binary and ternary rhythms must become the plain chant singer's second nature.

To solve any doubt as to the rhythm, some of the Exercises have been written in modern notation with accents.

Lesson VI. Bistropha, Tristropha, Mora vocis.

Preliminary Instruction, see No. 52, pp. 33, 34, and Nos. 72, 73, pp. 52—54. A note prolonged by the *mora vocis* is to be sustained for *precisely two beats* (cf. what has been said above concerning closes).

In order to get hold of the rhythm of the *tristropha* more readily, it is desirable to sing this neum *at first* like a *torculus* or *porrectus,* e. g., ■■■ =  or .

Tempo rather quicker than hitherto, perhaps M. M. 126 for the individual note.

Lesson VII. Intervals of a Fourth.

The fourth may be slurred a little *(portamento)* to accustom the pupil to produce a beautiful *legato* when taking the wider intervals.

Lesson VIII. Intervals of a Fifth. Pressus.

Preliminary Instruction: 1) Neums with 4 and 5 notes and 2 accents (see No. 52, pp. 34—36) not employed in Lesson IV.

2) *Pressus* (see Nos. 66, 67, pp. 46—48).

3) Single note (see No. 65, pp. 45, 46); *salicus* (see No. 54, p. 37). Displacement of the accents with the *mora vocis* (see No. 73, p. 53).

Delivery. When solfa-ing, the *pressus* is always to be sung as a single, sustained and accented note. Exercises 5 and succeeding ones include intervals of a fifth, in the same form as they appear in the ancient classical chants almost exclusively, i. e., *re-la* and *sol-re.*

When Exercise 3 for Lesson VIII. has been practised with the sol-fa syllables, all the previous Lessons, beginning from No. I. are to be repeated, in accordance with the plan for Course B.

Directions in Detail for Course B.

Preliminary Remark.

Course B is to train the pupil to sing correctly and artistically on a vowel (to vocalise) the long series of notes or groups which so frequently occur in Gregorian chant. Firm rhythm, fluent melody, neatly executed progressions, smooth connection of the notes, variety in the light and shade, perfect tranquillity — these are the requirements that have to be satisfied in rendering these *cantilene.*

With a view not to discourage the pupil by giving him too much to do, we start again with the simple Exercises in Lesson I. for connecting the tones, and thus combine the new work with that which has long been familiar. When it is evident that an Exercise does not go well, the pupil should sol-fa it again until the difficulty as regards time and striking the note has been overcome.

This Course more than Course A presupposes a competent master, who knows how to select the Exercises according to the needs and capabilities of his pupils. However desirable it might be, e. g., for those who wish to become efficient plain chant singers to practise every day Exercises for the shake (L. I., B) and the figured scales (L. II.—VIII., B), it would be incongruous to trouble ordinary singers with such things. There is no doubt however that children particularly like vocalising, and it certainly helps them to develop their voices; but then Exercises of so wide a range must always be sung *piano.*

Lessons I., II., III.

1. Attention should be paid to the following points:

a) Correct pronunciation (see Nos. 8 and 9, pp. 4—6, and Nos. 25—29, pp. 16—20).

b) *Legato* method of singing.

c) Careful accentuation (the final syllables softly).

d) Purity of tone *(do-re* and *re-mi* are often sung flat).

2. The *degree of force* is still to be *piano.* When an Exercise can be sung satisfactorily in every respect (precise attack, good vocalisation, a beautiful *legato),* it can be delivered *mezzoforte* and with various dynamical gradations.

Example:

3. With Exercises 5 and 6 pay more attention than heretofore to purity of tone and rhythmical precision during the whole of the time they are practised, especially if they are often repeated in one breath, omitting the last note, a highly desirable plan.

4. Exercises 7—10. These exercises on the figured scale should be sung in one breath and by degrees quicker and quicker, but in exact time. These must likewise be solfa-ed in the first place, and then vocalised. The vowel must have the same tone-colour whether on a high or low note (making allowance of course for the difference in the tonal position).

Lesson IV.

Exercises 5—10, like Exercises 7 and subsequent ones for Lessons II. and III., can be vocalised. The dotted closes and the pauses are then omitted.

Lessons V. and VI.

These Lessons require special attention. Each Exercise when vocalised must at first be taken slowly so that the rhythmic forms may be in evidence; then by degrees quicker.

Instead of the text, the names of the first note of the group may occasionally be used, as indicated in the Exercises. For the sake of variety, in addition to the usual syllables, we have inserted others, viz., the tone-syllables invented by Graun.

Lesson VII.

For Exercises 10—12 we give a number of short passages taken from the *Liber Gradualis.* They present no further difficulties as they contain nothing new for those who have learnt the foregoing Exercises, and they will gradually accustom the pupil to the liturgical books.

As regards the *quilisma* see No. 68, pp. 48, 49.

Lesson VIII.

Exercises 1 and 3 contain examples for the *up-beat* in the *saliscus* and some other forms of neums. Sing the Exercises with and without the syllables in small print.

For the pitch of the dominant (Exercises 9—11) take *a*, *b* ♭ or b ♮.

The Tract melodies (Exercise 16) in Mode VIII. should be intoned on *f* or *f* ♯ (major), those in Mode II. on *f* ♯ or *g* (minor).

Lesson IX.

For this Lesson we give Exercises with the *Do Clef* on the third line (see No. 36, p. 22).

Pitch for the dominant of the Antiphons (Exercises 1—4) as in Lesson VIII. The Gradual melodies (Exercise 6) are intoned on *f* ♯ or *g* (minor). The *tempo* should be much more animated than with the Antiphons.

The melodies here given contain most of the phrases occurring in Graduals, Mode II. (see No. 131, p. 106).

Lesson X.

The Gradual melodies in Mode V. (Exercises 1—3) should be sung a whole tone or a semitone lower than written.

Exercises 4—9 are typical *Alleluja* melodies (see No. 138 pp. 111, 112) to which have been added the initial words of the verse appertaining thereto under the *recitation note.* Choirs which are not in a position to *sing* the verse can render the *Alleluja* in this way (cf. also No. 135 pp. 109, 110). Moreover, weak choirs can select one of the *Allelujas* here given for use on Sundays and festivals, reciting the verse proper for the day in the manner indicated. The melody for Exercise 6, Mode II., should preferably be used during Christmastide.

Lesson I.

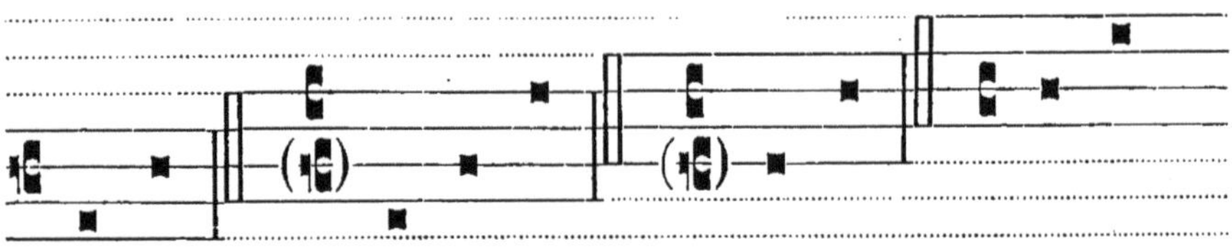

do fa. do fa do. fa do. do fa.

A and B.

1.

A. *do-re do-si do; re-mi re-do re; mi-fa mi-re mi;*

B.									
	1. *do-*	*do-*	*do;*	*re-*	*re-*	*re;*	*mi-*	*mi-*	*mi;*
	2. Sá-	ba-	oth;	A-	ra-	bes;	Gá-	la-	tas;
	3. *do-*	-	*do;*	*re-*	-	*re;*	*mi-*	-	*mi;*
	4. A-	-	dam;	a-	-	ra;	da-	-	ta;
	5. Ve-	-	re;	re-	-	ple;	me-	-	ne;
	6. Ti-	-	bi;	mi-	-	hi;	ni-	-	mis;
	7. Su-	-	mus;	fu-	-	sus;	su-	-	um;
	8. Lo-	-	co;	do-	-	mo;	ro-	-	go;

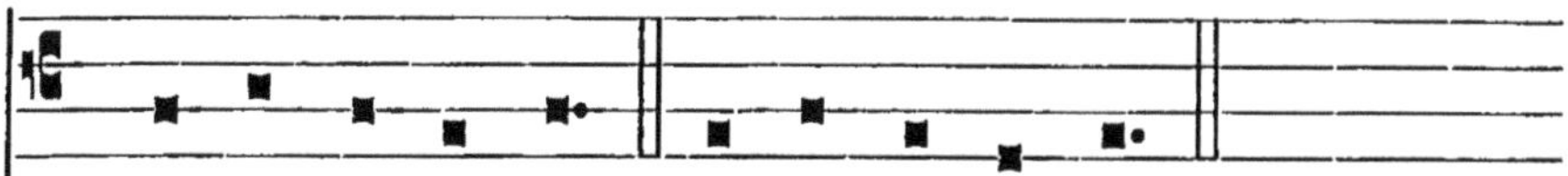

A.	*re-mi*	*re-do*	*re;*	*do-re*	*do-si*	*do.*

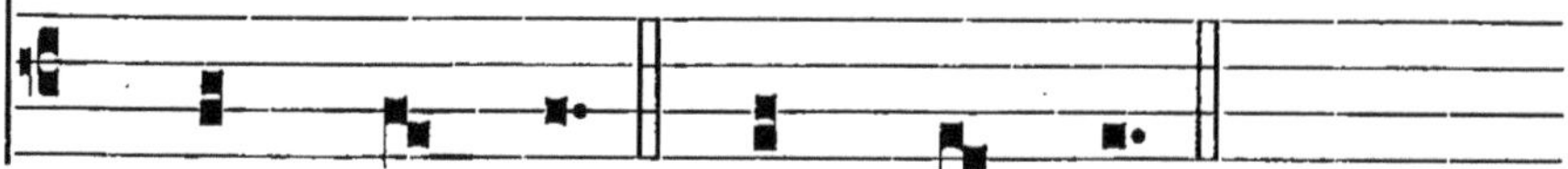

B. 1.	*re-*	*re-*	*re;*	*do-*	*do-*	*do.*
2.	Phá-	ra-	o;	thá-	la-	mum.
3.	*re-*	-	*re;*	*do-*	-	*do.*
4.	psal-	-	lam;	tam-	-	quam.
5.	re-	-	gem;	de-	-	gens.
6.	il-	-	li;	si-	-	tim.
7.	mun-	-	dum;	vul-	-	tum.
8.	po-	-	no;	o-	-	vo.

2.

A.	*do-si*	*do-re*	*do;*	*re-do*	*re-mi*	*re;*	*mi-re*	*mi-fa*	*mi;*
B. 1.	*do-*	*do-*	*do;*	*re-*	*re-*	*re;*	*mi-*	*mi-*	*mi;*
2.	E-	de-	re;	dé-	ge-	re;	ré-	ge-	re;
3.	*do-*	-	*do;*	*re-*	-	*re;*	*mi-*	-	*mi;*
4.	Sa-	-	lus;	na-	-	tus;	ma-	-	num;
5.	Fe-	-	ra;	re-	-	gna;	ter-	-	ra;
6.	Pu-	-	ra;	tu-	-	am;	cu-	-	ra;
7.	Vi-	-	ta;	i-	-	ma;	vi-	-	vam;
8.	So-	-	la;	vo-	-	ta;	cor-	-	da;

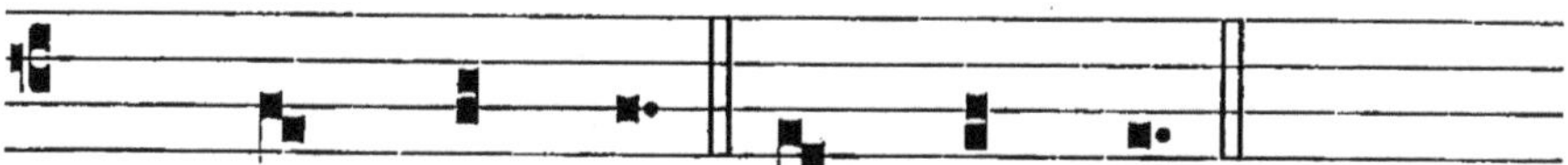

A.	*re-do*	*re-mi*	*re;*	*do-si*	*do-re*	*do.*
B. 1.	*re-*	*re-*	*re;*	*do-*	*do-*	*do.*
2.	fré-	me-	re;	sé-	que-	re.
3.	*re-*	-	*re;*	*do-*	-	*do.*
4.	pas-	-	sus;	ma-	-	gnum.
5.	e-	-	ram;	E-	-	va.
6.	lu-	-	dam;	ru-	-	bra.
7.	mit-	-	tam;	di-	-	gna.
8.	do-	-	na;	to-	-	ta.

3.

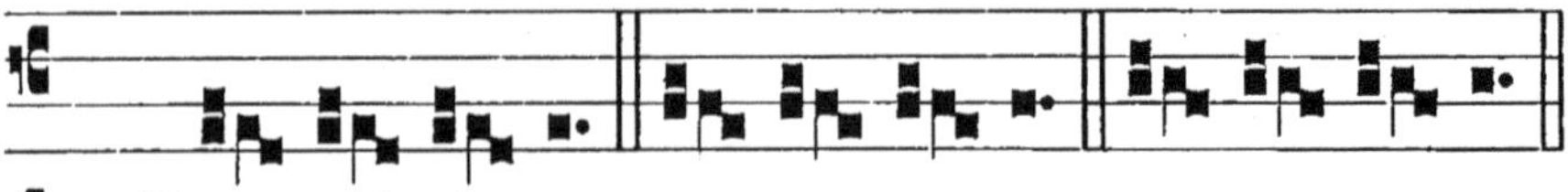

A. To be solfa-ed.

B. 1. *do- do- do- do; re- re- re- re; mi- mi- mi- mi;*
2. *do - - -; re - - -; mi - - -;*
3. *e - - -; œ - - -;* o *- - -;*
4. *i - - -; ue - - -; u - - -;*
5. E- go au- tem; exspe- ctá- bo; no- men tu- um;

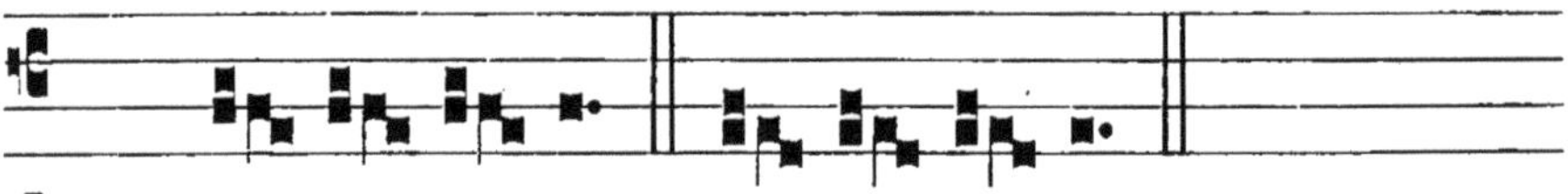

A. To be solfa-ed.

B. 1. *re- re- re- re; do- do- do- do.*
2. *re - - -; do - - - .*
3. *œ - - -; e - - - .*
4. *ue - - -; i - - - .*
5. Te- sta- mén- tum; in æ- tér-num.

4.

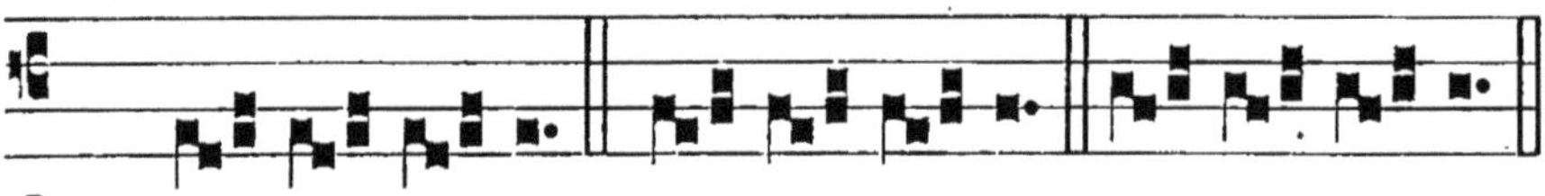

A. To be solfa-ed.

B. 1. *do- do- do- do; re- re- re- re; mi- mi- mi- mi;*
2. *do - - -; re - - -; mi - - -;*
3. *o - - -; œ - - -; e - - -;*
4. *u - - -; ue - - -; i - - -;*
5. Servum me- um; ma- nus me- a; con- ser- vá- bit;

A. To be solfa-ed.

B. 1. *re- re- re- re; do- do- do- do.*
2. *re - - -; do - - - .*
3. *œ - - -; o - - - .*
4. *ue - - -; u - - - .*
6. et de- có-rem; da- bo e- i.

B.

5.

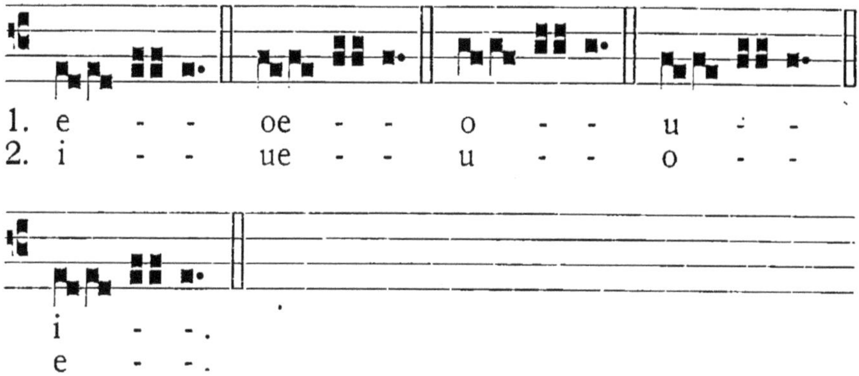

6.

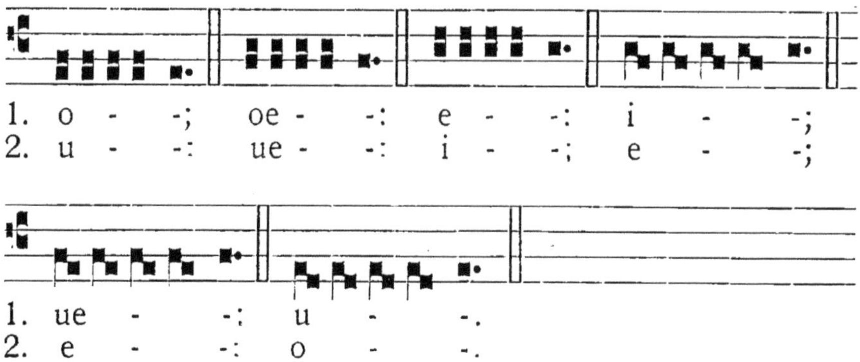

7.

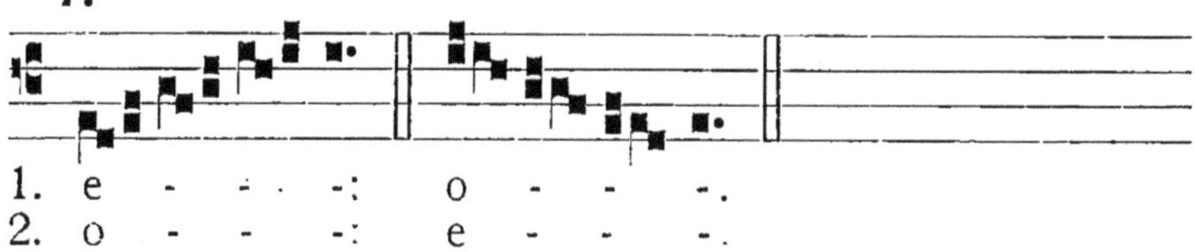

8.

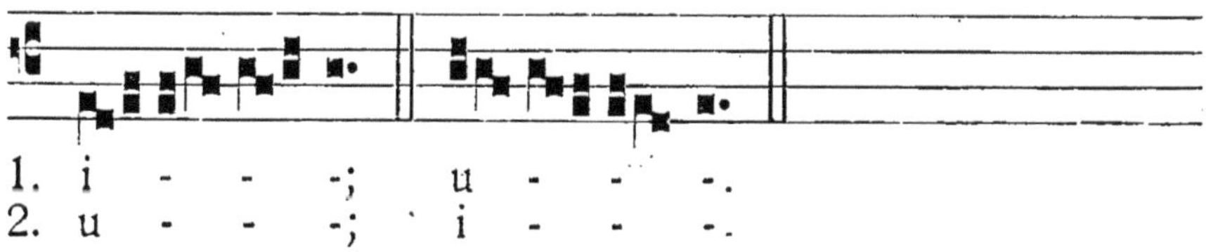

9.

1.	e	-	;	i	-
2.	o		-;	oe	-
3.	u		-;	ue	-

Lesson II.

A and B.

1.

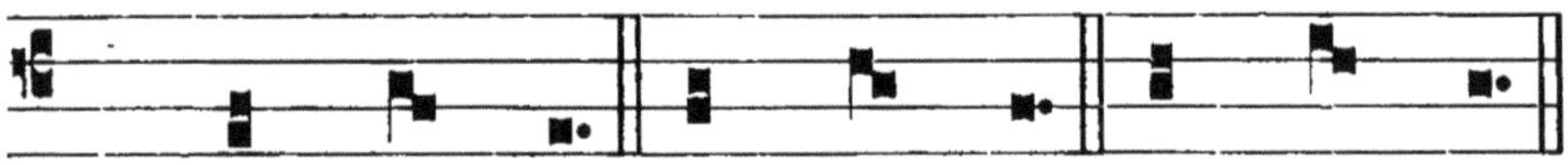

A.		*do-re*	*mi-re*	*do;*	*re-mi*	*fa-mi*	*re;*	*mi-fa*	*sol-fa*	*mi;*
B.	1.	*do-*	*mi-*	*do;*	*re-*	*fa-*	*re;*	*mi-*	*fa-*	*mi;*
	2.	Co-	ló-	nus;	o-	dó-	rum;	mo-	ró-	sus;
	3.	*do-*	-	*do;*	*re-*	-	*re;*	*mi-*	-	*mi;*
	4.	Cla-	-	vos;	pa-	-	ro;	da-	-	bo;
	5.	Di-.	-	ro;	li-	-	mo;	stil-	-	lo;
	6.	Ne-	-	mo;	ve-	-	ro;	se-	-	co;
	7.	No-	-	men;	mor-	-	tem;	pro-	-	pter;
	8.	Mu-	-	ro;	pu-	-	ros;	sum-	-	mos;

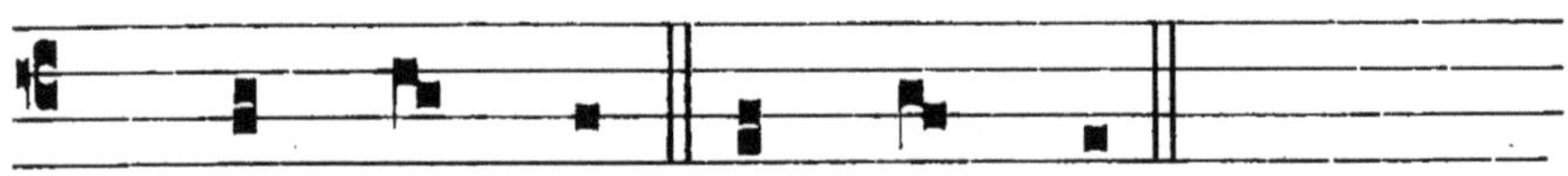

A.		*re-mi*	*fa-mi*	*re;*	*do-re*	*mi-re*	*do.*
B.	1.	*re-*	*fa-*	*re;*	*do-*	*mi-*	*do.*
	2.	for-	mó-	sus;	no-	dó-	sus.
	3.	*re-*	-	*re;*	*do-*	-	*do.*
	4.	va-	-	do;	san-	-	ctos.
	5.	ni-	-	tor;	vi-	-	no.
	6.	pe-	-	to;	de-	-	go.
	7.	o-	-	mne;	or-	-	bem.
	8.	mu-	-	to;	du-	-	ro.

2.

A. *do-si la-si do; re-do si-do re; mi-re do-re mi;*
B. 1. *do- la- do; re- si- re; mi- do- mi;*
2. Ví- ri- di; sí- mi- li; lí- li- i;
3. *la- - la; si- - si; do- - do;*
4. I- - gnem; di- - tem; ri- - gem;
5. Ve- - ni; he- - ri; se- - ni;
6. Fu- - mi; nul- - li; u- - bi;
7. Vo- - cis; o- - ris; so- - lis;
8. Na- - vi; sal- - vi; fa- - ti;

A. *re-do si-do re; do-si la-si do.*
B. 1. *re- si- re; do- la- do.*
2. fí- li- i; prín- ci- pi.
3. *si- - si; la- - la.*
4. vi- - de; vi- - tem.
5. men- - ti; ve- - lim.
6. dul- - cis; cru- - cis.
7. no- - bis; no- - stris.
8. na- - ti; pa- - ti.

3.

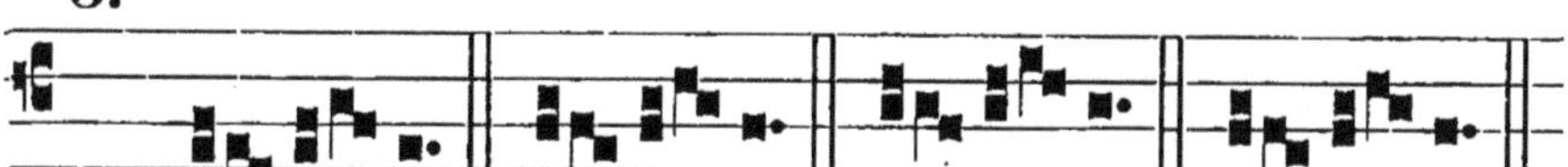

A. To be solfa-ed.
B. 1. e- - -; o- - -; a- - -; o- - -;
2. i- - -; u- - -; a- - -; u- - -;
3. A- nima; lá- bi- a; cá- pi- ta; á- tri- a;

A. To be solfa-ed.
B. 1. e- - -.
2. i- - -.
3. grá- mi- na.

4.

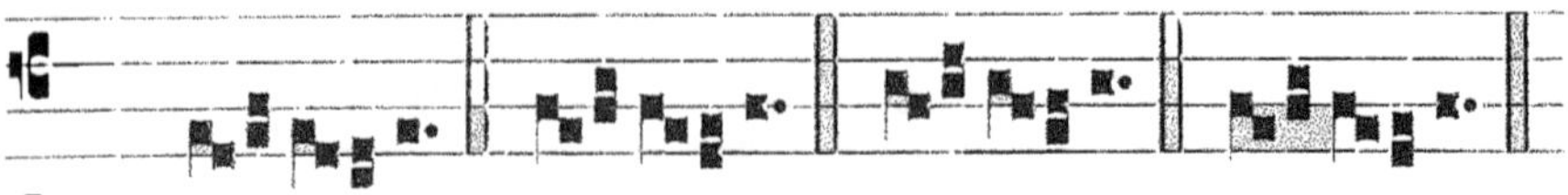

A. To be solfa-ed.

B. 1. i- - -; e- - -; a- - -; e- - -;
2. i- - -; a- - -; e- - -; a- - -;
3. Dó- minus; ó- le- o; pó- pu- lo; cómmo-do;

A. To be solfa-ed.

B. 1. i - -.
2. i - -.
3. ró- se- o.

5.

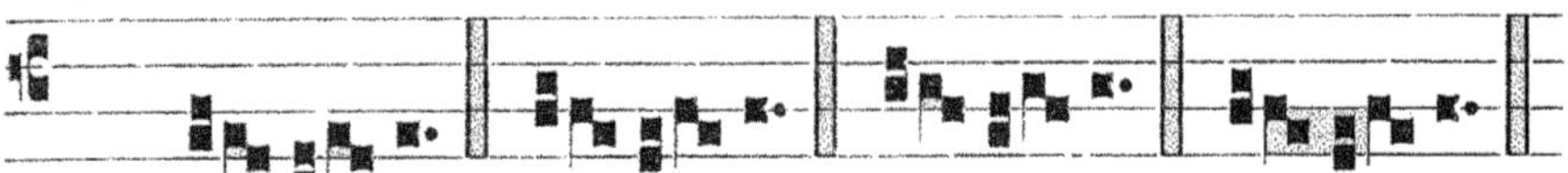

A. To be solfa-ed.

B. 1. e- - -; ae- - -; a- - -; ae- - -;
2. oe - -; o- - -; a- - -; o- - -;
3. U- ni-cum; ú- be-rum; tú- mi-dum; lú- bri-cum;

A. To be solfa-ed.

B. 1. e- - -.
2. oe- - -.
3. lú- mi-num.

6.

A. To be solfa-ed.

B. 1. o- - -; u- - -; a- - -; u- - -;
2. o- - -; a- - -; u- - -; a- - -;
3. Gé- ne-ra; té- nebris; vé- ne-ror; sé- ge- tis;

A. To be solfa-ed.
B. 1. o- - -.
2. o- - -.
3. déx- te- ra.

B.

7.

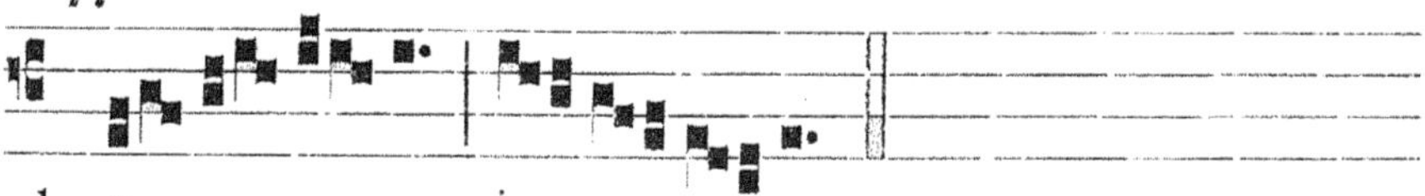

1. e i
2. oe ue
3. o o
4. a a

8.

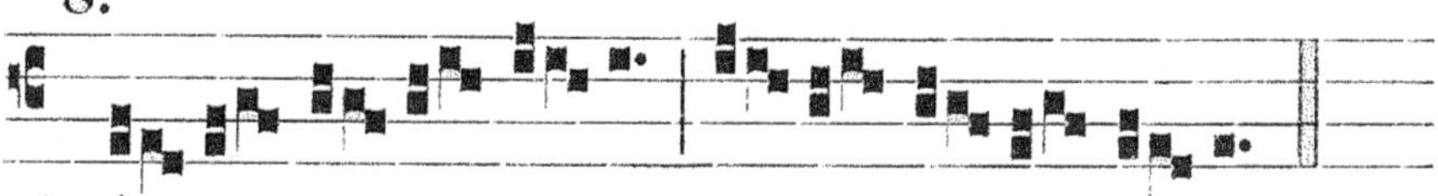

1. i e
2. ue oe
3. u u
4. a a

9.

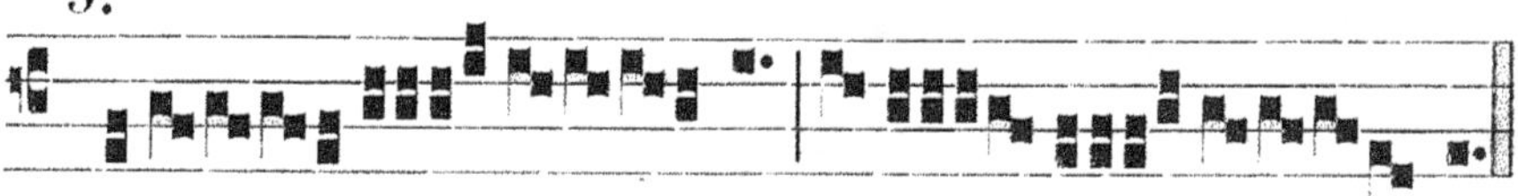

1. e 1. i
2. oe 2. ue
3. o 3. u
4. a 4. a

Lesson III.

1. **A** and **B**.

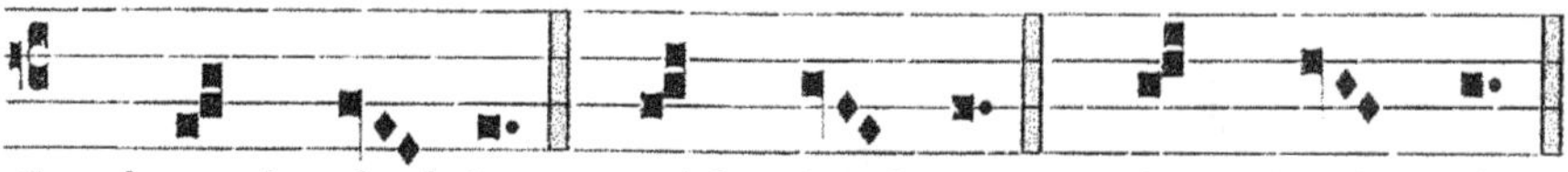

A. *do-re-mi re-do-si do; re-mi-fa mi-re-do re; mi-fa-sol fa-mi-re mi;*
B. Lá- pi- dem; rá- bi- em; má- ci- em;

A. re-mi-fa mi-re-do re; do-re-mi re-do-si do.

B. tá- li- ter; fá- ci- ens.

2.

A. do-si-do re-mi-re do; re-do-re mi-fa-mi re; mi-re-mi fa-sol-fa mi;

B. lá- que- um; áb- e- unt; cá- se- um;

A. re-do-re mi-fa-mi re; do-si-do re-mi-re do.

B. pa- tres sunt; mál- le- um.

3.

A. do-re-do si-la-si do; re-mi-re do-si-do re; mi-fa-mi re-do-re mi;

B. Pá- bu- lo; stá- tu- o; ám- bu- lo;

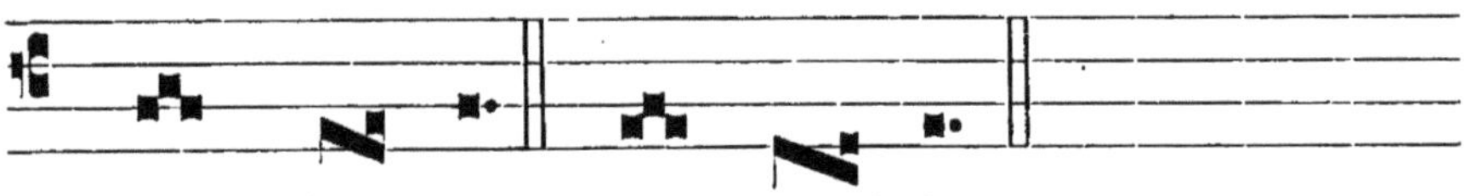

A. re-mi-re do-si-do re; do-re-do si-la-si do.

B. ár- gu- o; vá- cu- o.

4.

A. do-si-la si-do-re do; re-do-si do-re-mi re; mi-re-do re-mi-fa mi;

B. Quó- ni- am; gló- ri- a; ó- mni- a;

A. re-do-si do-re-mi re; do-si-la si-do-re do.

B. ób- vi- am; má- ri- a.

5.

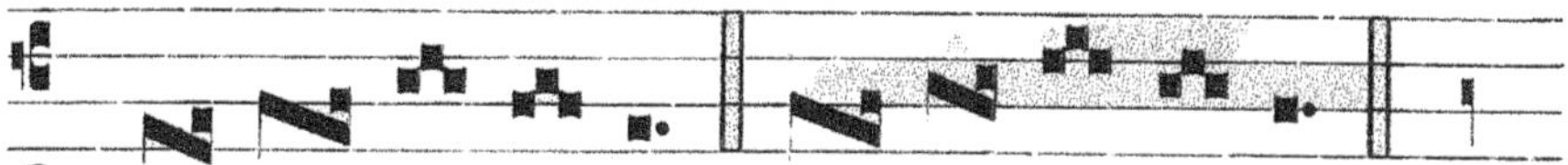

A. To be solfa-ed.
B. Vir- tú- te tu- a; læ- tá- tur ju- stus;

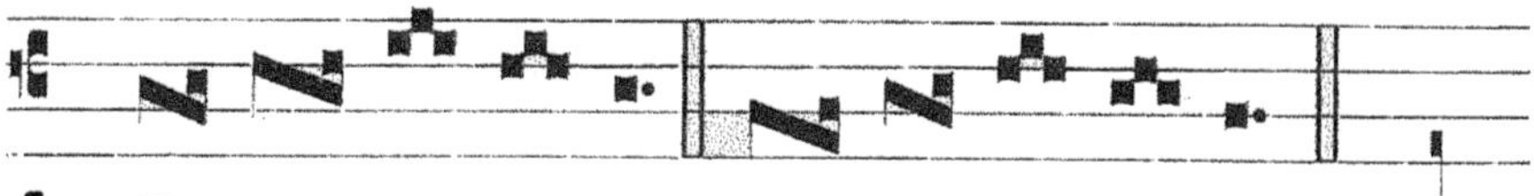

A. To be solfa-ed.
B. de- si- dé- ri- um; á- ni- mæ e- jus;

A. To be solfa-ed.
B. trí- bu- is e- i.

6.

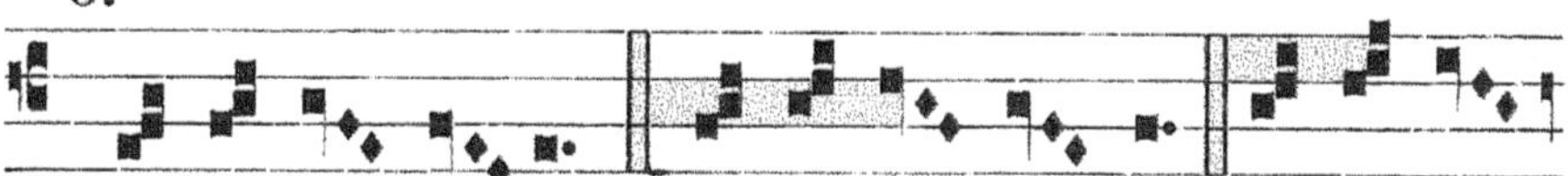

A. To be solfa-ed.
B. Dómi- nus di- cit; qui re- li- quí- stis; ó-mni- a;

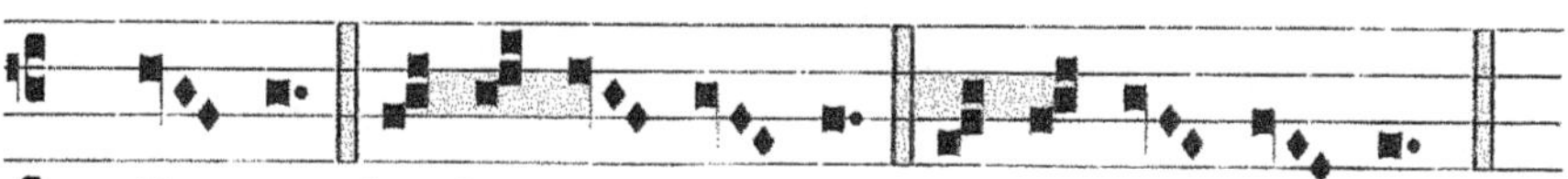

A. To be solfa-ed.
B. pro me; ac-ci- pi- é- tis; vi- tam æ- tér- nam.

B.

7.

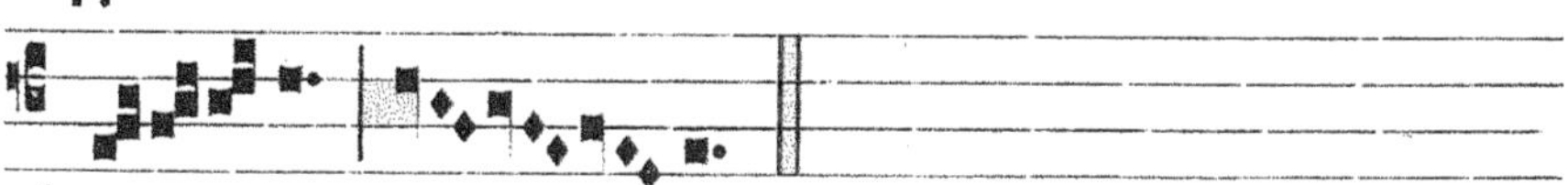

1. To be solfa-ed.
2. On a vowel.

8.

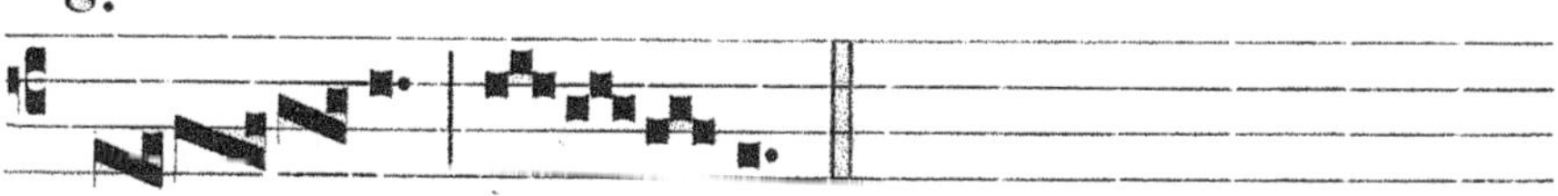

Same as Ex. 7.

9.

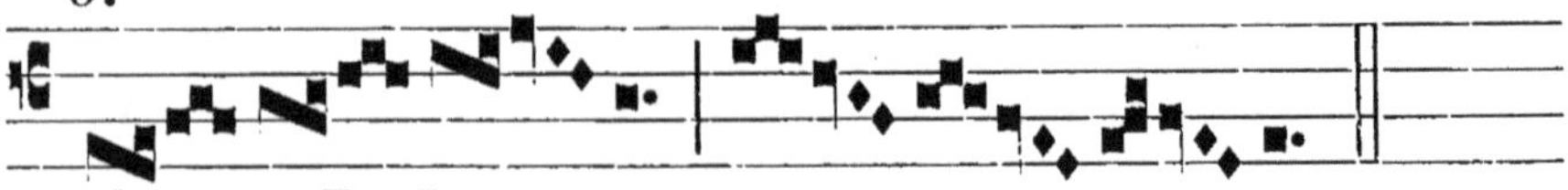

Same as Ex. 7.

10.

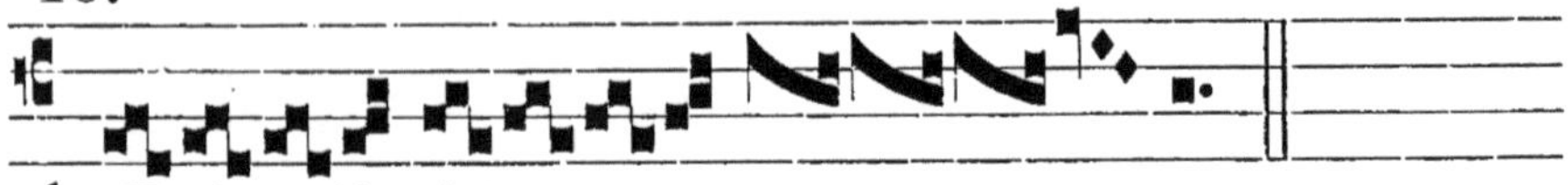

1. To be solfa-ed.
2. On a vowel.
3. a - - - e - - - i - - - -.

1. To be solfa-ed.
2. On a vowel.
3. a - - - - o - - - a - - - -.

11.

Same as Ex. 10.

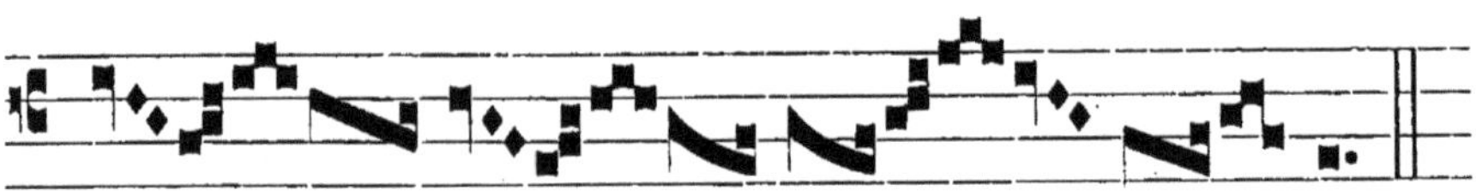

Lesson IV.

A.

1.

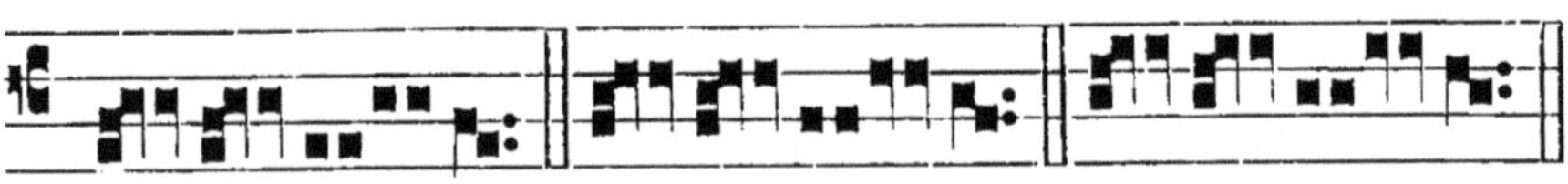

2.

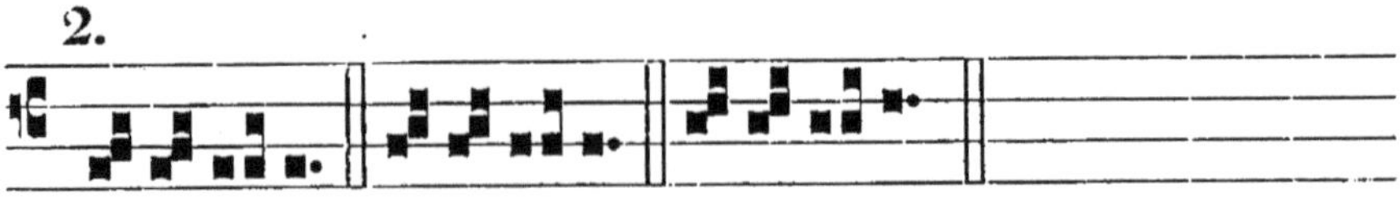

3.

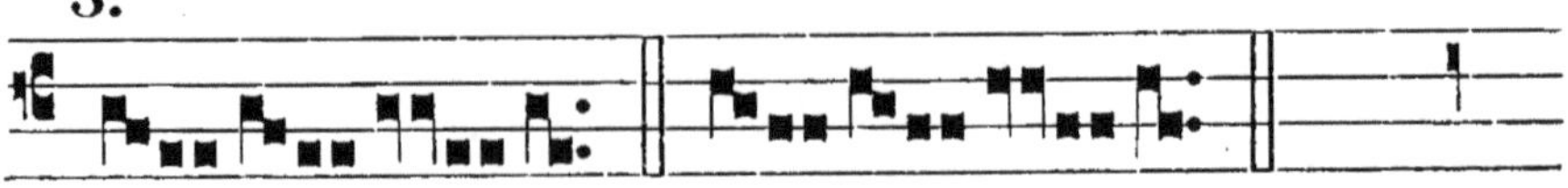

4.

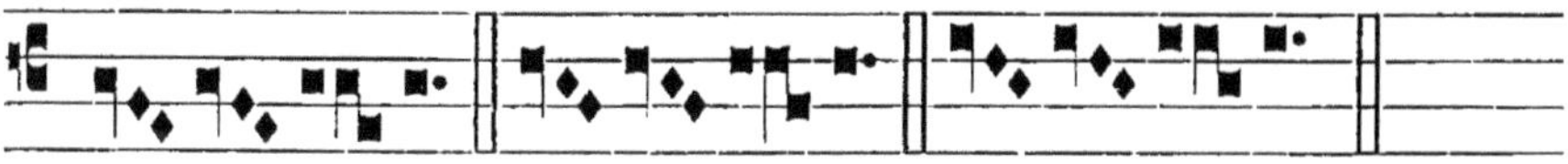

A and B.

5.

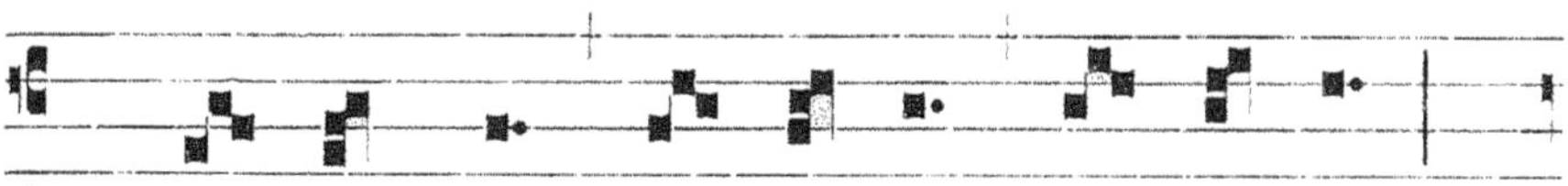

A. To be solfa-ed.
B. Fle- tis nunc; vé- ni- am; í- te- rum;

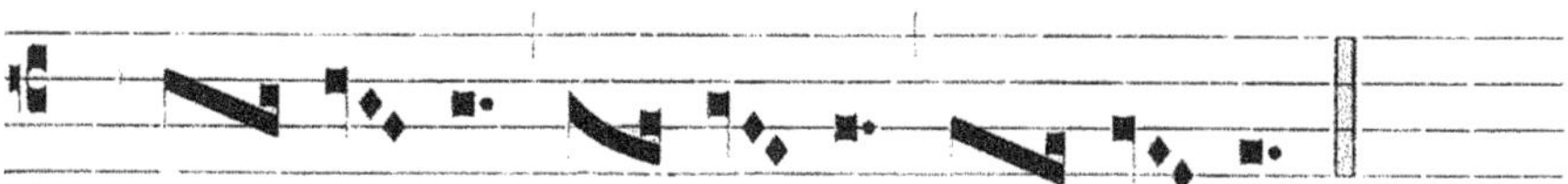

A. To be solfa-ed.
B. póst- e- a; gau-dén- tes; é- ri- tis.

6.

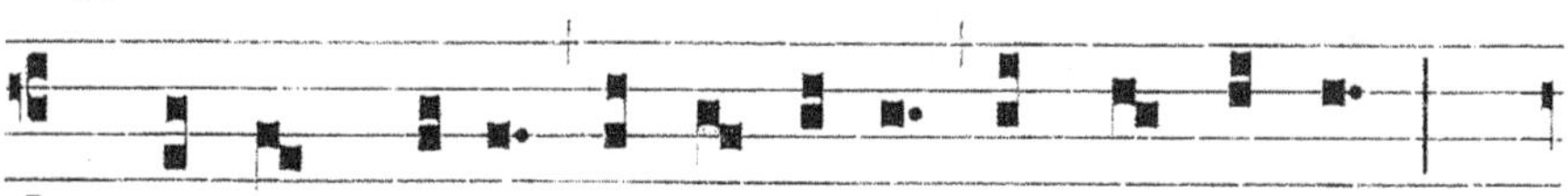

A. To be solfa-ed.
B. Do-mum De- i,; can-tá- ve- ro; in sǽ- cu- la;

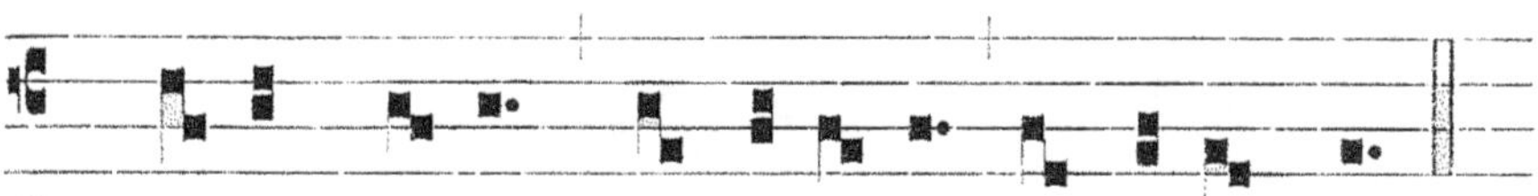

Ä. To be solfa-ed.
B. di- em ma- lum; non timé-bo; tu me-cum es.

7.

A. To be solfa-ed.
B. Dó- mi- nus; ló-qui- tur; Fi- li- us;

A. To be solfa-ed.

B. me- us es; re- gná- bis; in cœ- lo.

8. a)

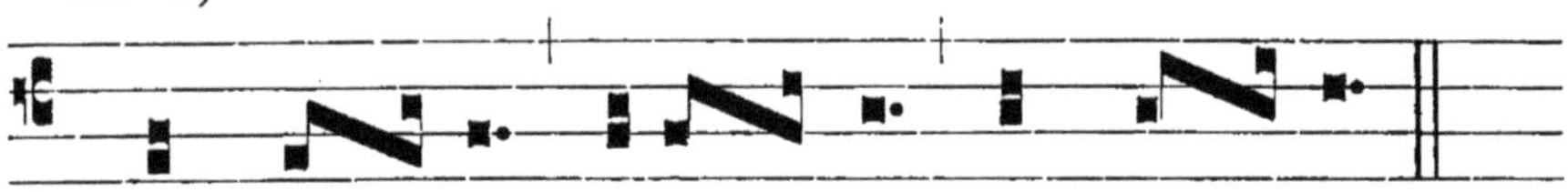

A. To be solfa-ed.

B. In De- o spe-rá- bo; pars me- a

b)

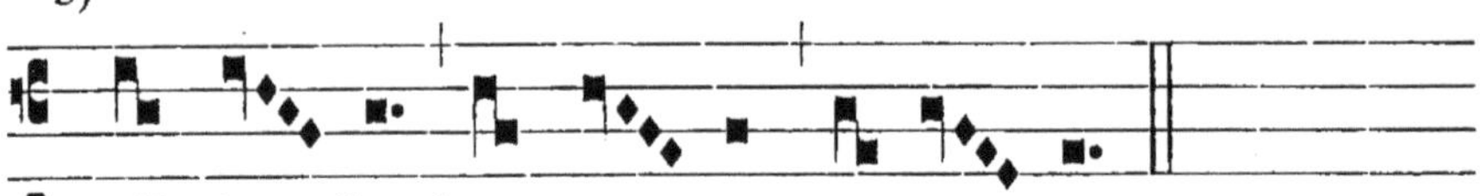

A. To be solfa-ed.

B. est ip- se et te- stis fi- dé- lis.

9.

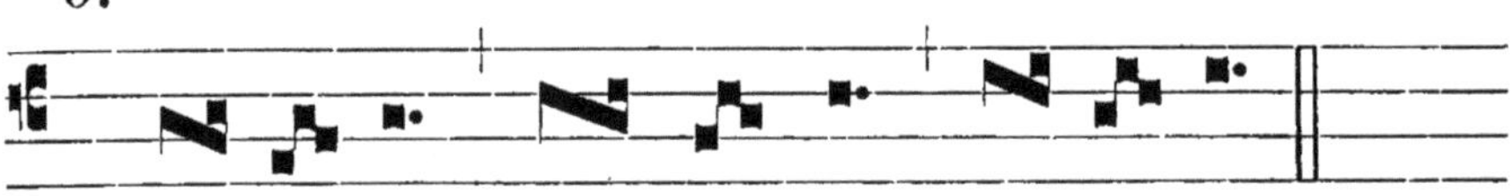

A. To be solfa-ed.

B. Stá- tu- it Dó- mi- nus Fí- li- um

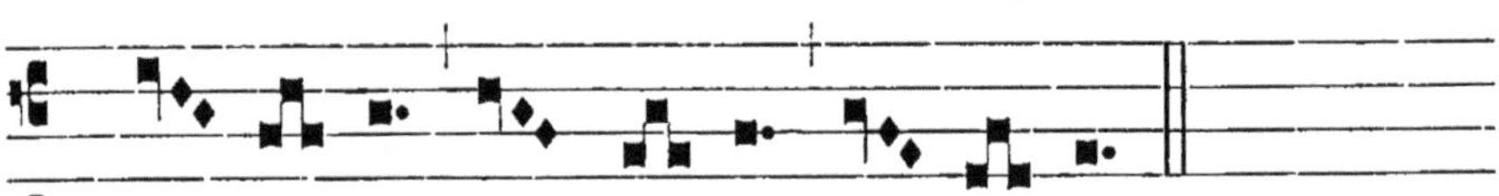

A. To be solfa-ed.

B. hæ- ré- dem et re- gem ó-mni- um.

10. c)

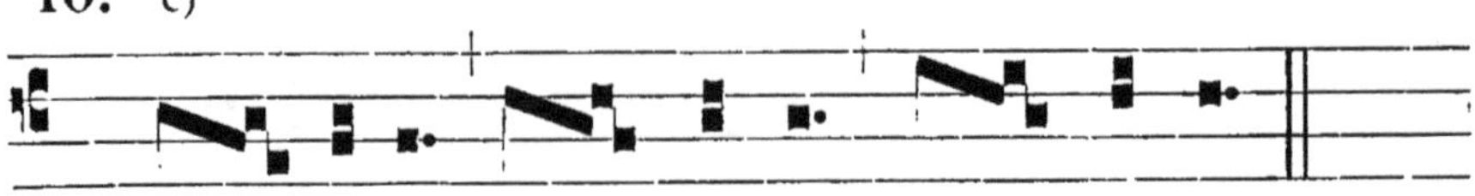

A. To be solfa-ed.

B. Pec- cá-vi; i- ní-que, per- vér-se,

d)

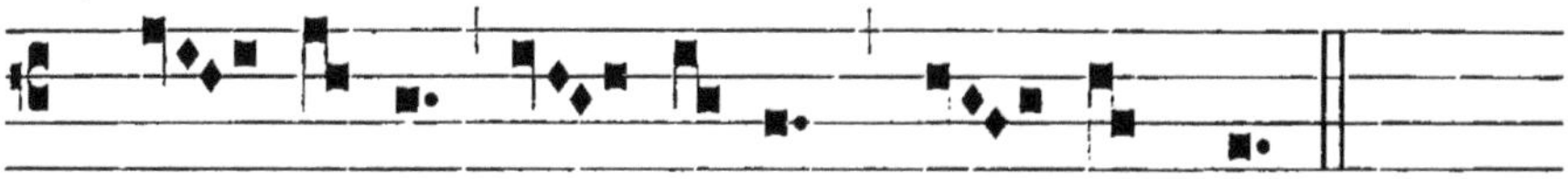

A. To be solfa-ed.

B. ím- pi- e ám- bu-lans co- ram te.

a) b) c) d)

Lesson V.

A and B.

1. a) b) c)

A. To be solfa-ed.

B. 1. La, la, la . . . .

2. Va________, vae________, voe________,

d) e) f)

A. To be solfa-ed.

B. 1. La, la, la . . . .

2. vo________, vu________, vue________,

a) b)

c) d)

e) f)

g) h)

A. To be solfa-ed.

B. 1. La, la, la . . . .
2. vi__________, ve__________.

2.

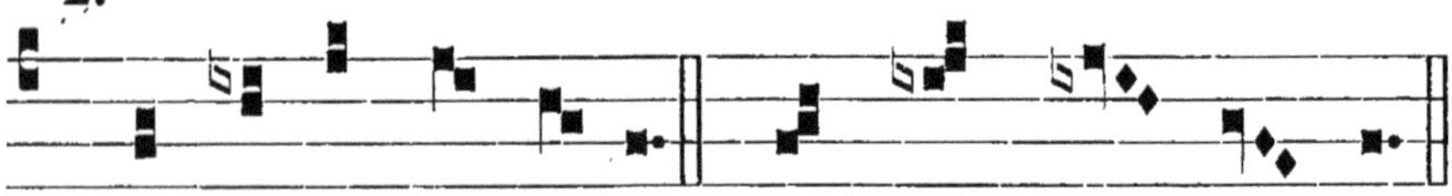

A. *fa-sol la-sa do-re do-sa la-sol fa.* *fa-sol-la sa-do-re do-sa-la sol-fa-mi fa.*

B. Ve__________________, vi______________________,

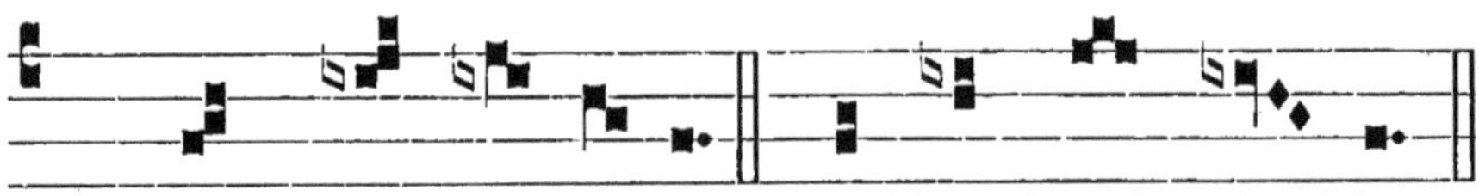

A. *fa-sol-la sa-do-re do-sa la-sol fa.* *fa-sol la-sa do-re-do sa-la-sol fa.*

B. vue__________________, vi_____________________.

A. To be solfa-ed.

B. vo__________, voe__________, vae__________,

A. To be solfa-ed.

B. va__________.

---

g)

h)

3.

A. To be solfa-ed.
B. 1. La, la, la . . . .
2. Do__________, re__________,

A. To be solfa-ed.
B. 1. la, la, la . . . .
2. mi__________, fa__________,

A. To be solfa-ed.
B. 1. la, la, la . . . .
2. sol__________, la__________,

A. To be solfa-ed.
B. 1. la, la, la . . . .
2. si__________, do__________.

4.

A. To be solfa-ed.
B. Da__________, me__________, ni__________,

A. To be solfa-ed.
B. po__________, tu__________, la__________,

A. To be solfa-ed.
B. be__________, si__________.

B.

5.

1. La, la, la, la . . . .
2. O________; u__________.

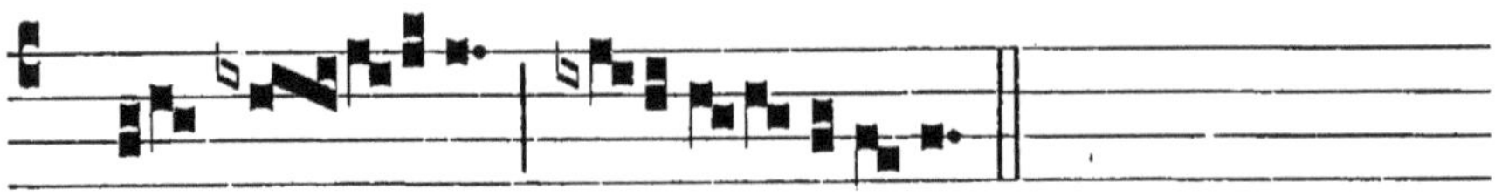

1. La, la, la . . . .
2. E________; e__________.

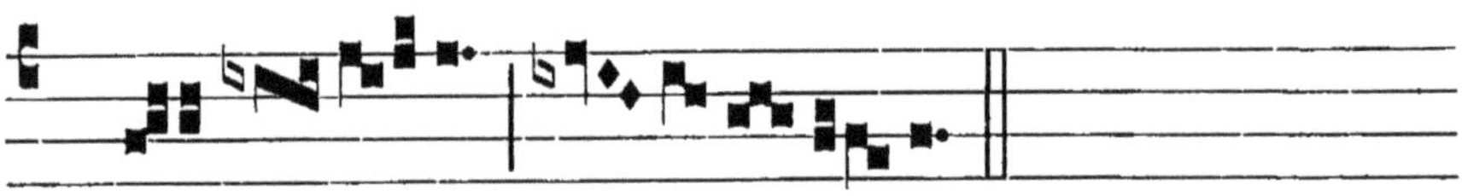

1. La, la, la . . . .
2. A__________; i__________.

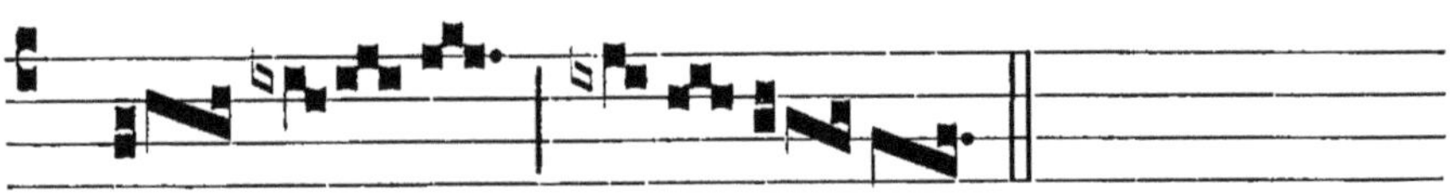

1. La, la, la . . . .
2. a__________; o__________.

6.

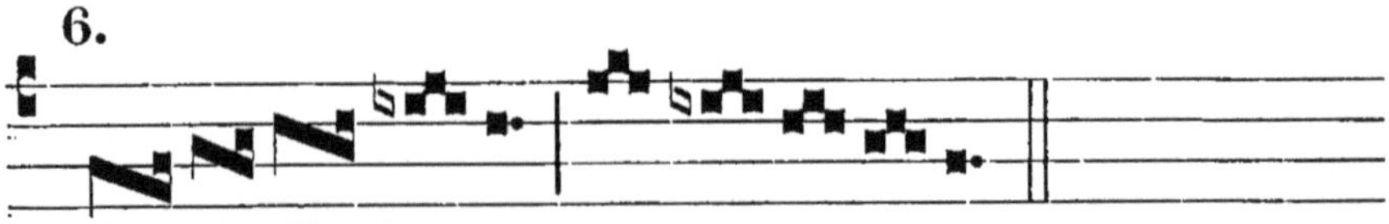

Same as Ex. 5.

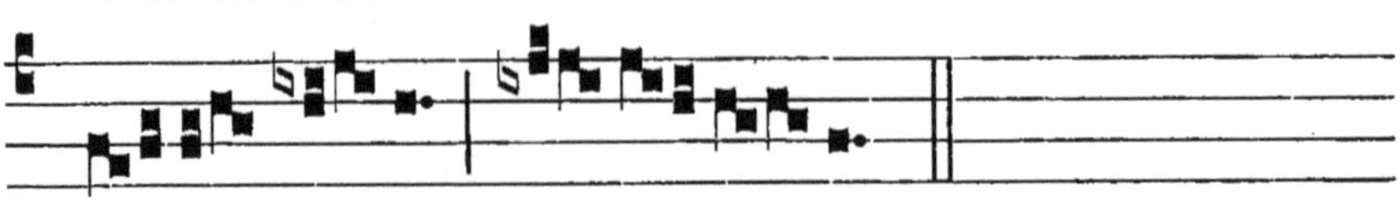

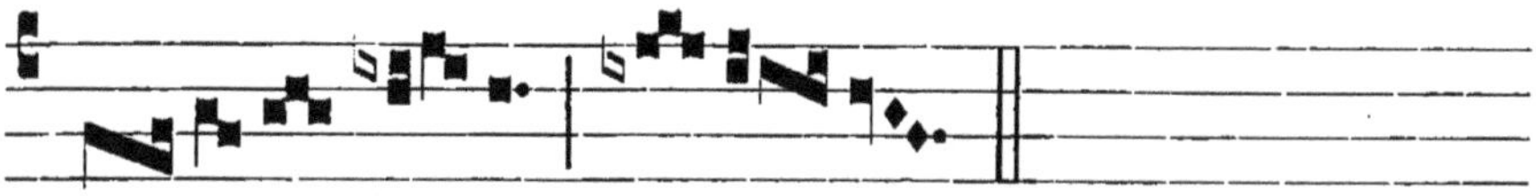

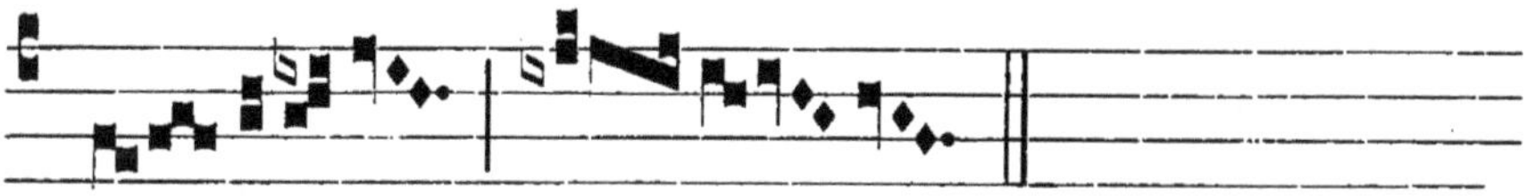

7.

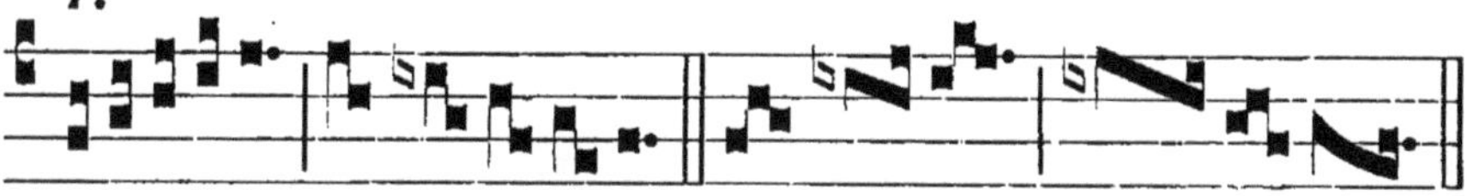

Same as Ex. 5.

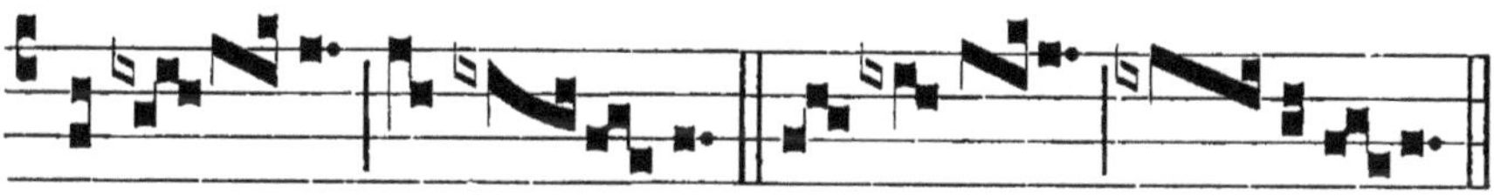

Lesson VI.

1. **A** and **B.**

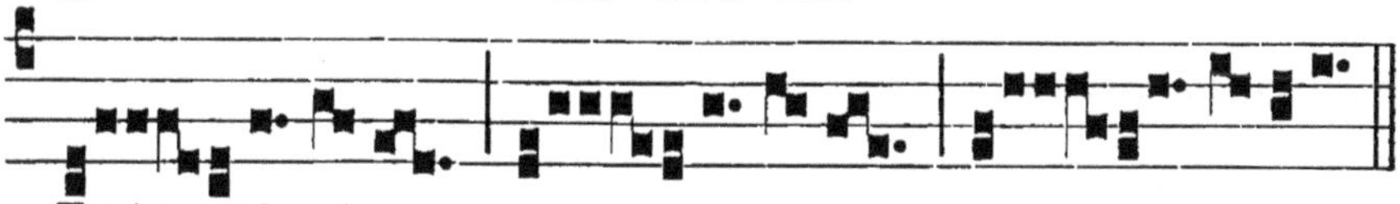

To be solfa-ed.

1. Do- fa sol-mi; re- sol la-fa; mi- la si-sol-si;
2. Da- po tu- ni; me- tu va-po; mi- va be-tu-be;

To be solfa-ed.

1. Do- sol fa-la; si- fa misol; la- mi re- do.
2. Si- tu pova; be- po ni-tu; va- mi meda.

2. a)

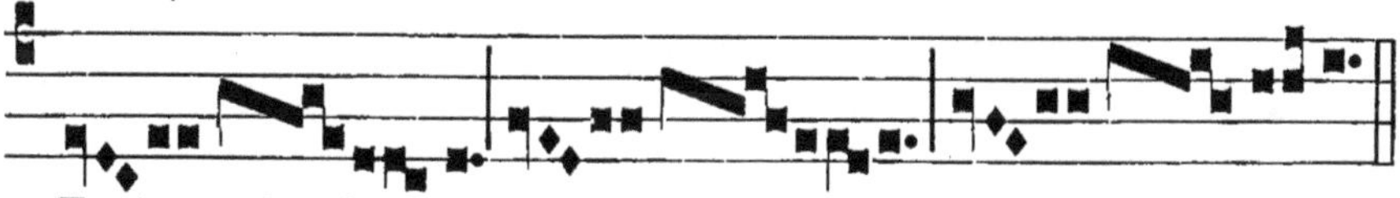

To be solfa-ed.

1. Mi- sol- re; fa- la- mi; sol- si- la- si;
2. Ni- tu- me; po- va- mi; tu- be- va-be;

b)

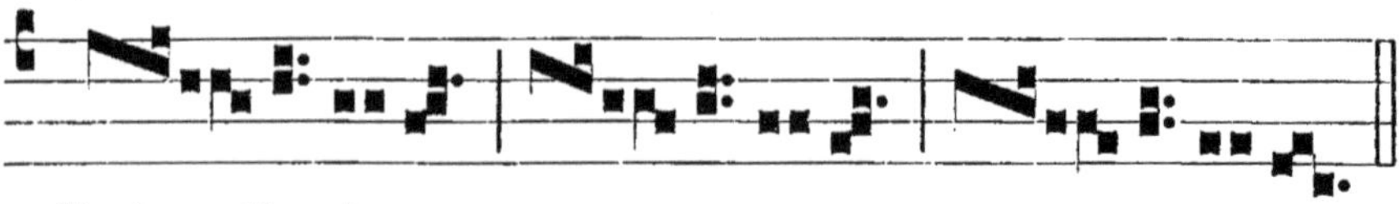

To be solfa-ed.

1. Do- la sol-fa; si- sol fa-mi; la- fa mi-re.
2. Si- va tu-po; be- tu po-ni; va- po ni-me.

3. c)

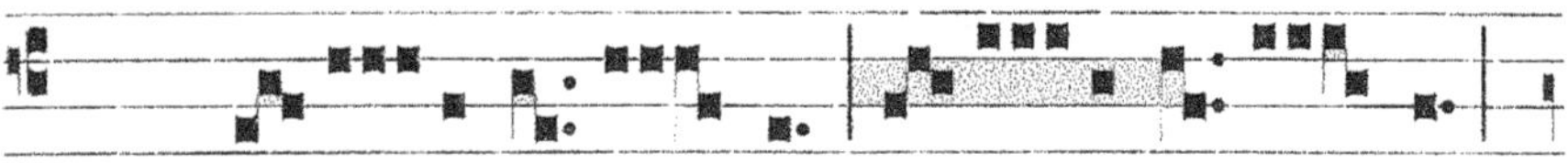

A. To be solfa-ed.

B. 1. Do- mi- do; re- fa- re;
2. Da- ni- da; me- po- me;

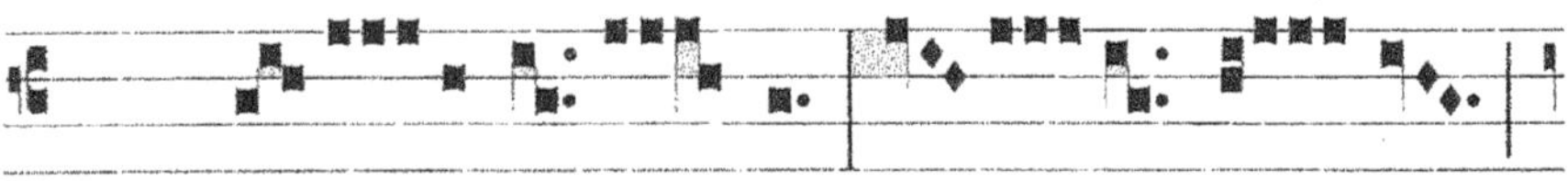

A. To be solfa-ed.

B. 1. mi- sol- mi; la- sol- mi;
2. ni- tu- ni; va- tu- ni;

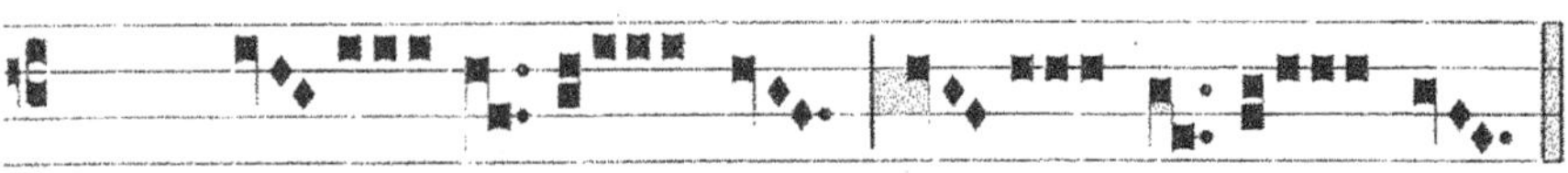

A. To be solfa-ed.

B. 1. sol- fa- re; fa- mi- do.
2. tu- po- me; po- ni- da.

a) b)

c)

4. d)

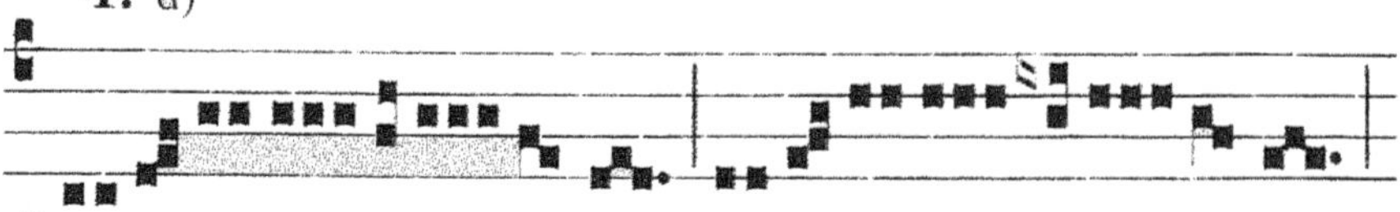

A. To be solfa-ed.

B. Do- re; re- mi;
2. Da- me; me- ni;

d)

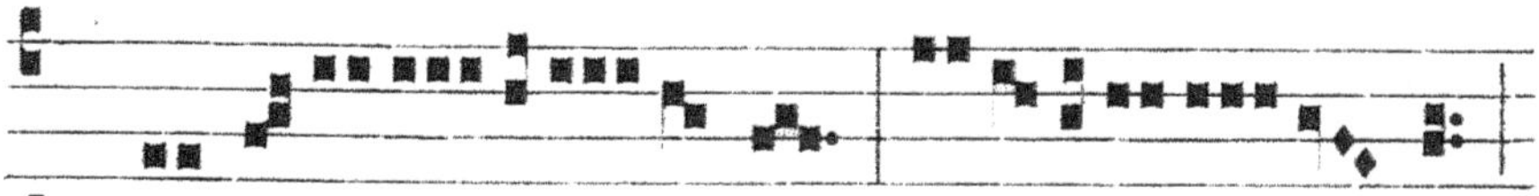

A. To be solfa-ed.

B. 1. mi- fa; do- fa;
2. ni- po; da- po;

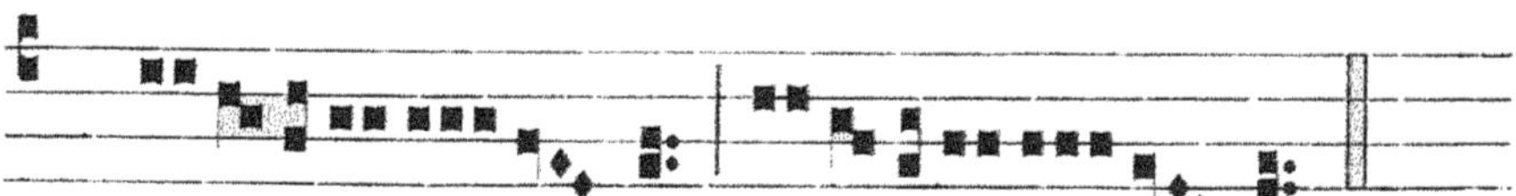

A. To be solfa-ed.

B. 1. si- mi; la- re.
2. be- ni; va- me.

5.

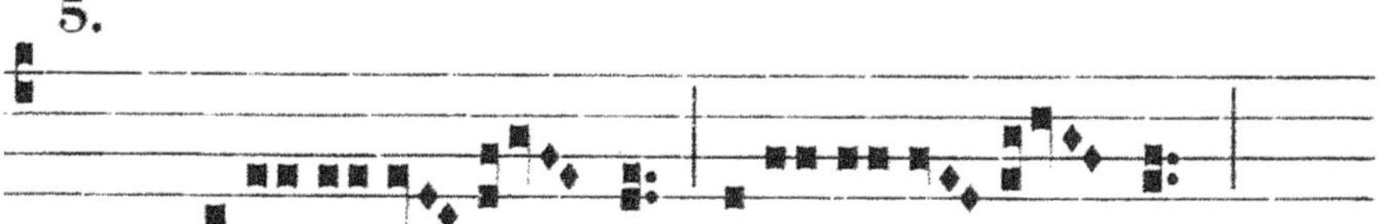

A. To be solfa-ed.

B. 1. Do- re; re- mi;
2. Da- me; me- ni;

e)

A. To be solfa-ed.

B. 1. mi- fa; la- sol;
2. ni- po; va- tu;

e)

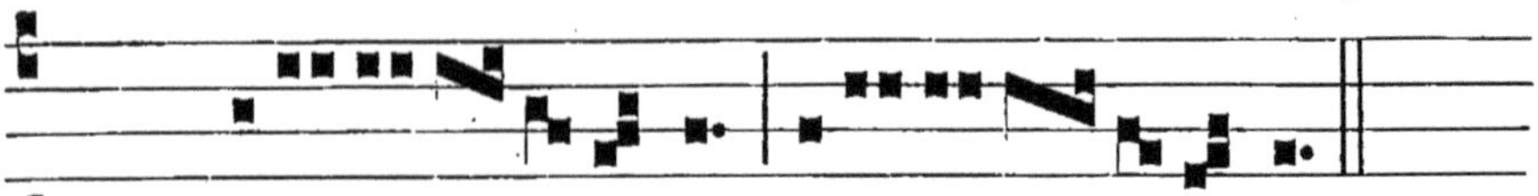

A. To be solfa-ed.

B. 1. sol- fa; fa- mi.
2. be- po; po- ni.

Lesson VII.

A and B.

1.

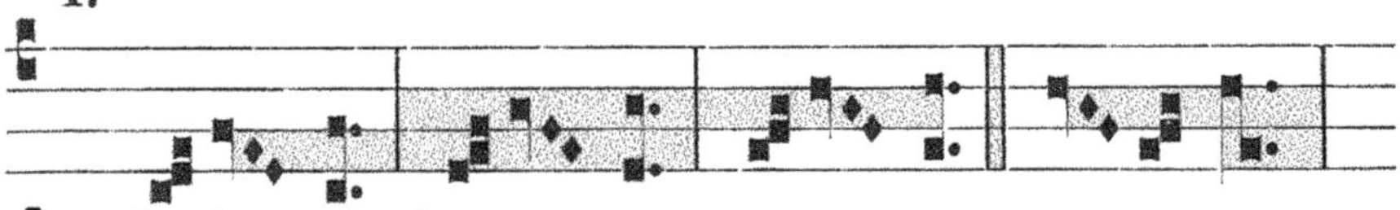

A. To be solfa-ed.

B. Do- fa; re- sol; mi- la; la- mi;

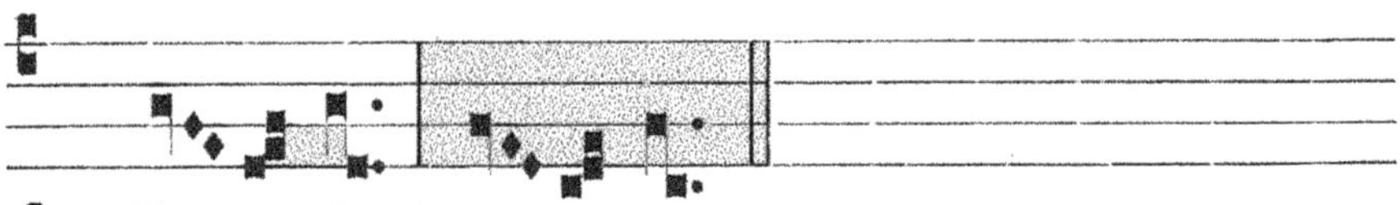

A. To be solfa-ed.

B. sol- re; fa- do.

2.

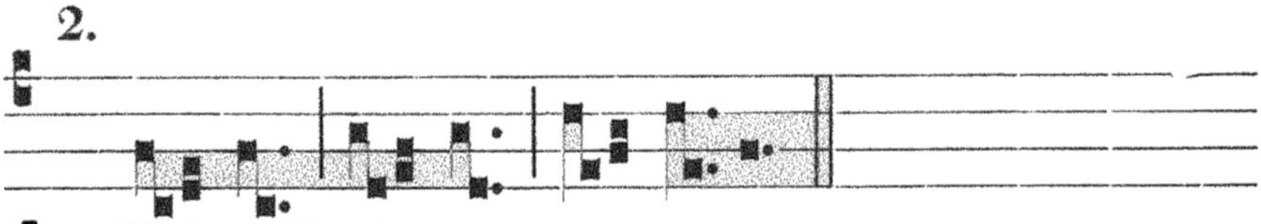

A. To be solfa-ed.

B. Fa- do; sol- re; la- mi- fa.

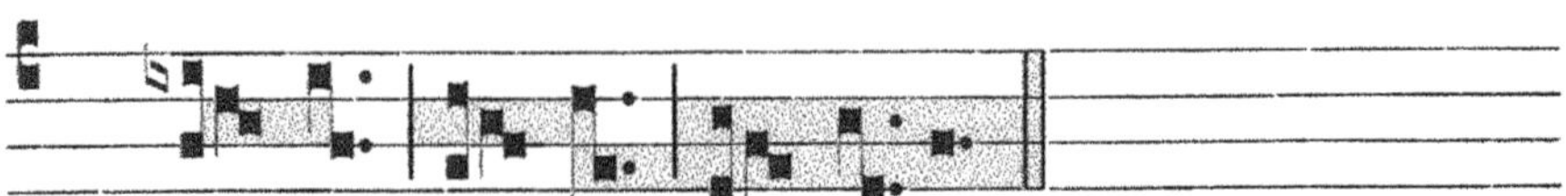

A. To be solfa-ed.

B. fa- sa; mi- la; re- sol- fa.

3.

A. To be solfa-ed.

B. Da- po; me- tu; ni- va;

A. To be solfa-ed.

B. va- ni; tu- me; po- da.

4.

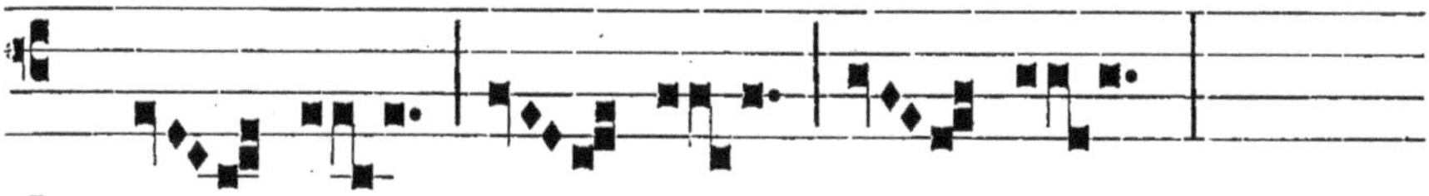

A. To be solfa-ed.

B. Le- sa; ri- ko; mu- li.

A. To be solfa-ed.

B. fo- ri; sa- le; li- da.

5.

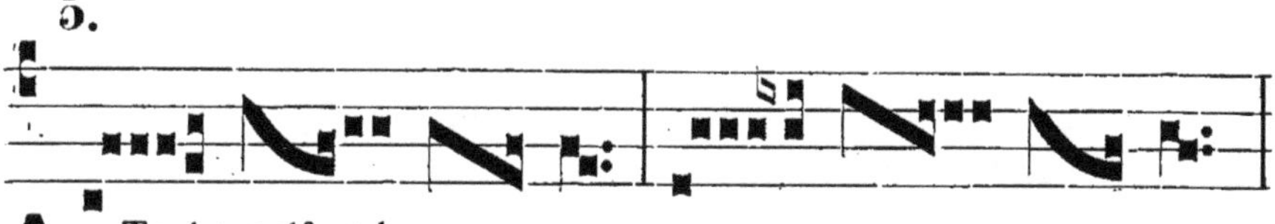

A. To be solfa-ed.

B. Fa- la- sol- mi; sol- sa- la sol;

A. To bo solfa-ed.

B. la- do- sol- re- mi.

B.

6.

E________________, e____________________.

Do- fa- mi- la- sol- mi; sol- fa- fa- mi- mi- re- do.

7.

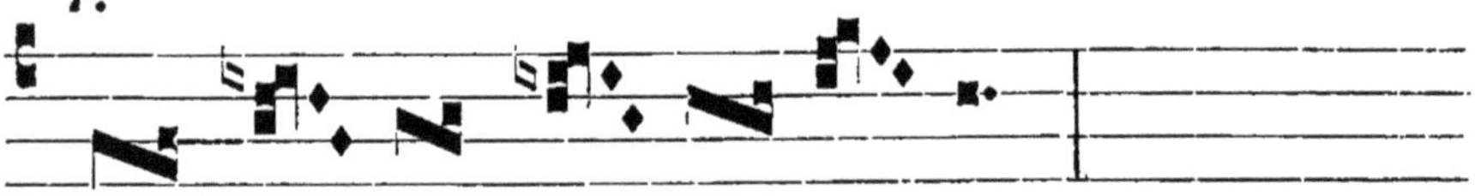

O_______________________________,

Fa- sa- sol- do- la- re- la;

o_______________________________.

do- sol- sa- fa- la- mi- fa.

8.

U________________, u______________.

Do- fa- la- mi; mi- re- fa- do.

9.

A_________________________, a_____________________.

Fa- re- sol-mi- la- fa- sa-do; sol-sa- fa- la- mi- sol- fa.

10.

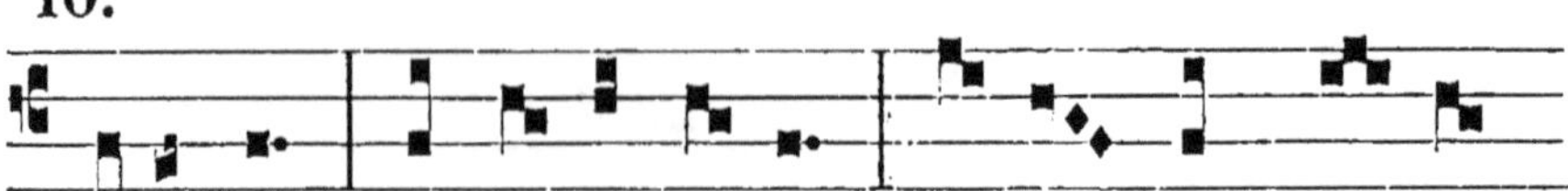

San- ctus; Dó- mi- ne De- us; Ple- ni sunt cœ- li

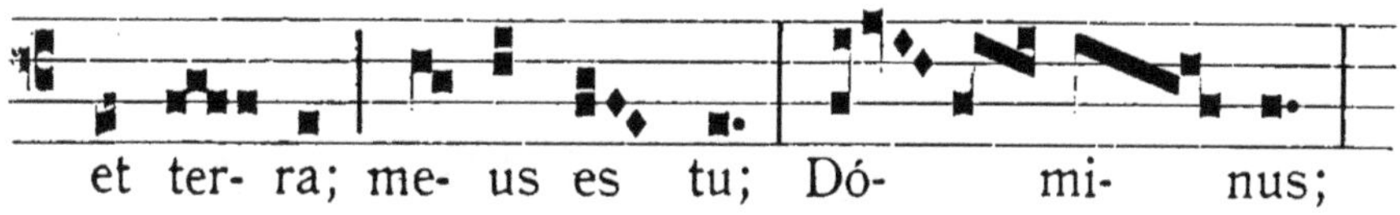

11.

12.

Lesson VIII.

A and B.

1. a)

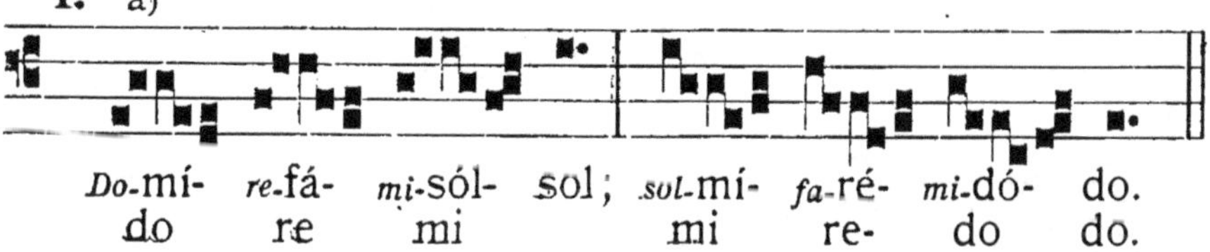

2.

Do- sol- do; re- la- re; mi- sa- mi;

b)

fa- sol; mi- fa; re- mi.

3. c)

Do-ré- sol- do; re-mi- la- re;
re mi
mi-fá sa la-sá-la;
fa sa

d)

Do- fa-sól-do; sa- mi-fá- sa;
sol fa

a)

b) c)

d)

B.

4. e)

f)

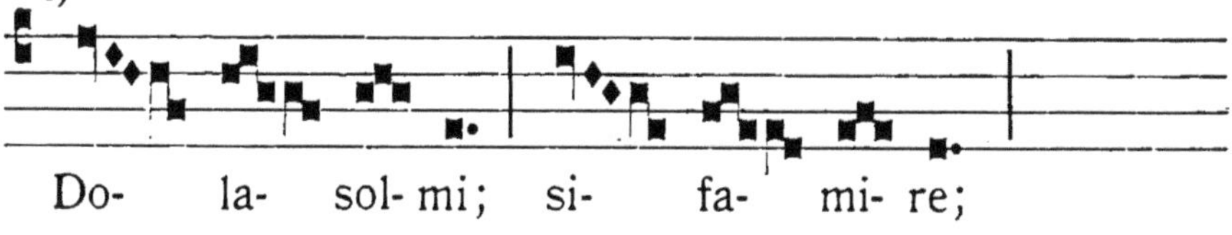

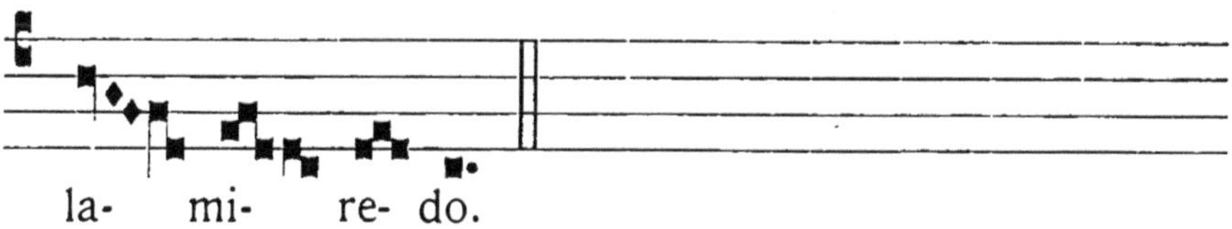

For Exercises 5—8, the *Gloria* melodies pp. 96—98.

For Exercises 9 and 10, the Antiphons *Jesus autem, Nos qui, Hæc est virgo, Bene fundata, Euge serve,* pp. 77 and 78.

For Exercise 11, the Antiphons *Estote fortes, Præceptor, O quam metuendus,* pp. 81, 83 and 84, and *Hodie Christus,* pp. 170, 171.

---

e)

f)

For Exercise 12, the Hymns *Crudelis Herodes, Salutis humanæ, Cœlestis urbs, Decora lux, Pange lingua, Te Joseph,* pp. 86—90.

13.

14.

15.

For Exercise 16, the *Tract* melodies, pp. 113, 114.

Lesson IX.

B.

For Exercises 1—4, the Antiphons *Sit nomen, Gratia Dei, Veni sponsa, Et ecce* pp. 77, 78 and 79; also *Puer, Bene omnia, Oppressit,* pp. 82, 83.

For Exercise 5, the Hymn *Veni Creator,* p. 87.

For Exercise 6, the following *Gradual* melodies in Mode II. (Lib. us. p. 411):

Lesson X.

B.

For Exercises 1—3, the *Gradual* melodies, pp. 107, 108.

For Exercises 4—9, the following typical *Alleluja* melodies :

4.

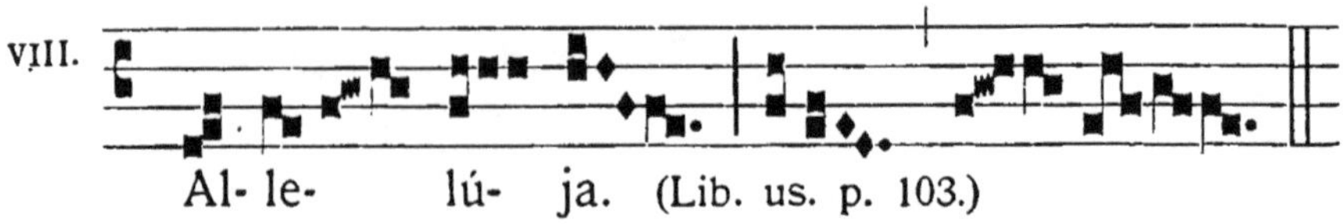

Ostén-de no- bis . . . .
5.
I.
Al- le- lú- ja.
(Lib. us. p. 713.) Di- lé- xit André-am . . .
6.
II.
Al- le- lú- ja. (Lib. us. p. 164.)
Di- es sancti- fi- cá- tus . . . .
7.
IV.
Al-le- lú- ja. (Lib. us. p. 457.) Ascéndit . .
8.
V.
Al- le- lú- ja.
(Lib. us. p. 949.) As-súmpta est . . . .

9.

VII.

For Exercise 10, *Alleluja,* pp. 110, 111.

For Exercise 11, *Alleluja,* Mode I., p. 158.

For Exercise 12, *Alleluja,* Mode VII., p. 159.

INDEX.

D.

E.

F.

G.

H.

I.

J.

N.

O.

P.

Q.

R.

W.

Y.

Z.

Lightning Source UK Ltd.
Milton Keynes UK
UKHW021543050219
336771UK00009B/193/P